# MEMORY AND LEGACY

*Annie at work, about 1895*

# MEMORY AND LEGACY

*A Thackeray Family Biography,*
*1876-1919*

JOHN APLIN

The Lutterworth Press

**The Lutterworth Press**
P.O. Box 60
Cambridge
CB1 2NT
United Kingdom

www.lutterworth.com
publishing@lutterworth.com


ISBN: 978 0 7188 9225 8


*British Library Cataloguing in Publication Data*
A record is available from the British Library

*For*

Juliet Anne Thackeray Murray

# CONTENTS

# LIST OF ILLUSTRATIONS

# PRELUDE AND
# ACKNOWLEDGEMENTS

In her second novel, *Night and Day* (1919), Virginia Woolf created in the character of Mrs Hilbery an affectionate if freely-drawn portrait of her step-aunt Anne Thackeray Ritchie in later life, remembering the time during 1910-11 when Lady Ritchie was working on the twenty-six-volume Thackeray edition published to coincide with the centenary of her father's birth. *Night and Day* came out in the year of Annie's death and caused some upset – Virginia said that Annie's son and daughter, Hester and Billy, were 'furious with me' (indeed, Hester never quite forgave her) – but whilst admitting that there were 'touches' of Annie, she also claimed that the fictional portrayal 'gets more and more away from the reality, and Mrs Hilbery became to me quite different from any one in the flesh.'[1]

Yet there is a persuasive truthfulness in Mrs Hilbery's devotion to her literary father's reputation, the daughter's life's work surrendered to the preparation of his biography, a responsibility which risks overwhelming her. And whilst Mrs Hilbery's daughter, Katharine, is certainly not modelled on Annie's own daughter, Virginia has fixed on just those qualities of patience and practical assistance required of Annie's family during work on the Biographical Edition and its successor.

> It was as much as Katharine could do to keep the pages of her mother's manuscript in order, but to sort them so that the sixteenth year of Richard Alardyce's life succeeded the fifteenth was beyond her skill. And yet they were so brilliant, these paragraphs, so nobly phrased, so lightning-like in their illumination, that the dead seemed to crowd the very room. Read continuously, they produced a sort of vertigo, and set her asking herself in despair what on earth she was to do with

them? Her mother refused, also, to face the radical questions
of what to leave in and what to leave out. She could not
decide how far the public was to be told the truth about the
poet's separation from his wife. She drafted passages to suit
either case, and then liked each so well that she could not
decide upon the rejection of either. (*Night and Day*, ch 3*)*

What Virginia got uncannily right, with an insight which crosses
generations, was this sense of a life in thrall to memory, of the
inhibiting power of duty. From her earliest years she had grown up
knowing and loving 'Aunt Annie', Leslie Stephen's sister-in-law
from his first marriage to Thackeray's younger daughter. After the
death of Virginia's mother, Leslie Stephen's second wife – Julia
Jackson had been the widow of Herbert Duckworth – Annie, though
no blood relative, embraced the role of aunt that came so easily to
her and which seemed to be expected of her, keeping a watchful,
interested eye on Leslie's talented and fragile daughter of this second
marriage, just as she continued to monitor the on-going care of Laura
Stephen, the vulnerable survivor from the first.

But this is looking towards the end of the story. We return first
to 1876, when a grieving Annie had reached the apparent certainties
and becalmed waters of middle-age. This biography of the Thackeray
family, which began in *The Inheritance of Genius* with the sixteen-
year-old Richmond Thackeray sailing to India in 1798, where his only
son would be born in 1811, picks up its narrative with Annie Thackeray,
Richmond's granddaughter, now placed firmly at its centre. She once
again found herself facing something of the same crippling sense of
loss which had come over her twelve years earlier, when her beloved
and eminent father had died from a sudden seizure at the age of fifty-
two. The death of her sister Minny in premature labour at the end of
November 1875, aged just thirty-five, presented her with the kind of
challenge that she had thought she had learnt to survive. How to go on,
soon to be forty, unmarried, alone? The future seemed bleak. The loss
of this adored sister with whom she had shared her father appeared to
have robbed her of any future possibility of happiness. And yet, almost
miraculously as it must have seemed, it turned out that there was a life
still to be built, a husband and family and opportunities for love and
hope lying just within her grasp, provided that for once she could place
her own happiness first.

In the second part of my account of this family, I am happy to repeat
my acknowledgements set out in the first. Not since Gordon Ray's
classic biography of Thackeray, written fifty years ago, has it been

possible to draw on so much previously unused and largely unseen material. As in *The Inheritance of Genius*, this domestic history draws continuously on the letters, diaries, journals and notebooks of the Thackerays and their circle. Apart from Thackeray's own letters, for which I am indebted to Ray's four-volume collected edition, as well as to the two-volume supplement edited by Edgar Harden, virtually all of the source material is newly transcribed. I have drawn on many archives, but three collections stand out. Early in my researches I was fortunate to meet Thackeray's great-granddaughter, Belinda Norman-Butler, who from the outset encouraged my work and maintained a lively interest until her death on Boxing Day of 2008, aged 100. She made freely available to me papers still in her possession, including her grandmother's (Annie's) journal and diaries, and permitted me to photograph Thackeray's pictures and drawings hanging on her walls. Her daughter, Catherine Wilson, has continued to encourage me in my work during its closing stages. Juliet Murray, another Thackeray great-great-granddaughter, has also been a wonderfully generous and hospitable friend, allowing me to use anything that I needed from her rich collection of letters, journals, drawings and other family papers. The opportunity to talk to her and to her aunt Belinda about people whose stories live on in the family memory has been a unique pleasure. Much from their collections has not previously been known to Thackeray scholars.

The third archive is the most extensive single collection of Anne Thackeray Ritchie papers, and was given by Belinda Norman-Butler to Eton College Library. It consists not just of Annie's letters, but also many of Minny's, a large number of letters from Thackeray's mother to her granddaughters, as well as correspondence from many family members and friends. I have spent seven years reading all of this material, and find it hard adequately to thank the Eton library staff for their generous assistance during this period. I want especially to credit Nick Baker, Linda Fowler, Rachel Bond and Michael Meredith. Michael's interest in my work has been generous and constant. He has freely shared his expert knowledge of the Victorians with me, and I value his friendship.

For this second volume, I am most grateful to the following for permitting me to quote from materials in their collections. The Joseph Milsand Archive, Armstrong Browning Library, Baylor University, Waco, Texas; Beinecke Library, Yale University; Bodleian Library, University of Oxford; Brotherton Collections, Leeds University Library; the Syndics of Cambridge University Library; Rauner Special Collections Library, Dartmouth College, Hanover, New Hampshire;

Duke University, Durham, North Carolina; the Provost and Fellows
of Eton College; Harry Ransom Humanities Research Center,
University of Texas at Austin; Houghton Library, Harvard University;
Huntington Library, San Marino, California; King's College Archives
Centre, Cambridge; University of Liverpool Library; John Murray
Archive, National Library of Scotland; Michael Millgate (private
collection); Morgan Library and Museum, New York; Heinz Archive
and Library, National Portrait Gallery, London; Department of
Rare Books and Special Collections, Princeton University Library;
the Masters and Fellows of Trinity College, Cambridge; Tennyson
Research Centre, Lincolnshire County Council.

I remain indebted to the late Belinda Norman-Butler, Catherine
Wilson and Juliet Murray for the right to use Thackeray and Ritchie
family materials, and to the following individuals and organisations
for allowing me to quote from items for which they hold the copyright:
Lady Delves Broughton (for Rhoda Broughton), The Carmelite
Monastery, London (for Baron Friedrich von Hügel), the Chichester
Partnership (for George du Maurier), the Provost and Fellows of
Eton College (for Sarianna Browning), Samuel French Ltd (for J.
M. Barrie), Henrietta Garnett (for Vanessa Bell, © Estate of Vanessa
Bell), Jennifer Gosse (for Edmund Gosse), Bay James (for Henry
James), Patricia Sedgwick (for George Meredith), the Selden Society
(for Frederick Maitland), the Society of Authors (for Leslie Stephen
© 2010 the Estate of Leslie Stephen, and for Virginia Woolf © 2010
Anne Olivier Bell and Angelica Garnett), and the Tennyson Research
Centre (for Tennyson family materials). I have endeavoured to trace
all copyright owners, and apologise for any inadvertent oversights.

I repeat my thanks for the many and various kindnesses shown me
by a number of people: Richard Aplin, Simonetta Berbeglia, Ian Brown
(National Library of Scotland), Richard Childs (county archivist, West
Sussex Record Office), Vanessa Curtis, Marion Dell, Colin Ford,
Veronica Franklin Gould, Elspeth Griffiths (Archivist, Sedbergh
School), Susan Halpert (Harvard College Library), Fr Kenneth Havey,
Lucinda Hawksley, Martin Hayes (Local Studies, West Sussex County
Council), Sue Hodson (Huntington Library), John Hopson (archivist,
British Library), Elisabeth Jay, Carol Hanbery Mackay, Jane Martineau,
Michael Millgate, Leslie Morris (Harvard College Library), Maureen
Moran, Xenia Murray, Christine Nelson (Morgan Library and
Museum), Hilary Newman, Christina Rathbone, Simon Reynolds, the
late Bryan Rhodes, Gayle Richardson (Huntington Library), William
Ritchie, Aaron Schmidt (Boston Public Library), Carrie Starren
(Leighton House Museum), John Sutherland, David Sutton (Reading

University Library), Grace Timmins (Tennyson Research Centre), Ann Wheeler (archivist, Charterhouse) and Derek Wood. I also thank the ever-courteous staff of the London Library. At the Lutterworth Press I have appreciated the interest of Adrian Brink and Aidan Van de Weyer, and benefited from the thoughtful advice of my editor, Ian Bignall, whom I also thank for his skilful design of both volumes. His successor, Charlie Livingston, took over the task gracefully and saw the project through to completion. To Peter Collister, who has lived with this project over the years, advised on drafts and steered me away from many of the crasser solecisms, I am more than grateful. He is not to blame for the faults that undoubtedly remain.

Throughout these volumes I have chosen to call Thackeray's eldest daughter 'Annie', even though her father himself wrote 'Anny'. This may seem perverse, but after the death of her sister in 1875 the only person regularly to spell it like that was Leslie Stephen, as did the children of his second marriage (including Virginia and Vanessa). Everyone else, husband, other family members and friends, kept with 'Annie'. However, I have not changed spellings of names in quoted letters. This means that in my own text I can reserve the name 'Anny Thackeray' for the daughter of Edward and Amy Thackeray, one of the two little girls who came to live with Annie and Minny after their mother's death. In my quotations from original manuscripts I have tended not to amend spelling errors or supply missing punctuation, although full stops have occasionally been silently supplied to assist meaning.

# One

# THIS SOMETHING
# COME INTO MY LIFE

## (1875-1877)

*One sees those who suffer enveloped in a sort of invisible cloud through which nothing human can pass but it loses all meaning & force: & all the goodwill & sympathy in the world are ineffectual to help. I learnt this lesson when still a boy when I used to be with Annie after Minnie died. And thus though it has not been my fate to lose part of my life by another's death I seem in a fashion to understand what sorrow is.*

Richmond Ritchie to his Sister, Gussie Freshfield
May 1891

When her sister Minny Stephen died at the end of November 1875 in the agonies of premature labour, Annie Thackeray was staying overnight with Margaret Oliphant in Windsor. Summoned by a telegraph to return to London, the intensity of her grief was fed by feelings of guilt. She had been lost in this dark tunnel once before, after her father had suffered his fatal seizure at Christmas 1863. The loneliness this time was acute. She knew that her duty was to support Minny's husband and child, and the pathos of five-year-old Laura's uncomprehending utterances was heart-breaking – 'Why does not my mommee come?' Annie told Emily Tennyson something of Leslie Stephen's tender courage. '[He] thinks of me & of little Laura & is so gentle & noble. I think she w<sup>d</sup>. be proud of him – as she always was.'[1] She and Leslie were never closer than in these bleak days, but she felt isolated and despairing at times. Months later, writing about Annie to Charles Eliot Norton, Leslie reflected that 'She is left alone of her family, though her mother – strange as it sounds to me – still lives & is apparently likely to outlive many of us.'[2]

And yet, retreating with Leslie to Brighton after the funeral at Kensal Green, Annie was able to experience a strange calm at times, wanting to believe that the healing had begun. 'I have had one or two little nervous attacks but nothing to speak of & Leslie mopes about but nothing to speak of. I think it will take a long time & every minute is a long time now. But I could never never have believed that one could have borne it so well.' She took comfort in traditional faith, imagining Minny joined with her father's dead cousin, Jane Ritchie, 'so plainly walking in the sunshine'. She mapped out an immediate future for herself, planning to return to Brighton for a more sustained period of recovery. And then she turned back to her father's death, persuaded that Minny's illness during her last weeks had some kind of genetic link to the poor health of his own final months, rather than being solely a crisis in her pregnancy. 'I believe it <u>is</u> true that my darling had some illness like Papa's. What should I do now if I had not those she loved.'[3]

When she returned to Brighton, she was accompanied by Richmond Ritchie, the second cousin seventeen years her junior. She continued to be pursued by the same feelings of guilt that followed Thackeray's death, for in both instances she had failed to be present during the final moments. She wrote to her father's American friend, Mrs Baxter, that 'it is my Fate – & she was dead when I came back next day, with tender closed eyes and a face so radiant. It was Papas illness killed her not her little baby, w[h] never was born, some convulsion – We had no parting only she had been so very tender – like a mother.'[4] Brighton seemed dreary once Richmond had returned to Cambridge, where he was a Trinity College undergraduate, but Annie strove to believe that her life would continue to be rich by virtue of her good fortune. 'What suddenly cheered me up just now about everything – was thinking what prizes I have drawn in Life – what dear dear prizes – no one ever had such a life as mine or such love in it.'[5]

Back in London, Annie and Leslie spent the rest of the winter at Southwell Gardens, but before long were planning to move, wanting to escape the sadness of a house in which Minny's influence was everywhere. There seemed no question but that they would continue together under one roof. Minny would have wanted this, and just then it was what both needed. During March and April of 1876 some of the pain eased, and Annie employed her normal strategy at times of loss – she converted the sadnesses into blessings. A sequence of short notes to Jeanie Senior, the social campaigner and sister of author Thomas Hughes, give an insight into her feelings.

> I like much [the] best to be treated as usual for now that time has passed & I have had a little silent time to face the truth I can only feel still that I & my Minny cant be separated death cant be <u>wicked</u> it doesnt undo her faithful tender love of years....
>
> I think you know what I mean when I say how <u>overawed</u> I feel at my own blessings, at the thought of Minnys love & tender trust in her old sister. I can only say in my heart to her Darling we can't be not together & then it seems to me as if we <u>were</u> heart to heart somehow. O pray God death is not death <u>there</u>, any more than it is here.[6]

And there was Richmond to divert her. Through that long winter and into the spring, his mix of maturity and youth could always lighten her, and he would come at a moment's notice from Cambridge, 'like new life in the darkness of gloom'.[7] Unfortunately, what she regarded as a delightful tendency to turn up unexpectedly tended to irritate Leslie, who never really took to Richmond. He always resisted the clannishness of the Ritchies, and probably would have preferred the Thackeray sisters to have lived less in their cousins' pockets.

Money was a worry, for since completing *Miss Angel* in mid-1875, her *roman à clef* about the painter Angelica Kauffmann, Annie had not earned much from her writing, and this new crisis left her in no condition to work freely. There was nothing in progress, and no major project planned. She found herself envying both George Eliot and George Sand for their ability to 'strike up & begin to tune their instruments, specially G. Sand who seems to me to boom & echo all through her prefaces & sweep one into her stupid books so that it doesnt matter how stupid they are'.[8] During February she noted that there was just £35 in the bank, of which £27 had to be set aside for her maid's wages. Well-intentioned measures to control her outgoings did not survive long, including a resolve to reduce the costs of correspondence by taking advantage of the lower postal rate for postcards. She also tried to make savings by planning inexpensive little treats. She told Richmond that 'we will only do nice cheap things no nasty expensive ones.... We will go & see Whistlers pictures too when you come, that is also cheap & within a walk.'[9]

Leslie Stephen was supporting her to a degree that Annie simply did not realise and which, despite his reputation for financial caution, he never thought of denying her. In marrying Minny he had taken on a household which included not just Annie, but on occasion the two little girls to whom the Thackeray sisters acted as honorary step-aunts,

Margie and Anny, the daughters from the marriage of their father's cousin, Edward Thackeray, to their former companion, Amy Crowe. Much later, Leslie described the financial arrangements in the private memoir he wrote for the children of his second marriage. He may be forgiven the tone of self-congratulation, for ever since his marriage to Minny, and until Annie's own marriage, he had met her household costs.

> I found it rather unpleasant to tell her of her debts to me. She did not quite approve of this practice. She thought or took for granted that I ought to be as careless as she was herself; and somehow it is not easy to present oneself as a creditor without appearing to be a curmudgeon. Here comes in my boast. I gave up reminding Anny of her debts, and was content to take upon myself much the largest share of the expenses – more, that is, than my proper share. I am always glad of this. From something which Anny said to me the other day, I find that she is still completely ignorant of the fact. She remembered and spoke with more than abundant gratitude of a present which I was afterwards able to give her. I gave her £500 to enable her to buy a house upon her marriage; and she talked about repaying this some day or of her children repaying mine. I mention this here, partly because I wish you to understand that should such a repayment be offered – which, I confess, strikes me as improbable – it is not to be accepted. I am too proud, I hope, to turn any gifts of mine into loans. But I wish chiefly to say that I have no cause of regret for any of my pecuniary relations with Anny. I avoided – I am thankful to say – that rock of offence: and though I may regret faults of temper, I cannot charge myself with a want of liberality.[10]

Yet, as Leslie conceded in a note added in July 1898, Annie would eventually refund him from the proceeds of the Biographical Edition of her father's works. She wanted to give him £800 (which perhaps indicated that she was rather more conscious of her indebtedness than Leslie supposed), but he would only take £400, and only then because Annie insisted upon it.

Late in October 1876 they sold 8 Southwell Gardens for £4,100, having by then moved to a house in Hyde Park Gate South which had been left jointly to Annie and Minny as a legacy from Thackeray's mother, Mrs Carmichael-Smyth. In acknowledgment of his portion of the Thackeray inheritance which came to him through Minny, Leslie now spent about £900 on the purchase of a house in Lingfield Road, close to Wimbledon Common, with the intention that Annie's mother might be placed there. Isabella Thackeray had lived with carers ever since the severe postnatal depression which followed Minny's birth in 1840, but for how long this Wimbledon house was used for her needs is unclear, for during most of her remaining years she lived with a married couple, Mr and Mrs Thompson, at Leigh-on-Sea, near Southend. It was a curious regime for Leslie, responsible not just for Annie but, when Edward Thackeray was away, for Margie and Anny too, now aged thirteen and eleven. Annie noted that when the girls were with them, 'Leslie used to take them to school every morning'.[11] Ten years later, after Margie had married Gerald Ritchie, Richmond's elder brother, Leslie settled 'quite a sum of money' on the younger sister, a generous gesture which caused Annie to 'cry with pleasure'.[12]

The domestic routine which Leslie and Annie now established together offered her – indeed, offered both of them – a framework of stabilising normality. In the end though, it was Richmond's support and love which saved her, once she saw that only he could supply the conditions for her renewal. The devotion which Annie had formerly lavished on her sister would be transferred to him, for she increasingly had come to value Richmond's family links, a year earlier sending him one of her father's letters to read. 'Do you know the last time I ever saw his dear face he sent me away. I just remember going back & standing by his bedside not thinking him ill, but looking at him & you see after eleven years I find you my dear to talk to about him & to be yourself too.'[13] Flattered, he succumbed to the intoxicating Thackeray genius worn so lightly and yet so authentically by Annie. He was quietly proud of being able to sign his schoolboy letters from Eton as 'Richmond Thackeray Ritchie', and he would have been pleased to realise that his own father had been Thackeray's favourite cousin. The trauma of Minny's death made any embarrassment about how others might view his and Annie's relationship seem trivial, yet there remained the discrepancy between their ages. When they married in August 1877, Annie was forty and Richmond a few days away from being twenty-three. Contemporary proprieties were undeniably shocked.

As the youngest of the four Ritchie brothers, Richmond was adored by his family. He was clever and handsome, reserved and thoughtful, but perhaps underneath it all a little too confidently assured in his views, suggesting complacency sometimes, character traits which resurfaced through his adult life. A formal manner hid real wit and a winning comedic gift, and Annie's droll self-mockery appealed to him. When he was a schoolboy she treated him as a young adult, and Edward

Lyttelton remembered him at Eton as a boy 'old before his years',[14] something which his school photographs tend to confirm. There was every reason to expect a brilliant future for him. He had been only eight when he won a King's Scholarship to Eton in July 1863, and was awarded the coveted Newcastle Medal in his final school year. His family called him Witz or Wizz, as did his own children later. President of the Eton Literary Society and a member of 'Pop' – the membership of which was determined by the boys themselves – Richmond went on to Trinity College, Cambridge, where he joined Hallam and Lionel Tennyson in their father's and Thackeray's old college. The expectations were great.

Howard Sturgis, his Eton and Cambridge contemporary, would re-member Richmond as being 'endowed from boyhood with the strength, the self-reliance, the maturity of taste and judgment which the rest of us hardly acquire with wrinkles and grey hairs. Nothing ripens the intelligence so early as that terrible ironic perception of the tears and laughter in things, which is called a sense of humour. Richmond Ritchie possessed that in an eminent degree, and had, moreover, one of the surest and most brilliant minds I have ever known.'[15] Sturgis was highly susceptible to Richmond's charm, though as Richmond's star rose his admiration was offered from a distance. When his ultimate appointment as Permanent Under Secretary at the India Office came through in 1909, Sturgis shyly offered congratulations. 'I follow your career from afar, like a little astronomer watching a comet through a telescope, but with a much warmer & more personal interest.... I should like to think that my little fluttered handkerchief, or thrown up hat has given you pleasure.'[16] He never forgot the affection of their undergraduate days, and Richmond's capacity 'to make me laugh, helplessly, rolling on the floor & begging him not to be so funny. Can you fancy that?'[17]

Thackeray had once been much amused to discover the boy of eight engrossed in *The Great Hoggarty Diamond*. But he was not just intellectually precocious. In September 1869, aged fifteen, and accompanied by his slightly older brother Gerald, he became the youngest person to climb to the summit of Mont Blanc – a feat recorded by the Alpine Club and which even Leslie must have admired. But in later life, the enormous demands of the India Office meant that his time for leisure was limited, though he was a successful golfer and keen bicyclist. He became a victim of Ménière's disease – probably many of the flu-like symptoms which plagued him derived from this debilitating condition which affects balance – and the constant stress of his work took its toll.

*Richmond Ritchie as a boy*

The months from about mid-1876 shaped the future relationship of Richmond and Annie, though at first she regarded her own feelings as having the kind of purity with which a mother loves her child. She wrote to him that 'loving people is the one thing of all things that seems to prove something beyond us in life – If anything is true, it is true that sincere & unselfish love does belong to the best & holiest of the impulses of life. I daresay to us both sometimes my foolish maternal

*Richmond Ritchie at Eton. He is standing in the front, on the right.*

sort of sentiment may have seemed absurd.'[18] Margaret Oliphant
thought that by the beginning of May Annie was at last 'looking
very much herself'.[19] All through the late spring and early summer,
simple, everyday activities could in a moment sweep her back into the
comforting safeties of the past. Out shopping for hats with Laura, Annie
gazed into the milliner's looking-glass. 'It was like some extraordinary
dream suddenly to see myself in a glass with a crown of pink roses,
for an instant it seemed as if everything had gone back years & years.
Its just like one of the dreams I have.'[20] Richmond pronounced on her
health with all the wisdom of his twenty-one years. 'Of course you
must try to get into a habit of seeing other people and helping them as
you did before; only you must take care and not overdo yourself.'[21]

Before accompanying Leslie to Kensal Green to see Minny's
headstone put in position, Annie wrote to Pinkie Ritchie, her favourite
amongst Richmond's sisters, picturing a free spirit happy near the
Tennysons' Farringford home at Freshwater on the Isle of Wight. Were
the horrors of the last months merely an illusion? The practical business
required at the cemetery reminded her that it was all too real. 'I can

imagine you quite well in the kind dear green glades. It seems to me as if <u>there</u> somehow my Minnie was still alive to me & all seems like a dream when I fly off in my mind to Ff^d & the big window & my dear Lady [Tennyson] in her corner. Give her my kiss.… I am now going to see my dear stone laid & to speak to the gardener about the ivy.'[22] She was even managing a little work now. Her constant concern for Leslie's comfort is touching, for when she planned a short visit away she asked Mrs Oliphant whether Laura and her father might go to her in Windsor during her own absence. 'I shall be so much happier if I think he is in y^r. kind keeping that it will make all the difference in my pleasure.' In this same letter she refers to Margaret Oliphant's current serialisation in the *Cornhill*, clearly finding meaningful associations in the story. 'I read Carita last night – O how well you write. There is not one vestige of us in it but it haunted me & haunted me.'[23]

In early June Annie visited the Elton family home at Clevedon, near Bristol, the location where many years before Thackeray had realised what Jane Brookfield meant to him. The wife of one of his oldest friends from Cambridge days, Jane had provided a focus for Thackeray's emotional outpourings until William Brookfield summarily put an end to the friendship. Annie first sought out her aunt Jane Shawe in Clifton, for her behaviour was beginning to cause concern. Clevedon was like a magic place, the pleasure which she experienced there on the terrace having an almost visionary intensity. She yearned for her father and her sister, but they were gone. The thought of Richmond offered a more immediate reality.

> Aunt Jane [Shawe] had got some mysterious fancy that I had said she had £70 in the savings bank & that I was counting on it – poor dear its distracting to think of such a waste of life & generous feeling & power of affection. She is exactly like L^y Sarah Francis in Old Kensington only much more dreary – But this isnt what I wanted to tell you about but something Oh! so lovely, a rainbow sort of Tennyson poem starting into life – w^h. is the terrace at Clevedon Court – the sweetest quaintest most exquisite thing with a fountain dropping into a marble basin with long rows of pink drowsy poppy heads, with a sight of all the summer in the valley & all the silver in the sea & the old grey ivy gables tumbling & piling in the hollow (Excuse the authoress). Darling, I longed for you & I wished so I had come with Papa & Minnie.[24]

She and Richmond were now exchanging love letters, though neither might have recognised them to be such. But there was something

decidedly clandestine about their behaviour. Richmond was treating
her letters secretively, preserving them carefully in a bureau bought
from a pawnbroker for £3, and discreetly destroying envelopes, perhaps
fearing his relatives' irritation at the evidence of their on-going correspondence. In one letter, he conjures up conventional lovers' images
on returning to Cambridge from a country visit –

> all your letters are comfortably installed in an absurdly small
> receptacle which has got a special key and if you are alarmed
> you may have it in your keeping. However I did resolutely
> burn a pile of envelopes and the ashes are still reproaching
> me in the little grate with little sparks running about like
> fairy good wishes.... [W]e drove back through the sunset
> and the stars blazed and a little crescent moon hung ever so
> high up; and I had only just time to rush to my school; and
> after that I thought of you and went to bed and to a sound
> sound sleep instead of writing.[25]

Annie, Leslie and Laura spent most of July at Coniston, in the Lake
District, staying near Leslie's old friend Victor Marshall from where
Annie paid more than one visit to Ruskin. She admired the simplicity of
Ruskin's style of life, and his 'lovely little aesthetic encampment here.
They are all as kind as they can be in fits of delight over <u>scraps</u>, not the
lake & the mountains but a gooseberry or a feather off a chicken's head
or something of the sort..., Ruskin has beautiful old bibles & missals
& above all such nice strawberries at his house. He says if you can
draw a strawberry you can draw anything.'[26]

The tranquillity of the surroundings made her feel Minny's absence
acutely. 'It would have made Minny O so happy to be here and every
little flower & cloud & tint seemed to ache for her.'[27] She was also
missing Richmond, and made arrangements for a number of his
family to come to Coniston to take summer lodgings. 'I think I shall
wait till you come to feel it all tho' I <u>see</u> how sweet & fair & fresh
& exquisite everything is.' Mrs Ritchie and Richmond eventually
joined them, together with his unmarried sisters Pinkie and Elinor. In
sending birthday greetings to another of Richmond's sisters, Blanche
Warre Cornish, she admitted to having been suddenly struck by
Laura's resemblance to Thackeray, a consoling sign of heredity and
what Thomas Hardy calls 'the family face'. 'This morning as I was
looking at her asleep she made a little face that was so like Papa, it
came over me with a happy sort of ache to think that the children
carry about some positive real true identity of the dear still dearer
ones whose life they live & still are. No children can ever ever be to

me what their parents are & have been, but how much Ah how much, I never knew till now. I am very glad I had a little talk with my Min about it once.'[28]

She sent a note to Ruskin at Brantwood during the morning of 28 July, inviting him to call. Later came his reply, which Annie carefully kept and pasted into a leather-bound book which in 1890 she presented to Richmond to remind him of that precious time. The original diary entry for that same day she would later cut out and paste in her journal, its record of another vivid dream the reason for its preservation. 'Last night I dreamt that it was Papa's funeral over again. There was a strange clanging music. I stood by the grave & people came & shook me by the hand, & somehow they took his hand too. I mean to think no more of Death till it comes. If I die I hope L: will marry somebody – Julia Marshall perhaps.'[29] She did not die, but she would leave Leslie and he would get married again, though not to Julia Marshall.

Annie also kept another small portion of her diary for the end of November, when Richmond came to be with her for the anniversary of Minny's death. It was always going to be an important time, and it seems that they moved towards a common understanding of what their future might be.

> *27 November* Went to the station and waited ½ an hour for R who was very very very glad to see me. Caroline dined. and then R. & I had a long and <u>most interesting</u> conversation.
>
> *28 November* R basely deserted me and went to Eton to play football. I trolled over the S.K.M with Miss Villis protégés and was very ill and had to go to bed. R payed me a little visit [*This was the anniversary of Minny's death*]
>
> *29 November* On the sofa but very happy. R spending the day out. He went to the play in the evening leaving me again stranded.
>
> *30 November* R went and was very very very sorry to go away. He enjoyed his visit very much and so did I.

Through the course of this first sad year, the endearments in their letters had grown ever more affectionate; 'dearest' becomes 'darling', and by December he is addressing Annie as 'sweetheart'. The year ended far more calmly than Annie can ever have felt possible at its start. On New Year's Day she went with Leslie and Laura to stay for a week with Dr and Mrs Jackson, Julia Duckworth's parents, at Frant, near Tunbridge Wells. Saxonbury was a lovely house, surrounded by woodland. Annie was much taken with Julia's mother, ill though she was, for she 'seemed to be much more alive than anyone else [and] inspired one with new interest in ones own life & belief in goodness'. Her instinctive and unsophisticated sympathies, together with a love of friends and family, chimed happily with Annie's views about what was important. 'She loved her children passionately & she loved her friends fervently & Poets & the Past & she was not religious but Religion somehow was so intense so tender & merry & unworldly. M^rs. Jackson would be carried down of an evening & we would all dine by lamplight & go into the dark morning room where we all sat round & talked & she quoted Poetry & Leslie responded.'[30] The next day came exciting news that Fitzjames Stephen, Leslie's brother, had been given a baronetcy, followed on 3 January by a letter from Richmond 'about what Willy said'. Presumably, Richmond had discussed his possible future with his eldest brother, but we do not learn what advice he received. Later that day, Leslie, on good form, recited Thackeray's poem 'The Chronicle of the Drum' to them all. It had been a happy visit. Back in London, Annie took time to have 'a long talk with Leslie'; again, this must have been about her future, and how Richmond might feature in it. It is impossible to know whether marriage was yet part of their plans.

At the end of a fortnight in the Alps, where he always found solace and refreshment, Leslie urged Annie to keep to a measured regime, knowing how easily she could overreach herself. 'Never on any account whatever go out before luncheon & never allow anybody to come in – just sit at home & be idle. Always take a short walk after lunch, whoever comes to see you & don't go out to dinner. If you will stick to that (making no exceptions) for the next six months, you will thank me for the advice.'[31] During this month, Richmond prepared for an examination at Trinity, and once it was over came to London and took Annie for a walk in the dark. Leslie returned from the Alps on 30 January, and just two days after Annie and Richmond's night-time walk, he witnessed the 'catastrophe' of them kissing in the drawing-room at Hyde Park Gate South. Accounts of this event and its aftermath have always drawn on Leslie's highly partial recollections, where, as he freely admits, his principal concerns were selfish ones, tinged by jealousy. He hated the idea of Annie marrying 'perhaps, as Julia suggested to me, partly because all men are jealous and I might feel that I was being put at a lower level in Anny's affections; I certainly thought that it would make a widening gulf between us; I hated it because men at least always hate a marriage between a young man and a much older woman; and I hated it because the most obvious result would be the breaking up of my own household'.[32] But what upset him most was a feeling that he had been compromised: he had seen the kiss and felt bound to insist upon a resolution to the situation. Leslie's distaste also reveals an underlying prudishness, for the overt affection which this particular relationship had reached made him require Annie 'to make up her mind one way or other'. Perhaps he expected a different outcome, but his ultimatum resulted in Annie telling him that same afternoon that she and Richmond were engaged. On 31 January, Leslie and Julia Duckworth talked to Richmond, presumably exploring his prospects if marriage was to be a realistic proposition in the near future. Leslie was now determined that the marriage should advance quickly, Annie's age meaning that time was not on her side. 'Soon afterwards I read in the paper that there was to be a competition for certain public offices. I wrote to Richmond, suggesting that this was a good chance for obtaining something to marry upon. He entered accordingly and won a clerkship in the India Office.'

In fact, things did not move quite as fast as this suggests. Nothing was made public for some months, and the engagement – if it really was as formal as that – was not widely known within the family. Richmond's mother and Jane Brookfield called, and they were probably told. Annie admitted to feeling 'quite overdone'. After so many months of uncertain feelings the sudden change in her prospects seemed to bring her close to breakdown again. It was convenient that Julia Duckworth was Annie and Leslie's immediate neighbour, and only too ready to minister to Annie who moved in with her for some weeks. It was all very comforting. 'Came to sofa, tea, jelly care.'[33] A stay of a few days extended itself from early February until the beginning of April, and Annie was able to work once more. It was the decisive period of recuperation, at the end of which she could tell Mrs Oliphant of her return to normal life, and of the good health of Leslie and Laura – 'she is very well & so is Leslie, & so am I at last. I came home really yesterday for I had been staying on at Julia Duckworths & it is so nice to be free again & able to walk & talk & come & go without always thinking about my health.'[34]

Annie lost another old friend when Jeanie Senior died on 24 March after a long illness. There had been sickbed visits, and Jeanie's courage was inspirational. 'Seeing her did me good for it was all sunset & gentle & I could cry & sit by her bed in the window. She has a grey room full of Azaleas & all her hair shines & her face looks like an angels & little Harry Hughes was deep in an arm chair reading Vanity Fair.'[35] Annie was deeply affected to observe an alternative means of dying, so unlike the cruel suddenness of Minny's going. 'She died at 7 o'c on Saturday as she lived, loving them sparing them – no crepe she said for me no mourning only flowers. Carry me away on Monday.'[36]

In April she spent some days with the Rothschilds at Mentmore Towers in Bedfordshire, and wrote to Richmond on notepaper borrowed from Hannah Rothschild, having removed what she could of the black-edged border. 'The more I think of it the more I feel as if a day might come when people will think of death with love & blessing & gratitude for the past & with less sorrow & gloom.' She gloried in the signs of the burgeoning spring when she walked out. And at night, she found it an easy transition from thinking about Minny to contemplation of Richmond, for there he was, mystically transfigured in the heavens and the flashing stars. He was looking out from his Cambridge window at just that same moment, surely?

> There was a great field full of lambs & hares yesterday & chestnut trees in bud w$^h$. put me more in mind of Minnie than all the gloom that ever was massed together.... I did like it so – & then last night, when the day was over I woke up about one o'clock & my room was full of smoke & I got up & opened the window wide & then it was you I seemed to see for all the stars were lighted up & a silver crescent was dropping & a sort of faint flame seemed to come from the horizon.... It was so lovely & you do like starlight nights dont you – Oh I hope you looked out of window last night.[37]

Duty cut short her visit, and she returned to London having been told by Jane Brookfield that Laura was unwell and Leslie 'very low'. The needs of others would always come first.

Much as the prospect of the change to his own circumstances distressed him, once Annie had made her decision Leslie fought her corner, for several of the Ritchies were implacably opposed to Richmond's marrying a woman so much older than himself. Mrs Ritchie had a different concern, for although she loved Annie dearly she feared for her son's glittering Cambridge prospects. Annie removed herself to Freshwater, Richmond returned to Cambridge, and Leslie worked on the Ritchies. This was perhaps the most unhappy part of the business for him, finding himself accused of precipitating the engagement and of encouraging Richmond to give up Cambridge for a civil service position. 'They complained of me for ruining his degree by suggesting the public office: though if he had neglected the chance the marriage might have been indefinitely postponed greatly to Anny's injury. The fact was that if they hated the marriage, I positively loathed it. I could not speak of it to Julia without exploding in denunciations.' He might easily have stood aside and let the relationship drift towards collapse; his refusal to do so speaks well of his commitment to Annie's best interests. Julia doubtless softened his views, for having Annie as a house guest for two months had shown her that Minny's death was not the real source of Annie's present malaise. This very different emotional crisis required a different solution.

The best of Leslie emerges in the surviving correspondence. If his personal objections to the marriage remained, not least to Richmond as a suitable husband for Annie – 'I would do anything in the world for her, but I cannot and shall not feel close to her after she has taken up with that boy'[38] – the painful honesty of his letters to Annie show him disinterestedly advising on her own best actions. The news came through on 1 May that Richmond had been successful in the civil service examinations, and Annie and Jane Brookfield sought Sir Henry Cole's advice about which office Richmond might try for. Until she heard his views, Annie was un-persuaded that work of this kind was the right thing for a man of Richmond's talents, but Cole convinced her both as to its value and social standing. He did not favour the Post Office – 'tiresome humdrum drudgery'; he felt that the Record Office certainly had its attractions for a studious, serious man with its interesting documents offering opportunities for literary work; but for someone of Richmond's capabilities 'he should unhesitatingly recommend the India Office or the Home Office. In the India Office there are all sorts of wide interests stirring, a man can make his own mark in a little time.'[39] Once he had pointed out that it was answerable to a senior government member – for it was responsible for the administration of the most powerful regions within the Empire – Annie registered its 'different social standing'.

Richmond required no further prompting, and three days later sent a telegram to Freshwater announcing an opening at the India Office. Mrs Ritchie's agreement that he should give up Cambridge for this opportunity was essential if the marriage was to proceed. Having already argued so strongly for this course of action, Leslie maintained his re-solve, prompting his conflict with the Ritchies. There was still a part of Annie which contemplated delay, doubtless because she was conscious of Richmond leaving Cambridge for her, but Leslie was adamant.

> I have an extreme repugnance to talking about R. with you, because I hate all talk about such feelings & because in this case my sympathy is so imperfect that I am afraid of being hurried into some remark wh. would shock you. It is useless to ask what you & he ought to have done & I wont think more about it than I can help. But as matters are, I do urge you in spite of all your protestations to the contrary, to be married as soon as possible.

I say so first, because a year hence you will be in no better position than you are now, or at least the difference in your position will be infinitesimal, & quite useless to take into account. Assuming that you are to marry at all, I can see no shadow of a reason for putting it off.

But 2ndly, the intervening time would be most trying. You would have all the Ritchies at you, worrying & pestering & talking nonsense & piling up scenes. You will always be proposing to unsettle everything that has been settled, & in short, it will be a year of worry & excitement – than wh. nothing can be worse for you. Why prolong anything so unpleasant? If you could give it up altogether, well & good – I should be delighted; but short of that I would do it at once.[40]

He also disabused her of any thoughts of delaying her departure on his account, or of establishing a joint home. 'I really dread the strain upon my temper, if I am to have Richmond always about the house & Ritchies buzzing in & out & ranting interviews & thrilling explanations & all the rest of it. The sort of divided allegiance wh. you will owe to R. & to me would be really irritating.... It is very awkward to be always a third person, & especially an unsympathetic 3d person.' He might have expressed it better, especially as Annie had been the third person during all the years of his marriage to Minny, but that was not in his thoughts when he wrote so frankly about Richmond, who was quite a different proposition. Then he played his trump card. 'I wish you to do whatever will make you happy & I should think myself unfaithful to Minny if your happiness were not one of my first objects in life.'

Annie took his objection to Richmond's presence rather to heart, feeling that she ought to look at once for her own house, for she had not grasped that Leslie had been looking ahead and imagining the married couple living with him into some indeterminate future. The idea of her immediate departure was almost worse.

You seem to fancy that I expect to be so much bored by R & you, that I would rather have you out of the house. At least, that is the only way in wh. I can account for your plan of taking a house. I object to the plan altogether, because I entirely deny the truth of your assumption. I should be deeply annoyed at your leaving me before your marriage.... I really could not bear it. No, you <u>must</u> stay with me till you marry. I ask it of you as a special favour & I will be as

*William, Blanche, and Gussie Ritchie, about 1860.*

good as I can in regard to Richmond. The separation would vex me far more than his presence. I would rather even that he lodged with us till his marriage than that you went away from me.... I implore you not to think of parting from me till the parting is necessary. <u>That</u> would really make me feel as if I were not fulfilling my duty to Minny.[41]

She felt thankful, having no wish to upset Leslie any more than her decision to marry had already distressed him. What cheered her most was the knowledge that people were at last speaking the truth to each other. Whether others approved of it or not was almost a secondary matter. 'I feel suddenly quite relieved & sleepy & peaceful & the sea has begun to flow & the hedges to give pleasure & your ladyship to realise the blessing w$^h$. is hers.'[42]

Meanwhile, Leslie was fighting their battle, and eventually triumphed on 11 May, a long day producing two letters and resulting in a noble victory which could only have given him considerable personal anguish. In the longer first letter, written during the morning, he assured Annie that she must ignore the objections of other people, including his own. 'You ought to decide it entirely upon the considerations of your own happiness & Richmond's & to leave my fancies out of sight altogether & also the fancies of R's family.' He was concerned that some of the Ritchies, principally Richmond's sisters Gussie and Blanche, were urging delay, for he feared that Annie's health would not withstand 'a year more of uncertainty & vexation with the Ritchies.... They are young & talk as if years were of no importance. They delight in making scenes, wh. is a simple torture of your nerves.' Leslie insisted that Annie should remain objective.

> Make up your mind, of course, but leave us to give it effect & to deal with Mrs R. & Gussie & Blanche & the whole kit of them. What you & R decide upon will be accepted by me as fine. I will then do all the fighting for you & the sentimentalizing & the discussion of ways & means & all the rest of it. Dearest Anny, I ask this as a right. I feel that I have inherited Minny's position & your father's. I wish that I had their power of making you happy; but at least you must let me do what they would have done had they been with us still.

He could not have come up with words that were more persuasive.

Later that day he talked to Mrs Ritchie, and his idea that Richmond might continue to work for his degree away from Cambridge seemed to clinch things for her, prompting his second letter of quiet triumph.

> [M]atters have much changed since I wrote. I have seen Mrs Ritchie, who is incomparably the most sensible of the lot. She talked pleasantly about you & will do everything that is wanted. I have no doubt that she will consent to anything that you & Richmond may determine. She said that she

should allow him his £200 a year & was otherwise perfectly judicious in her remarks.... I shall only say that I think he had better go in for his degree or, at least, promise to consider it, because it will please his mother & might be useful.[43]

Annie was sitting quietly in Watts's Freshwater studio listening to Thoby Prinsep talking of his early life in India when the clinching telegram arrived from Richmond – 'Mother consents I am appointed to the India Office'.[44] She went to share her news with Jane Senior's mother in her cottage at Colwell Bay, and with the Tennysons at Farringford – 'they were all very kind'. The effectiveness of Leslie's work behind the scenes is borne out by Mrs Ritchie's own letter, which was wholly loving and generous towards Annie. If lingering anxieties remained, there could be no doubt but that Annie's happiness was assured by this particular endorsement.

> Well darling I suppose it is all settled. I am sure you know by y$^r$. self that I have many conflicting feelings but this is certain & uppermost that I love you most dearly and that I know you will be the dearest & most loving wife my Richmond could have won for himself – & that I most earnestly pray & hope that your love for each other which has certainly been well tested will keep you as it has now <u>brought</u> you to the same <u>level</u> as it were. The dear fellow has been two days with us and is very happy & radiant – I had a talk with Leslie yesterday and he was very kind & full of love for you and solicitude for y$^r$. welfare.... We have not yet heard when R. will have to begin at the India Office but I am sure I can get him leave to finish this term at Cambridge & he will then have resided long enough to take his degree.... Of course he cant take such a good place as I hoped he would when he began his College career but he says himself that if he is able to go on reading he ought to be in the 1$^{st}$. class.... This will hardly bring you nearer to us than you are already, and have been for many years that you have been like a sister to the girls and a daughter to me.[45]

Even Leslie mellowed, and later in the month he gave a more considered assessment of Richmond's virtues to Charles Eliot Norton, who had been a regular correspondent ever since Leslie's first trip to America in 1863.

> He is many years her junior – a fact wh. is the only objection to the marriage, for he is a thoroughly able & honourable

man & devotedly attached to her. The story of their affection is a long one, and I have seen this coming for many months, though it is only of late that I saw it to be inevitable

People will of course be surprised & probably some will be displeased. Women are not allowed to do such unusual things without criticism. On the other hand, the unusualness is in itself a proof of the strength of the feelings wh. have brought it about; & upon that side I have no fears. I am as certain as I can be of anything that the marriage will be as happy as mutual affection can make it. That is of course the great thing – almost the only thing.[46]

News of the engagement spread quickly – it was probably already a poorly-kept secret – and within days letters arrived in great numbers. Some people had to be told in person, and once Annie left Freshwater she went to explain things to Margie and Anny. It would have been a poignant meeting, as was her visit to Wimbledon to her mother on 26 May. And then Richmond arrived, Annie recording in her journal for 29 May '1ˢᵗ HAPPY DAY'. She meant two things by this. Recent uncertainties were behind her, and her lonely vigil since Minny's death was at last ending.

Even her anxiety about others' prejudices was dissipating, and she told Pinkie Ritchie, whose support had always been strongest, that

I had a horrid bout of purgatory & doubt but the moment I saw him a sort of conviction of blessed peace & reality came over me & he too said that he had been afraid I meant to put off & off & so slide away for ever.... Dear my worst doubts were for him. For me I never could pretend to have any except indeed some very insignificant ones as to what people may think.

She had already sent Pinkie the briefest of notes from Freshwater, on this one occasion permitting herself a selfish thought. 'O my darling I can only cry because I am so happy.... O my dearest it ought to be you not me – no I wont say that but only God bless you my own Pinnie & give you the love and happiness you give to others.'[47] To Nina Lehmann she quietly rejoiced at 'this something come into my life wʰ. seems to make it full of gratitude & reality', even as she wondered at the sacrifice that Richmond was making for her. 'I do feel so sorry for Richmond sometimes yet I cant when I see him, he is so happy & singleminded & it does seem such a miracle.'[48] She wrote to

Browning's friend, Joseph Milsand, just days after the engagement was made public. 'When my sister died I had no more courage left to refuse the familiar comfort & help of his presence & most youthful affection …. I do not think Richmond will care less for an old wife than he has done for his old cousin & in that case I think he will be happy. I am sure I am.'[49] Perhaps she was right to be sensitive, for when the news spread into the gossip columns the one thing that was stressed was their ages. One regional paper was unable to resist malice. 'The chief fault of the gentleman is that he is twenty years [*sic*] the junior of the lady, and all London is shaking its head at the alliance and talking of the blunders of love in consequence.'[50]

Annie knew that it would be difficult to win the blessing of Charlotte Ritchie, whose attachment to her Ritchie nephews and nieces stretched back to the time when they had been sent in turn from India to her charge in Paris. In 1874 she had scolded Annie in Florence for monopolising Richmond's attentions, voicing the family doubts which only now were being resolved. Knowing that news of the engagement would be bitter-sweet for Charlotte, Annie nevertheless yearned for her approval. 'It seems like a sunrise after the long darkness & my heart is very full of him & of all that I have here & <u>there</u> too. Dearest you will write & say god bless us and when I die I think it will seem as if no one had been so blessed as I with such wonderful love – indeed he looks happy & says he is happier than he has ever been and people do not seem so shocked as I expected but on the contrary every one is kind & full of sympathy.'[51] Richmond sent Charlotte his own eloquent testimony to the saving power of Annie's love, compared with which the difference in their ages – so much a matter of concern for others – was of no importance. In that she was able to offer him 'a real life', Richmond had felt himself as much in need of rescue as did Annie herself.

I am sure that if at Florence you had known our hearts, you would not have wished for any alteration in them, and now I am equally sure that when you see our happiness, if without seeing you cannot believe, you will rejoice as much as anybody in our happiness. How anyone who knows Annie can fail to envy me in my blessed fortune I cannot see. Willie the other night said 'You are going to marry the most charming creature alive, and you cant expect to have everything'. But for Annie it is different – I can quite understand and even sympathise with people who fear for her; all I can say in answer to their doubts is that myself I have such entire faith in our mutual love that my heart is quite secure from all apprehension....

For myself I can only say that for the first time for years my heart is perfectly light. I may have for a while sometimes forgotten, but the anxiety was always there waiting. It is all over however, thank God, and I can begin to think of leading a real life. Annie is as happy as I am, if not happier as her anxiety was far worse than mine: but she cannot help having misgivings of the opinion of the world at large. As for the happiness of those who really love her and her happiness, I tell her that it is doubting their love if she thinks it possible they should not rejoice with her rejoicing.[52]

In the years to come, as they both grew older, he may have reflected on this blithe confidence. The difficulties would inevitably come, and the marriage was tested. As Annie moved towards old age, he found himself enjoying the company of other, younger women. But as he sets out on the journey there are no doubts, and after a morning in the gardens of Kings College he candidly confronts the matter of her age. '[E]ven when I am bothered about you most, the blessing is still there; and the feeling that there is nothing to hold on to and cling by has gone right away out of my life – and my blessing goes on till you die. There is no reason to think that if you live to be as old as Methuselah, my feeling for you will alter; or as far as altering goes, if you die.'[53]

As the letters of congratulation arrived, many people expressed delight that at last Annie had someone to care for her, and some made a point of saying that Minny would have wished it. Richmond's youngest sister Elinor was enthusiastic, feeling that it was 'rather glorious' that he was able to do this. Meta Gaskell, elder daughter of the novelist Elizabeth Gaskell, wittily likened him to the most doting of Thackeray's creations, though Richmond might not have found the allusion flattering. 'You will make the very dearest, sweetest, tenderest wife possible; and M[r]. Ritchie is indeed a happy and lucky man. As for tales that I have heard of <u>him</u>: if I did not count it blasphemy, I should liken his devotion to Dobbin's!'[54] Annie told her father's old friend, William Synge, that Richmond 'is years & years younger than I am but who has cared [for] me so long & with such wonderful fidelity & unchangeableness that I have no courage to say no to the happiness it will be to us both to belong to each other.... I have wondered & wondered what my Father would have said – I think perhaps – if he had known all – he might have agreed.'[55] Fitzjames Stephen rejoiced that Annie had come to know 'the greatest happiness of life. I think that to see you happily married would have been the one thing which could have increased dear Minnie's happiness if she had been spared to us all.'[56] To Mrs Oliphant, Annie managed to compress all of the troubled history of the last months and years into a few lines, with just a hint that this joyful outcome might not protect Richmond from some regret in the years to come. 'That night as I sat by the fire with you I thought shall I speak about it & I couldnt & then you know what his wonderful tender fidelity has been all this time & now that it is settled – I dont quite know how by Richmond himself & Leslie & dearest most generous M^rs. Ritchie who has only thought of him & of me in all this – Now that it is settled I can only pray that he may never be sorry. He is so happy now & I am too thankful for words. My Minnie would have understood how it has come about.'[57]

Annie came finally to believe that it was the right choice for Richmond, reflecting on something which Charles Eliot Norton had written to Leslie, 'how a happy marriage could make life again & bind all that was shaken together once more, & dearest I do indeed feel this & as if for Richmond too there had been so much reality in his love for me that if he had left me & married someone else, what he might have gained in youth he might have lost in truth of feeling'.[58] But Leslie himself remained a worry for her. Though their common and established bonds could not be broken, she felt as if she was deserting him, and that inevitably she was hurting him. And there was Julia too, whose care had helped Annie towards recovery. Since Herbert Duckworth's death in 1870, Julia had devoted herself to her young children and guarded the dignity of her widowhood. Her friendship with Leslie had grown in recent months, to the extent that at the beginning of February, having startled himself with the sudden recognition that he loved her, Leslie made a declaration to Julia, though it took a year for her to agree to marry him. At one level Annie and Leslie were oddly similar, each uncertain about the likely outcome of a wished-for relationship, the possibility of happiness seeming so elusive and fragile. Shortly before her engagement was at last made public, it was of Leslie and Julia that Annie thought first, almost as if she feared that her own happiness was to be gained at their expense.

> Darling I went to see Julia after you went away – I ended by crying this time not for us – but because it is so sad for her & Leslie & she doesnt know what to do – She said they envied us so this morning, & Leslie said that isnt parting & that we both looked so happy.... Im afraid Leslie is very very unhappy he says Julia has healed his wound but she cannot

put back the blood.... Dearest as I think of you my heart
overflows with thankful happiness. There is Leslie more
lonely than I was & his happiness seems so precarious, there
is Julia not knowing how to help him.[59]

As wedding presents began to arrive and 'that horrible bugbear of
parting' with Leslie began to approach, she found that she was not
alone in dreading the separation. They had shared a house for ten years,
and there had developed between them deep bonds of trust founded in
the honesty of their friendship. Living apart would not weaken this
loyalty, but they must have feared that something of what Minny had
meant to them would become ever more impalpable if they were not
together to share in the common memories. When he had told Norton
of Annie's engagement, Leslie was frank about his own position. 'So
long as Anny lived with me, I seemed to preserve part at least of the
new element wh. came into my life with my marriage. When she goes,
I shall have a terrible gap between me & the past.'[60] A fortnight before
the wedding, Norton wrote to Annie with his good wishes, regretting
only 'the new loneliness that it would bring to Leslie'.[61]

Leslie spent his summer holiday that year at Coniston with Laura
and his sister, but as he prepared to interrupt it to be alone with Annie
for a last few days before she started her new life he feared that even
this time would be denied him. There is something childishly wilful
about his clinging for as long as possible to the mood of melancholy
content in which he and Annie had learned to rub along since Minny's
death.

> I hear rumours from Julia that Mrs R & Pinkie are to come
> to stay with us from Tuesday. Now I do object most strongly
> & it is the last time I shall be able to object to anybody
> coming to see you. Therefore I think my wishes ought to
> be respected. I object selfishly because their presence will
> effectively keep me away from Julia, whom I am longing
> to see. I object on your account & my own, because I really
> think these days ought to be as quiet as possible. You should
> not be flurried & hurried & over emotioned by wellmeaning
> friends. I should like to have a chance of talking to you
> occasionally in peace & comfort & I cannot do it when P.
> is sighing in the background & Mrs R. talking affectionate
> platitudes all over the house.
>    Surely they might just as well go to Stanhope Gardens
> instead of pigging together in our back-cupboards. If you
> can possibly get rid of them, I shall be most grateful.[62]

In the next breath petulance is swept aside as he presses £500 on her in order to buy a property, 'if not for the house, then towards expenses at starting'.

Annie and Richmond were married at Kensington's ancient parish church, St Mary Abbot's, early in the morning on 2 August, 'one of the many bank holiday couples'.[63] Lionel Tennyson was best man. It was a simple, happy affair with a deliberate absence of fuss, about which Annie herself tells us hardly anything at all. Fortunately, there are accounts by Henry Bradshaw and Pinkie to give a flavour of the occasion. A week or so later Bradshaw wrote to George Smith, the friend and publisher of both Thackerays, father and daughter. 'The bride looked more charming than ever (you must know that she won my heart the very first moment I ever saw her). There was no ceremony, no wedding breakfast, and the result was that instead of being a very dull and miserable affair, as weddings too often are, it was one of the liveliest I have ever known.'[64] Pinkie found an appropriate lightness of touch to capture the mix of informality and intimacy which reflected Annie's own personality and her capacity for giving simple happiness to others. Mrs Brookfield arrived too late, Leslie embodied gloomy resignation and Julia made few concessions to her customary severe mourning, but Annie was oblivious of anything but the mystery of this moment which had been given to her.

> It was a dear little wedding, with just the amount of true friends that ought to have been there. Annie and Richmond seemed as utterly lost in each other and unconscious of anybody listening to them as if they had gone off by themselves, but then, the Service did barely last four minutes. Was it an omen that Annie, for the first time in her life, was before her time? It was hard on Mrs. Brookfield to find the Service just over.... Annie looked delightful and quite calm, I thought. Her gown was very becoming, made all in one sweep and tight-fitting, but her bonnet of muslin and lace rather trying. Richmond looked to me a perfect bridegroom, strong and tender, and when they joined hands they seemed to enjoy a long romantic 'shake hands!' One thing struck me, the contrast between Richmond's best man at the right hand, and Annie's supporters on the left – poor Leslie, who looked very deplorable, and Julia Duckworth, who wore the thickest black velvet dress and heavy black veil, and gave the gloomiest, most tragic aspect to her side of the chancel.... I placed myself as Annie's bridesmaid at the side of the children, who were most pathetically upset at the

emotional scene; dear Margie's teeth chattering, little Annie
sucking lozenges to stifle her sobs, Stella Duckworth with
her mother's tragic mask, and Margaret Cornish with tears
streaming down her cheeks. However they all became happy
on being given champagne by Richmond.[65]

There would be a more extended wedding tour later in the year,
but for now the only time that could be spared for a honeymoon was a
few days at Newlands Corner, near Guildford. Then Richmond began
to travel daily up to Waterloo to the India Office, while Annie stayed
for another week or two in the Surrey countryside, revisiting places
which had become familiar during Leslie and Minny's marriage. They
also managed a few days in Sussex staying near Julia's parents at Frant,
Richmond still commuting. Leslie returned from Coniston, and they all
met up. Annie could not help but register how, by Richmond's side and
in comparison with Leslie and Julia's kind but serious manner, she began
to feel what being a young married person might be like. 'Leslie came
to the station to meet us.... It seemed so strange to watch him & Julia
flitting down the little street together, & then I looked round & there was
my dear young Richmond in absurd tender delightful spirits.'[66] Towards
the end of the Surrey leg of their stay she had heard from a Godalming
neighbour, George Eliot, who asked Annie to visit her when she was
back in town again, 'for I have been long wishing that some sign of
remembrance from you would fall to my share. No one has thought of
your twofold self with more sympathy than "meine Kleinigkeit" or with
more earnest desire that you may have the best sort of happiness.'[67]

About three weeks after the wedding, and shortly before Annie
left for town to look at a possible house in Young Street which Jane
Brookfield had discovered, she had one of the vivid dreams which
came to her at the important moments in her life. She wrote of it to
Gussie Freshfield, Richmond's eldest sister, reflecting on these first
days of marriage, confident at last that she had done the right thing.

> Last night I dreamt that we hadnt been married & that I said
> to Minnie – no I wont do it Im afraid of what people will say,
> its too great a responsibility, Ill go & you must tell Richmond
> Im gone & you mustnt tell anyone & then I went away with
> a curious ache & scorn, it was so strange & vivid. Dearest
> Gussie I woke up & I went to the window & looked out at
> the dawn & felt this much – that even if ever we are less
> happy w^h. I don't expect for one instant – we shan't ever love
> each other less or feel that we were not honest people.[68]

Two

# SHADOWS OF THE PAST
## (1877-1881)

*There is no greater happiness in the world, and no one who could appreciate it so much perhaps as you dear Annie, who have so much love to give.*

Kate Perugini to Annie
5 June 1878, on the birth of her daughter

Leslie's wedding present to Annie was a new portrait of Minny, and in October she called on George Frederic Watts's studio to collect 'the dear picture'[1] which succeeded in capturing the tranquil, introspective side of her sister's temperament. Three months after the wedding, Leslie was still finding it hard to adjust to his 'hermitage'. His sister, Caroline, was out of town, whereas Julia was 'well enough but has anxieties & worries – as usual'. The old comfortable certainties had gone, and in his melancholy he pondered on his memories of lost content. 'I only know that one has got to hold on – pleasant or unpleasant – & that I have no right to complain of life, even if I never have another happy day. The days go quickly now & the slow ones were very happy.'[2]

Annie and Richmond now took a delayed wedding trip to the West country, starting at Exeter and travelling as far as Lands End before returning via Bristol and ending at Haslemere. They were uncharacteristically careful with their money, logging the costs of accommodation, meals and fares. In early November they rented 'a happy little house' in Gloucester Road, a base until they moved in the spring to Young Street, where Leslie's £500 bought them No. 27, opposite the house where Annie had lived with her father and Minny thirty years before. Although the end of another year brought the sad associations that could never wholly leave her, Annie was entitled to feel hopeful. 'We <u>are</u> so thankful and somehow the very thought of all the sorrow & desolation w^h belongs to this time of year makes all the blessing of tender love seem even more great & more dear to me.'[3] She was expecting her first child, having become pregnant very soon after the wedding.

Mindful of the history of Minny's difficult pregnancies, Annie decided that she had to stay in London rather than accompany Richmond to Paris where Charlotte Ritchie's life was drawing to its close. At the end of January 1878, her nephews and nieces gathered round her, and Richmond was touched at his dying aunt's concern that Annie should stay strong. '[Mrs Brookfield] told me that she had been talking to herself about the little baby that was coming, & saying she must take great care. It is a very beautiful thing that the minds instinct can change from selfishness to unselfishness, & that in the most entirely natural state conceivable, possessed by disease, can disregard the suffering unassisted by will & turn to entirely external objects, as being the really important ones.'[4] Annie wrote regularly to Pinkie and Blanche as they maintained their vigil, keeping them up-to-date with happier news, for early in the new year Julia Duckworth, the long-term friend of the Thackeray sisters and a widow since 1870, had at last agreed to marry Leslie. If Annie was left with pangs of regret as Leslie's memories of Minny began to retreat, all she articulated were genuine expressions of pleasure at the new possibilities of happiness for her dear friends and for Minny's child.

> My hope is for Leslie & Julia's happiness & for sweet Memekins. I think it very noble & generous of Julia to give up her liberty & her prestige & her money & everything to comfort & cheer up Leslie. I am very very thankful she has agreed at last after all her natural long hesitation. Leslie is very grave & very dear – He seems to turn to me & Richmond – He has never urged Julia, but matters have evolved themselves the governess question brought it about. He says it would be very painful to them both to get presents or to have it treated as a first marriage but do write to him a word of sympathy. He had held an interview with D[r]. Jackson at the thought of which I cant help laughing.[5]

Charlotte Ritchie died on 29 January, and Annie was saddened to lose this close family link with her father, of whom she had dreamt once more during the night. 'I wish I was with you, I fear it is so lonely & silent for you & yet what a speaking voice Chatties will ever be.... All last night while you were in such anxiousness I was dreaming of Papa & talking to him just as if 13 years had not gone.'[6] In describing Charlotte's last moments as being like a child falling asleep, Pinkie was struck by the devotion of those Parisians amongst whom her aunt had worked selflessly for years – 'it seemed such a perfect summary of her glorious life, to see her with that radiant calm in the room where she has suffered and loved and lived in her heroic loneliness'.[7]

Leslie and Julia married on 26 March. Annie found the occasion exhausting, for reasons that are not hard to imagine. 'I seemed to be so utterly done up after the marriage w$^h$. was as you may think very trying with all the blessing it brings in that I went to bed at nine & fast asleep, for I had been awake the night before. Julia looked marvellously beautiful in her lovely grey & Leslie very happy & I think they are all quite happy about it now.'[8] Leslie simply moved next door to Julia's at 13 Hyde Park Gate South, and Annie and Richmond lived briefly at No 11 until Young Street became available.

In these early months of marriage Annie worked her contacts, writing to the influential Lord Houghton – formerly Richard Monckton Milnes – aware that Richmond had surrendered his Cambridge career for her. Changes at the India Office made her grasp at possible openings.

> L$^d$. Salisbury is going & L$^d$. George Hamilton is going & new private Secretaries are being appointed – Do you happen to know who will be L$^d$. George Hamiltons successor. Dear Lord Houghton you help so many people in so many different ways, could you make Richmond a private Secretary? I know I am writing nonsense, but when I think of all he has given up for me & of the blessing of faithful tender affection & happiness I owe to him after all my bitter troubles, it seems to me that if others only knew him as I do, & his steadfastness & quiet grasp of mind & determination of character they would not think it unnatural that I should long for him to be trusted & promoted in the career he has chosen.[9]

It was rare for her to seek preferment, and in this instance she was thinking of Richmond's career and not of herself. In turn, she reached out a helping hand to a friend who had been a rock of support at the time of Minny's death. Aware that the novelist Margaret Oliphant was distressed by the illness of her son Cecco and having to write to meet pressing family expenses, Annie proposed lifting some of the burden from her shoulders. She offered to write for Mrs Oliphant, not by filling the role of a copyist but by undertaking some of the creative process itself. It was an act of exceptional generosity and a candid revelation that this was something which Minny had once done for her. 'Do please tell us if ever ever we can go anywhere or get anything that c$^d$. save you in any way. Sometimes writing does not do as well as sending people for things – once when I was distracted about other things Minnie did a chapter or two for me. It seems too preposterous but if you were hard driven & sent me any rough notes Im sure I could at least put them together.'[10] It is a reminder of Minny's own early writing ambitions, quietly put aside when she married, but surviving as a small collection of notes and odd pages from incomplete stories. The occasion when Minny helped her out is not known, nor whether Mrs Oliphant now took up Annie's offer. But it shows that neither writer had any pretensions about her craft, regarding it (like Thackeray) as essentially a technical process. Annie's own writing had still not emerged from the virtual silence which had fallen in the two years since Minny's death. Apart from a few short magazine pieces, the period saw only the republication of her earlier 1868-9 *Cornhill* novella *From an Island* in a collection of other reprints.[11]

The couple took possession of 27 Young Street just before Easter, left carpet-fitters and a gardener at work, and went off to the Hand and Sceptre Hotel in Tunbridge Wells for the holiday period. By the time they returned they were able to move into the house which would come to have many happy associations as the family home where Hester and Billy were born. Now demolished and replaced by a multi-storey car park, the house adjoined the old Greyhound Inn. Across the road Annie could look out on her childhood home and remember the scenes of thirty years before. Some former neighbours, including their family doctor, John Jones Merriman, were still residents in adjacent Kensington Square, as was the expert in public health, Sir John Simon and his wife. The community retained something of the genteel village atmosphere of its 'Old Kensington' past, and for Annie it was the happiest of locations. They became residents in time for the traditional local May Day celebrations, and Annie was once again able to delight in the Jack in the Greens dancing past the window down Young Street. Theirs was a comfortable house, with a long garden at the rear and 'an ancient medlar tree with a hole in it. There was also a lovely tall acacia tree. In those days before Kensington Court there were other gardens full of birds & trees beyond the walls & the tall spire of the church.'[12] Just a month later, at 4.30 in the morning of 1 June, Hester Helena Makepeace Thackeray Ritchie was born, a healthy child whose birth caused her mother, shortly to be forty-one, no distress at all. A midwife was there to assist, and Mrs Brookfield brought the baby to Annie to hold, pointing out the 'beautiful brown eyes like Richmond'.

Friends sent their congratulations. Dickens's daughter, Kate Perugini (remarried since the death of her first husband, Charles Collins) was delighted that at last Annie was experiencing 'all the wonder and delight of having a dear little creature of your own to love and watch over'.[13] Pinkie, who would be a godmother, anticipated great things from this unique combination of Thackeray and Ritchie genes – 'it is very nice to think she <u>must</u> be a Thackeray there is so much more of that in her composition than in all the other children'.[14]

A rare correspondent was the reclusive George Crowe, the younger brother of Amy and Eyre Crowe, who ended his days in an asylum. Urging Annie to maintain her own writing despite the new responsibilities of motherhood, he remembered Thackeray's pride in her first published efforts. His linking of the writing of father and daughter would have resonated with her, though she was always modest about her own achievements. He warned her that

> it is all very well giving "Richmond" dear little daughters & sons, but this won't excuse you from going on with your & our other family – How delightful they are! I never read them without <u>his</u> voice heavy in my ear – you are the daughter of his mind. How proud he was of that paper in the Cornhill.... Is it not a comfort to see how secure his place is now?[15]

Hester was christened in St Mary Abbot's at the end of June, her godparents (in addition to Pinkie) being Lady Martin (the actress Helena Faucit, wife of Theodore Martin) and George Smith. 'At the last moment by Lady Martins request we called her Hester Helena. The Martins drove us to the church & Hester had a tremendous fit of crying just before she started, w[h]. delayed the ceremony a little.'[16] They walked across Kensington High Street for tea in Young Street and later still, when the guests had all gone, Hester's nurse reported the appearance of an unknown lady who had dropped a white shawl over the baby. Annie realised at once that it came from 'my dear Mrs Cameron'. On a visit from Ceylon, Julia Margaret Cameron's return had coincided with the birth, leading to one of her heartfelt notes. 'That inestimable precious gift of yr little Hester will be one more of those glorious gifts which fill the soul of us poor Mortals with Gratitude. It is a trembling joy is it not this sacred possession of children of one's own.'[17] During that summer, they saw a lot of her at Young Street, and also of the newly-married Lionel Tennyson and his wife Eleanor Locker. Whilst the Tennysons looked for a house, Annie and Richmond put them up. She told Pinkie of her fondness for Eleanor, although it was wonderful when they had the house to themselves again. 'I cant tell you how nice Eleanor has been. She puts me very much in mind of her mother in a certain courteousness of mind & general human kindness and it is delightful to hear her laugh.... Last night as I went up to say goodnight to Eleanor in the little attic room I thought for a moment somehow that I sh^d. find you there tucked up in the little old bed. It was rather scrimmagy for Eleanor, & I sometimes wonder whether we shall ever be in order quite.'[18]

These summer meetings were the last with Mrs Cameron, who returned to Ceylon in October and died three months later, the news reaching Annie in the middle of February. Poignant reminders of this imaginative spirit came with the arrival in Young Street of yet more gifts, sent from Ceylon.

Annie and Richmond eventually mastered the right feeding regime for the baby, but only through a lengthy process of trial and error.

> Somewhere about this time Hester was ordered a bottle by the D^r. We dined at the Trevelyans & when we came home the baby was awake & crying & the moment seemed come. I tried to mix it. Richmond it was who tackled the problem, cooked the water on the stove & mixed Hesters first draught. She liked it. We had no end of adventures goats donkies bottles & mixtures before we hit upon Nestles food which suited her – It half poisoned Billy afterwards – One can never tell exactly.[19]

Although they had domestic staff, the Ritchies were less dependent on nursery-maids than might have been expected. Annie did not complain, finding motherhood wonderful in almost every way, but physically exhausting, especially when coupled with the neuralgia attacks and headaches which plagued her throughout her adult life. Important events in Hester's progress came to be recorded with pride – 'Friday 7 [March] 1879. Baby stood up by her little chair all alone.'

Annie encouraged Richmond to consider other kinds of work, perhaps not convinced that his temperament suited an office job. Matthew Arnold, the poet and prominent cultural critic, was brought by his own experience of drudgery to disparage thoughts of a school inspectorship, 'which your husband is mad enough to desire'. Instead, Arnold endeavoured to press one of his reviews of her, and flatteringly linked her with the infamous French female novelist George Sand. 'One gifted woman should see what is said of another; I think, if I find when we next meet that you have not read me on George Sand, I must ask you to let me give you the new volume which contains my notice of her.'[20] It is unlikely that Annie would have taken his praise too seriously.

She had now fully resumed her former social life, abandoned since Minny's death. Within the course of a few days in January 1879, she attended the christening of Lionel and Eleanor Tennyson's first child (called Alfred after his grandfather), was at home to Anthony Trollope (who probably called about the short book on Thackeray which he was about to write for Macmillan's *English Men of Letters* series), and entertained Robert Browning to dinner 'rather successfully', as well as herself being a guest of the George Smiths where Browning recited a new poem to the company. The novelist Rhoda Broughton became a new acquaintance, despite Richmond's inauspicious first encounter with her as fellow dinner guests. 'He was sitting next her on the opposite side of the table to me, & when I introduced him she paid no attention. He – I believe we are being introduced. She – How very disagreeable.'[21]

Henry James's presence at this same dinner, hosted by fellow writer Hamilton Aidé, went unrecorded by Annie. Their friendship was embryonic, and on his side ambivalent as yet. He was initially uncomfortable in the presence of this 'boy-husband', with his apparent mix of diffidence and arrogance. 'Miss Thackeray is at any rate very happy and satisfied in her queer little marriage. Her husband is, superficially, an ill-mannered and taciturn youth; but he improves much on acquaintance.'[22] Nor could he quite fathom Annie herself. A year earlier, shortly after Julia had agreed to marry Leslie and become 'the receptacle of his ineffable and impossible taciturnity and dreariness', James dined with Leslie, Julia and the Ritchies, Richmond 'even out-silencing Stephen', whereas he judged Annie to be 'the very foolishest talker (as well as most perfectly amiable, and plainest, woman) I have lately encountered. Compared with her conversation, *Miss Angel* is Baconian!'[23] A few weeks later, a full two months before Hester's birth, James was discomforted at meeting Annie 'further advanced towards confinement... than I have ever seen a lady at a dinner party'.[24] There are few hints here of the subsequent close and sustained friendship which would lead James to write of Annie in 1906 that 'I cherish the thought of being so with <u>her</u> – she's one of the women in the world whom I've most loved'.[25]

Annie's attempts to write met with mixed results, for Hester's needs came first. 'I think if Richmond were to beat me I might begin to write again but I dont think Goethe himself could have written while Wolfgang was a baby.'[26] But she worked when she could, finally completing a short book on Madame de Sévigné, the seventeenth-century letter-writer whose correspondence had appeared in editions since the mid-eighteenth century. Annie was already an admirer before agreeing to contribute a biographical study to Blackwood's 'Foreign Classics for English Readers', edited by Margaret Oliphant, flippantly claiming in 1875 that 'I think Minnys letters are quite as good as

M^me de Sévignés that [St Beuve] praises so'.[27] Leslie did his best to dissuade her from the task, not because the subject was unworthy, but because he thought Annie ill-equipped to undertake it. Fearing that she would fall short, he wanted her to dedicate herself to the fiction with which her name was properly associated. He did not mince his words, exposing a professional suspicion of genteel lady writers who, without a university background, lacked the required scholarly discipline.

> Do pray leave Mme de Sévigné alone. I cant bear you to do things that you cannot do thoroughly well. Rd ought to make you understand the difference between cram & real knowledge. Why should you do what will put you on the level of every wretched scribbler who can remember dates & facts? To write about Mme. de S. you ought to be a thorough critic....
>
> The one thing that vexes me about your work is that you haven't enough respect for [your] talents & your calling & are content to put in bits of sham & stucco alongside of really honest work.
>
> You profess to believe me to be a critic, this is the very ABC of the doctrine. I feel it very strongly. It doesn't matter if people like me do a bit of penny-a-lining sometimes for bread & butter; but you artistic people ought to stick to your strong points.[28]

Annie was not so discouraged as to set the idea aside, although the book would not be finished until 1881. Its successful completion would shape her future direction as an author, giving her the taste for biography and memoir which increasingly preoccupied her and led to two fine editions of her father's works. It is not hard to see why the personality of Madame de Sévigné should have appealed to Annie so directly and sympathetically. In describing the qualities of the Frenchwoman's letter-writing, the unnamed author of an old encyclopaedia article might just as well have been writing of Annie, so closely does his account of Madame de Sévigné touch on her too. 'She had an all-observant eye for trifles and the keenest possible appreciation of the ludicrous, together with a hearty relish for all sorts of amusements, pageants and diversions, and a deep though not voluble or over-sensitive sense of the beauties of nature. But with all this she had an understanding as solid as her temper was gay.'[29]

In the early summer of 1879, Annie and Richmond stole away to visit Dutch picture galleries for two weeks, leaving Hester in the care of grandmother and unmarried aunts at Mrs Ritchie's Bracknell house,

Brock Hill. They were absent for Hester's first birthday, returning on
6 June. They revelled in Rubens, van Dyke and Rembrandt – 'so fine,
so disjointed', and enjoyed the railway travel, as it permitted 'a sight
of a hundred spotless interiors & their 10,000 windmills & cows'. The
Franz Hals pictures at Haarlem put Annie in mind of Millais, 'such
kindred spirits'.[30]

Later in the summer she left Richmond in London and took Hester
to Devon, to the Lynton summer house of her cousin Blanche and
husband Frank Warre Cornish. The day after her arrival it poured with
rain so she sat by the fire and 'read for M.$^{me}$ de Sevigné'.[31] She also
read James's *The Europeans*, 'w$^h$. is pretty but very slight & not nearly
so good as his later things', and 'a wonderfully good story of G. Eliots
Behind the Veil & a very stupid one called Brother Jacob'.[32] But just
as she seemed ready for serious work she was told to rest, for at the
age of forty-two she found that she was pregnant again, and she was
now suffering from crippling headaches. Her solution was to propose
to Margaret Oliphant that she might undertake the Sévigné book collaboratively with Richmond, which also served her continuing hope of
finding more creative outlets for him than those offered by the India
Office.

> [T]he D$^r$ said I musnt write a word for a long time to come. I
> think, if you dont object (only this of course alters the whole
> case & might not for many reasons be convenient to you)
> the best chance both for the book itself & for me & M$^{me}$ de
> Sevigne w$^d$. be to announce it when it does come by M$^r$. &
> M$^{rs}$. R.T.R. or by R & A Thackeray Ritchie if that w$^d$. be more
> explanatory. He really writes capably & M$^r$. Greenwood has
> paid him some most delightful compliments. I could do the
> sentimental biographical & he c$^d$. do the resumés & point
> the morals.[33]

Mrs Oliphant must have gently turned down this suggestion, for it
is not mentioned again, and the book continued to be largely a solo
project.

It was from Lynton that Annie wrote to the former actress, Fanny
Kemble, on hearing of the death of her sister, Adelaide Sartoris, herself
once a celebrated operatic soprano. Both women had been good friends
of Thackeray and subsequently of his daughters. 'When I look back
almost to the very beginning of my life so much of it seems interwoven
with her & all her goodness to us; all the voices of my dearest seem
to sound again & it seems to me as if I had a sort of right to tell you
how my heart is with you & how I long to know that you are made

able to bear this bitter hour.... My little one is laughing & chattering as I write. May she have such dear & noble friends as her mother has had.'[34] Mrs Kemble replied from France a few days later.

> I suppose I <u>believe</u> the world is always full of finely & nobly endowed human beings – but in our lives we each of us gather but one harvest. Mine <u>has been</u> a very rich & full one – alas for this last fallen sheaf of very glorious good grain.... I have just finished reading for the third time your father's book of Esmond & while I read it I often thought of his early friendship for my brother & <u>us</u> – & his great constant kindness to me – he was part of my harvest too – I have had a very rich life – its memories make me rich & very thankful still.[35]

Annie shared her sadness about Mrs Sartoris with Henry James, and urged him to visit Lynton. 'Do think of it if it is at all possible & if the house full of children & babies doesn't frighten you.'[36] He did not come.

A continuing anxiety for Annie was how to deal with the public interest in her father's life. She was all too conscious of his injunction that there should be no biography, and the weight of responsibility pressed heavily on her. She disliked Anthony Trollope's *Thackeray*, which led to a coolness between them, although both she and Leslie appear to have felt that, if it had to be done at all, a short book in Macmillan's *English Men of Letters* series with Trollope as author seemed a good choice, in that his genuine admiration was as much for the man as for the writer. Trollope had told Frederick Chapman after Thackeray's death in 1863 that 'I loved him dearly'. But when it came to making material available, Annie was predictably reticent. She released none of her father's letters, and when Trollope submitted a list of questions she offered only sketchy answers.[37] It was less than helpful. He started work on 1 February and finished within two months, not a little puzzled by Annie's caution, telling John Blackwood that 'there is absolutely nothing to say, – except washed out criticism'. It was not helped when such a potentially useful source as Edward FitzGerald, the poet and translator and Thackeray's closest friend at Trinity College, Cambridge, claimed that he had destroyed all of his early letters from Thackeray, and had forgotten much of what he once knew. 'It had to be done (as Thackeray's inner circle intended) with almost no material',[38] and Trollope necessarily fell back on his own anecdotes. He dealt with personal matters delicately enough, skirting the problem of Isabella's mental collapse and ignoring the open secret of Thackeray's passion

*Annie with Margie and Anny Thackeray, about 1867*

for Mrs Brookfield. Yet he still managed to offend Annie, principally it would seem for mentioning the 'comfortable income' of £750 which Thackeray was able to leave to his children, a figure which Annie herself appears to have supplied. With heavy irony the *Pall Mall Gazette* reviewer castigated Trollope's poor taste. 'It must be a source of satisfaction to Thackeray's children to be assured on Mr. Trollope's authority that "the comfortable income" – the precise figure is stated – which he left behind *was* "earned honestly, with the full approval of the world around him".'[39]

A story was passed down from Trollope's granddaughter that 'Anne Thackeray or rather Ritchie went to Grandpa at Waltham House and besought him herself to write it as she said no one would do it better than he. He did not want to write it. But to Anne's entreaties he finally yielded and then was cruelly abused by Richmond Ritchie in some article.'[40] Victoria Glendinning assigns this to family mythology, not least because 'the review was most unlikely to have been by Anny's husband', but on those grounds at least the story may be accurate, for Richmond was indeed reviewing for the *Pall Mall Gazette* during these years, much to Annie's satisfaction, and the reviewer's traditional anonymity might well have been used as a disguise for his wife's disapproval. It took three years for good relations to be restored. In the year of his death they met once more. 'Anthony Trollope came & stood by the fireplace very big & kind & made it up. He said Billy was like his grandfather. I never saw dear M^r Trollope again. I said to him I'm so sorry I quarreled with you. He said so am I my dear.'[41] Annie continued to feel that she had behaved badly, and eventually set the record straight in a short piece written for *The Illustrated London News* of 20 June 1891, 'Thackeray and his Biographers', recognising that although Trollope saw her father 'from a very different point of view from mine… he writes with an affection which never varied, and which was ever constant to my father's children, though not untried, I fear, by the present writer'.

This morbid sensitivity to things written about her father had very deep roots. In 1871, with the memory of his death that much fresher, she had taken offence even to James Fields's affectionate essay in *The Atlantic Monthly*, urging him to make changes before republishing it in *Yesterdays with Authors*.

> There are passing words & actions w^h. cannot help seeming different when they are told alone with emphasis & without all that may have led up to them & varied ever so slightly by the impress of a different mind. My Father was so much in the habit of trusting his friends & of laughing at himself that many persons may have taken words as seriously meant w^h. were only sarcastic or they would never have been spoken by the person, who of all those I have ever known had the justest & manliest mind & the greatest dislike to over-speaking & exaggeration. Leslie Stephen said some time ago he thought I may have been over sensitive in regard to some of the things

that have been said about my Father. It is so painful to me to discuss him in any way that I avoid doing so when I can & I would not trouble you now with this letter if it were not that perhaps you would rather that I write it than not.[42]

But the Trollope episode made Annie see that future requests for information would become increasingly hard to resist. However much she felt bound to honour Thackeray's own veto on potential biographers, the only certainty was that her privileged access to his papers combined with a unique knowledge of her own family history would die with her, and that his memory might be served better by some kind of authorised account which could both protect and shape his reputation. According to FitzGerald, when Trollope had been seeking out materials, Annie had 'misinformed him in many ways'.[43] She was beginning to see the attractions of managing rather than suppressing the story, and that could only be done by writing it herself. It took a long time for the specific idea of the Biographical Edition to surface, but this was one of a number of defining moments which prompted it.

Four years had passed since Minny's death, but Annie never stopped regretting her decision to be away from home that fateful night. She reflected on the changes in her own life since then – marriage, motherhood, and a second child expected. Pregnancy had always been a dangerous time for Minny, yet Annie was remarkably untroubled by it, despite her age. Already cautioned by her doctor during the summer, she would have been realistic about the risks as her own pregnancy advanced. Death was not something to be feared – Thackeray had taught her that – though she knew only too well the permanent sadness for those left behind. She feared for Hester, though knew that many would love her, and probably believed that Richmond would re-marry in time. At the turn of midnight on Minny's anniversary, she wrote a letter to be put aside for the day when Hester might wish to learn of the mother only dimly remembered.

This is the first letter I have ever written to you my darling child & I can hardly find words to tell you what a blessing & happiness you have been to your old mama. My sweetheart may God keep you safe & good all your life. I think you will grow up ready to love & trust & you have your dearest Father to shield you & love you even if I am gone –

Dont be afraid if troubles come.

My little darling if you are hurt or lonely in life, <u>make your heart large</u> & take in all the love that comes your way & all its comfort.

> If you want a woman to go to – I <u>think</u> you will best understand what y<sup>r</sup>. aunt Magdalene w<sup>d</sup>. advise & there are Margie & Annie who will love you always & Aunt Minnies Laura & your own aunts. Be occupied my darling & may you be blessed my sweet sweet delight – & make your Daddy happy for your loving
> 
>      <u>Mother</u>.[44]

In fact, Annie grew more robust as the weeks went by and was able to work quite steadily at Madame de Sévigné, noting less than a month before her confinement that she had written six chapters. Mrs Oliphant was warmly approving. 'The beginning reads charmingly, and I am sure it will make a delightful volume.'[45] Annie maintained the same full social life which had raised Henry James's eyebrows before Hester's birth. She attended the christening in Westminster Abbey of her godson Charles – Lionel and Eleanor Tennyson's second son and the future biographer of his grandfather – the next day going to dinner with the Holman Hunts, and a week later called on Watts and Frederic Leighton and lunched with the Tennysons.[46]

There was a final excitement the day before she gave birth, when the Young Street chimney caught fire and 'the fire engines came thundering up'. The midwife arrived a few days before a boy was born in the early hours of 18 March, and Annie proudly noted her approval of him as 'a very observant child…. He put the cloth away from his little face & looked round the room, taking everything in.' Richmond provided a more matter-of-fact account of the uncomplicated birth for his sister, Blanche. 'A little boy was born this morning about 4 after a very short struggle. Annie is perfectly happy & well, and the child is very big, very ugly, and with big eyebrows.'[47] Catching up with her correspondence a few weeks later, Annie was still enchanted by

> my sweet little son … I like him quite as much as a daughter. He is so good & so close up to one. I think he will be rather dreamy & easygoing with a grateful imaginative little heart, & Hester will settle things, & Billy will back her up…. Thank God for inventing little children & big ones. How I wish everybody had children, I feel quite ashamed now when I see those who have not got my blessings.[48]

On 31 May she went to a grocer's shop on Camden Hill to register the baby's name, and until the last moment was undecided as to its exact format. The registrar was patient – 'Take your time Mum' – and then she confirmed the entry as William Thackeray Denis Ritchie.

'William' was somehow inevitable, and the addition of Denis – a name which in his teenage years the boy sometimes preferred to use, but later abandoned – nicely suggested a completion to the imaginative work which his grandfather had left unfinished, *Denis Duval*. But from the start he was known in the family as Bill or Billy, never by the more formal William. As the children grew, their parents had various pet names for them – Codge or Coak for Hester, Bung or Billiki for Billy, and a collective term for the pair, 'the Cobungo'. From the beginning there was a delightful informality about this family group, and both Richmond and Annie had great fun as parents, spending as much time as possible playing with the children who were not abandoned to the care of their nurses, but grew up informally and un-complicatedly, surrounded by love. The Thackeray model for living, honestly and without pretensions, was their grandfather's greatest gift to them. His example was not something that Annie was ever likely to forget, but she was always happy to have unexpected reminders of it, such as the occasion a couple of years later when she met a lady who remembered Thackeray's attentiveness to his daughters. 'This old lady says Papa was so proud of us that he always took us both when he went anywhere – could you imagine another Papa doing the same thing?'[49]

A month before Billy's christening, there was much chatter amongst George Eliot's acquaintances at her marriage to the banker John Cross on 6 May, George Lewes having died in 1878. Annie was sensitive to her parallel situation insofar as she too had married a much younger husband. Contemptuous of those who had gushed over George Eliot's writing whilst judging her harshly for living openly with Lewes, and who now professed horror at the supposed irregularity of her marriage choice, Annie told Pinkie about meeting George Lewes's daughter-in-law.

> She said M^r Locker says it is the clique who always treated her as a Royal Supernatural gigantic illuminated being who are now so furious with G.E. all except Herbert Spencer who hasnt turned & rended her to shreds as all the rest of her old devotees have done. M^rs Charles [Lewes] said with her eyes all full of tears remember that she is an Englishwoman of the middle classes imbued with English prejudice, & perhaps to her the name of <u>wife</u> may have seemed a refuge from all the agony of years. She told me that she used to <u>tremble</u> when she met anyone alone she felt it all so bitterly. She had given up everything good position respectability for M^r Lewes....

I wish it was otherwise but those people who were so silly in their raptures have no business to be so pitiless now. We may say what we like – at least you may darling as for me my only excuse was that I did love Richmond & he did love me & didnt shirk the price – but I musnt talk of poor G.E. except at home. Only I always forget & begin.[50]

The christening was set for 7 June at St Mary Abbots. His godparents were Sir John Simon, Pinkie, Jane Brookfield and Herbert Stephen, and at the very last minute Annie pleaded a special favour.

My beloved M[rs] Tennyson. After a good deal of uncertainty we have been obliged to settle tomorrow for the Christening & now I am going to do a very audacious thing & ask you if when Billy grows up some day I may tell him that he had you & M[r] Tennyson for Godparents. I should like to think my little son had some link with you and I think & believe as he is his mothers son he will – if you say yes – love & be proud of it: & of all your long goodness to her. He has a godfathers gift to come to him already, so that all that will have to be done will be for dear King Alfred someday to write little Billys name under ours in the beautiful golden books....

He is such a beloved little man, quite grey eyed & he laughs into my face & right thro' ones old heart. [51]

She cannot have been expecting the Tennysons to turn up at the church at such short notice, but sought to commemorate her own affectionate link with the poet's family by adding the talisman of their names to her son's list of supporters. The ceremony itself was thoroughly down to earth, and Billy had an early introduction to the mix of informality and confusion which was typical of the Ritchies' way of doing things, for during the service Hester decided to run off, pursued by Annie up the altar steps to the far end of the church. The service continued in their absence, 'and when at last we came back the Christening was over!'[52]

Later in the year, after Tennyson had sent her his new collection of poems which included a dedication to his grandson, Lionel's two-year-old boy, she thanked him and asked for one more privilege. 'I dont exactly read but I seem to live into these noble poems & to read them all with my old selves as well as my new self, & nothing else that I know of could bring my Fathers & my sisters dear faces before me so vividly as the sound of your voice does speaking here & stirring my old heart & everyone elses. The dedication is so dear and, please my dearest M$^r$ Tennyson will you write my little W$^m$ Thackeray Denis's name on the book for him for he too is a little poet – Will you write it on a bit of paper for me to paste it in & for him to know what a Godfather & Mother are his.'[53]

During this summer of 1880, Richmond thought hard about his career. He was willing to contemplate exchanging the India Office for more creative challenges, for something which felt more like 'real work', but if he was to make it through his writing he knew that he needed to devote himself in a more committed way than hitherto. He had undertaken reviews for the *Pall Mall Gazette*, including a rather cool assessment of James's *The Europeans* in 1878, but he was pulled up short when an article was turned down. He wrote to Annie from Paris.

Of subjects which are really within my reach I suppose I can manage as well as the ordinary penny-a-liner. But I haven't got the facility of expression or the inventiveness of a real writer; and when those gifts are not present by nature, their place can only be supplied by tough work, & the substitution of knowledge for inventiveness. My own private belief is that nobody who has not written bad poetry in his youth is worth a damn. But I think I've enough talent to get on in a respectable way, if I work sufficiently hard, which hitherto I've never done. I don't know why I write you this rigmarole, but I've been devoting a good deal of serious thought to the charming subject of myself & my prospects in life. You see my fault has been to let things slide & to take it easy. For years when my character was forming, I was in love with an old pong of my acquaintance & thought of nothing but how I could make her & myself happy. Circumstances were at first so unfavourable that it was only in daydreams that our happiness was possible; and then they became so difficult that they absorbed me entirely; and when I got what I wanted, I was content to remain quiet & enjoy what I had got. In most cases, I suppose, when things go easy, a man has time & liberty to get a second object in life; so that even when happiest, he has a profession or occupation before him. But I've not got that & my nominal profession is not a real one. So the time has come, I see, when I must take a definite path for myself – dont think it unkind of me to say this. If it were not that I was so completely happy with you, I would not be in danger of letting my life slide away in the happiness of each succeeding moment. I would be perfectly happy going to the office & coming back to you. But then there's a beastly little grain of energy or ambition or something which does not let me be content with that only – & that's the real rub of a profession like a Public Office which occupies your time & tires you without satisfying the desire of doing something real, which everybody has who is worth a straw. I do hope & trust that the Coak & Billyboy may find real work to do.[54]

He took the family to Coniston in mid-June, staying with his friends the Spring Rices at Patterdale and the Deverells at Bossington, 'a lovely summer baked place with garden & trout streams & animals for Hester to play with'.[55] They saw something of Ruskin, though his first meeting with Richmond misfired. 'I had not the least idea who it was, – but thought it was some one probably staying with M<sup>r</sup> Marshall – and I think you ought to scold him a little for going away in his lovely boat like the captain of the Phantom ship, in that solemn manner!'[56] Richmond returned to London before the rest of the family, and at the end of July told Annie of one article in progress and of plans for others. It was frustrating that Lionel Tennyson, his charmingly dilettantish India Office colleague, was reviewing books for the *Nineteenth Century*, work which was not arduous but moderately lucrative, and it raised Richmond's hopes for something similar. 'I am writing a rather good article, with translations from Saint Simon about an idiotic story in one of those many 3 volumes – and have got my ideas about 3 more articles into very good working order. The 19<sup>th</sup> Century has given Lionel £15 for his choice of reviews in this month's number. It seems to me very easily earned for 7½ pages, and the reviews very stupid.'[57] In wanting to develop in the direction of literary journalism, his model was likely to have been Leslie rather than Annie.

His hopes for a different future survived at least until 1881, when Pinkie praised his 'admirable review of Washington Square' in the *Pall Mall Gazette*.[58] And then the reviews seem to have faded away. Mentions of his writing disappear both from his own and from Annie's correspondence, and as the India Office began to turn into a real challenge and promotions followed, his true career became fixed. When in January 1883 Richmond was appointed Private Secretary to Kynaston Cross, MP and Under-Secretary of State for India, he put aside any ambition of achieving anything through writing. His energies became completely absorbed by the demands of his salaried position. Annie was in Worthing when Richmond telegrammed confirming his

promotion, and she went '& walked along by the sea with an overflowing heart'.[59] She took an almost motherly pride in a success
achieved entirely on his own merits. 'O my dear dearest. It is nice to
think of you getting your steps & grades & I never leave off thinking of
it all day long.... I've been drinking Hesters Port wine to pick myself
up these last few days & I drink M$^r$ Private Secretarys health and am
his loving M$^{rs}$ P S.'[60]

The Thackerays and Ritchies had long become reconciled to the
idea of their male relatives departing for extended periods of service
in India, continuing an almost unbroken link since the time of the
first William Makepeace Thackeray, the grandfather of the novelist,
but there was a special pang for Annie when Pinkie, her dearest
Ritchie sister-in-law, left to support her brother Gerald who was in
low spirits at Gopalgunge in Bengal. She sailed in November 1880
and would not return until the spring of 1882, but she corresponded
regularly with Annie and also with Hallam Tennyson. Knowing that
she would miss her terribly, Annie wrote a last letter before Pinkie's
departure, but delayed its sending in order that it might reach India
once the spirits of the traveller were reviving after the long journey
out. 'I think it will be less horrid for you when you get this than these
days before and now only the joy of living joy is before you.'[61] Two
months later she would be telling Pinkie of George Eliot's death,
so soon after the marriage that had turned heads. But first there was
her note of sympathy to John Cross to write, so encouraging and
honest, in which she urged him to embrace the transforming power
of love which drew its strength from sadness. 'May I say it to you
that death seems to lose its terrors when one has love to give hope.
Before Richmond & I were married everything seemed hopeless &
utterly miserable & now I seem to owe him something more even
than the happiness he has given me.'[62] George Eliot's funeral was
on 29 December, and although she had not been an intimate Annie
was quite affected by her reflections on the occasion. She thought of
attending, but the weather made it impossible for her. 'It is absurd,
but I do feel George Eliots death very much. There is nothing to
be sorry for – all is at peace for her poor Soul but it haunts one
somehow. She was buried in a great storm of wind & rain or I think I
sh$^d$. have gone to the funeral.'[63] Some years later she discovered that
her doctor and his wife had attended the funeral, and in the driving
rain had seen another mourner nearly slide into the grave. 'He was
quite quite tipsy & so slippery from rain that he could hardly be
raised up. I dont know why I tell you this dreary story but there is
something friendly about it too.'[64]

Scarcely a month after George Eliot, Thomas Carlyle too was dead, two mighty voices silenced. Asked to rank them, Annie saw that her regard for Carlyle set her a little in the past. 'Of course to my generation Carlyle is a far more powerful influence. George Eliot seems more to me like an expression & interpretation than an actual influence, but Richmond & Blanchie feel differently. Scribner sent to ask me to write about George Eliot but I didnt feel up to it & Fred Myers is to do it.'[65] Annie was brought up short when, on a visit with Billy to see Carlyle's great-nephew and namesake, she was suddenly struck by her own son's fleeting resemblance to her father, convincing her that the loved ones who have gone never quite leave us. She scribbled off a postcard to India. 'The little Carlyle baby is very like his g$^t$. Uncle. He gave a grunt <u>exactly</u> like him & Billy opened his eyes & laughed & looked like his grandfather for a moment. It was the oddest most affecting moment to me. There were the two babies in the dear old room & old me looking on & the new like a shadow of the past.' Pinkie appreciated the anecdote, but was perhaps more down-to-earth in her sympathy for the Carlyle child's inheritance – 'what a heavy mantle of a name for that little baby to bear!'[66]

For a few years virtually nothing is heard of Laura Stephen, who of course was now living with Leslie and her stepmother, Julia. Just as Isabella Thackeray had slipped from the scene once she had been placed in safe care, so Laura's voice is silenced for a time. It was only after Minny's death that Leslie began to realise that things were not quite right, claiming that before then none of them had feared problems, 'though she was obviously a backward child'. In fact, Minny's frequent anxiety about Laura's slow physical growth and increasingly wilful behaviour may have given her a deep-seated concern about her 'normality'. Perhaps she never shared these fears with Leslie, nor ever quite understood them herself. It certainly comforted him to believe that Minny had never thought anything amiss. 'I can remember, though they are too sacred to repeat, little words of Laura's mother which prove to me conclusively that no suspicion of any worse incapacity had entered her mind. I am happy to remember them, for the maternal blindness saved her from a cruel pang.'[67] Even now, it took time for Leslie to accept that his vague concerns were beginning to be more serious than his usual tendency towards 'morbid anxiety'. A single telling reference in Annie's journal – 'Beginning to be very anxious about Laura'[68] – indicates that she, at least, accepted that something needed to be done, but for some time neither she nor Leslie could decide what this should be. He had many family responsibilities to preoccupy him. There were

*Page from Annie's journal with sketch and some of Hester's hair, 1881*

Julia's three young children to incorporate, Gerald, George and Stella Duckworth, and before long the children of their own marriage began to arrive. Annie feared that in time it would be difficult for Laura's special needs to be met, and that within the competing demands and complex dynamics of the Stephens' growing household it would become unclear how she would cope.

By contrast, the Ritchies' family life was remarkably ordinary, or
at least it was in its early years. Hester was physically sturdy, resisting
most childhood illnesses, though Billy was less fortunate. He had a
ringworm infection as a baby, resulting in an elaborate Browning joke
about 'the ring and the bookworm' which, seeing its funny side, Annie
repeated to several people. He also contracted mumps – this time in
company with Hester – and also the highly infectious scarlet fever, or
'scarlatina' as Annie always called it, remembering her own childhood
attack in Naples. These diseases were always treated seriously by
the Victorian middle-classes, usually leading to voluntary quarantine
followed by house fumigation. When the children had mumps in
May 1882, Annie stayed with them upstairs in Young Street, and
Richmond – who presumably had managed to avoid the disease as a
child – took temporary lodgings elsewhere; then Annie took Hester
and Billy to convalesce in the country environment of Hampstead.
Remembering the way in which her father used to divert Minny and
herself as children, Annie conjured origami fishes and horses and carts
from her morning paper and, in good weather, took them out for walks
and encouraged their imaginations to range freely. 'I kept them in till
lunch then after the storm & East wind suddenly came a lovely burst
of sunshine & softness & we went to Italy & Switzerland & fed a goat
& a donkey.'[69]

Billy's scarlet fever was potentially more serious. Richmond took
Hester to the safety of lodgings on Campden Hill, whilst Annie spent
the Christmas of 1882 alone with Billy in Young Street, which at least
allowed her to tidy up her biographical article about Tennyson. 'Billy
was beginning to recover & we had a turkey & he had a little plum
pudding all to himself…. Later Richmond & Hester came & stood in
the Street outside & we waved to them from the nursery windows. In
the afternoon I sent off my proofs of the Tennyson article to Aldworth
how well I remember the proofs all steeped in Carbolic.'[70] Before he
was four, Billy had minor surgery, which she remembered later as being
'less severe than the Jewish ceremony but of the same nature',[71] and
shortly before his fifth birthday both he and Hester caught whooping
cough, a common and not an especially dangerous childhood illness.
Annie regarded him as a frail child, so that when the time came to send
him away to school it caused her significant distress. In fact, he would
prove to be remarkably resilient.

*Madame de Sévigné* was completed at last in February 1881.
When she was told of Mrs Oliphant's delight at receiving the final
manuscript, Pinkie said just the right thing, knowing what a struggle
it had been for Annie. 'I think that is a triumph for the mother of

Hester & Billy to have accomplished.'[72] Pinkie had helped with some translations, though Annie had done most of her own from the popular Didot edition of Sévigné, getting Richmond to scrutinise her versions. The book is modest in size and ambition, but Annie was proud of this new venture, and must have felt vindicated after Leslie's discouraging words of some years before. 'It is a very small mouse out of a mountain but even small as it is there will be a thousand inaccuracies I fear, but it <u>runs</u> all the same that I do lay to my flattering unction.'[73] The dedication to Hester and Billy is dated 18 March, Billy's first birthday. Mrs Oliphant was generous in praising the manuscript to William Blackwood, believing it would sell well, and that it had found its ideal author. 'It is not only Madame de Sévigné, but it is thoroughly Sévigné-ish.'[74]

This year saw something of a revival in Annie's published output, for *Miss Williamson's Divagations*, a collection of previous *Cornhill* pieces going back to 1876, appeared on 28 March. With the single exception of *Mrs Dymond*, published in 1885 but with origins going back ten years, there would be no further serious flirtations with fiction, virtually all future writings being memoirs or biographical studies of one kind or another. There is even something of the fictionalised memoir about the title piece. 'Miss Williamson's Divagations' is told in the first person, Young Street has become Old Street (where she lives), and the choice of the name 'Williamson' by the daughter of William Makepeace Thackeray lends a kind of gender ambiguity to the narrative voice. But Annie cannot have been encouraged by the opinions of the *Times* reviewer, who though identifying many 'pretty little incidental touches' noted that the pieces 'have all the delicacy of gossamer as well as its flimsiness'. Credit is given for the subtle evocations of place, but as fiction the individual items lacked substance, scarcely sufficient to command the reader's attention, 'and the difficulty we found in following the author through the "Divagations" was to get up even a languid interest in them'.[75] Annie was never so confident about her talents that she could easily shrug off even relatively mild criticism like this. It would have rather dampened her pleasure in the praises of her friends, which, usually for one so modest about her successes, she trumpeted to Pinkie in India. 'Everybody is asking me to dinner & begging for copies. They didnt think there was so much life left in me.'[76] As for *Madame de Sévigné*, it took about a year for the *Times* to notice it, but it was pleasingly favourable. 'Darling did you see todays Times with a good column to Sevigné. I wonder if that will help the sale – It might have done so if it had come before.'[77]

A change in Gerald Ritchie's fortunes brought great happiness. As Pinkie's Indian trip drew to its close, she became anxious about leaving her brother alone again, believing that a tendency towards depression would only be defeated once he was married. She was therefore overjoyed when he became engaged to the eighteen-year-old Margie Thackeray, who had travelled out to India in October 1881 with her father Edward Thackeray and his second wife, and by mid-December Pinkie was telling Hallam Tennyson about the match. It was an outcome that she had longed for – 'in a way wonderfully unlike most visions the vision has come true and as delightful, simple & straightforward a romance as could be imagined has come to pass'.[78] Understandably, Annie's reactions were almost those of a mother giving up a daughter, but she was deeply happy at the thought of the ties drawing the Thackerays and Ritchies ever closer. 'I thank God my darling Migsie is so blessed & Gerald indeed is fortunate & he will have a sweet young wife & Pinkies dear heart will be at ease for him. Richmond says he quite expected it – I had – I suppose – thought of it often but so vaguely that it never occurred to me as a thing to be thought about.'[79] Annie felt a little anxious for Margie's sister, 'little Anny', in the same way that she always had hopes for Pinkie herself, who had so faithfully watched as one after another her brothers and sisters married and left.

There was a strange episode when Pinkie did eventually get back to England, for she appeared almost by accident to have drifted into an engagement of her own, one from which she was too polite to detach herself. Charles Lutyens was the older brother of Edwin Lutyens, with whom Richmond later had many dealings relating to the architectural works in New Delhi. It is difficult to see how an attachment ever came about, as there was a marked lack of enthusiasm from all quarters. We only have Annie's later journal account to go on, but there seems every reason to suppose that Pinkie had had a fortunate escape.

> After some weeks Pinkie arrived from India engaged to Charles Lutyens & we went to stay in the von Hügels house at Hampstead.... Charles Lutyens came to see us.
>
> The wedding was fixed, but nobody was very happy about it. He was in financial difficulties, he did not like our family, he considered that most of us w$^d$. be damned among other classes. Also we were not sufficiently well dressed.
>
> Within a week of the wedding Captain Lutyens came to Gussie & said, if it wont break her heart break it off break it off – He is not good enough for her tho' he is my son.

Poor R^d. had to take this message to Brock Hill. Pinkie who was reading started up not heart broken but more relieved than words can say.

On the evening of what sh^d. have been her wedding day R & I were sitting by the fire after dinner when we heard the cab drive to the door. It was Willy who was bringing Pinkie to stay with us, & she remained for some days quietly getting used to the new state of things & resuming her old life once more.

Three

# AFTER ALL A LIFETIME
# (1882-1885)

*It touched me when I was at Vaux & M<sup>me</sup>. Marochetti said how*
*with all ones love interest & life in those who are ones life now she*
*felt she lived as much with the gone as with the living and I feel*
*this more & more as I get older & nearer the Kingdom come.*

Annie to Pinkie Ritchie
May 1883

One learns how to negotiate the journal which Annie began to com-
pile in the 1890s. It was put together later than most of the events
described in it, and consists of a synthesis of original diaries which
were then destroyed – she burnt some of them in 1899, though others
seem to have survived until 1915 – which presents some problems of
interpretation. A few fragments from the old diaries were preserved
and stuck in, just a day here and there, but most of the journal's
material is either a verbatim copy or a rewriting from memory of
events for which the diaries served as prompts. Some incidents were
suppressed, but Annie revisited others in the light of hindsight. The
implications of a passing comment can be hard to decode, unless
other evidence gives shape to the context. At the wedding in June
1881 of Amica Milnes, Lord Houghton's daughter, the bland statement that she 'met M<sup>r</sup> Swinburne again after a g<sup>t</sup> many years'
suggests nothing beyond the record of a pleasant reencounter. They
had last met in September 1865, although we would not know this
from the journal. On that occasion, when she and Minny had stayed
with the Houghtons at Fryston Hall, Swinburne does not even merit
a mention, though he was a fellow guest. After Fryston, the sisters
went on to the Brookfields at Somersby. The events of these days are
contained in a simple factual statement, devoid of all nuance: 'We
went to Fryston and Somersby & then we came back'.

What the journal pointedly conceals is the true effect that the 1865 Fryston visit had on Annie, and in particular the encounter with Swinburne. The reality is startling. In the letter of thanks sent to Lady Houghton from the Brookfields, Annie was still recovering from an intoxicating mix of Swinburne's poetry and personality. There is a tangible frisson, an awakening coinciding with the end of a long period of withdrawal since her father's death in December 1863. Just a fortnight earlier she had heard of Amy Crowe's death in India, but Fryston had managed to sweep even that aside for the moment.

> I have brought some paper & a pen & some ink out into the windy garden to try & say once more thankyou for everything & for all the kindness – I dont know <u>what</u> we should have done if we had not come away to a dear sympathetic audience that is not yet tired of hearing every single thing M<sup>r</sup> Swinburne said, & all the Archbishop [of York] said and all the names of the books in the library, & everything that happened every day over & over again, and how very very good you & Lord Houghton have been to us for w<sup>h</sup> I wont say thankyou anymore because it sounds like phrases – It has been like a little awakening to us – all sorts of things which had seemed to cease to concern us almost, have come to us out of our dear little visit, & coming here is like a delightful little moral to it. There is quite absurdly nothing to tell you about Somersby – every moment is almost exactly alike – an old grey horse who was standing at the farmers gate has walked away ... There is a continual hum of a steam reaper & hay-maker – all about the place there are horrible machines instead of peasant maidens. I think the harvest moon may as well cease to shine.[1]

Nor was this the first visit to Fryston. Annie and Minny had gone there once before, with Thackeray in April 1863, and this too is noted in the journal, again with no mention of Swinburne as being of the company despite the names of other guests being listed. In information given to Edmund Gosse for his 1917 Swinburne biography, Annie claimed that it was on this earlier occasion, in her father's presence, that she first met the poet. But either from confusion or by design, she has collapsed the two visits into one, for almost certainly it was not until 1865 that the highly-charged encounter occurred. Swinburne's effect upon her seems to have led Annie – in her much later account for Gosse – to incorporate an element of fabrication and concealment. Gosse noted that 'Lady Ritchie dwells on Swinburne's "kind and

cordial ways" during this amusing visit to Fryston. She had never seen
anybody so disconcerting or so charming, and when Thackeray [*sic*]
and his daughters had to take their leave, while Swinburne remained at
Fryston, the ... author of *The Story of Elizabeth* burst into tears.'[2]

Gosse thinks that he is writing of the 1863 visit, but his story, a
source for all subsequent biographers of Swinburne, depends solely upon what 'Lady Ritchie recalls for me'. It is extraordinarily
misleading, but he had no reason to doubt its authenticity. It is hard to
think that Annie can have accidentally confused the occasions, for by
shifting the encounter backwards by two years she assigns to her dead
father a wholly imaginary role as chaperon. Praise by 'Thackeray' for
the young poet's intellect lends respectability to this almost mythic
creature whose appearance Annie found so striking. 'She was in the
garden on the afternoon of his arrival, and she saw him advance up
the sloping lawn, swinging his hat in his hand, and letting the sunshine
flood the bush of his red-gold hair. He looked like an Apollo or a fairy
prince; and immediately attracted the approval of Mr. Thackeray by the
wit and wisdom of his conversation, as much as that of the two young
ladies by his playfulness.' At dinner, on the Sunday evening, he recited
poems which shocked the Archbishop of York, while Annie and Minny,
'who had never heard such sentiments expressed before, giggled aloud
in their excitement'. Then there were the tears at departure, Annie
portraying herself as a susceptible adolescent, rather than a woman
aged twenty-eight, only two months younger than Swinburne in fact.
Presented with a world of alluring new possibilities, she felt unable to
understand quite what it all meant. But in introducing her father as a
calming presence at an occasion which he never witnessed, her original
memories were sanitised and could be made available to Gosse who
took on trust this strange reworking of the actual sequence of events.
There is no reason to believe that Thackeray and Swinburne ever
actually met, though Annie may finally have succeeded in persuading
herself that they did.

We do not know what she felt on seeing Swinburne again in 1881,
nor if anything of the old excitement remained. The intervening
sixteen years had changed so much for her. She had been overtaken
by marriage, motherhood and middle age. There is no hint in anything
that she later wrote about Swinburne, nor in her letters to him, of the
electrical charge of that first encounter. She was alert still to his sartorial
dash – 'Swinburne came to see us one day in white stockings & low
shoes w[h] fascinated me all the time'[3] – though it merely amused her
now. They became good friends during their later years, she living in
Kensington and then Wimbledon, he in Putney with Theodore Watts-

Dunton. Early enthusiasm for his writing had given way to a more measured appreciation, and in 1905 she thought that his novel *Love's Cross Currents*, originally published in 1877 as *A Year's Letters*, lacked substance – 'it is like Newcomes & an <u>immense</u> deal of water – too much'.[4] She would invite him to meet women friends, including Rhoda Broughton at 'rather a highly flavoured swarry',[5] and once quizzed him about Spenser for her Browning essay, knowing of his specialist knowledge of the Elizabethan poets.

> I heard a story from Dean Stanley which interested me very much – That when Spencer [*sic*] died the poets his friends stood round & flung their pens into his grave. Did you ever hear this story? – A great friend of mine M[rs] Strachey who <u>loves</u> Elizabethan literature & your Webster (& who I <u>should</u> <u>so</u> like to bring to see you) declares she cant reconcile this 'fine story' with the fact that Spencer died hungry & in destitution. As you I do believe were alive then (I dont know <u>who</u> you were my dear old friend, perhaps Marlowe or Webster himself) will you please give me your impression of the facts. I want it – to tell you the present facts – for a little article I am writing about dear M[r] Browning. My quill spluttering as it is I fling with the rest of the swans, gooses & steel nibs & better than these the <u>hearts</u> affectionate sympathy w[h]. belong to him.[6]

She remembered a farcical occasion when, on the way to catch a train to Eton, she took a visiting American keen for an autograph to see the now almost deaf Swinburne. 'I <u>shouted</u>. Here is a friend who has brought a book all the way f[m]. America for you to write your name M[r]. Swinburne! – & only 5 minutes to do it in! <u>Swinburne</u> & unfortunately I have no less then eighteen letters in my name! M[r] M[c]Cabe shouting "And every letter famous, M[r] Swinburne". We caught our train notwithstanding.'[7] After Swinburne's death, Annie was one of the few closer acquaintances whom Watts-Dunton singled out for a careful reply to her letter of sympathy. Too ill and upset to respond in person, he commissioned his wife to send telegrams to 'special friends', and Clara Watts-Dunton remembered sending 'an especially long one' to Annie.[8]

The success of *Madame de Sévigné* encouraged Annie to undertake more biographical work, particularly when she could draw upon personal memories. An interest in Maria Edgeworth eventually led to a series of introductions for various of her reissued works, beginning in 1895, but first came 'Miss Edgeworth' for the *Cornhill*. At the start

of 1882 she wrote to Edgeworth's sister, grateful for the loan of family
books but frustrated at the constant interruptions to her work – 'I suffer
from prostrating headaches w^h. prevent me from writing or reading'.
She was irresistibly reminded of her own childhood encounters with
the novels. 'The stories were my first playfellows & one of the early
things I remember is being ill with sore eyes & my Father reading the
little Merchants to me in a darkened room at Paris.'[9]

The friendship with Tennyson stretching back into her childhood
had grown stronger since her father's death. His trust was such that
once when walking with her in 1882 he asked her to write an article
about him for the American publishers, Harpers. 'I could tell you
things he said.'[10] Coming from someone so resistant to the queries of
potential biographers – as touchy as her own father in this regard – this
was clearly an invitation not to be passed over, though its demands
competed with work on Maria Edgeworth. Within weeks she was
collecting materials, and arranging interviews through the agency of
Hallam Tennyson. 'I wonder if I sh^d. find y^r Father tomorrow morning
if I come abt 11. I have bought a little pocket book in case he will tell
me anything more.'[11] This was the essay which she was completing
at Christmas 1882 when Billy had scarlet fever. In the following
March, Harpers sent her £50, but hoping for more she returned the
cheque and asked for £100, to which they agreed without demur. She
only had happy memories of this project, and of going to Aldworth
for Tennyson's final approval before publication. 'He read, he said
flummery flummery, he corrected a word here & there. I was not
Dante but He most assuredly was Virgil & it was joy to have such a
convincing lesson in style. Simply given & indisputably felt by me.'

Tennyson had no cause for complaint when this supremely inoffensive study appeared. Its republication ten years later, in a volume which
also included her reissued Browning and Ruskin essays, was followed
almost at once by his death which contributed to high sales for the
book. All the same, Annie had been nervous about writing it, sensitive
always to what could be said and what should be tactfully avoided.
She told Richmond that 'I tremble about my Tennyson – Happily it is
very short & vague and absolutely slight'. She was right about its lack
of substance, which was precisely why Hallam so approved of it when
preparing himself for writing his own monumental *Memoir.* 'I have
just been reading your delightful sketch of him again – I wish that it
might stand as the only life, but "ghouls" have begun to dig – & my
Father was anxious that some authentic life shd be written to keep out
penny-a-liner lies. He hated the biographies of literary men as a rule as
much as your Father did.'[12]

*Letter from Annie to Richmond with sketch of Hester and Billy, about 1882*

In April 1882 the Ritchies went to stay with Charles and Emma
Darwin, a visit described in some detail in the journal. It had been
prompted by her Maria Edgeworth researches, for both Darwin and his
wife, born Emma Wedgwood, had ancestral links to the Edgeworths.
It was the last time Annie saw Darwin, an occasion made memorable
by her getting the date of their invitation wrong and arriving a week
early. Later she decided that fate had been at work, for Darwin fell
ill with his final illness on the day when they had been scheduled to
arrive.

> We drove to the door the Butler hospitably said M$^r$ & M$^{rs}$
> Darwin are sure to wish you to remain, pray dont go, & M$^{rs}$
> Darwin & M$^r$ Darwin came out and called us in, & M$^r$ Darwin
> said youre as welcome as can be & you must forgive me
> for laughing – I cant for the life of me help laughing. There
> never was a more charming little visit nor a more delightful
> host & hostess. He told us about his travels with Ad$^l$ FitzRoy
> he told us about birds he told us about Fishes. How the little
> new starlings lead off & seem to know the way when the
> time of migrations arrives & he told us about the tortoises in
> the Island of Ascension hatched from the eggs in the sand &
> starting off & plunging into the sea – & by Jove he says the
> little tortoises without compass or experience sail straight
> across by nearest way to Algiers its perfectly wonderful he
> cries. Then he said he should go & rest – These ladies he said
> are good eno' to carry me off & read me to sleep when they
> think I am getting over excited ...
>     The day we should have really gone he was taken ill with
> his fatal illness – those 2 happy days were the last bright
> flash of that glorious life.

She wrote in characteristic vein to Darwin's daughters, moved
at the passing of a heroic life and as always drew on more personal
memories. They were all blessed in having the best models. 'My
own dearest Father has taught us how to love the best & the greatest
things ... Here is one great man to love indeed without fear, & to teach
our children to look to & to live towards.'[13] It was harder to draw
noble conclusions from the death of Magdalene Ritchie after her new
baby was born, following 'terrible weeks of suffering and fever'. Her
journal sketches out with stark grimness the appalling rituals of a
Victorian death-bed scene, with the children brought in one by one to
kiss their dying mother, and the melodrama of Annie herself hurrying
outside in those last moments to quieten the barrel-organ boy who had

been playing music in the street for the children to dance to. Annie had grown close to Magdalene over the years. As the Brookfields' daughter there was all the history of her father's old passion to be borne, but once Magdalene had married into the family as the wife of Richmond's eldest brother, it helped to ease former heartaches. This was the girl to whom as a baby Thackeray had charmingly sent 'my very best love and compliments upon your appearance in this world, where I hope you will long remain, so as to make your Mamma & Papa happy'.[14] Now she too was gone, at the age of thirty-two.

The occasion of Edward FitzGerald's death is not recorded in Annie's journal, but it was another significant departure. One of her father's earliest friends, as young men they had enjoyed an unusually passionate relationship. Its precise nature cannot now be retrieved, for FitzGerald destroyed many of Thackeray's letters, particularly those early ones which might have told so much, and Thackeray was himself always careless about retaining correspondence. On FitzGerald's side at least, the early relationship had a homo-erotic dimension, hinted at in a coyly sentimental poem celebrating the day 'When first I saw Willy and Willy saw me!' Though the men saw little of each other in later years, once FitzGerald chose to cultivate the life of a Suffolk recluse, the affection between 'Fitz' and 'old Thack' lasted until Thackeray's death, and the intensity of FitzGerald's loyalty led to a significant legacy for Annie and Minny under the terms of his will. Upon his death in June 1883, £500 came to Annie, 'for love of my father'.[15]

When she learnt from Leslie that the librarian of Trinity College, Aldis Wright, was compiling FitzGerald's official biography, she wrote from Hampstead to offer her support.

> I am almost sure I have some old letters – a very few – to my Father f$^m$. him – would you care for any to me – He wrote so well & so characteristically that every note seemed to be unlike other notes. I have only seen him once in twenty years when to my great pleasure I grasped at him in a crowd.
>
> Our house is let & I should have to hunt through old put away papers so that it w$^d$ not be for another month that I could look for the letters w$^h$. I seem to remember tho' I have not looked at them for years.[16]

She must have seen the irony of offering up letters to help with a FitzGerald life, governed as she was by her father's enduring censure on publication of his own papers, a project now long overdue. Just weeks earlier she had been asked to consider allowing the American publication of one of the few Thackeray letters which, instead of destroying, FitzGerald had preserved and given to Annie. She now asked George Smith for advice, shifting the decision onto him as owner of the copyright.

> I once showed Mr. Fitzgeralds book of my Fathers old letters &ct to Mr. Bowker & I have had several notes from him about one of them … w$^h$. he is very anxious to get. I said at first I wasnt inclined to publish & the letter was Mr. Fitzgeralds & finally the copyright was yours.
>
> I wrote to Mr. Fitzgerald however on the very day he died after receiving a second & 3$^d$. letter on the subject. The papers are now mine as he has left them to me dear kind old friend – & some money too – & as I have rec$^d$. this again from Messrs Harpers I send it on to you please to settle.[17]

It would be some months before Annie had retrieved the FitzGerald letters at Young Street for Aldis Wright, time enough to have begun to question the wisdom of publishing them. Although she sent Wright some letters, she withheld all but one of those to her father, sending instead transcripts of FitzGerald's to her, despite her instincts that these were not really suitable either. It was frustrating not being able publicly to acknowledge his loyal friendship to her father.

> One of my letters to M$^r$ FitzGerald (to wh. the enclosed is an answer) was written after I had found out from some old letters of my Father what a friend he had been to my Father. At the time of my mothers illness & even before he had helped him with money loved him encouraged him & my Father who was as well able to <u>take</u> generously as to give when the time came, in all his troubles writes back in a brave & grateful & noble way which almost makes me cry even now after all a lifetime, but you will see even in these few notes how nervously M$^r$. FitzGerald shrank from publicity, just as my own Father did he so often says 'do not quote this' & though I long to show you what a generous true friend he was I hardly know how to do it – I wish I could have found more.[18]

Two days later, she suggested that Wright might approach Fanny Kemble for letters, but she was already doubting whether even the little which she had herself sent was too much. She was clearly relieved that Wright was finding no shortage of materials. 'A great many qualms have seized me about the passage I copied out: I am going to ask Leslie what he thinks about it. I am so glad you have so many letters.'[19] When it came to it, Wright would use none of FitzGerald's letters to her, and only one to her father, and in thanking those who had loaned material, his characteristically Victorian avowal of caution suggested a reserve attuned to Annie's own. 'It has been my endeavour to justify their confidence by discretion.'[20]

It was natural for Annie to have thought of Fanny Kemble, for the Ritchies had decided to build a house in Rosary Gardens, and Mrs Kemble lived close by in Hereford Square. The increase in salary which came with Richmond's promotion perhaps made them ambitious for a move, and they had noticed that living next door to the Greyhound Inn in Young Street was supplying rather too rich a mix to Billy's growing vocabulary. Hester later provided a description of the new custom-built house, to which they would move in August 1884. '36$^A$ Rosary Gardens was a most pleasant medium-size brick house, with a big hall and a well staircase. It faced south, and the sun poured in, and M$^{rs}$. Kemble's back garden came up to the drawing room window. According to the fashion of the day, the wall papers were W$^m$. Morris papers. The "Pomegranate" in the Dining room, the yellow "Venetian" in the drawing room.'[21] Not for the last time they found themselves overstretched. Annie would ask George Smith for an advance to cover the costs of the move and, bizarrely, to help pay for the erection of a weathercock. Scarcely a year later they had to move in with Richmond's mother and Pinkie in order to generate a rental income from Rosary Gardens. The Young Street house was also let to tenants, including at one time to Edward Burne-Jones's daughter, and what with her share of Hyde Park Gate South, Annie and Richmond had useful assets tied up in property.

With Rosary Gardens still in the early stages of planning and construction, for much of 1883 they rented for extended periods at Kew and then Hampstead – where they occupied the Heath Street house of the leading Roman Catholic layman, Baron Friedrich von Hügel. In September they took guest-house rooms in order to join an augmented family party at Lynton. During a storm on Lynton Moor Annie determined on the title of her latest collection of republished essays, this time on women writers, for which she was already correcting the proofs. 'I thought of Macbeths 3 witches & then it suddenly occurred to me that my book ought to be called A Book of Sibyls by Mrs RR.'[22] Only one of the essays was new, that on Mrs Opie; the other three were a revised version of 'Jane Austen' (first written in 1871), 'Mrs. Barbauld' (1881) and 'Miss Edgeworth' (1882).

There were two special pleasures for Annie during this Lynton holiday. She witnessed the growing romance between Richmond's youngest sister Elinor (Nelly) and the political writer, Herbert Paul, later a Liberal MP, and she met Richard Doyle again, the original illustrator of *The Newcomes.* She would encounter 'dear Dicky Doyle' just once after this, shortly before his death. 'He dined with us he seemed so tired but tired or not he was always a charming presence.'[23] As for Nelly, she and Herbert Paul were married within the year, Hester being one of the twelve bridesmaids. A violent headache prevented Annie from attending, but Richmond represented them, and she sent him a telegram for the happy couple – 'Love to Mr and Mrs Paul. JOB counts upon us for a lift home' – which much to her amusement came out garbled as 'Love to JOB. Count upon us for life'.[24]

Hallam Tennyson became engaged in November, and when Annie wrote excitedly at the news of his father's peerage, just as she was sorting through the FitzGerald letters for Aldis Wright, she also urged Hallam to choose books from the forthcoming sale of FitzGerald's effects as her wedding gift to him. There had been a past awkwardness between herself and FitzGerald – about what we do not know – which the smoothly diplomatic Hallam had helped resolve, and she thought her gift might be appropriate. 'I am so delighted by the news. I quite approve radical though I am, literarily & personally – I think England will look all the more respectable for doing her best to honour her great men … I wanted to ask you to mark some of dear M[r] Fitzgeralds books on the catalogue for my wedding present. I hear they are old & yet I dont think you will mind but theres a Molière & a Sevigné in good condition. I shall always feel grateful to you for making up my difficulty with him w[h]. was more serious than I had any idea of.'[25]

FitzGerald's long interest in Madame de Sévigné may have helped fuel Annie's. His two-volume *Dictionary of Madame de Sévigné* would be published posthumously, and in the sale of his books she bought his annotated copy of the 1853 edition of the Sévigné letters, which as Hallam had not wanted she kept for herself.[26] She also bought his personal copy of the 1882 revision of *Euphranor*, which as Hester later noted included 'Marginal notes & corrections by EFG … with much matter not in the 1st & 2nd edns especially about Tennyson'.[27] Tennyson and FitzGerald had been close since their shared Trinity College days, though their paths (like those of FitzGerald and Thackeray) had rarely crossed in later years. Annie was pleased during that long summer of 1883 to enjoy the calming influence of Aldworth. Tennyson read to her the lines on FitzGerald which he had tactfully kept from his friend, 'afraid he might not like the end',[28] a poem whose original ending alluded to FitzGerald's sometimes frank criticisms of the poet's more recent work. Tennyson fondly if a little regretfully recalls 'When, in our younger London days, / You found some merit in my rhymes, / And I more pleasure in your praise'.[29]

Although the past was important for Annie, she did not live in it. Her essentially optimistic outlook meant that she delighted in the absurdities and charms of everyday living, and as the mother of young children she shared in their encounters with a newly-minted world, relishing the inventiveness of their language and the sharpness of a vision untouched by cynicism. Billy's solemn aphorisms were copied out with particular care, such as this page from her journal for 1884.

Billy reflectively Angels isn't <u>true</u>. They's only dreams

Billy in bed Listen to the wind its going all over the trees and into the world

Billy wouldnt kiss little Mary Spring Rice. I apologetically He is shy you see. Billy looking up from my lap where he had hidden his face. Ise not shy – Ise Rude.

Hester to charwoman: M<sup>rs</sup> Brown how old is your eldest son
He is 19 Miss
And your other son M<sup>rs</sup> Brown
He is 17 Miss Hester
And how old is your daughter
She is 14 Miss
And which is your favourite child M<sup>rs</sup> Brown?

Billy log. And when Adam had eaten the apple did he know how far Inja was & about the Earth going round & round & everything.

13 March. I tell the children the story of S<sup>t</sup>. Elizabeth of Hungary & the Roses. B. Did you hear it in church No I read it in a book. Oh! it <u>isnt</u> true then
19 March. Get on Billy do your copy look at Hester she has nearly finished. Billy: Hesters the Hare. Ise the Tortoise.
7 May. Geralds treat to the Crystal Palace, to all the families – Diver from the bottom of the water throws up a pipe. 'Would any gentleman or lady like to ask the Diver any question through the pipe.' Small Bill steps forward takes the pipe & says 'Diver. When is a door not a door?' <u>Diver</u> Cant say Im sure Sir.

Billy charmed their Hampstead friends the du Mauriers, whom the Ritchies got to know well during their stays in Heath Street.

*'Punch' cartoon by George Du Maurier, 'An Indignant Disclaimer', May 1884*

George du Maurier illustrated for *Punch*, before failing sight caused him to turn to writing. He immortalised the occasion of Billy's refusal to kiss Mary Spring Rice as a *Punch* cartoon, in which 'Mamma' also features, Billy turning from a lady offering him chocolates and retreating into the safety of his mother's lap. 'I have today been designing the wicked Billy saying he was not shy but rude; someday, when he is a KCB, or an admiral of the blue, or whatnot, he will show the drawing in Punch with contrition, & say: "you might not have thought it, but I was that boy!"'[30] 'An Indignant Disclaimer' bears the caption:

> *Mamma.* 'Now, Billy, you mustn't be shy, you know!'
> *Billy.* 'I'se *not* shy – I'se *rude*!'[31]

Annie and Richmond followed the serialisation of the immensely popular *Trilby* when it appeared in 1894, and she took the final number to du Maurier who wrote on it after the last line of the novel 'And so good-bye, dear Mrs. Ritchie'. They had the set of numbers bound, and Hester Ritchie would annotate this copy many years later.

> My mother Anne Ritchie took the number of Harpers Magazine in which the last chapter of Trilby appeared to

Hampstead & I remember how she asked M^r du Maurier to write his name.

I remember how he pointed to the spectacles with one black glass & told her he had lost the sight of one eye. And I remember too how he sadly pointed to the word FINIS.

Then to my mortification he told my mother that on no account was she to allow me to read Trilby. I was 16 years old.[32]

They moved at last to Rosary Gardens late in August 1884, but only three days later set off for the north, visiting Edinburgh and Durham before staying with their friends Hugh and Florence Bell in Redcar, a town Annie visited often in the years to come. It typifies the Ritchies' curious attitude to money. Instead of reining in their holiday plans, they abandoned for weeks the new house which had already drained their funds so exhaustively. Richmond does not appear to have been much more resourceful than Annie in controlling the family finances. Despite frequent good resolutions about cutting back, no lasting savings were ever made in the things which might actually have made a difference, such as running their household with fewer servants. And because it did not occur to them to ask that kind of question of themselves, the danger of living beyond their means was never realistically addressed. They may not have had ideas above their station, but they certainly assumed a lifestyle beyond their income. Other members of the family, who perhaps were no richer but who budgeted more carefully, occasionally might help them out, a touching example being an unsolicited offer from Willie and Magdalene Ritchie late in 1881. 'Uncle Willy came in one evening very shy & apologetic to ask a great favour. He brought £100 in bank notes in his pocket & the favour was that we should take the money! They were both so eager & generous that we compromised & kept £30 as a present – I said to dear Magdalene "We should only pay our bills with the £100, you may as well pay yours & she rather ruefully – well since you put it so – but the 30 you must promise to spend".'[33] Annie and Richmond had to face the truth of their limited means when ten years later Billy was sent to school at Sedbergh rather than Eton, in part at least because Eton's fees were beyond them. Even paying for Sedbergh required Annie to sell some of her father's papers.

They were not back in Rosary Gardens until mid-October, when the sixteen-year-old Gertrude Bell,[34] attending school at Queen's College in Harley Street, came to stay for a few days. She was taken to see the revival of the Gilbert and Sullivan comic opera *The*

*Sorcerer*, and accompanied Annie to the National Portrait Gallery to view a picture of Thackeray. Annie also took Gertrude on a little tour of Kensington, pointing out those parts which featured in *Old Kensington*, and showed her Thackeray's Young Street house as well as the grander Palace Green. Gertrude lent a hand with putting things straight at Rosary Gardens. 'Their house is so pretty, the rooms have all sorts of funny comfortable corners. It was nearly all arranged, only pictures to hang and piles and piles of books to put in the shelves.' Richmond's natural reserve sometimes made his manner distant, but it did not put off Gertrude, with whom he set about arranging the books. 'How nice he is. I thought at first I did not like him at all, but after I had seen a little of him I quickly changed my opinion.'[35]

As money was in short supply, it was timely now to secure the promise of £400 from Alexander Macmillan for *Mrs Dymond*, to be Annie's final novel, serialised in *Macmillan's Magazine* from March 1885, particularly as George Smith then matched the price for the book rights. This was her first venture with Macmillan's, though others would follow, and apart from *Madame de Sévigné* for Blackwoods, it was her first move away from the Smith, Elder stable. Nonetheless, it was Smith who for virtually her entire writing career underpinned her income, crowned by a staggeringly generous sum for the introductions to the Biographical Edition of her father's works. As she struggled with *Mrs Dymond*, the origins for which go back to the Franco-Prussian conflict witnessed in her visits to Paris a decade earlier, Annie was afflicted from the middle of January 1885 by crippling pain which then affected her intermittently for years to come. She had long suffered from 'headache' which she assigned to neuralgia but perhaps some of which can be attributed to migraines, and now leg pains prevented her from walking. She described this incapacity as sciatica, but the frequency of its recurrence suggests that it may have been arthritic. In February things were not made easier when she fell down stairs and 'loosened all my teeth, worse luck'. Richmond also became ill about this time, early signs probably of the Ménière's disease which periodically would result in him having to be brought home from the India Office.

Annie was at her worst during April, was administered morphia which caused severe nausea, and had to be looked after by Richmond's mother and Pinkie at Southmead, their Wimbledon house. She returned to Rosary Gardens later in the month, but was still unwell, wracked by sudden spasms of pain. The loving support of her family was comforting, but she was feeling her age – two months off forty-eight. She transferred to the quiet and fresher air of Hampstead as she began to feel stronger, but it had been a trial of endurance.

May 3. M^rs Kemble visited me. Out with R in a bath chair. As I w[alke]^d along I could see R smiling with pleasure.

Monday. Woke up pretty well, began to dress, horrible seizure. Pain all day. R nursed me, made me tea & comforted my soul. One leg in hell all night. Thought it was General Gordon.

5. Perfectly squashed galvanized – nurse came. Hester came & said How pretty & white your hair has grown Mama & she kissed it – Was there ever a sweeter way of growing grey? – Pinkie stayed on.

6. Lay still – Billy peeps in 'I sor you with your agonies momom'.... R came & played Patience by my bedside.

May 8 Woke up into sunshine after a delicious sleep – sorrow endureth for a night. Children & Towser breakfasting with Richmond downstairs          .

Wednesday to lodgings at Hampstead in a fly – ever so much better. R came to see me. Kate Greenaway, von Hügels, Fields. Writing M^rs. Dymond again & home again.

Just before leaving for Hampstead, fresh from the benefits of a session of galvinism – the treatment so much favoured by her grandfather, Henry Carmichael-Smyth – she sent a note to her new neighbour, Fanny Kemble, indicating something of the depths from which at last she was emerging.

> I am sure you will like to know that for the first time today I seem really to be coming out of my slough of despond – I had a horrid relapse after that day you came, but at last I seem to be at the end of the long lane. I am going away at once for a few days to Hampstead & when I come home I mean to come & see you ... The children acted a little play to amuse me today. Hester was a schoolmaster flogging Billy. I was amused when he cried out indignantly 'Hester! how badly you act – you are thumping me instead of the chair'....
>
> I am scarcely able to believe my happy good deliverance from Evil. The Demon went away suddenly this morning after being galvanized – I can eat – I can hobble I could almost jump for joy.[36]

Not until 7 June was she able triumphantly to record that 'I take a walk for the first time in a month & get to the Pond & back again'.

Despite only having been in Rosary Gardens for a few months, they were already finding its running costs crippling – '[we] began to think we must not live on in it'. She put on a brave face to her American correspondent, John Field, claiming that the £150 addition to Richmond's salary as a Private Secretary 'just makes the difference of size & comfort in our 4 walls'.[37] But £150 could only go so far. The year had begun well enough, she and Richmond having exchanged houses for the Christmas holiday period with Blanche and Frank Warre Cornish at Eton. On New Year's Day they enjoyed extracts from *Messiah* in St George's Chapel, Windsor, Walter Parratt accompanying Botticelli-like ladies playing violins. Annie admired the flair with which Blanche had decorated their Eton house, in some ways as startlingly unusual as the conversation for which she became famous amongst generations of Eton boys. She noticed 'Blanchies great charming drawing room the jardin the Italian pots the tapestry – delightful quasi-Roman interior',[38] so different from the dark and cluttered décor of many Victorian living spaces. Once back in town, Hester and Billy started their formal schooling by attending a kindergarten, though with mixed results. 'Billy says he doesnt like it because they talk Politics to him.'[39]

It was a moment of sweet irony when Leslie approached her to write the article on Elizabeth Barrett Browning for the *Dictionary of National Biography*. After all his discouragement over Madame de Sévigné, Annie can be forgiven a quiet smile of triumph, even if she was his second choice.

> I enclose you a letter from Miss Zinneker which, I think explains itself. She was supposed to be especially well informed about M[rs] Browning & I am rather put out by having everything on my hands again. Do you think that you could do it? The life would have to be as short & with as many facts for Dryasdust as possible – dates of birth death, marriage, books published &c. & with criticism only subordinate. If it suits you, I think that your writing it would be the best solution &, of course, one life might be a little less dry than the others without injury. There is no hurry at all. You might take a year I should think, if you wished it. I must find some one to do it soon or to undertake it soon. I cant write it well myself – chiefly because I dont care about Mrs B's poetry & should, I fear, make my indifference clear. Browning himself would, I am pretty sure, prefer you to any one & indeed, expected you to do it originally.[40]

By the end of January she was working on the article when she felt well enough, and sent Leslie a first draft by May. He was probably mightily relieved that Annie had been able to rein in her inclinations towards whimsy, realising that she had no real feel for 'our dismal work', but his editorial pen still intervened. One of his problems was his lack of sympathy for the subject. 'After all I cant believe much in Mrs B. She shrieks too much. I dont think it necessary to say anything of her "spiritisms" – damn it.' But there is genuine praise for Annie in his summing-up, for he thought it 'very well done indeed'.[41]

As she made revisions, Annie sought information from Browning through his sister, Sarianna. When she wrote in September, Leslie had already been at work on her second version. 'I sent it to Leslie who has sent me my shorn lamb without any tempered winds but I see that I shall be able to reprint my article somewhere with all my little rigmaroles which are at least genuine and mean the loving & grateful remembrance of some thirty years.'[42] It proved almost impossible for Annie to write a dictionary entry according to the 'Dryasdust' formula and not to dwell on the person, especially one known to her. She asked for Elizabeth's date of birth, which she did not know. Surprisingly, nor did Robert and Sarianna, or at least they would not until they had returned from their stay in the Valle d'Aosta. 'I am sorry that Robert cannot give you, till he returns to London, the precise date of her birthday, which was in March. She avoided sensitively all talking of a past that to her had not been happy, – We lost her on the 29th June. I know your kind feeling for her, and share it. No sister could be kinder than she was to me, and I loved her deeply. If you purpose writing an article less arid than a Dictionary record, I shall be very glad – She had a great affection for you, and without some love there is no insight into character.'[43]

Not until the end of November did Annie get the clarification she sought. 'Her birthday was the 6th. March – Robert only discovered it just before we left town, in a little memorandum she had made of her brothers' and sisters' birthdays. She died the last day in June.' She had already sent proof sheets for Browning's approval, and Sarianna reported back his pleasure. 'No one could have done it with more affection ... The only suggestion that Robert would make, is, he would feel gratified by enumerating, among the recognitions, the enthusiastic praising of Aurora Leigh by Henri Taine, in his work on England. It is rare to find a Frenchman so appreciative of foreign poetry.'[44]

When Leslie had checked at the end of July on the progress of the revisions, he also explained the outcome of Laura's recent assessment by Dr John Langdon Down, the authority in mental health problems in children and adolescents after whom Down's Syndrome was named. Leslie had at last accepted that Laura's difficulties were not simply those of a slow learner. As the young children of his second marriage grew up around her, Laura's differences were starkly evident, and she was the victim of the sort of unkind treatment that clever children can mete out on those less able. She had become a figure of fun, and almost certainly was bullied. Leslie and Julia endeavoured to shield her, but like most Victorians they would have coped so much better with virtually any kind of physical illness. It was especially hard for Leslie to accept that a child of his might have some kind of mental incapacity. He set out the facts, still determined to persevere with his attempts to get Laura to read and to learn, but was now close to admitting failure. Without articulating what the future might entail, institutionalisation must already have been in his mind, and had probably been raised by Langdon Down. For Annie, who feared for Laura stranded in this family where she was conspicuously different, it was a relief that Leslie was addressing the matter seriously. Inevitably she would have had constantly in her mind the pathetic example of her own mother and her many decades of removal from the family home, which continued still. It made Leslie's letter especially painful.

> I should have been glad to talk a little about Laura. We thought it desirable some time ago to let Langdon Down see her again; & I wished to tell you about it viva voce, because, to say the truth, it is not very pleasant to write. However, I dont wish you to be in ignorance longer. Briefly what he said, came to this; 1st that she had changed less than he had expected, 2ndly, that his impression was that she would not develop much further.
>
> Now, I do not think much of Dr L.D. He did not impress me as having an opinion worth much more than my own. Still he has great experience &, what I must confess impressed me was that his view was to some extent a confirmation of my own suspicions. He could throw no particular light upon treatment.
>
> I do feel & feel it the more from this that such hopes as I have tried to cherish will be disappointed.
>
> She improves in some ways but the improvement is small & I seem to see definite limits to it's [*sic*] possibilities. There are, that is, certain things in wh. she seems to make no advance. I watch her closely & daily & though I catch at every ground of hope, this is my definite opinion. We must go on doing what we can but I greatly fear that we can do little …
>
> It is all very trying & the outlook for the future is not pleasant. All I can say is that I shall not give up making her

do what she can do; because she <u>may</u> still advance & equally because, as soon as she is left to herself she falls back & becomes more apathetic or babyish.

I should have liked to talk to you. When I think of some things I remember it makes me wretched & yet glad too that the future was so hidden from us in old days.[45]

In the late summer Annie took the children to Cromer as guests of the father of Eleanor Tennyson, Frederick Locker and his second wife. Hester and Billy revelled in the seaside, 'like two delicious bunches of seaweed', but Mrs Locker's religious earnestness was a little daunting. Annie did her best to be diplomatic, recalling the energies pointlessly expended during the many years of her grandmother's own religious preoccupations. 'But I do like people whose hearts are in their lives & having firmly tho feebly exclaimed my own state of mind I shall avoid all discussions in future … It was quite curious to feel exactly the old Paris Grannie feeling come over me w$^h$. I had forgotten for years.'[46] To her mingled shame and amusement, Billy rather exposed the holes in his scriptural education when finding himself under scrutiny. 'Painful scene on Sunday. M$^{rs}$. Locker surrounded by children: & what did S$^t$. Paul wear? Godfrey: the breast plate of faith; & on his feet? – Dorothy: Preparation of Righteousness, & what did he hold in his hand. Billy promptly, "The Union Jack"; dismissed in confusion.'[47] After Cromer they went north, meeting Richmond at Doncaster and proceeding first to Redcar, then on to Edinburgh and St Andrews, where Richmond spent his time on the links. Golf, and later bicycling, were his relaxations in rare breaks from the India Office. During this trip Annie completed *Mrs Dymond*, and having returned to London they accepted the inevitable and arranged to lease Rosary Gardens, securing a tenant for £200 a year from the following Easter.

Leslie and Julia encouraged them to consider returning to live next door to them at Hyde Park Gate, to the house which Annie still part-owned. It would have made good sense, but they decided against it, and instead moved in with Richmond's mother and Pinkie at Wimbledon. They had not lived in Rosary Gardens long enough for it to have felt like home, but leaving it seemed like a defeat. Annie liked to remember some of its novel features, such as the speaking-tube arrangement which linked the drawing-room to the children's nursery. Billy's mastery of the device had the occasional startling result. 'I was entertaining some smart company on one occasion when a shrill whistle came down the pipe & Billy's voice. Are the horrid visitors gone yet?'

Towards the end of the year, Lionel Tennyson, accompanied by his wife Eleanor, embarked on the long passage to India, part of his endeavour to seek preferment within the India Office. He would never see England again, succumbing to fever and liver failure on the return journey. There would be quite unforeseeable consequences for the Ritchies, giving a new twist to the family's long relationship with the sub-continent. In the months following Lionel's death in April 1886, Richmond and Eleanor appear to have become entangled, though quite what their relationship involved is impossible to know. For a while the contentment which Annie had discovered in her late marriage and young family was shaken. Stability would be restored quite quickly, for it was inevitable that Richmond should choose Annie over Eleanor, if choice indeed was required, but it was sufficient for her to doubt the happiness in which, perhaps complacently, she had been becalmed.

# Four

# THE LIGHTS OF THE HILLS
## (1886-1889)

*We must all die, but kindness does make one feel so alive, & I like to think of it existing in some mysterious way handed on almost with an independent life from that of the giver.*

Annie to Margaret Oliphant
28 November 1888

After *Mrs Dymond* there would be no further novels. Biography and memoir took over. It had been a gradual but decisive change of focus, attributable in part to Annie's poor health making the completion of large-scale projects difficult. She enjoyed the process of researching materials for her essays on Tennyson and those women writers making up of *A Book of Sibyls*, and even meeting the more precise brief of preparing an entry for the *Dictionary of National Biography*. But her finest single achievement still lay ahead, a self-imposed challenge which at times she feared she might never complete. The Biographical Edition of her father's works and its successor, the Centenary Edition, both of which included her elegant prefaces, opened the doors for modern Thackeray scholarship, not just by the scope and insight of those introductions, stamped with her inevitably privileged authority, but in the glimpse they offered of the richness of the materials which in due course became available to later students.

Although ten years would pass before serious work began on this project which culminated in monthly publication of the Biographical Edition volumes during 1898-9, from the mid 1880s her responsibility for the Thackeray legacy increasingly preoccupied her. In the months immediately after her father's death, George Smith had given good advice in warning off unwanted early biographers, though his caution which was timely then, was scarcely adequate now. 'Your Father's life will be written; and it is desirable that the writer should be one, who can do justice to your Father's memory and also would have the advantage of your aid and of reference to papers and documents – It is not necessary to decide on the author nor desirable that the Book should be immediately commenced but it would be well to warn off Biographies by announcing that such a work is in preparation.'[1] More than twenty years later, it was no longer a credible position. 'What a nuisance my Fathers biographers are' she complained to Richmond in November 1890, when a book undertaken by Herman Merivale was nearing completion. The nuisance lay principally in being prodded towards a decision which could not be shirked for much longer.

Whereas Annie might continue to withhold materials, she had no control over those Thackeray letters owned by others, the copyright to which she and Minny in any case had assigned to Smith, though she certainly endeavoured to exercise a moral authority when friends raised the topic of publication. Less than a year after her father's death she was urging restraint on Mrs Baxter, whose many Thackeray letters included a number in which his naïve infatuation for Sally Baxter is evident. 'I can only tell you that we ourselves must not publish one word that he has ever written home. He told us that he did not wish it & said to me one day when we had been speaking of a memoir of a friend of ours <u>Mind this</u> there is to be nothing of the sort published about me when my time comes. And so we have been firm though many people have spoken to us on the subject. Dear M$^{rs}$ Baxter if it is not too late I cannot help hoping that you too will keep what he has written.'[2] Annie succeeded in postponing publication of the Baxter letters, but in 1885 they resurfaced when she was responding to queries about new Thackeray attributions from the bibliophile and lawyer, Charles Plumptre Johnson. He had heard of the existence of this American material, and her response implies frustration in having always to sound a discouraging note, 'but I have always been obliged to refuse to have anything to do with any republication of letters &ct'. More than forty years after Thackeray's death these letters finally appeared.[3]

Jane Brookfield presented rather a different kind of problem, and one which would not so easily be solved. The letters she owned were far more personal in nature, revealing the extent of Thackeray's passion which, if in the strictest sense not illicit, was very far from orthodox. Her financial difficulties since William Brookfield's death had made Jane see the publication of extracts from the letters as a useful supplement to her income. Alarming as the idea was, Annie would not have wished to upset 'Aunt JOB', who had continued to be close to Thackeray's daughters and had supported Annie when Minny died. In 1887 Jane sold a group of letters to Scribners, who published them both in *Scribner's Magazine* and as a volume. The letters were inaccurately transcribed and heavily cut, with the more sensitive material removed, Mrs Brookfield herself seeing the project through the press.

She had been contemplating their publication for some time, Annie all the while seeking tactful means of persuading her father's old friend towards discretion. Something of the prehistory of this episode emerges from Leslie's reply to George Smith, who as copyright owner had been approached in 1886 either by Scribners or by Jane herself. Smith sought advice, valuing Leslie's not exactly disinterested opinion, and already knowing what Annie's view would be.

> I shall be very glad to read the letters in question if you care to let me see them.
>
> Several years ago, Anny showed me a collection of letters belonging to Mrs Brookfield. They were honourable to Thackeray and some of them very interesting; but clearly impossible to publish, as I thought & as, I am sure, Anny thought too. Mrs B. was, I also think, equally convinced that the letters should not be published <u>as they were</u> but she seems always to have hankered after some publication. I have heard about it at intervals & did what I could to throw cold water. I guess, however, that the letters now produced are the old letters wh. I saw, with all the interesting passages cut out.
>
> I fancy Anny's position in the matter to be that she disapproved of the publication all along; but could not say so to Mrs Brookfield – a phenomenon not without precedent. I very much wish that she had put her foot down firmly for once.[4]

Smith's personal affections and business instincts rarely clashed, but over this he would have had some difficulty. The year before there were hints of a tension, probably relating to an even earlier attempt by Mrs Brookfield to gain his support. Even if it concerned some other putative Thackeray project it still shows a rare difference of views. From Cromer, Annie sent Richmond her proposed response to Smith, which evidently was sharper than her normal tone. 'Your retort to G Smith is I think very good & I have posted it. That you didn't pounce down on him for not consulting you is no excuse for his not consulting you, and if he has made a mistake by trusting too much to his own judgment, he must take the consequences.'[5]

Richmond was more prepared to be confrontational than Annie, for she remained conscious of George Smith's history of fair dealings and of his loyalty to her father, but she could be assertive when required.

She explained to Charles Johnson that so far as copyright was concerned, permission needed to be sought from Smith, the generosity of her comments being no more than he deserved.

> I should be very glad to help you, but the copyright of my Fathers drawings &ct. are I believe <u>entirely</u> in Messrs Smith, Elder's hands & I could only help you in any small way in my power with their permission. I had rather <u>you</u> asked for this directly than that I did. When we sold our rights to them it was because we could not in the least manage the publishing or work it, & it was of greatest help to us to get their help at the time.
>
> Now there are some things upon which we have occasionally different views, & I am very loth ever to raise any possible question of the sort. M$^r$ Smith is one of my oldest & kindest friends but of course one cannot expect different people to see things in the same light invariably, tho' on the whole we have disagreed far less than most people.[6]

Jane Brookfield's friendship with Annie suffered no lasting damage. Once the letters had appeared in America, the book was also issued under the Smith, Elder imprint. The American edition had included a somewhat grudging prefatory note from Annie, but it was dropped for the English edition. 'I am very glad to hear that you have made a satisfactory arrangement for publishing your selections from my Father's letters. I am of course unable myself by his expressed wish to do anything of the sort.' In the end, nothing indiscreet was published. 'I am so much happier & <u>calmer</u> now that M$^{rs}$ Brookfield has so kindly <u>burnt</u> everything that seemed more confidential & private than that w$^h$. has appeared that I dont get into the same miserable state of nervous fuss I did before.'[7]

Propriety was preserved. Indeed, Annie seems to have been softened by the book's reception, and found herself responding to notes of praise. Fanny Kemble recalled past happinesses, and it reassured Annie that no harm had been done. 'Papa's are dear letters aren't they & I'm so glad you have liked them.'[8] It also brought back voices from the past, such as Emma Taylor Lamborn, sister of Bayard Taylor, who on reading the letters in *Scribner's Magazine* was reminded of their visit to London in 1857, of meeting Thackeray and his two daughters and visiting Onslow Square. 'The British Museum, London Bridge, and the Tower are not so clear to my mind as the genial presence of your dear Father on that day, and your own kindness to the two American girls whose short stay in London was made so memorable. Many times I have wished to tell you how much your stories have charmed me, especially the sweet, sad one of "Elizabeth".'[9] The broader critical response was also encouraging. One reviewer appealed directly to Annie to release more letters as a way of preventing merely speculative biographies, believing that '[Thackeray] himself would surely prefer an authentic record'.[10]

The most intelligent support came from the critic and future Liberal MP Augustine Birrell, who would marry the widowed Eleanor Tennyson in 1888. Having heard that Annie had been pestered by people for allowing publication, he assured her that she had done the right thing.

> Authors (the rascals) are so full of artifice – but these letters, read as they will be read by thousands, just as they stand, fill me with a kind of joy that he should have been the kind of man they shew him to have been – When all these silly pottering people shall have died of their enlarged egotisms these letters will be read with love and joy & an almost total indifference to everything contained in them – except the great man himself.[11]

It was exactly what she needed to be told, and perhaps Birrell was just the man to say it. Thirty years later, after resigning as Chief Secretary for Ireland following the Easter uprising, Lytton Strachey saw him as 'decidedly a Victorian product. Large and tall and oddly like Thackeray to look at.'[12]

Any awkward moments with George Smith were probably caused by nothing more than Annie's unworldliness in matters of business. Although he had secured a watertight agreement when Thackeray's daughters sold their father's copyrights to him in 1864, this was to protect the unpublished materials against his commercial rivals, rather than limit the family's wishes about what should appear in future. The only 'new' work to appear thus far was *The Orphan of Pimlico* in 1876, for which Annie had written an Introduction. His working of the copyrights had the effect of protecting Annie's interests as much as his own. A characteristic instance of Smith's thoughtfulness occurred in 1890, when the theatrical impresario Savile Clarke wanted to stage *The Rose and the Ring* as a children's pantomime. Not only did Smith support Annie's wish for this to proceed, he transferred to her his own royalty entitlements so that she was sole financial beneficiary. 'As regards Mess.rs Smith and Elder you are perfectly right in saying that the copyright is theirs, but as I told you they told me it was to be mine for this occasion & that I was to make my own bargain.'[13]

Annie had not enjoyed good health in 1885, and the next several years were not to be much better. During the summer of 1886 her

consultant sent her for six weeks to Ramsgate and then to the French
spa town of Aix-les-Bains. 'He assures me I shall get well in time
… I find that in some curious way one gets used to pain. It doesnt
hurt ones feelings as it did at first – only ones legs.'[14] In a year Annie
would be fifty, and was aware of age holding her back. Though himself
prone to attacks that would incapacitate him for a day or two at a time,
Richmond was just thirty-two, a young man still. The age difference,
dismissed as unimportant when they married, continued not to matter
with a young family to distract them, but with the passing years Annie's
extended periods of debilitating illness could only serve to make the
gap seem bigger. She breezily signed off in her letters to Richmond as
'your old Pong', but now there were things which he could do with the
children when she simply had to sit and watch.

People from her own generation and younger were beginning to
fall away, and the death of Lionel Tennyson whom Annie had watched
growing up in Freshwater was a hard moment. He was Richmond's
contemporary in the India Office, although had never really made much
of himself there. Within a few years of marrying, Lionel and Eleanor
appear to have drifted a little apart, and there was a sense that things
were not quite right between them. They began to follow independent
lives, leading Richmond to wonder whether his own tendency towards
solitariness had held Annie back. He often dined with the Tennysons.
'[Eleanor] gave me a long account of her health and her wish to repose
in a suburb. Lionel it appears loves society. Do you wish I did? It made
me feel horribly selfish as she talked, and I felt as though, if I managed
better, you would be better and stronger.'[15] If Eleanor confided in
Richmond, Annie was closer to Lionel, for she had known him for so
much longer, and he had been a favourite of Minny's. During Billy's
quarantine with scarlet fever she had talked to Lionel in the back garden
at Young Street. 'He was very sad & so was I.'[16]

There is something mythic about the end of the life of the laureate's
son, succumbing during the return voyage from Calcutta after surgery
for an abscess on his liver, his body being lowered at last into the
Red Sea. His going to India was his mother's doing, Emily Tennyson
having ambitions for her younger son which he did not share. Probably
her anxiety for his future was prompted by Tennyson's acceptance
of a hereditary peerage, which would pass to Hallam. Friends like
Annie would have seen the irony in this, as in many ways Lionel
was altogether more lively than the more dutiful Hallam. Soon after
the peerage had been made public, she sent New Year greetings to
John Field, and shared her thoughts. 'Hallam will make a much better
career as a Lord than as a bart, for he is a good well educated average

man & not specially brilliant & just fitted to be a liberal sensible peer. Lionel seems to me to have much more natural gift.'[17] In different circumstances Lionel might have made a modest success in the theatre, but we get the measure of the deadening expectations placed on this lively and amiable man when we learn that as a boy his mother had expressed hopes that, 'as your Father's son' he would do 'some good service in the world'.[18] She had written in 1884 to the new viceroy of India, hoping that there might be a place for Lionel on his personal staff, leading to the Indian tour. He and Eleanor went out in 1885, and Pinkie heard from Gerald and Margie that the Tennysons were proving a welcome diversion in Calcutta. 'At a ball, Gerald says "The sight of Lionel gazing about him, with an air of mild surprise is a most refreshing contrast to all the military little grigs".'[19] But by the time Pinkie wrote this Lionel had already fallen dangerously ill. Eleanor feared that they would have to delay their return to allow him time to recover from malarial fever and liver complications, but following surgery his doctors insisted that he should leave for England without delay, as the approaching summer heat in Calcutta would be unendurable. They began on 4 April, Lionel sedated with morphia, and just over a fortnight later he was dead.

Murmurs and rumours have attached themselves to that return journey, 'of Eleanor dancing through the night on board ship while Lionel lay dying'.[20] It is flimsy gossip and lacks credibility. Contrary evidence comes in the form of Gerald and Margie's testimonies; they insisted on accompanying their friends for part of the return journey, Margie until a week before Lionel died. But Margie's harrowing eye-witness account, sent to Pinkie from Colombo where she left the ship, praises Eleanor's support through Lionel's final desperate weeks. Through Margie, Eleanor despatched a telegram to Hallam spelling out the hopeless situation. Some weeks after Lionel's death, Pinkie transcribed Margie's letter for Hallam.

> He quite gave up too caring to be read to for the last few days & he slept almost all days on the deck where he was carried up when it was cool & he was well enough ... They told Lionel he was in greatest danger & he spoke to the nurse about it & said to me 'They tell me I shall very likely not live to reach home, but I don't see why I shouldn't, I feel I have strength'. He told the doctors not to tell Eleanor that he knew about his danger. When she was ill, I went always very early in the morning to see how he was for her & one day I waited a moment before going to tell her & he became excited & said Go at once &

tell Eleanor – I <u>swear</u> she is waiting to know. – When he was
brought up on deck, she used to lie on her chair beside him &
he put out his head & laid it on her shoulder … My last days
on the steamer were agonizing to her – there was <u>no</u> place
where she could hide herself from people advancing with
kind inquiries, until the day before I left when she completely
gave way, the captain said she might use his cabin on deck &
then she found peace – The passengers & ship officers were
extraordinarily kind & would have done anything for either of
them – Two men gave up their cabin to Eleanor that she might
not be crowded with other ladies – I felt almost as if I were
committing a murder when I sent off the cruel telegram here
from Eleanor – I have never come near anything so sad in my
life & it haunts me night & day.[21]

Annie's journal record of Lionel's death, written long after the
event, is surprisingly matter-of-fact, but she was reluctant to open
up the still raw associations of old memories. The sad facts reached
her when she was at Mrs Ritchie's Wimbledon house, prostrate with
sciatica. 'Then came the news that he had died at sea. Margie saw
them off at Calcutta, & could not keep away & went on board with
them as far as Ceylon. He died when they reached Aden & was buried
at sea.' But the news of Tennyson's vulnerable, wayward son had
affected her deeply. Pinkie recorded that 'Annie, whose love for him is
so very great has been made ill again in her weak state by the news'.[22]
Earlier, as Lionel lay sick on the ship, Annie had complained of her
own depressive state, in words which seems remarkably prescient. 'I
have been ill enough to feel that <u>double</u> life which is round about us all
& to wonder what might be in store.'[23] In mid July she addressed the
painful subject of Lionel's death directly, anxious that Eleanor should
find comfort in her children. 'I have seen her she has her three sweet
little ones to cheer her – little Charlie is the <u>image</u> of Lionel of whom
I can hardly think or speak without crying – at least that feeling which
swells ones heart when one loves people either dead or alive.'[24]

As the Tennysons' good friends, it is natural that she and Richmond
would have made themselves available to support the young widow and
her children. But Annie's journal does not mention Eleanor, and there is
no hint of any difficulties over the summer when Annie was away trying
to get well. Nor do contemporary letters help. After the crisis – if crisis
it was – records would have been sanitised, a process which Hester later
continued by removing entries in the journal from certain years. There
was no need to censor the 1886 pages, for nothing was said. The story

that has attached to this year is therefore based on scant evidence, and recent accounts spin out a breathless love story between Eleanor and Richmond told as if the events are clear cut. They are not. The history of the episode relies more upon family folklore than anything verifiable, and Winifred Gérin, who set the hares running, was disingenuous in asserting a sequence of events which she had no means of verifying. It is highly likely that something happened between Richmond and Eleanor. What this was, how it came about, whether it was more than an intensity of feelings, and quite how it was resolved is not known.

That Richmond enjoyed friendships with other, younger women, is not in doubt, and later in his life there was one close relationship which possibly had a sexual dimension. But mostly these were mere flirtations, an outlet for this hard-working man who was beginning to rise in the India Office, who enjoyed the company of attractive women and was flattered by them. Annie made light of the friendships – or learnt to do so – even on one occasion referring to his fondness for Lisa Stillman (daughter of William Stillman and stepdaughter of Marie Spartali) and suggesting that Hester's jealousy of Richmond's ladies was typical of daughters and fathers, as she herself could bear witness. 'Hester laughed over Lisa's snuff much pleased. Have you discovered that the Codge is extremely jealous of her. We always were of Papas ladies tho' we liked them afterwards all the more.'[25] It was a remarkably accurate prediction, for – not without causing some pain to Annie in the process – Hester subsequently grew unusually intimate with the two women with whom Richmond formed his closest extra-marital attachments.

There was no hint of impropriety in his new friendship with the budding novelist Mary Cholmondeley, a close correspondent during these years as she sought to place her first books with publishers. Not normally one for long personal letters, Richmond made an exception here, advising on drafts of her books, finding time to write unhurriedly after long days at the office. She seems to have encouraged him to adopt a sometimes paternal role, but eventually her persistent advice-seeking began to bore him. 'Miss Cholmondeley was there, more aggravatingly humble, vain, conscientious & literal than ever. But she is very nice when she is thawed.'[26] It is strange that it should have been Richmond who gave technical advice on writing fiction, with no experience beyond that of any intelligent reader. Annie was prepared to be blandly encouraging, but then it seems Mary got passed over to Richmond. Mary was too timid to suppose that she was being patronised.

> I have been reading the story w[h]. is <u>very</u> pleasant & well written – I wonder whether the Graphic w[d]. like it for its

Christmas no. – But wouldnt it be improved by a little chasting. When I was your age (I always write to you like this) I remember my Father told me (& it really was a pang to me) to cut out all <u>jollys</u> & all the slang & I think y$^r$ hero w$^d$. really seem more romantic & handsome still if he didnt talk quite so much slang – R$^d$. was very much interested, & amused and he said when I asked him that he never heard anybody say 'sugar' except as a boating term ... I neednt tell you how glad I should be if I could help you in any way.[27]

In that summer of 1886, as Annie went to Ramsgate to begin weeks of recuperation, Richmond proved indispensable to the work of the India Office, even assisting in the re-election campaign of its government members. In June he travelled to Thornbury Castle in Gloucestershire with the Parliamentary Under Secretary of State, Stafford Howard, 'to help him canvass & concoct the Indian Budget at the same time',[28] his letters to Annie giving a flavour of Victorian electioneering. 'This afternoon we are going to the first Liberal meeting. The Tories led off yesterday. Plump for Plunkett is their cry.... M$^r$. Howard has gone off to preside at a dinner of the Local Society, which has been marching round & round the Castle all the morning playing tunes.'[29] It was a welcome change in his routine. Back in London, he compiled the speech that Howard had to make to the Commons. As he prepared to join Annie for a few days in Ramsgate, his weariness was palpable. 'The speech was dull but sound. And I am quite satisfied though I am not sure M$^r$ Howard is ... I am still not awake from the work & rather in a dream, but agreeably conscious that it is a dream.'[30] It was normal for him to work inordinately long days, often dining at the Garrick Club before returning to the India Office until late at night, sometimes reaching home after midnight, only to work on papers into the small hours. An ability to think through complex problems and arrive at rational conclusions, coupled with thoroughness and conscientiousness, would eventually gain him the position of Permanent Under-Secretary. His career path, so uncertain just a few years earlier, was now fixed.

Ramsgate did Annie good. 'This is the first time I have walked out without any pain at all & O how I did enjoy it.'[31] She began to prepare for her trip to Aix-les-Bains, and Richmond took himself off to Ambleside to stay with Victor Marshall and his family at Monks Coniston, where he picked up news of Ruskin – 'they say the light has now gone completely out of him, and he is quite happy & foolish, wanting nothing & not even coming down stairs'.[32] Annie crossed to France on 22 August in the company of the French educationist Marie

*Richmond with Hester and Billy at Beavor Lodge, Hammersmith, home of the painter, William Richmond, about 1886*

Souvestre, whose pupil at Allenswood Academy Hester later became.[33] Their train from London sped by 'like a cannonball' watched by Sir John Simon and his wife, who stood at the trackside and waved, and then wrote sympathetically to Richmond – 'it can't be nice for the best of you all to be away!'[34] Billy confirmed this neatly. 'It's a pity the old gel isn't here.'[35] It was unfortunate the way in which things had worked out, for Richmond's leave was tied to the requirements of the office, and it had concerned him that Annie's visits to Ramsgate and Aix made a proper family holiday unlikely that year. '[C]ould you put off going till the last 4 weeks of the children's holidays, which would give us a bit together. That would be the nicest as 2 months is a horribly long time to be away.'[36] This does not sound like a man tired of his wife's company so much as one who feared habitual separation.

Based with his mother and Pinkie in Wimbledon, Richmond could accept invitations in the knowledge that the children were well looked after. A couple of days after Annie had left he was at a dinner where the writer and art historian Vernon Lee (Violet Paget) was of the company, 'a sort of cross between Howdy Sturgis & Oscar Wilde who rushed in & proceeded to discuss the best routes to Clapham Junction. It is a great mistake, with a passionate nature to have a large pasty white face.' The Ritchies had made a vivid impression on her when they had been fellow dinner guests at Edmund Gurney's four years earlier. She had seemed horrified at the idea of their marriage, and of Annie as an ageing mother. Henry James's squeamishness during Annie's first pregnancy was as nothing compared with Vernon Lee's outburst in a letter to her mother. '[S]he is Miss Thackeray the novelist, he her godson and twenty [*sic*] years younger, and she is the thin, sentimental, leering, fleshy, idealistic old person who would marry her godson, and who seems quite brimming over at the idea of having babies at an age when she ought to be ashamed of it.'[37] After this second meeting, Vernon Lee and Richmond probably had the measure of each other.

Nearly twenty years later in Florence, Pinkie's own encounter prompted a rather more admiring portrait than her brother's.

> Vernon Lee I forget if you know, – She is very amusing and very interesting in her conversation … and if Rhoda Broughton were half foreign and impersonal she w$^d$. remind me more of her – she looks such a funny little sort of old sorceress talking the metaphysics of art smoking her cigarette in a stiff man's collar & cuffs – with a portrait of herself by Sargent like a boy, with her mouth open talking – and one of her great friends Miss Ethel Smythe the composer with her mouth wide open singing – also by Sargent.[38]

Annie was installed on the second floor of the Hôtel Thermal at Aix, especially convenient for the baths. Princess Louise, Queen Victoria's daughter, had a suite on the floor below, and Fanny Kemble made a point of joining Annie for about a week, holding court in the Hôtel d'Europe. Annie put herself in the care of a Dr Blanc, who prescribed a course of fifteen baths for the three weeks of her stay. She described (with sketches) the rituals to her daughter. 'I had such a funny bath yesterday the water all squirted out of pipes out of the ground. It comes up from the Earth all ready boiled & then when I had been squirted all over they wrapped me up in a blanket & two men came & carried me off through the street under a hood & tramped upstairs to my bed room & took me up & popped me into bed. Dont be afraid Madame they said – You are not the first lady we have carried up.'[39] Marie Souvestre's seriousness had become rather wearing. 'She is a good soul but there is something so abrupt & <u>do not breathe</u> it to anyone – common in her ways, tho' she is most generous & scrupulous about any money transactions, that I dont feel as if I could ever be really intimate tho I am really grateful for her kindness.'[40] Keen to be friendly, Princess Louise asked Annie to drive out with her, taking her on one curious occasion into a peasant's cottage where she was evidently a familiar visitor – 'she walked into a wonderful old Rembrandt Jan Steen cottage with an old woman lighting a fire & the cows dragging up & the oil lamp swinging'.[41]

She was home again on 18 September, but telegrams giving plans and changes of plans had left Richmond unsure quite when to expect her. He seemed tangibly relieved at the prospect of her reappearance and of the familiar intimacy restored. 'It is extraordinary what a difference it makes. My cold at once got well & my lump began to subside again. The Cobungos planned the places we should occupy respectively in the Family Pongo Grand Nuptial Bedstead. Will it be Friday? Hooray. But dont knock yourself all to pieces travelling too hard.'[42] It seems that there may have been something he needed to talk to her about, and it involved Eleanor. Had Richmond and Eleanor fallen 'mutually in love' in Annie's absence, as Gérin puts it? – probably not. Had they become aware of the dangers of a growing intimacy? – very likely. This was threat enough, but it was probably no more than that. It pulled Richmond up short, and he did not hide things from Annie. Despite what others have claimed, there is no evidence that Annie sent him off to Brighton to decide between herself and Eleanor, and that 'he sent her a laconic card', choosing her.[43] There is no card, no record of a Brighton visit. All that survives is a single undated letter, written on India Office notepaper. It suggests that Richmond may have been at Southmead, and that it was Annie who had gone out of town with the children. His job had made him skilful at thinking a problem out. And this letter reveals much hard thinking.

> Pinkie has been talking about Eleanor, who has been pouring out to her. I wrote her a line myself when she left Sthmead in which I said that she knew my life had not been spoilt, thanks to you, & that when I saw her with her children I could not but hope that the difficulties of her life had been

lightened. And I said she wasn't to answer except with the truth. And this is her answer.

Pinkie has been talking in the same strain. I know now by experience that nothing I can do is of any avail, which is the pity of it. And I will be all right in a day or two. Only if you don't mind I shan't come till Monday, when I shall have had 2 days to myself.

Dont you be frightened but write to me about yourself & the children – Next week I shall rise up & wash my face & eat like King David. There is no book like the Bible. 'But no man can deliver his brother or make agreement for him: for it cost more to redeem their souls, so he must leave them alone for ever' – If I hadn't had you for an anchor, God knows what would have become of me.

Send me a telegram here when you get this.[44]

This acknowledgement of Pinkie's assistance is not surprising, for she was a good friend of Eleanor's as well as being Annie's closest ally in the Ritchie clan. Richmond had been challenged, had acknowledged his susceptibility, and had turned back, for he was unable to console Eleanor at the price of pain to Annie. The crucial passage from Psalm 49 is one he would use again, in a letter to his sister Gussie after the death of her young son in 1891. On this later occasion he is rather more explicit about his meaning, acknowledging that sympathy cannot relieve the burden of another's misery.

One sees those who suffer enveloped in a sort of invisible cloud through which nothing human can pass but it loses all meaning & force: & all the goodwill & sympathy in the world are ineffectual to help.

I learnt this lesson when still a boy when I used to be with Annie after Minnie died. And thus though it has not been my fate to lose part of my life by anothers death I seem in a fashion to understand what sorrow is.

Our helplessness for one another is all told in the Bible. 'No man may deliver his brother nor make agreement for him for it cost more to deliver their souls so that he must leave that alone for ever.' In one way this is a selfish saying, in another it is not. I know that many times you must have thought me selfish and cruel. But I hope it has never really been that.[45]

He had set constancy and nobility of character above youth and physical beauty, just as he had done when he married Annie. In that sense, nothing had changed although everything would now be different.

She knew all about the fragility of happiness, and what Richmond had given up to marry her.

As for Eleanor, being married to Lionel had never been easy. The expectations placed on her by Emily Tennyson saw to that, just as it was made unnecessarily hard at times for Hallam's wife, Audrey Boyle. The assumption was that, as Tennyson women, their interests were surrendered to those of the Laureate, something which Eleanor was never quite prepared to do. When she remarried in 1888 she discovered real contentment with her new husband, Augustine Birrell, once he had managed to win the Tennysons' acceptance of him as stepfather to Lionel's boys. The rumour-making connected with whatever went on between Richmond and Eleanor in 1886 may well have originated in whispering on the part of Emily Tennyson and some of the Ritchies – Richmond's sisters Gussie and Blanche would be the prime suspects – supplying Eleanor with a reputation for flightiness going back to the days of her marriage to Lionel. That way, Richmond and Lionel emerged if not as innocents, then relatively unscathed. Eleanor remained a topic best avoided with Emily Tennyson, as Pinkie saw at Easter 1889 when she was at Farringford, though poor Audrey, Hallam's wife, was now bearing the brunt of Lady Tennyson's sometimes sour observations. 'I paid dear Lady T. a delightful long visit in the afternoon. We avoided all heart-burning subjects, Eleanor, Home Rule, the new railway – she says Hallam never wished for a child – that he is entirely contented with his nephews! – but that Audrey has such a passionate desire (with a slightly scornful turn of the mouth) that she hopes her wish may be fulfilled.'[46]

Nothing broke Annie's surface calm. The news of Watts's engagement to Mary Tytler gave her pleasure and perhaps reassurance too, and she wrote at once to 'Dearest Signor' to send her congratulations 'for one does feel the marriage of true souls in this'. He was seventy, Mary thirty-six, a reason for celebration and not for any kind of prurient speculation. She felt especially affectionate towards Mary, 'a sweet woman & true artist appreciating the best & dearest things in those whom we all look up to & love – some of us a little more than others'.[47] Watts's reply is gracious and warm. 'Your letter is like yourself & I need not say how dear to me the affection it proves is.... When my life is changed I shall hope to see you often for I shall find it easy to put down my brushes & run over to Wimbledon.'[48] In a note to Gussie at Cannes she touches on the 'absolutely natural and reasonable' news of Watts and, more significantly perhaps, on Richmond who 'is quite reviving at last – after all those trying tiresome weeks & his cut is being allowed to heal'.[49] It suggests some kind of surgical procedure on the 'lump' that had troubled him through the summer. Perhaps his recovery meant no more than that, just as, when she wrote to Tennyson a month later, it is unnecessary to look for significance in Annie's first mention of Eleanor since her return from India. 'I saw your beloved little trio the other day & Eleanor whose progress seems most satisfactory and I have just heard of Watts on board his ship looking <u>younger</u> than his bride.'[50]

Tennyson had sent her *Locksley Hall Sixty Years After and The Promise of May*, for there was no reason for awkwardness between these old friends. The poetry was both a reassurance and a comfort. The anniversary of Thackeray's death approached and memories were much with her. 'When I think of the past of the dear companions so dear so much younger than I, of my Daddy whom I have now caught up in life of the unspeakable reality of goodness & generosity in which they have lived and had their being, then the <u>wings</u> seem to come to your noble thought, & all that has been & will still be so heavy at times grows calm & simple & wide once more as they touch one suddenly with their pinions.'

The success of her Tennyson memoir in *Harper's New Monthly Magazine* led to a further commission. According to her journal, where dates can be unreliable, she decided to write on Ruskin in 1886, although if so it took her an age to complete. Ruskin would send his 'full & total permission … to say <u>anything</u> about him, or this place, that you please', even offering to provide Annie with a sketch of Brantwood.[51] Just as Tennyson had previously encouraged her, knowing that he could count on Annie's discretion, so now it was satisfying to be told by Ruskin's cousin, Joan Severn, that 'nothing would give him greater pleasure, than that <u>you</u> should do the article'. His friends were approached for information, Annie telling Octavia Hill that she was hesitant about taking on the task, but that 'indeed it is my duty'.[52] Mary Watts observed that her new husband's admiration for Ruskin was not unqualified, believing that the complex personality of her subject would make Annie's job a hard one.

> Great as Signor believes Ruskin to be, & he often says he is one of the men through whom this age will be called great, he as often deplores his unreasonableness & says that while he has done so well in telling us that there is something more to live for than the making of money, & that man does not live by bread alone he destroys his own case by going so far as to say that Adam Smith was an idiot – What a difficult task you have got yourself. Ruskin said to Signor once that he must always contradict himself three times before he was worth believing![53]

Reminiscence worked in both directions, and as she got older Annie was asked for her own recollections of her father's contemporaries. For though she wore her own celebrity lightly – such as when she was photographed 'for the absurd purpose' of a series on authors in *The Graphic*[54] – she took seriously her responsibilities to that revered generation. To an unknown correspondent she sent her memories of Dickens, which she also drew upon for one of her 'Chapters from an Unwritten Memoir'. She had really only known Dickens through her friendship with his daughter, Kate, who had been close to both of Thackeray's daughters.

> After my Fathers death – only a short time after – M[r]. Dickens's daughter M[rs] Perugini took me once to S[t] James Hall to hear her Father read the storm in David Copperfield.... When the reading was over M[rs] Perugini took me into the back room & M[r] Dickens very quickly came forward & took my hands; he was weary excited exhausted, panting a little but I never shall think of him without remembering the bright look of his kind circling eyes the cordial & almost magnetising sympathy of his fatherly friendly greeting to my Fathers daughter.[55]

Annie and Richmond took the children on their first foreign visit at the end of May 1887, staying at the Hôtel du Nord in Boulogne. As she walked with them along the ramparts, recalling her own childhood visits with her father, Hester and Billy were 'radiant'. It proved hard to escape from their fellow English. 'We have enjoyed our little outing immensely the children open their eyes quite round at the caps & wooden shoes & the French & the fish & the general delightful chatter – Hester said "I didnt know the French people were all English" when we first landed but up in the old town one can get away from ones shady compatriots – odious creatures.'[56] They celebrated Hester's ninth birthday with a cake from the pâtisserie and welcomed Fanny Kemble, who called on them on her way to Switzerland. They were back home on 3 June after a very rough crossing, in time for the Queen's golden jubilee. But this was a disappointment, for although Richmond and the children left the house early for a good view of the procession, the vast crowds meant that they got no further than Hyde Park Corner. Annie had turned down a seat for the Westminster Abbey service because she feared that it would exhaust her, but, as she noted in her journal, so much did during these years. 'My health was so broken the whole time, that I was not able to keep any regular way – perhaps if I had been well I might have failed equally.'

In the late summer they holidayed on the East Anglian coast at Aldeburgh where Richmond could enjoy some golf, and for part of their stay they were joined by two of the Strachey children, Pernal and Lytton. Lytton Strachey at this time was a friend of Billy's, and his elder by just seventeen days. Billy was a gregarious child, and an optimist too, trusting in his mother to find a way to give birth to six-year-old children. 'I wish you would. We might have such games.'[57] This early acquaintance with Lytton did not survive into adulthood, though Annie was godmother to Lytton's brother, James, subsequently Siegmund Freud's English translator. At Aldeburgh Annie suffered almost constant headaches. Their first lodgings at Tiffany House were contaminated with foul 'poisonous' smells, and after a midnight consultation they decided to quit the house without delay. A transfer to The Esplanade came with its own problems, for later 'horrible discoveries' were made first in Billy's hair, and then in everyone else's, but not until they had returned to London were the children discovered to have ringworm. At the time however The Esplanade had seemed ideal, a 'charming little untidy house by the edge of the sea w$^h$. washes & hushes & throbs all day long at our door'.

This was Edward FitzGerald country, and Annie shared her discoveries with Fanny Kemble, one of his former correspondents.

> They tell me that it was not a fact that M$^{rs}$ FitzGerald forced him to marry her. She urged him to break it off, but he from some sense of honour would go on with it & it was more than he could bear. He left some letters to this niece [*Annie Kerrich*] evidently wishing that the truth should be known. Miss Lynn said he would never come in to see her in that he used to sit outside the window & talk to her till she became so Rheumatic she said to him you really <u>must</u> do an act of charity & come inside. I can no longer sit at the open window talking & then he came & she used to read to him & he used to laugh & laugh & be more delightful than ever.[58]

An even richer find was the fisherman and fishmonger, Horace Basham, who showed her his letters from FitzGerald. She determined to make copies for Aldis Wright, whose book was still in progress. 'It seems such a pity to leave out all <u>that</u> part of his life fm the memoir.'[59]

All through these years, headaches would drive Annie in search of sea air, if not to 'Dr Brighton' then to some other resort on the south coast. She worried about Billy's 'thinness', so in March 1888 at Worthing she was pleased to see his response to the bracing conditions.

1888.

Jan 4. Laura came to stay

Jan 6 Pretty ball at the Holman Hunt morris dancers little Hilary the most charming & George Gladys with a helmet on perfectly lovely Effie Stillman in the Pot of Basil

American proofs of Ruth

Jan 18.ᵗʰ The children being rather dull and cut off by their R.W. & the house being ailing we had a little entertainment to cheer us up. Colonel Loraine came down from town to conjure for us, a being by affable drawling

*Page from Annie's journal for January 1888*

'O dear me how I do enjoy seeing Billy <u>drawing</u> up every instant –
pink cheeks a little extra skin over his skeleton.'[61] Her walking was
still not good, and each day a kindly retired cavalry officer pushed her
along the promenade in a bath chair. One day they were driven out to
Goring Castle, home of Shelley's grandfather, and Annie imagined the
poet roaming the neighbourhood 'disguised as a soldier'. During the
quieter moments she read, enjoying Maupassant's newly-published
*Pierre et Jean*, 'a wonderful piece of writing.... Books do become so
good at Worthing.'

On her birthday she treated herself by calling on Robert Browning,
and was touched by his kindness to Billy and Hester. 'He kissed
them & was most charming.'[62] She saw a good deal of Browning
in his last years, passing on to Pinkie his praise for Pen's wife and
describing his relationship to his godchild, Lionel Tennyson's eldest
son. 'RB described his daughter in law so warmly & happily & also a
correspondence he had had with little Alfred T. Being his godfather he
sent him a present & a letter at Xs saying "you have three names. One
is a good name one is a glorious name one is an affectionate name" &
Alfred wrote back & said thank you for the present but your name is
not only affectionate it is a little glorious too like mine.'[63]

During this year the health of Richmond's mother became a concern,
but hers was a peaceful decline. Since Annie and Richmond had left
Rosary Gardens in March 1886, the shared arrangements at Southmead
had worked well enough, despite some trepidation on Annie's part.

> Perhaps Pinkie might have been happier in a smaller
> home with her mother alone – but Grannie could not have
> moved again & she liked the new interests & gaiety of a
> larger household & I don't know what I could have done
> without Pinkies constant valiant friendship. There were
> some rubs, but very few indeed.... Pinkie began to help
> me over my Ruskin divided <u>rule</u> worked well on the whole,
> there were occasional small tugs at the reins among us
> younger people.... I had a lovely bedroom with a lovely
> view over the lawns, & a wonderful echo of birds & the
> distant hills.[64]

Annie read to Mrs Ritchie and enjoyed the garden with her, developing
in these years an even greater affection for the woman who had
thrown in her support when Richmond determined to go through with
his unorthodox marriage. The story of Augusta Ritchie's last days is
not dramatic, but it is touching, and Annie was profoundly moved
by Richmond's private vigil at his mother's bedside. She began to

weaken from about the middle of October, and one of her last actions was to instruct her gardener to have a lawn laid just where Annie had hoped for one.

> Sunday Nov. 4 I awoke about 5 & got up at 6 went to dear Grannies door. The nurse said she has had a horrible night. She looked very calm & sweet & pleased to see me. She said wrap yourself – I said Do I tire you. She 'I like it'; a great light like a wing came into the Eastern sky & she lay looking at it. She asked for drink & I gave her a little brandy & water; later she said she wanted the nurse & to be moved & I went away & back to bed thinking – 'How we shall love her she is going to get better' When I woke at 9 R was by my bedside. He said you saw my Mother this morning. She is dead. She died as you left the room.
>
> Gussie told me that she stood outside the door as they laid her in her coffin, but she heard a sort of low breath. Richmond had stood in the room all the time.
>
> He came into my room afterwards & lay down half fainting on my bed. In his deep heart he is so tender & so afraid of showing it or shamming that it makes him seem stern & cold when he is not one bit.

Annie took to her own bed, distressed and unable to attend the funeral. A day or so later Pinkie went to Cannes to join her sister Blanche Warre Cornish, who was close to the nervous collapse from which she took some months to recover. Already plans were being made to sell Southmead, the proceeds from which would be divided between Mrs Ritchie's children. Annie was acutely aware of the special meaning that the death would have for Pinkie, the one unmarried daughter still living in the family home.

> Your mothers end seems to me like a sweet radiance shining brighter as her sun set behind the horizon & lighting us all up to the last as her dear thoughts travelled from child to child & to all of us who belonged to her who were not her children. I shall always think of her as a sweet light shining for us all. When Hester & Billy & I sit in the drawingroom as usual I try to think of her in her corner still – I have never got used to Minnies death or Magdalenes – Hers seems to me already like an event that happened years & years ago – Tho for you my darling Pinkie it is all different & has to be <u>endured</u> thro' as you will with your heart full of others.[65]

Pinkie provided hopeful news about Blanche, though she was still far from well, and Annie's reply is perhaps a measure of the disappointment in her own recent life. 'One cant hope for <u>perfection</u> of health & spirits, but if one is fairly content with a certain amount of imperfection one can get on, & accept the life God sends one. I wonder if it is the Devil makes one ill & how one is able to get thro the troubles of life & make the best of it – That must be the secret of Providence w[h]. is hidden in the heart of people things & feelings as well as in the lights of the hills.'[66]

Richmond was very low, 'so dull & sad' that Annie looked for ways to distract him, involving him in the great task which for years she had been minded to undertake, the organisation of her father's letters and manuscripts. The process led her inexorably towards a decision as to what her role in his legacy should be. It seemed to draw Richmond out of himself, '& we both cheered up over my daddys handwriting, <u>sorting</u> all the MSS & lectures &ct all over the dining room table. It is delightful work'. She had learned something about Richmond, but also about herself in these last days. After the deaths of her father and sister, grief had initiated a state of clinical hysteria from which recovery was slow. Richmond's calmer handling of his no less profound sadness affected her deeply, and her love was enhanced by the example of his stoicism.

On the anniversary of Minny's death she wrote to the person with whom she had been staying on that appalling night. With characteristic kindness, Mrs Oliphant appears to have been offering to accommodate the family as they searched for a house.

> <u>If</u> this house were to be let furnished I cant tell you what a boon yours would be, but all is so uncertain that Im afraid to accept your goodness <u>materially</u> tho' the soul of it, I do keep & R & I both, very dully sitting there last night planning our next move, <u>did</u> feel your coming in with your dear kindness <u>much</u> more than I can tell you. It was just as if you had opened the door & walked in....
>
> I sometimes long that she should have known how deeply Richmond has felt her loss how silently he stood by, making no signs or fuss, but never leaving her, not when all the saddest part of such parting was happening & I had run away to my room. His heart is as true as hers tho he says so little & the others all so very much prefer Willy &ct – (Please burn this)....
>
> And now again dearest M[rs]. Oliphant thank you & thank you – We must all die, but kindness does make one feel so

> alive, & I like to think of it existing in some mysterious
> way handed on almost with an independent life from that
> of the giver.[67]

They took a short let on a house in Lexham Gardens until the beginning
of February, and were able to accommodate Gerald and Margie and their
baby daughter, Theo, during their visit from India. There was a great
gathering of Ritchies in the new year, when Gussie and Douglas hosted
a children's performance of *The Rose and the Ring* at their house in
Airlie Gardens. Gussie enjoyed the material comforts which marrying
Douglas Freshfield had brought her, and though occasions like this were
fun, at other times it is evident that even Richmond – who was very fond
of his oldest sister – could find her grand. The undisguised costliness
of the hospitality at Airlie Gardens was a little overwhelming for the
poorer members of the family. But Gussie would be almost broken by
the death of her young son Hal from meningitis in May 1891. In a terrible
reminder of Lionel's death, Theo Ritchie too would die of peritonitis
returning from India in May 1896. In compiling her journal at the end of
the century, with the memories of these young deaths still vivid, Annie
recalled that Airlie Gardens pantomime. 'Hal acted Bulbo with such
fun & spirit. I held Theo in my arms to watch. The play was a great
success: & so sweet to think of now when those two darling children
have passed away.'[68] Pantomime had always been a New Year tradition
for Thackerays and Ritchies, so ten days later, and shortly before their
return to India, 'Gerald took <u>all</u> the family to the pantomime cheering in
an omnibus. Crowds & crowds of people came to see them & us. It seems
to me like the Beleaguered city now as I think of it, so many familiar
names & faces passed from <u>this</u> city to that great unknown world.'

On 4 February they moved into Kingsley Lodge in Lingfield Road,
Wimbledon. It was bitter weather, and within days of the move Annie's
sciatica had returned, for which she tried a course of seaweed baths.
Not until early March was she able to walk out again. Fanny Kemble
insisted on coming to visit, but failed to locate the house. 'I was sitting
by the fire with M[r] Oscar Wilde of all people & there we sat on little
guessing that you were close by.'[69] Aldis Wright's book on FitzGerald
was finally about to appear, and until the last moment Annie remained
anxious about the accuracy of her recall in things relating to her father,
and pleaded caution. 'Miss Kerrick told you exactly what I told her,
but then again as I think it over the very exact words seem to go – what
I think he said when I asked him w[h]. of his friends he had cared for
most was "There was dear old Fitz – & I was very fond of Brookfield
once" & then I know he added "we shall be very good friends again in

*Laura Makepeace Stephen, about 1885*

hell together" – But this of course isn't to publish & that is why I sh[d].
be glad if you could quote Miss Kerrick's letter rather than mine.'[70]

Auberon Herbert lent them a house at Ringwood in the New Forest
in June, and there was something idyllic about their short break amongst
the wild ponies, deer and yellowhammers and at Billy's enchanted
discovery of four snakes coiled up together. 'It is unlike anything I

have ever done before & we are living in a fragrant wooden house full
of books at the edge of the beautiful forest with an old farmer and his
wife & 2 or 3 <u>shaker</u> workmen.'[71] Laura came there to stay for a few
days after Richmond returned to London. She would be nineteen in
December, edging towards adulthood yet trapped in her child's world.
She was now spending several months of the year away from the
family home, for Leslie and Julia placed her as a resident with a family
in Paignton; by 1893, even these extended periods were insufficient,
and she would be admitted to the Earlswood Asylum for Idiots and
Imbeciles at Redhill, Surrey. Annie would visit her niece regularly and
took her for drives, or had her to stay for a few days at a time. This
relationship with Laura was not simply a necessary duty – for who else
would do it? – but a precious link with the past.

Her respect for the survivors from her father's generation – Tennyson,
Browning, Watts and Ruskin – rarely fell below an unquestioning
adulation, but Annie's opinions on past worthies could at times be less
than reverential. She ploughed dutifully through the three volumes of
William Knight's *Life of William Wordsworth*, but emerged with no
great affection for its subject. 'Is it worthwhile writing poetry if that is
the life you have to lead to do so? – When one reads bits here & there
one feels it <u>is</u> worth & then it all gets on my nerves & I much prefer
Coleridges – life & opium pipes – but O how lovely W. Ws poetry
is. I shall send you a vol. for y$^r$. cottage only sometimes feel as if I
should like to throw stones at them as they sit in a row outside Dove
Cottage.'[72] It made her the more attached to the familiar certainties,
and she settled down to read Wright's work on FitzGerald, unaware of
the storm that would blow up as others read the book.

> I have read a little further & I feel as if I must say one word
> about the <u>change</u> people spoke of in my dearest Father. He was
> <u>never out of pain</u>, he never complained, it made him always
> sick & languid; he used sometimes – very rarely to go to a
> smart party – because we liked it & enjoyed it, and couldnt
> go without him. More than once we have driven to the door
> & driven home again, – it seems so hard to me remembering
> how he fought on with this constant suffering that so many
> of his best & oldest friends called it <u>changed</u> – changed he
> was indeed dear Father. Sir Frederick Pollocks book <u>cut</u> me,
> & just so much does M$^r$. Fitz's faithful tenderness fill ones
> heart with affectionate pride.[73]

Aldis Wright had included a letter in which the news of Mrs
Browning's death prompted from FitzGerald the comment that

there would be 'no more Aurora Leighs, thank God'. On reading it, Browning's wild rage led to a savage attack on FitzGerald in the form of a poem in the *Athenaeum,* written at speed and probably published too hastily. Friends rushed to Browning's support, whilst believing that the sentiments were not typical of FitzGerald's gentle kindliness. It seemed easiest to unload the blame on to Wright for choosing to include the offending letter. Even Annie, so warm thus far in her praise for his work, decided that Wright and the *Athenaeum* were the villains of the peace, and in a startling sleight of hand links Henry James and Wright as writers whose bachelor status hampered their judgments about matters of feeling. A note of understanding to Sarianna Browning produced a reply from Browning as well.

> I have heard from them both – two very touching letters, & indeed from the first I sympathised with RB's cruel pang – He says he only thought of the woman his wife – not of the writer – <u>She</u> says she w<sup>d</sup>. have prevented the verses had she known of them, 'for one hasty word does not undo another' but they have both suffered cruelly, & alas as he says when people praise dear EFG. it only makes the pang worse. He took up the book on a garden seat, 'being anxious to know more of this man so many of his friends cared about' & <u>it opened</u> (cursed spite) on the sentence. He says he will try & think more as we all do & 'forget one of the most odious incidents of his life & so begins & ends his acquaintance with EFG.' Indeed we all know how he was of all men the one who would have most shrunk from giving pain or being indiscreet. It was a wild metaphor just as people talk of quartering Gladstone. I am even sorry for Aldis Wright.... Henry James blamed Browning but I felt vext with H. James, how <u>can</u> a bachelor <u>feel</u> what people feel – what women feel – a spinster lives the life of her home, a bachelor has a comfortable well cooked establishment in a cottage or a mansion & except where his own friends & loves are concerned cant realise the passion people put into their lives – No bachelor ought to be allowed to Edit a life, & if A Wright hadnt been a dried up little misogynist – (tho' I do like him very much) this wouldnt have occurred.[74]

FitzGerald's niece had written hoping that Annie would tell Browning that 'Uncle Edward never really meant to be hard – he would ask his pardon, yours, whoever he has unwittingly pained if he only could and I do it, for him',[75] and was angry with 'Aldis Wrong' for including inappropriate material, a view shared by Sarianna, who nevertheless believed that her brother should have kept his silence, 'for one hasty word is not mended by another', but was in no doubt that the blame fell on the publisher and editor. 'It is strange that during the whole time the book was passing through the press, there was not a single person to recollect that there were those living who loved her, – to whom even jokes about her death would be profoundly painful.'[76]

There is a final irony to this sorry tale. Mrs Sutherland Orr's 1891 *Life and Letters of Robert Browning* included a Mrs Browning letter which Annie read as a swipe at her father, to her mind as bad as FitzGerald's offending comment. 'There is a little passage about Papa w[h]. has given me a real pang – for I loved her & do love her & I suddenly feel as if the dear woman had thrown a stone at me – "If anybody wants small talk by handfuls, of glittering dust swept out of salons here's M[r] Thackeray besides!" … and then some dots. Its not a bit like him either. I'd <u>much</u> rather she had said Thackeray is dead – no more Vanity Fair –, & she <u>knew</u> him too, but I suppose she had no humour & liked everything dull.'[77]

When Sarianna heard that Annie was upset, and with memories of the previous dispute still fresh, she wrote believing the remark to have been innocently meant, offering to amend future editions.

> I have not the book with me – the only passage I can recall in which your father is mentioned is where she says he brought them 'glittering (or golden) dust from the salons.' So far from considering the phrase as disrespectful, on the contrary I thought it implied that he turned into something sparkling and precious even the commonest talk when he reported it. No one could suppose his own conversation was dust. In that sense I read the words myself, or never would I have transcribed them. How it would have grieved Ba who loved you dearly, to have caused you pain…. I remember Robert's putting down once, a volume by a popular novelist and remarking to me 'though I like the man, I cannot get through his book; but Thackeray never wrote a line I could not read with pleasure!'[78]

Annie agreed to take another course of treatment at Aix-les-Bains at the end of the summer of 1889, and this time Richmond would join her for the last two weeks of her stay. She set out with a German companion on 28 August, and in the fluster of their hurried departure managed to forget their tickets. By the time she arrived at Aix she was 'annihilated', but quickly fell into the familiar routines of the Hôtel Thermal and the care of Dr Blanc. Hamilton Aidé was also staying at Aix, and proved to be reviving company. They went to the theatre together and he would collect Annie for drives out in his carriage after her bath. 'I go in sick I come out cured.… Miss Bagot here told me she was Eleanor Birrells bridesmaid. She is very pretty with an <u>awful</u> tight waist an expression of agony passes over her face & she lays her jewelled fingers upon her aching ribs.'[79]

Richmond reached Aix on 16 September, much to Annie's joy, and they set about making a holiday of the time remaining. In his letter to Hester and Billy, he caught the eccentricity of the hotel's ex-patriot community in the comic vein which was shared by family members old and young.

> I saw [Momm] carried in from the Baths this morning in one of the covered chairs & shot into bed like a sack of potatoes.… She is quite well & we are enjoying ourselves very much – Only there are too many old cats in the hotel – Billy will know what sort I mean – with only two legs but with a double allowance of claws. There was one frostbitten old spinster – Lady Helen Stewart – who bleated out to Momm at dinner 'I don't know whether you have observed it, but I have only one eye'. At which I exploded, but everyone else seemed to think it was a charming, charming topic of conversation.[80]

Annie likewise amused the children with her often self-deprecating wit in which a dry observation of social nuances played such a strong part. As they returned via Dijon, they stayed a night in the plush Hôtel la Cloche, opened just five years earlier, and she suspected that the splendour of their room was meant as a judgment on the modest contents of their travel cases. 'Papa says it was exactly like Brown Jones & Robinson arriving. We have got the grandest room we ever had Papa says it is exactly like the room where Brown was attacked by musquitoes & it has 4 windows with yellow satin curtains 2 golden beds a washstand all over lace & golden sofas & chairs & chandeliers – Our poor little lacquer things do look shabby on the yellow chairs. We ought to have had blue satin vests at the very least.'[81]

At the beginning of November, Billy started at Charles Olive's preparatory school in Wimbledon and Hester at the high school, though the latter was not a success. The day's auspiciousness was marked by her choosing to tell Richmond about it on a piece of Palace Green notepaper, preserved from the old days. She had lain awake much of the previous night, unable to sleep 'from sheer excitement at being the Mom of a <u>real</u> schoolboy – It was so odd – Bill seemed quite changed last night, exactly like you when you used to get y$^r$. prizes at Eton', with the result that she then missed Billy's early morning departure. 'I fortunately packed Billys last night with y$^r$. old Eton Bible in w$^h$. I wrote his name & a small atlas & I am going round to the school in the course of the morning to clear up minor points.' But there was also the worrying news of Leslie's fainting fit at the Athenaeum, constant overwork on the *Dictionary of National Biography* taking its toll. 'It didnt last long but the Doctors say he <u>must</u> give up the Dict. Julia has told no one. She says we know what a blow it is to him but she doesnt even tell me what the attack was tho I know too well.... One comfort – only I dont know if it is a <u>reality</u> or only a consolation of theirs – the Doctors say no it is <u>organic</u> disease [*sic*] but a predisposition to be guarded against most carefully.'[82]

There was an urgent summons from Eastbourne where Jane Shawe was taken ill and died on 2 December. Unwell herself, Annie had not been able to go down to see her aunt during her illness, but nor had she realised the seriousness of her condition. She had grown used to these intermittent emergencies, only the previous year hurrying to Clifton where Aunt Jane had caused upset by moving from one nursing home to another, leaving 'in high dudgeon at the nurses want of proper respect'.[83] Annie was left with feelings of guilt and regret. 'I felt unhappy ashamed that I had not done – not <u>more</u> perhaps for I <u>did</u> what I could, but even less with a more willing heart.'[84] Richmond took control of matters, attending the funeral and arranging for Jane's papers to be sent to Wimbledon where he and Annie made them available to the Shawe relatives, though it was just the start of a protracted squabble over money matters oddly reminiscent of Thackeray's trivial yet draining battles with his mother-in-law, old Mrs Shawe.

When Annie read that Browning was seriously ill in Venice, she wrote immediately to Sarianna for news – on the day of his death, as it turned out – trusting that the newspaper report was an exaggeration. As she waited to hear more, she distributed Christmas gifts, copies of her short piece, 'The Boyhood of Thackeray'. It was her first specific writing about her father's life, and she sent it to the Tennysons, to Mary Brotherton, and to Fanny Kemble.[85] The Tennysons' copy appears to have been delayed, but Lady Tennyson responded by thanking Annie for promising it to Alfred – 'You know Child he had a true affection for your Father'[86] – and Tennyson himself hurried to his neighbour to read Mary Brotherton's copy. 'Your delightful little paper in S$^t$. Nicholas (was it you who sent it to me?) was most touching & interesting to me. – I only wish there was more of it – just as I wished there were hundreds more of "Fitz"'s letters. The dearly beloved Laureate has walked off with S^t. Nicholas – "None of those things should be written, – but I should like to read it", said he.'[87]

The news of Browning's death had by this time reached Annie, and she wrote once more to Sarianna.

> How blind I was to the gravity of the bad news. I <u>couldnt</u> believe it somehow & when I wrote to you I seemed alas so <u>convinced</u> that what I had read was exaggerated that such vigor & might as his could not succomb & now I am beginning to realise you, & Pen, & his wife, & the darkness which must have fallen – and yet those noble farewell words are in ones heart – in all our hearts. It seems to us, not like death but like some translation from December gloom into glorious Christmas above. I can only thank God for having known him among those who live in my soul's life & you too dearest friend I love & am grateful & proud to count my friend.[88]

In the New Year, Sarianna returned to England and thanked Annie for her messages. 'You knew him when you were a child, and he loved you and your sister.'[89] Touched by these words, and moved by the examples of Sarianna's courage and of Richmond's reaction to his mother's death, she reflected on the nature of her own response to loss.

> <u>You</u> are a Browning & your courage & steadfastness make me cry. I was only in hystericks when I lost my Minnie & I grudge it so now & feel how near I might have been to her, to the greater life & I only thought of my pain & not of that blessing of love & tender devotion w^h. was & <u>is</u> still I do believe. Once when Hester was a baby it seemed to me Minnie <u>was</u> there – & I just said out loud forgetting everything isnt she a darling baby Minnie – & then tho' I remembered in a moment I <u>felt</u> as if she indeed had blessed my little one.[90]

When she posted her little Thackeray article to Fanny Kemble 'as a Christmas card from your old friend's daughter', she dwelt on the sad news of the death of their mutual friend. 'As each person I love dies it seems to me like another bit of <u>oneself</u> gone "speed, fight on, fare ever <u>There</u> as here" he says & his own words seem to take away the pang of parting & to give me hope & trust flowing from that large nature into weaker ones.'[91]

Five

# MY LITTLE DREAM
# OF AN EDITION
# (1890-1893)

*[I] found Bill in a grand draught & shirt sleeves & open window
performing hairbreadth antics & refusing to appear till our
company w^d go – There is something very ludicrous in discussing
why Papas memoirs sh^d. or shouldnt be written while his grandson
is catching Influenza in the next room.*

Annie to Pinkie Ritchie
March 1891

The start of a new decade brought an improvement in Annie's fortunes.
Her constant headaches disappeared, for a time at least, and the pain
in her legs diminished. Her journal hailed the end of 1890 as a year of
grace, and she noted that three of the previous five decades had started
with significant births.

31 [December] We opened the doors to welcome in the
New Year. Thank God, for all the happiness & mercy in this
1890.

1840 Minnie born.
1850
1860
1870 Laura born
1880 Billy born
1890

Nevertheless, the year had opened with influenza outbreaks, and the
Kingsley Lodge household was laid low. Nor did Freshwater escape.
In a message to Emily Tennyson which betrays tellingly her time and
class, Annie rejoiced to hear of the slow recovery from bronchial

*Annie with Billy and Hester, about 1885*

pneumonia of 'my dear King Alfred ... I <u>was the only</u> person in the
house who escaped – Bovril was our last resource & what good stuff it
is the cook was just well enough to mix it up.'[1]

Watts congratulated Annie on the publication of her Ruskin essay
in March, but was guarded about its subject. 'What a time you must
have had! but you seem to have got happily through it. Pray encourage
your little ones to take pleasure in dancing & physical exercises. No
doubt Ruskin and Rossetti suffered much from want of healthy safety

valves for mental high pressure.'[2] He thanked her for new photographs of Hester and Billy, and was startled by their growth. 'When one is brought suddenly in some way with proof of times progress how alarming it is, doing one's very best it is impossible in any degree to keep pace with the unfaltering steps.' These family photographs are noticeably different from the usual posed and formalised frozen portraits of the Victorians, who grouped figures almost like statuary. Annie is recognisably modern in wishing to document the children as they changed and grew. 'I am going the first fine day when I am up to it to take them to be photographed for its a shame not to keep the dear little vision of life as it fleets – It cant ever be so sweet again.'[3] She would slip photographs into her letters – to Pinkie when she was in India ('a punkah waving over my head as I write & look at you holding Hester in that dearest of little pictures on my table'),[4] and to the dying John Field in America ('"Our youngest child" as Billy calls the little dog is also there as you see & I think the whole performance creditable to the Wimbledon Photographer').[5] A picture of Annie seated with the children, taken around 1885 in the garden at Southmead, is natural and charming. She holds a confident Billy who looks with curiosity out to the photographer, whilst Hester presses more shyly against her mother, gripping an enormous if compliant cat. Annie seems distracted, but probably was concentrating on holding everyone in place.

She took the children to Freshwater for Easter. It was her first visit since her marriage, and initial impressions were a little disconcerting – 'it seems to me far more bother than it used to be & the island has certainly grown'. But the children's pleasure reassured her that she had been right to return. 'It is certainly nice to see them going thro' all my own old raptures.' They stayed in lodgings rather than at The Porch, and it began to seem quite like old times for a number of Ritchies were at Freshwater, including Pinkie as well as Gussie with her family. She was proud to see Hester admired, both by Hallam and Tennyson himself who thought her 'the prettiest little girl he knew'.[6] Annie had arranged for Laura to join them for some days, where she would be free to wander on the downs and gather primroses in the lanes. A horse and carriage took them to Yarmouth to meet Laura and her carer, but first off the boat was Oscar Browning, 'with a strange halo of modesty like an aureole'. Having offered a lift she found herself asking him to lunch if invitations from the Tennysons or Gussie were not forthcoming. 'It was rather absurd for he said – "Count upon me. Even if they <u>do</u> invite me I shall come to you" – To w<sup>h</sup>. I – idiotically – O no – no – please dont come if they ask you anywhere else.'

The artist and illustrator Helen Allingham was also at Freshwater, and Annie observed her in the road executing one of her cottage paintings – 'you never saw anything so quick so pretty'. At dinner Mrs Allingham told an intriguing story about Froude's monumental Carlyle biography and Carlyle's niece, wife of Alexander Carlyle. 'F. asked M$^{rs}$ C to let him see the papers to correct any of the mistakes w$^h$. <u>she</u> asserted existed. She agreed but said that neither he nor she should decide but 2 other people of some standing who should be <u>paid</u> & if the mistakes were important <u>he</u> sh$^d$. pay & if they were unimportant she sh$^d$. pay. However this Froude wouldnt agree to. She says there are whole scenes (quite immaterial) w$^h$. are his invention altogether such as his conversation with Carlyle on the death of his brother – Whereas F was in Devonshire & Carlyle in Scotland.'[7]

Although they had only been in the Lingfield Road house a year, she and Richmond were already contemplating a further move. They remained until 1894, when they built yet another new house, but meanwhile it did not stop them looking around. It was important to get the neighbourhood right; somewhere like Cheyne Walk, where Pinkie had taken a house after the death of her mother, had its drawbacks. 'Pinkie says the great objection is the <u>horrible</u> population at night. It was disagreeable in Young S$^t$. even and this is much worse. That is one reason the rents are so low in C. W. – now in Rosary [Gardens] except for that mysterious singer, there was never anything under a butler to be met with.' As always, money was the crucial problem. In May, her journal records another ritual panic, with a solution which made no lasting difference to their outgoings. 'Bankers book came. Cold perspiration. 3 maids in future, cut off ladies maid.' But it started a more painful cashing in of assets, for early in June Annie sold some of her father's manuscripts to a dealer, realising £70. There would be a lot more of this in years to come, although she never parted with letters. She also negotiated with *Harper's Magazine* to publish a group of Thackeray's drawings, 'The Heroic Adventures of M. Boudin', for which she wrote an introduction and received £150. She had no compunction about publishing material in America for which Smith, Elder held the copyright at home and in 1888, George Smith agreed, perhaps reluctantly, that she was free to do this. 'I have of course nothing to say to the publication of any letters, or anything else, in America.' The enactment of the international copyright law in 1891 would inhibit future deals of this kind.

It was at this point that Smith waived his rights to the pantomime version of *The Rose and the Ring*, planned for the end of the year. His largesse extended to the whole family, with the arrival every New Year of a gift of chocolates or other luxuries, to the excitement of children and adults alike, and Annie's letters of thanks were as charming as the gifts which prompted them. But this year he also acknowledged Hester's twelfth birthday with a cheque for £1,000. Annie was stunned by the size of the gift and all the associations that went with it. Probably she remembered her own legacy from FitzGerald, and it occurred to her that, had Smith similarly willed the sum to Hester, she might never have known of this exceptional generosity.

> I have brought my writing block out into the garden to thank you, for the house did not seem large eno' somehow to hold all the many things w$^h$. I have been feeling – Dear kind generous friend – all these years I have known that I could only love you for all your unendingness & unfailingness & now comes this great gift which I scarcely feel we ought to take only we have become so used to your kindness dear Mr Smith dear Lizzie. And this comes with a rush somehow. I think of what my Father would have felt & how shall I say it – that it might have happened & I might not have known it & – Even the garden doesn't quite hold it all.[8]

She told one or two people, including her mother. 'You will never guess – It is the most splendid present that ever was made – from her Godfather £1000! not £100 not £10 but a whole thousand in a cheque to "Miss Hester Ritchie".'[9] Annie's own generosity meant that she was careless about money, the trait which Leslie had found so challenging during their years together, but she was never wilfully extravagant. Both she and Richmond enjoyed simple, inexpensive gestures, and this seems to have been inculcated in the children for one senses that they too favoured the kind of surprises that were not costly. On the morning of her birthday that year, she had heard music as she lay in bed. 'Woke to a delicious serenade. Hester & Billy on accordions.'

'My Poet' appeared in *Macmillan's Magazine* for July, the first in the occasional series which she called 'Chapters from an Unwritten Memoir', hinting at bigger things to come from the resource of materials and personal memories at her disposal. Most of the 'Chapters' are charming and inoffensive, taking us back to her early life in Paris and Kensington and touching on her father to a greater or lesser extent. It was becoming easier to write about him, for he had featured in the essays on Tennyson and Ruskin, as he would in her 1892 piece on the Brownings. They were important stepping-stones in being able to write about those close to her, including people still living who had featured in her past. One such was Frederick Locker, Eleanor's father, who thought his appearance in the first of the series 'very kind, & very flattering, & a very pretty picture. It is pleasant to think I have known you so many years.'[10] His son-in-law, Augustine Birrell, picked up on Annie's trademark vagueness about details. 'One seemed to see the scene – & yet there seems the greatest doubt as to <u>when</u> it could have been. Lady F. Baillie [and] Mr Locker can't concur within five years – What does it matter? It <u>happened.</u>'[11]

Birrell's principal reason for writing now was to seek contributions to *The Speaker*, a new weekly, 'on men of letters of this present time.… The Managers of the enterprise are very anxious you should do <u>Ruskin</u>.' The offer was from a newspaper rather than a magazine, the payment was not good, but Birrell astutely identified Annie's qualifications for this work. 'No detail is expected – no fussy enumeration of writings, but a broad & generous treatment in bold outline – There may be an <u>under-current</u> of acidity if desired – but the main object is to forestall the criticism of 2000 AD.… If after you have done J.R. a wild desire seizes you to do the same kindly office for almost anybody else – Miss C. Rossetti or whom you like – the thing can be managed – but this as you like – Please entertain first the idea & then the Readers of the "Speaker".' A fortnight later, the Ruskin piece was written. The £5 payment may not have been much, but *Macmillan's* were only paying £10 for each of the early 'Chapters', later increased to £18.

Annie was amused by the name of their boarding-house at Littlestone on the Kent coast, selected in August for its golf course. As she put their address at the top of a letter to George Smith – 'Ellesmere (Robert?), Littlestone on Sea, Kent' – she alluded to a Smith, Elder publishing phenomenon, Mrs Humphry Ward's *Robert Elsmere*, which enjoyed huge sales from its first appearance in 1888. While Billy followed his father on the links, she drove out with Hester to 'old romantic seaport towns & churches left <u>wrecked</u> high & dry, with their old corners & pebbles to show what they once were'.[12] In reasonable health at last, she hoped for nothing more than that this present calm should continue. 'I am getting just a little bit what shall I call it – rested? but I w$^d$. enjoy the rest of my life here if I c$^d$. see them all looking so well & brown & happy.'[13] She had learnt not to wish for too much. A three-day stay with Elizabeth Gaskell's daughters in Manchester in mid-November, where she managed to talk at cross-purposes to her lunch partners, mistaking the Russian prince on one side for the Lancashire anarchist on the other, was extended into a trip further north when she travelled to the Bells at Redcar. Margaret Oliphant sent her usual letter on Minny's anniversary, leading Annie to dwell on her friend's own struggles and resilience. 'This is my own darling Minnies day & last night as I sat alone by the fire thinking of it all there came a letter f<sup>m</sup>. M<sup>rs</sup>. Oliphant which seemed to belong to the past. O such a pathetic letter it seemed to go <u>echoing</u> thro the room poor dear dearest woman.'[14]

The episode of Thackeray inviting Charlotte Brontë to dinner at Young Street became the fourth of her *Macmillan's* 'Chapters', but cautious as ever she sent the draft to George Smith, who had brought the writers together. Her casual enjoyment in this examination of the past is interesting, and perhaps the bigger project was already lurking in her mind. 'I dont mean to do any more for the present – nor shall I publish this unless you don't dislike it. Of course it would come in very naturally with the rest when the memoirs are published collectively by the children some day. Meanwhile I send out an occasional chapter which amuses <u>me</u> & does no one any harm.'[15] *The Rose and the Ring* pantomime was a delightful triumph, and Annie wrote with a childlike excitement at being fêted as the author's daughter. 'I laughed & cried & clapped. How I thought of my daddy & <u>longed</u> for him. I was presented with an <u>enormous</u> bouquet, ices, tea programmes appeared every 5 minutes.'[16] Just one ripple disturbed this tranquil surface, when FitzJames Stephen's son, James (J.K.) Stephen appeared uninvited during a lunch party at Kingsley Lodge. He had enjoyed a brilliant career at Eton and Cambridge, but in December 1886 was struck on the head by a pumping machine, after which he sank into a long mental decline. It led to erratic and disturbing behaviour, such as this impromptu visit to the Ritchies. 'Dear Jim Stephen ashy pale & distraught, walked in like a ghost & the company fled before him. It was like Shakespear.'[17] He would die in February 1892, 'such a sudden end to so much fear & so much hope'.[18]

The better health of 1890 would not last. During the winter London was once more full of influenza, and by mid-January it was cold enough for the children to skate on the pond on Wimbledon Common. Annie was concerned both for Billy, who seemed 'very thin & delicate', and for Richmond, who began to fall victim to the dizziness and nausea of Ménière's disease, suffering 'constant breakdowns' whilst his India Office responsibilities increased, particularly when, later in the year, he became Private Secretary to George Curzon, Parliamentary Under-Secretary of State. Annie took the children to Brighton to try to strengthen Billy, and arranged for riding lessons for them both. 'It is a comfortissimo to see Bill his own little self again. Another time I shall not wait so long & shall simply bring him off without more ado. His pony danced off with him this morning but he sat beautifully & was complimented by an old thunder & blazes who said he was as right as a trivet.'[19] Her pride in Billy's growing expertise as a rider is expressed in terms unexceptionable for the time. 'It seems quite [a] waste that Billy who hasn't either a pony or leggings or a first & second coachman should ride so very much better & more easily than the little Jew boys who have!'[20] She had so many hopes for her son, and worried at his perfectly adequate though average school reports, for it was assumed that he would follow Richmond and go to Eton. Despite mediocre marks, however, he certainly had the Thackeray quickness of wit.

> Billys repartee 4. March 1891 Billy: tell me a story about when you was very young.
> Sententious Mama. I went to see M[r] & M[rs] Browning at Paris & M[r] Aide who was there said – Well Miss Thackeray when are you going to write a book and M[r] Browning said 'No doubt it will come in good time. The Roman ladies sat at home & spun wool. Now-a-days ladies spin wool in other ways'.
> Billy. I dont call that a story Mom. I call it a yarn.

While Annie was in Brighton, where Julia's mother was also then resident, reviews of Herman Merivale's book on her father started to appear.[21] This had been a curious enterprise, for Herman's weak health had made her feel more generous towards the project than she might otherwise have done, and she even released some materials to him. But mid-way through writing he suffered a complete breakdown, and the book had to be completed by Frank Marzials. Herman had set out in a spirit of affectionate respect, and Annie felt that the book was probably harmless enough.

> Leslie says he sh[d]. like to kick poor H. I dont like some things but I do think it is done with feeling & a certain amount of judgement. I was talking to M[rs]. Jackson last night who asked me what had really happened. She said 'I cant see why because a man has written books all his private life & feelings are to be dragged into publicity for every newspaper to have its criticism. Its a vulgar fashion.' – I myself should like the children to have the money & think that then after my generation was passed there c[d] be no great objection or want of dignity in it all but I feel very luke-warm abt it.[22]

To Charles Plumptre Johnson, who had spotted some obviously forged Thackeray letters in the book, she admitted to being pleased on the whole with its publication. 'It is a real picture as far as it goes – sadder than he was, except during those last two years of his life when

Herman Merivale saw most of him – but very touching to me.' Her more cautious public view was that the book 'is full of very real and true things', though she missed 'the fullness of the impression of the earlier days'.[23]

Richmond sometimes slept at his sister Gussie's house in Airlie Gardens when Annie was out of town, and did so this time, 'abominably genteel' though he found it. He took a knowing snipe at Pinkie's new friendship with the writer and social reformer Edith Sichel, with whom she lived until Edith's death in 1914; predictably, Gussie was more hostile still. 'Gussie abused Pinkie & Edith, who, I said, had been as bad as an engaged couple when they stayed there: & that I had been tempted to suggest to them to retire into the diningroom, – where the lovemaking of the upper middles is carried on in England, as in a temple of Venus Respectabilis.'[24] His less robust health was probably behind the Ritchies' adjustments to their Wimbledon regime. After one of Annie's dinners, where the maids managed well despite there being 'no waiter & no assistant cook', Richmond implored that they should refrain from dinner parties for the time being and she agreed.[25]

The death from meningitis of Hal, Gussie and Douglas's son, was terrible and sudden. Annie wrote a series of comforting letters to Gussie, and a touching one to Jane, Hal's sister, knowing that her confusion might be lost in the general family grief. '[T]o love is not only to see people but it is to be with them in ones spirit & <u>after the first</u> I have never felt away from my sister who died just when you were born, but I seem nearer to her as days go on.'[26] She did not hide the pain of loss in such letters, but wrote with such generous honesty that the recipient was allowed to feel that not just sympathy but a real understanding was being offered. And, of course, it was the memory of her own dear losses which gave her words such pointed authenticity.

> I like to think that the day may come when Hals love will once more fill your hearts with sympathy for life & with peace & when the world will be to you what you <u>have</u> of him not only what you have not....
>
> After my Father died I was haunted for two years by such a tiny little thing; that he had once put out his hand to me as I went by & that I had tapped it with the paper-knife I held – I used to wake up in the night with his dear hand before me. It is so cruel to think that when every nerve is strained & aching imaginary things sometimes take an importance which they never never really had. As if the reality was not enough.[27]

Pinkie and Edith Sichel had spent Easter in Italy, that magic land for Annie. Pinkie's description of Lucca on Easter Sunday triggered all kinds of suggestions, of 'a sort of odd feeling of former existence I cant describe' though it was not somewhere that Annie herself had visited. 'I cant remember – but the Storys will tell you & do ask them from me – were not <u>they</u> there with the Brownings & a whole colony of dear past spirits.'[28] Pinkie moved on to Rome and the Hotel Minerva, the mention of which swept Annie back to Easter 1869, when she and George Eliot had both been in Rome but had not met. Minny was scornful at the time of George Eliot, but only now do we learn of Annie's aborted attempt to see her. 'I remember the <u>Minerva</u> perfectly & I went there & either did or didnt leave a large bouquet of rose-buds for George Eliot. It was in my mind to do so & I bought the flowers & went to the door with them & then I think my courage failed & it seemed to me affected.'

She was working on her Browning essay and completed it later in the year, although it would not appear in *Harper's* until May 1892. Her self-deprecating account of her working-method actually offers an astute and accurate summary of her particular strengths, for the essay's power derives from its being a lived record rather than a portrait of the kind which had been undertaken by Mrs Sutherland Orr. 'It is rather egotistical for I had to tear up all I tried to write that <u>wasnt</u> personal, for it was so dull & also it was only a faint repetition of M^rs. Orr's book, so it became all <u>personal</u> reminiscences at last.'[29] Meanwhile a new commission had come from Macmillans for an introduction to their reissue of *Cranford*. She visited Knutsford in early October, having already sought guidance from Elizabeth Gaskell's daughters about Cranford's original.

> You ask about the topography of Knutsford – and I want to say, as distinctly and emphatically as ever I can, that my mother <u>never</u> drew portraits of either persons or places. Some tiny trait in either she might draw from reality; but she <u>never</u> directly copied Nature – and so though of course Knutsford is Cranford in a general sort of way, there was no attempt to record either special people or special places. When we go home, at the end of July, I could send you the exact date of the writing of Cranford – which was begun in my dear Father's study, a dark room lined throughout with books – (on the right of the front door as you go in) – I will send you a charming account of Knutsford, written at the time when my Father was laid beside her in the little grave-yard there....

> I cannot tell you <u>what</u> pleasure it gives us to think that you
> are writing the introductory preface. You will do it so very
> beautifully – but oh! Annie! <u>those drawings</u>! Don't tell the
> Macmillans, <u>please</u>; but neither Julia nor I can endure them
> – They give so <u>entirely</u> the wrong flavour to the humour –
> although I see, of course, how clever and well-drawn they
> are.[30]

There was also preliminary reading to be done for an introduction to
Madame d'Aulnoy's fairy tales, published by Lawrence and Bullen
in 1892, while Herman Merivale's book prompted a short piece for
the *Illustrated London News* on 'Thackeray and his Biographers' –
she borrowed her title from Andrew Lang's review of Merivale in
*Longman's Magazine*. It was an industrious year, but one which saw
the return of her headaches; as she noted in the journal, 'I was working
& the hard work & the headache seem to go together'. Her mother,
Isabella Thackeray, who had been living with carers ever since the early
1840s when Thackeray had realised that her frail mental health made
it impossible for her to continue stay in the family home, continued
to be the recipient of Annie's letters, which, unsurprisingly in the
circumstances, maintain a resolutely optimistic tone. 'I am sure you
will like to hear how <u>very</u> well I go on keeping. I do enjoy it more than
I can say. It seems quite <u>curious</u> after being ill so long to be well able
to come & go.'[31] She was regularly employing the secretarial services
of Eva Irving to transcribe her chaotic manuscripts into versions which
publishers might comprehend. Mrs Irving had previously taught Hester
and Billy whilst they had lived with Richmond's mother, though with
limited success. As a copyist however she was exemplary, 'a Martha
matter of factedly toiling from morn to evening, I an impotent old
Index of other peoples feelings'.[32]

Rhoda Broughton now became a close friend. Although they had
been acquainted for some years, it was only when Rhoda moved from
Oxford to Richmond on the edge of London that the opportunity for
meeting regularly arose. Despite an unpromising first encounter in
1879, Richmond also got on well with her, and Annie would teasingly
refer to her as his '<u>other</u> lady'.[33] He was the first to visit after her
move.

> Rhoda has the most fascinating little house – like the old
> ones in Kensington Square – at the very top of Richmond
> Hill, nearly opposite the Star & Garter & quite opposite
> the view. £80 a year, but on clay & very unwholesome. My
> voice went clear out during the 3 hours I was there, & came

back again by degrees when I went away – it is so awfully relaxing. She has been very friendly & nice: but quite old: & said she couldn't write an improper novel now if she tried; whereas M[rs] H. Ward, who cut her at Oxford for honor of Nancy, is now determined to have a thoroughly improper side in Elsmere's successor & uses Ethel Arnold as a sort of moral barometer to see how far she may go.[34]

New Year was spent at Redcar, and as the bells rang out at midnight Annie spotted the Plough in the night sky. They normally stayed with the Bells at their house Red Barns, but this time there was a houseful of visitors so the Ritchies took lodgings, which may have been a blessing as the Bell children caught scarlet fever. Fearing that Hester was displaying symptoms, Annie sent Richmond and Billy back to London and stayed to nurse her, which delayed their own return until 15 January, and soon after Richmond went down with a bout of influenza. The threat of infection led them to arrange for Billy to board at Charles Olive's school, while Hester stayed at Allenswood with Marie Souvestre, whose pupil she had been since the autumn.

The on-going series of 'Chapters from an Unwritten Memoir' and a growing friendship with the *Macmillan's* editor, Mowbray Morris, led to a new relationship with the parent firm. As well as securing Annie for *Cranford*, Macmillans commissioned prefaces to *Our Village* by Mary Mitford (1893) and to a series of Maria Edgeworth's novels (1895-7). More immediately, Macmillans collected into a single volume her three essays on Tennyson, Ruskin and the Brownings, also published in America by Harpers. She did not conceal from Hallam Tennyson her pleasure at the terms offered. 'They have been very kind & liberal about it & have given me £200 & I <u>may</u> perhaps get as much fm America w[h]. I dont think likely.'[35] It would prove to be one of her most successful publications, its appearance in 1892 followed shortly by Tennyson's death at the beginning of October helping sales. Macmillans would also republish her 'Chapters' as a book, although she had to add to it to fill it out. Over the years Annie grew more confident in looking beyond the comfortable support of the Smith, Elder stable, although was not always realistic in her expectations, particularly when she dealt directly with American publishers. She sought advice about local practices from William H. Forbes, the husband of Emerson's daughter, Edith, when tentatively exploring an American deal for what later turned into the Biographical Edition.

My wife has read to me your letter asking about prices &c from our publishers.

I have for so long a time had nothing to do with such matters that my opinion is not good. Mr Emerson had twenty per cent of the retail price and Edward Emerson has the same for his Father's books and I think he has the same for what he is doing himself....

If you will authorise me to do so I will see Mr Houghton of Houghton Mifflin & Co and tell him confidentially what you propose to do and if you like, try to get an offer from him.[36]

Annie seemed increasingly determined to maximise her income from her publishing deals, and became cautious about assigning her copyrights unconditionally. But in negotiating over the book publication of the 'Chapters', Frederick Macmillan was keen to ensure that his firm secured a watertight arrangement in light of the new international copyright law.

We should like very much to publish your volume of Memoirs, but I am afraid that without some additions the chapters that have appeared in the Magazine would hardly make a volume sturdy enough to run alone. I estimate that the nine chapters which have appeared in 'Macmillan' are not equal in bulk to more than two thirds of your book on 'Tennyson Ruskin & Browning' and I do not think the book ought to be shorter than that which as you remember needed the assistance of large type and ample margins to occupy 250 small 8$^{vo}$. pages.

This however need be no serious objection for I have no doubt you can find material for four or five new chapters which will not only have the advantage of making the book more than a mere reprint from the Magazine, but as they would be published for the first time in the volume would enable us to obtain for it a Copyright in the United States under the America Copyright Act....

There was good reason why the American Edition of the other book should be in Harpers hands for the articles of which it consisted were originally written for and appeared in their Magazine. But these papers have all appeared in 'Macmillans' (where I remind you, they have been paid for at an exceptionally high rate per page), and it seems to me not unreasonable that the publication of the book in both continents should be left in our hands....

As regards terms, I understand you to say that you would like to retain an interest in the book, an arrangement that we shall be happy to fall in with, but I need hardly to say that when an author continues to remain part proprietor of a copyright, he cannot expect to receive such a large sum on publication as when he sells it out and out. We are anxious, however to deal as liberally as possible with you, and on condition that you can see your way to supply more chapters so as to bring the book up to the size of 'Records of Tennyson etc', & to enable us to secure an American copyright, – & that you will leave the publication of both the English & American Editions in our hands, we will pay you £200 down on account of a royalty of 10 per cent in America & 15 per cent in England and a further sum of £50 for the Colonial Library Edition. That is to say you would receive at once £250 with the prospect of further profits contingent on the sale of the book.[37]

The deal on offer was by no means disadvantageous, but Macmillan's firmness with Annie may have been salutary in underlining George Smith's customary lightness of touch.

A week or so before they went to the ancient smuggling town of Deal for Easter, drawn by the golf and the coastal walks, Annie heard of the death of Julia Stephen's mother. The Jacksons had supported her after Minny's death, and as Julia Margaret Cameron's sister, Maria Jackson had been part of the network of links to earlier happiness. It saddened her, but Deal was reviving. 'I feel that one must be satisfied with the <u>existence</u> of dear people here or in ones heart, & not expect more than life has to give: or indeed than one has to give oneself and one must try to accept <u>oneself</u> with ones own infirmities & limitations.'[38] They were fortunate in their boarding house. The cooking was excellent, with freshly-caught shrimps for breakfast and potatoes like 'poems'. As Richmond and the children walked, she took little drives out and pottered around the town, imagining the houses with sea views they might one day buy, and she sat and read Henry James – 'Its so good' – probably his latest collection of tales, *The Lesson of the Master*. The quiet of the boarding house and dearth of human dramas meant that 'my visions of writing a story like Henry James about the Boarders have not been carried out'.[39]

Back in London she was ill for two weeks, but consulted the society physician, Sir Andrew Clark, under whose regime she benefited significantly. His prognosis was generally encouraging. 'No butter no marmalade otherwise rather liberal diet. <u>1 sp. of whiskey</u> a day – green vegetables, indeed everything I have always taken – no fruit, hardly any pudding, no little &cts. He found nothing beyond a weak heart w$^h$. accounts for my vagaries & general debility & was most sensible & encouraging – to walk ½ an hour a day "& encourage cheerful activity".[40] By early August she was able to announce to Tennyson, to whom she sent birthday wishes, that Clark had prescribed medicine to counteract her headaches, 'the first that <u>ever</u> cured me at all & I have been extraordinarily better ever since'.[41]

She certainly was working more consistently through these years, producing essays rather than anything more sustained, the focus upon memoir and reminiscence suggesting that her former caution about biographical work had all but gone. Important in this regard was her 'Chapter' dealing with Dickens and her father – she did not, of course, touch on the Garrick affair – in which she remembered *David Copperfield* appearing in its monthly numbers 'and how glad we were when they came to our hands at last, after our elders and our governess and our butler had all read them in turn', and described the parties to which Kate invited the Thackeray girls – 'nothing came in the least near them'. Arriving once to collect his daughters, Thackeray was cheered by the assembled company of children who lined the stairs and crowded the hall, all orchestrated by Dickens. She sent Kate her draft to check her memories. Did it quite happen like that? Was she remembering correctly? It was a chance for Kate to revisit her own almost-forgotten past.

> I have a sort of vague remembrance perhaps of the party you speak of but so misty that it vanishes entirely when I try to fix it in my mind; but I feel confident that your description of it is accurate, or nearly so, for I can see my father turning to yours and saying with the twinkle in his dear eyes, I remember so well – 'This is for <u>you</u>' – and all honour to those boys 'the thousands of boys' who set up a cheer for your great and dear Father! – Those boys knew what they were about. If your account of that famous party is not quite correct – it is correct enough to charm your readers I am sure – and as the fault of most Memoirs – (to me at least) – seems to be that they are too census like in their dull veracity – I thank you in my heart for trying to make that party a little more delightful perhaps than it really was – You have a wonderful memory dear Annie.... Then I remember a hayfield at Boulogne. I was sitting behind a haystack with a volume of Shakespeare – and you and Min & your Father came into the field – you had been calling at our house & found Papa away from home – I saw you – but whether you saw me and I got up

and talked to you – or whether I hid away still more behind the haystack (which would have been more like me in those days) I cannot remember but I do recollect that I felt very keenly how your Father would have roared to find a small girl in very short petticoats sitting under a haystack on a bright sunny afternoon studying Hamlet![42]

Billy was twelve in 1892. Although no final decision needed to be made for another year, Annie and Richmond began to doubt whether Eton would be right for him. In June, a short visit to the Warre Cornishes at Eton gave him a flavour of what school life might be like. 'I am getting less & less enthusiastic as Bill settles down more & more to the situation…. He says he thinks it w$^d$ be much nicer coming properly to school here than going to S$^t$ Pauls. So I said yes if we could afford it – but we should see how things turned out.'[43] There was the real problem of expense to be considered, for it was unlikely that he would be in the running for a scholarship, and this raised the matter of his academic ability. Would he cope with Eton's challenges and the heavy load of family expectations that would be placed on him? Annie shared this worry with Tennyson, aware that his grandson and namesake – his 'wonderful good Alfred' – had just gained an Eton place as a King's Scholar. 'Oh! how I envy his getting into College. I want to send my Bill, but it will be a fearful tight fit, & I know he could never get into college. However he is doing nicely & is well in the average & that is no little to be thankful for.' She ended this final birthday letter to Tennyson by sending 'half a century of love'.[44]

She put on a brave face in congratulating Eleanor on Alfred's scholarship. 'I hope if we can screw [Billy] into Eton he may be able to help with a scholarship or something in time. He is captain of the 2$^d$. 11 at his school which is very good for his dear lungs but one cant make a living by it.'[45] She was also pleased that Augustine Birrell had been re-elected to the House of Commons. Irish politics would loom large in Birrell's future career, for he became Chief Secretary for Ireland in 1907. The Irish question was a live issue in the 1892 election, and Annie approached it from the perspective of her own family politics.

Nobody knows the Irish whose cousins are not the Shawes as mine are – because one sister ordered a tombstone for my poor Aunt Jane who had previously refused, immediately another ordered a second much more expensive so as to keep up her dignity & the people wont take the first back for w$^h$. we shall have to pay half. Do you wonder I am beginning to think they are not quite accountable beings.

Before she took the children for the summer to Bamburgh Castle in Northumberland, she finally raised with George Smith the project which had been stirring into life for some years. In 1891 Annie had at last acknowledged Jane Brookfield's collection of Thackeray letters as being 'the nearest approach to an autobiography' that had so far appeared,[46] her view prompted in part by the inadequacies of Merivale's book. This greater confidence had come from the encouragement of those she respected, including Andrew Lang who had opened his review of the Merivale biography by identifying the person best-suited to write one. 'It is generally understood that Mr. Thackeray wished no biography of himself to be written. The only contemporary author who could write that life as it should be done has therefore been obedient to her father's desire.'[47] Even as long ago as 1875, after the appearance of the anonymous collection *Thackerayana* to which she and Minny had taken such objection, Henry James had been publicly urging her to set the record straight. 'Why does not Miss Thackeray attempt a biography of her illustrious father?'[48] With such advocates, it was hard to resist concluding that enough time had elapsed, but there was a yet more powerful persuader. Annie's anxieties over money were about to increase with the additional costs of Billy's schooling, and the new copyright laws embracing America made it impossible to resist the likely financial benefits.

> I was going to write & tell you something I have been thinking about which I should like very much & w^h. American copyright will make practicable I hope. Dont you think – when you are ready for it – & yr. other stores are practically sold out – that a final cheap edition of my Fathers books with notes biographical or otherwise by me – with quotations from his letters & original sketches added (such as those we have to 'Cornhill to Cairo' &^ct) w^d be a good thing. It might be a little income for me f^m America & it might also suit your plans over here. I saw one of the Harpers Magazine managers yesterday. I said I was thinking of asking you about this: & it was quite true for it had been vaguely in my mind for some time past. He seemed to take to the idea w^h. however w^d. want to be thought about.[49]

It was Annie's idea from the beginning, and never the case, as has been asserted, that George Smith had to persuade her to undertake an edition of this kind. Indeed, he remained to be convinced.

Richmond had already left for his own holiday, calling at the Freshfields' summer home in the north between visits to Coniston and golfing at Dornoch. He interrupted his trip for a few days to assist George Curzon in his re-election at Southport, picturing himself as Fred Bayham in the election campaign from *The Newcomes*. Neither he nor others seem to have scrupled at the ethics of a civil servant assisting his parliamentary masters in their party elections; Curzon was a Conservative, but Richmond had been equally loyal some years before to his then Liberal chief, Stafford Howard. He admired Curzon's stamina, and amused Annie by reports of the hustings. '4 meetings he managed last night – at one of which a rustic radical described how he was buying a sheep's head for supper – & he said to the butcher "Mind I want a Tory one" – whereupon the butcher took the brains out of the head and said "Here's a real Tory one".'[50]

Annie still had business to do before she left for Northumberland. The sadness of Hal Freshfield's death more than a year before was still much in her mind, and she continued to feel for his mother. Experience had shown that grief feeds upon itself, and that the bereaved required the company of other people. She tried to distract Gussie with news of her own doings, telling her about Lucy Baxter's visit from America and of bringing Lucy and Eyre Crowe together again after forty years. If Annie is to be believed, when serving as Thackeray's travelling companion and secretary during his 1852-3 American lecture tour, Crowe had been as charmed by Lucy as his employer had been with her elder sister, Sally Baxter.

> I cant help remembering one time when Minnie & I were quite alone & apart from every one & everything & how it strained our strained cracking nerves. One doesnt feel it, one <u>wants</u> to be alone & yet one becomes a sort of bogie to oneself – at least I do – & it is only by seeing others & thinking about them that one gets ease from oneself…. My dear unknown interesting Lucy Baxter spent the day yesterday. My Father was so fond of her as a girl – she knew all our old stories. She has piles of his letters & I actually conjured up her old admirer Eyre Crowe out of the dim past to meet her at tea. She is very American very handsome with an odd elaborate coiffure & old fashioned ways, a <u>real</u> lady delicate high bred.

Mrs Oliphant had also been visited, and Annie recognised something heroic in the constant struggle to generate sufficient income, a problem she saw reflected more widely in the lives of women writers.

> She said this clever pretty story she is now writing in Blackwood was <u>lost</u> by Blackwood for years. That M[r]

Blackwood seeing some money to her account put it down as a Debt – That she said she had never borrowed anything in her life f^m. him & that the MSS had been sent for the money & this money was only on acc^t. a part of what she was to receive. But she told us that she has had to be content with this old payment as a whole – even when after much delay the MSS. was at last discovered. People do make one ashamed. M^rs. Lynton who has slaved, told Laura Colmache she had never earned more than £300 a year & I know she has worked & worked night after night at her desk.[51]

On 11 July she visited her mother at Leigh-on-Sea, near Southend, where she lived with the couple who acted as her carers, and was back there a fortnight later as Isabella was 'ailing again'. She came away happier in her mind, for her mother seemed to revive in her company.

As Annie, Hester and Billy journeyed north by train to Belshill in Northumberland, her work went with her. She would write a couple more of her *Macmillan's Magazine* 'Chapters', planned some other essays, and even told Richmond that she was minded to 'tackle my novel again', an aspiration which bubbled up now and then over the years and came to nothing. But her major holiday task was represented by the large package of her father's letters which accompanied her, for only days after writing to George Smith she had started the process of 'sorting them for the Edition'.[52] Ever since the time in 1888 when she had read some letters through with Richmond, a moment when she was transported across the years by the charms of 'my daddys handwriting', it would continue to be here, rather than in the published, public works, that she would encounter her father. Whilst her desire for a Thackeray edition was driven by pragmatism and the necessities of her personal circumstances, the project enchanted her, as through the filter of his witty, indiscreet, sometimes painful and always honest correspondence, the raw materials of his life were set before her, including the role she and her sister had played in it. She was able to make immediate use of the letters, for one of the 'Chapters' completed in Northumberland was on Carlyle – 'I have found such a pretty little bit about him in Papas letters'.

Meanwhile she enjoyed the holiday. Her entirely respectful Ruskin essay did not diminish her own private interest in the gossiping and rumour-mongering that surrounded the disaster of his marriage to Effie Gray, later Millais's wife, and she passed on to Richmond what she had picked up, a second-hand story purporting to come from Ruskin's cousin. 'He isnt an eunuch a bit but as soon as they were married M[rs] Ruskin said to him that she was in love with a gent[n]. in India so says he, we are not married, we shant be married until you tell me you care for <u>me</u> – Then M[rs]. R. gets a divorce. Then R. says he cant in the eyes of the Bible marry again unless she had committed A. Then the Severns (who are really very fond of him, but also of his inheritance) do <u>everything</u> they can to prevent his marriage. But if he had really wished it surely they couldnt have done so. Then Kate Greenaway goes on her knees to him to marry her, she adores him so. Amor omnia, alas it doesnt vincit.'[53]

It was time to press home her enthusiasm for her project, and she wrote to George Smith from Belshill.

> I have been thinking over my little dream of an edition with notes of my Fathers works. I brought a great parcel of his old old letters down here to look thro' and there are so many things w[h]. w[d] be of interest – as to when & how V.F. was written for instance – as to his view of Ireland & Home Rule – notices of the books he is reading & so on – all this with the dates of where he was & where he wrote his various books & a few very few little fillagrees [*sic*] of mine w[d]. I do think add to the interest of the books. You see how well those little scraps of things in Macmillan do, & this w[d]. be such a good way of saying anything one wanted to say – It might even be an edition without pictures so as not to interfere with those w[h]. exist, but with notes so as to add a certain biographical value. I don't imagine there w[d]. be eno' to say about <u>all</u> his collected papers but if one took the novels & the lectures & Roundabouts – some 10 or 12 volumes.
>
> It may not be worth your while to reprint a new edition, with the added expence of <u>me</u> – (taking each as an article it wd. be about 80 or 75 a volume) but please think it over dear Mr Smith & tell me what you think.[54]

We do not have Smith's replies, but Annie sent on his queries to Richmond. There appear to have been concerns over costs and viability, with Annie depending on the American rights to boost returns. 'Here is his this mornings letter – I fear you are right but with America it w[d]. make near £1400.' She again raised the problem of getting Billy into Eton, and of perhaps needing to change their plans for him, but now the Edition is seen as a possible salvation, or otherwise the sale of some more Thackeray manuscripts. 'I am sure to be able to get 400

*Thackeray carte de visite, endorsed by Annie. 'This is the photograph which seems to me most like my Father's <u>habitual</u> expression.'*

out of my Fathers things. The annotated edition w$^d$ be the thing.' It was becoming something of an idée fixe.

Annie wanted Richmond to tackle Smith, hoping that face to face discussions might be easier than negotiation by letter. 'I wrote to George Smith once more about the Edition. I wish you w$^d$ (if you were moved to it) go & see him as it might make it easier for him to discuss it.'[55] But Richmond was himself preoccupied by the inevitable shuffling of jobs at the India Office which followed a new administration. Curzon was returned, but replaced by George Russell as Parliamentary Under-Secretary of State, whose son became his private secretary. It left Richmond temporarily without a promoted position, but his talents were such that the Permanent Under-Secretary, Sir Arthur Godley, whose job Richmond would inherit in 1909, invited him to be his private secretary from the end of September. 'I am heartily glad of a change of work and no longer to be the fag of young men on their promotion. And it is bound to serve me for promotion also.'[56] Annie was delighted. It gave Richmond security – though no more money – and Godley had chosen him on his merits. 'Its very nice to feel so proud of ones husband & I trust if the Coak ever marries she will have as proud a young heart as mine is an old one, when people appreciate & show it.'

Reviews of *Records of Tennyson, Ruskin and Browning* were beginning to appear, and those in the major nationals were all encouraging. But it was Tennyson's death on 6 October which provided the greatest stimulus to sales. Annie was distressed, and relieved that her essay had initially appeared several years earlier, and with his blessing. 'It prevents any sting but at this moment I should like to hug myself in silence & never have printed a word about him.'[57] She was in two minds about attending the Abbey funeral, but in the end she went to say farewell to this early friend of Thackeray's, who had become even closer to his daughters. She sat between Margaret Oliphant and Ellen Terry, letting the latter weep on her shoulder.

When Hallam told her at the end of the month of his intention to write a memoir of his father, with his mother's assistance, it boosted her own commitment to a Thackeray edition, taken on as a similar biographical duty despite her father's proscription. 'I have just been reading your delightful sketch of him again – I wish that this might stand as the only life, but "ghouls" have begun to dig – & my Father was anxious that some authentic life shld be given to keep out penny-a-liner lies. He hated the biographies of literary men as a rule as much as your Father did.'[58] The provision of an 'authentic life' chimed true with Annie. Her reply makes explicit for the first time her frustration at the constraints which had been placed upon her, and a readiness to set them aside now. 'I often

wish I had been older & more matured when my dearest Daddy spoke
to me abt his life: & that I had asked him to leave it to our discretion. In
his case there were so many complications – not the least my Mothers
illness & possible recovery even then – To write a true life was alas
impossible & a make up one omitting all that was most real was no
good.'[59] Late in November, as Minny's anniversary came round once
more, Annie wrote to Lady Tennyson. Hallam's work on the Memoir
had begun in earnest, and Pinkie had been asked to pass on anything that
he might be able to use in his work, for in recent years she had visited
Farringford and Aldworth far from frequently than had Annie.

> Pinkie tells me she has been writing down all she can find
> recorded of His dear words.... Monday is the day my Minnie
> left us 17 years ago & all this time always seems to me holy
> somehow & as if <u>now</u> more than at any time I may write to
> you dear dear Lady Tennyson.... How people do love & feel
> his greatness & how they will prize anything of him you &
> Hallam give to the world to his friends & loving followers.[60]

Public gestures of commemoration were important for Annie.
She approached Watts about a possible Thackeray portrait for Trinity
College, Cambridge, for although she had heard rumours that he felt
unable to undertake it, she needed to ask him herself – 'dearest Mary
& Signor I know so well that it may be utterly impossible that dont
even answer this except one day to tell me how you both are'.[61] She
can hardly have been surprised at his reluctance to execute a portrait
from memory. He recommended that she approach Millais instead.

> I would have given much to have painted your Father &
> asked him to sit more than once.... I cannot undertake any
> portraits excepting such as are to be devoted to the object of
> helping to form a true national Gallery. A portrait now unless
> painted on these terms would make me so nervous fearing
> failure that I should be sure to fail; also though I knew your
> Father my memory for faces & characteristics is so curiously
> bad there would be no chance of my doing any thing that
> could possibly satisfy.[62]

Richmond's attacks from Ménière's disease returned during the
early part of 1893. The Ritchies left Wimbledon to stay for a short
while at Cheyne Walk with Gerald and Margie, home from India for a
few months, so that Richmond was closer to work and able to consult
his doctors more readily. Billy boarded at Olive's, although when in
February he and fellow pupil Gilbert Woods fell ill, presumably with

influenza, Annie decided to bring both boys home for nursing, a kindness for which Woods's father, the Master of Trinity, Oxford, was very grateful. 'If you were an Aunt you could not have done more for him.'[63] It was an eye-opener to discover that not all parents treated children as informally or so affectionately as did she and Richmond. That, at least, seems to be the tenor of her comment on a letter from Mrs Woods. 'Poor Gilbert, no wonder he isnt expansive towards his parents.'[64] This was a year during which Annie had two principal preoccupations – a growing concern over Richmond's health, and the pending decision on Billy's future schooling. She felt troubled 'about Rs nerves & my own nerves & impressionableness', grateful that throughout these months 'Pinkie [was] always full of love & help coming steadily all the time'. As for Billy, they got as far as identifying a possible place in an Eton House for him. The options had at first seemed to diminish when Frank Warre Cornish was elevated to Vice-Provost, surrendering his former role as a House master, although Mowbray Morris urged Annie to set this consideration aside. 'It had been pleasant for you, of course – though I am not so sure if it had been best for Bill – to know that your son was under the care of one of the family. But there are many other good houses nestling under Henry's holy shade.'[65] Two months later, Annie felt sufficiently optimistic to be able to tell Emily Tennyson that

> I hope he may get to Eton in the autumn as M^r Lowry has a vacancy. I think his father who has been his constant companion minds the parting even more than I do.... It is a happy time tho' I have a good many anxieties just now & Doctors & Eton Masters seem the most important people in the world & ones heart sinks many a time when one imagines what <u>might</u> be & then come blessings one never dared dream of.[66]

But Blanche's coming to them some time during the summer of 1893, 'strongly opposed to Eton for Billy' was probably decisive.

With such distractions, it seems hardly credible that they should have chosen this as the year in which to instigate elaborate plans for moving house. Concerns about school fees did not prevent them from deciding to build two adjacent houses on a plot in Wimbledon, one of which was intended to provide a regular rental income. Nor were they deterred by their Rosary Gardens experience, of having being unable to afford to live in the house once built. The Wimbledon houses would not be completed until well into 1894, at a cost of more than £3,000,[67] but construction was under way by the middle of 1893. In May, they decided against a Queen Anne style house – presumably Annie had at one point hoped to emulate her father's 1860s project at Palace Green – and instead 'determined on the Jacobean farm-house w[h]. was eventually built'. This would become The End House, in Berkeley Place, and they would be very happy there.

Despite her enthusiasm, little progress was made with the Thackeray edition during 1893. Apart from these preoccupations, a further reason for delay was a project which Richmond had taken on, based on his professional knowledge of India and his occasional journalism and reviews. Sir William Hunter had initially asked for a specialist military history to be published by the Clarendon Press as *Lord Amherst and the British Advance Eastwards in Burma*. Annie was thrilled at this chance for him to write something substantial, worthy of his talents, and for which his expert knowledge made him appropriate. 'I am so excited about L[d]. Amhurst. You are quite quite right & you will do it admirably.'[68] But by March, he had suffered a series of distressing attacks attributed to nervous exhaustion acting on the liver, and Hunter acted to remove any sense of pressure. 'I lose not a moment in assuring you that the book will remain in your hands until you feel really able to write it, without imperilling the progress which you have already made towards convalescence. Dismiss it from your mind till then, & only take it up anew when you feel that you can do so with comfort to yourself.'[69] By July, Hunter had agreed to Annie's involvement, at first with the intention that she should work collaboratively with Richmond, although in due course she took on the bulk of the research, visiting the London Library to read memoirs and diaries. This was a time of great anxiety for her, suggested somewhat cryptically in her journal. 'In g[t] indecision & trouble of mind. Home – Schools – money health – fearing to upset R.' Hunter's initial breezy reassurances were now replaced by talk of deadlines. 'I had hoped that it would be issued long before Christmas: but a work from your joint hands is well worth waiting for. I trust you are feeling stronger, & with pleasant anticipations of an interesting and valuable book <u>not later</u> than five months hence.'[70]

It was about as far from the kind of topic that Annie would have chosen for herself as might be imagined, but she undertook it without complaint, glad to relieve Richmond of worry. She could manage the biographical detail, but the military history – which would have been his portion – was beyond her. Richmond reflected on their current troubles, coloured perhaps by other memories. 'R said speaking of our perturbations. "Thro it all I have felt the only mistake I <u>didnt</u> make was in marrying." Ah! Thank God in heaven for that & Amen & Amen (& I write this in 1899 looking back & thankful to remember).' By November, the Amherst book was still notionally a joint project, though

Annie knew that Richmond was unlikely to be able to clear enough time to complete his part. 'I am trying to get Lady Amhersts diary finished for Richmonds book. But I want him to give it up, for his own work is quite as much as he ought to attempt & he is much too tired at night to set to work again. Anyhow my half will be there for Sir W. Hunter.'[71] In December, she finally told Hunter that Richmond could not finish the task, at which point he arranged for Richardson Evans to take on the outstanding parts. The book was eventually published as the joint venture of Annie and Evans.

Although not her only work during the year, it was the most demanding. A couple of pieces appeared in *Macmillan's Magazine*, including another 'Chapter' prompted by the death of Fanny Kemble, but she was not very satisfied, thinking the essay 'much too long & diffuse', and was typically modest when she read Henry James's tribute to their mutual friend, 'a mountain top quite beyond my level'.[72] She may have been startled by the strong feelings that Fanny Kemble could provoke, even in death, for the editor of *Macmillan's Magazine*, on the basis of just two brief meetings with Mrs Kemble, called her 'the most disagreeable woman I had ever encountered'.[73] Annie also provided some 'Reminiscences' by way of an introduction to a collection of Julia Margaret Cameron's photographs,[74] and her preface to Mary Mitford's *Our Village*. But always the great task loomed over her, and in her journal she records how in March she was 'puzzled ab'. everything, about Edition & correspondence', and that she had resolved to work on no more than one introduction at a time.

The year's great achievement was in finally settling on a school for Billy. After the months of anxiety, he started in September at Sedbergh School, beautifully situated on the edge of the Yorkshire Dales and just a step from the Lake District. He proved to be ideally suited to Sedbergh, which was small and run almost as a family enterprise by headmaster Henry Hart and his wife, a sister of the Ritchies' friend, Henry Lawrence. It had a sound academic tradition, recruiting sons of northern business men in the main, and without the competitive drive of Eton where Billy was unlikely to have succeeded. The bracing location certainly helped him to thrive after earlier concerns about his thinness and susceptibility to illness. They had decided in principle by the end of July that Sedbergh was the answer, having been told by Mrs Hart that Billy could become a member of their own School House, and it remained only for Annie to visit to decide whether this was indeed the right place. She went alone on 2 September and stayed for four nights, her first impressions being favourable. 'It is a sweet green place which has something Swiss about it very silent fresh clean a little damp a sort of Zermatt feel. Every thing is bright green & the climate is something like Coniston but bracinger. As for the schoolhouse & the little wooden boys rooms & the long dining room it is all anything one could possibly wish – Its <u>smaller</u> than I expected but none the worse for that.'[75] She discovered that only one Sedbergh boy had ever had to leave because of 'delicacy', ironically that being the son of their own former Young Street doctor, John Jones Merriman. She was rather alarmed to hear of the regular runs on the moors, undertaken by the whole school, but the beauty of the moors was striking. 'I am a little less enthusiastic for last night the cold damp of the mist woke me up – & I have been thinking that a 10 miles run before afternoon school is very tremendous but of course it is on these lovely delicate moors, & M$^r$ Hart often goes too.'[76] By the time she left, she had seen enough to feel confident that it would do. 'So I have left the signed paper for M$^{rs}$. Hart & one can only say ones prayers & do the best. He will like those hillsides there are 9 new boys coming.'[77] On her return, she and Richmond talked until midnight, and agreed that Sedbergh was the right thing for Billy – 'a gulp, agreed'.

She was reassured by their friend James Cropper, who lived close to Sedbergh, his comments on the boys and their family backgrounds offering revealing detail on the perceived pecking order and social nuances of contemporary public-schooling.

> In the matter of learning, I am sure Sedbergh will satisfy you. In the matter of care by masters, there seems to be nothing lacking, and the isolation of the place keeps these men to their work and helps the public spirit which is so manifest there.
>
> There is a manliness about the whole school, which I think makes war with loafing & cliques – and though I consider that a considerable number of the boys are sons of what may be called second class (not second rate) people, yet I gather from a lady friend who has a son at Sedbergh, that there is no lowering of manners, & no want of attention to the niceties of life.
>
> We all want so many things for our children, and above all that grace which is part a heritage, and part an infection, but perhaps even more, a result of the inspiring influences of both books and women.
>
> Your son will in any case have those, and he will also have opportunity of knowing & choosing his friends at the University.[78]

Just a fortnight later she returned to Sedbergh, this time with Billy, and as they arrived the hills 'looked like Heaven'. While he sat a preliminary examination to determine his form, coming out 'good second class', Annie needed to calm herself. 'Many qualms about the over-strain of school. Dont expect more than is possible. Love & dont fuss & trust in God & trust in the <u>Self</u> he has given you & in R's love & the childrens.' She stayed a few days, and then left early on the Monday morning, watching as Billy walked up the hill to start his new life as a public schoolboy.

During Billy's first term his parents made separate extended visits, staying at the White Hart in Sedbergh. Their active affection for both of their children was notable, and in the midst of their busy lives they never cut them out. Some of Annie's most charming letters are those she wrote to Billy during his Sedbergh years, for she missed him terribly, and Richmond too kept up an affectionate and amusing correspondence with 'my dear Billiki', signing himself 'Wizz', admitting to Annie that on leaving Sedbergh after his first visit in October he had 'blubbered like a seal'. Richmond's view of the Sedbergh boys seemed to confirm James Cropper's, though quite on what he based his estimate is hard to say − not on their haircuts alone, presumably. 'The boys of course are not up to the Eton level, but there is nothing to be ashamed of in them. They all have their hair cut by the cricket professional who employs a sort of mowing machine, Billy says; & as he had just gone his rounds, they all looked rather like convicts.'[79] Each end-of-term was anticipated with great excitement, and at the end of this first one Billy was welcomed home to Wimbledon with fireworks, which spooked the horse pulling his luggage from the station.

On Christmas eve, as Annie reviewed the previous twelve months for Emily Tennyson, she was simply grateful that the year was closing so much more calmly than it had started off.

> Bill has come home well and grown in every way, broader − stronger − happy. It was such a <u>pinching</u> anxiety sending him off − I can use no other word, that to have him back so improved & so comfortable in every way is an indescribable relief....
>
> It has been a year of such anxiety that I dont know how to believe that all is ending so peacefully & I feel very very thankful & my heart very full − R[d]. is <u>ever</u> so much better tho he is only out of Influenza now again, & so am I, for I too succombed.... I have finished one or two

little undertakings too, but the longest & most difficult –
the Edition of my Fathers books w[h]. I want to put together
with notes & quotations from his correspondence – seems
farther & farther off. I often wonder how Hallams book is
advancing. I do hope it does not try you both very much.
One changes so. Some days I can write other days every
thought seems to jar.[80]

Her one disappointment was that, as yet, the Edition had not progressed
much further than being her little dream. When she had written to
Emily at the start of the year, she had been nervous and cautious about
Richmond's health, about Billy's future, and about her work in hand.
She had turned round this last anxiety into encouragement for Hallam's
work on the Tennyson memoir.

How I do look forward to reading what you will give to all
who loved him. I think that means all who ever came across
his dear path. I do feel so much for Hallam. When I, old &
tough as I am, try to put things together about my Father I get
paralysed but if I begin about something else & let the things
come, not feeling sure whether or not I shall publish them
then I can write, & I believe if he wrote a very great deal for
his children & himself & afterwards took out what was fitted
for publication (& so little makes such a great difference) he
w[d] find it easier. Forgive my boring suggestions & dont repeat
them if you think they will worry him, but I am sure one has
to adapt oneself to oneself as much as to other people.[81]

To suggest that it was necessary to write uninhibitedly about those
closest to one in order to 'let the things come' was doubtless good
advice. If she could only follow it herself she would be well set up for
the serious work which faced her.

# Six

# THAT HISTORY HAS LASTED ON
## (1894-1895)

*What a difference these last five years have made in my life &*
*my way of life. My mother's death has made me feel like an old*
*woman. Till then I felt ill but not old.*

Annie's Journal
1894

Half a century had passed, a whole lifetime since Thackeray had con-
cluded that it was no longer possible for Isabella to continue living
at home with him. For all of these years she had been separated from
her family, forgotten by all but Annie who visited regularly. She was
not institutionalised, so in that sense was more humanely treated than
Laura, who became an inmate at the Earlswood Asylum for Idiots
and Imbeciles. It is quite possible that grandmother and eldest granddaughter never met. Isabella's dangerously unpredictable behaviour
after Minny's birth seems not to have been repeated in later years,
and she lived out her time peacefully and simply in the home of the
Thompsons, her permanent carers, in Leigh-on-Sea, near Southend.

Only Annie documents this continuing life, noting her own visits
as well as the times when Isabella, accompanied by Mrs Thompson,
would come to stay. There are also letters, gentle communications of
great affection, giving her mother news of Hester and Billy, of her
writing projects, her holiday plans, sending thanks for birthday wishes
or for Mrs Thompson's 'most delicious jam'. They are optimistic and
encouraging, conscious of their fragile, unworldly recipient, although
Annie did touch on Tennyson's death, inviting her child-like mother
to recall memories of earlier times. 'We all feel very sad to have lost
our dear poet our dear old friend Tennyson. You must remember him
young & with thick brown hair – but indeed until he was near 80 he
remained young, as Browning did. Poets dont grow old somehow &
drink in new spiritual life & youth from the nature around them.'[1]

Much had happened since those early married years, when Isabella had doubted her domestic skills as she struggled to meet Thackeray's expectations of his young wife. Much had happened, that is to say, in the lives of husband and children, whereas for Isabella nothing had happened at all, not for fifty years. Overwhelmed by post-natal depression, the charming and naïve voice had fallen silent as life moved ahead without her. We know virtually nothing of the intervening years, neither her reaction to her husband's death, nor to Minny's – assuming that she was told of either, or that she was capable of understanding what they meant. Years later, Hester remembered an occasion when some dim flickering of memory prompted her grandmother to say that 'once I had a little daughter just like you'.[2] Yet the tone of Annie's letters suggest that her mother was capable of rational understanding, and that her mental health actually stabilised as she grew older. A few previously unknown letters in Isabella's own hand, prompted perhaps by Mrs Thompson, indicate a sketchy grasp of the world beyond her own, without showing any desire to rejoin it. She writes, for instance, with affection and a studied formality at Christmas 1887. 'I read with great pleasure the account of your expedition across the common with the blessed merry skittish Donkey. You put me in mind of Moore's ballad of Love with a humour. M^rs Thompson begs your acceptance of two of her prettiest cards for Hester & Billy. With our united best wishes for the year to come and for a happy Christmas and prayers for your health and prosperity. I remain ever your affectionate Mammy.'[3] Her last surviving letter shows a quiet contentment in her small routines, and a continuing interest in the doings of her grandchildren.

I am sorry to say that we have been tormented here with a very nasty cough. I am advising barley water or gruel & nitre to get rid of it…. So Billy has attained his 9th year and Hester will have attained her 11th next year, and so he is learning the Carpenters art. It must be very interesting. I recollect having 2 country hats made for me of wood shavings!!! This is just the dull part of the year for Leigh. We had 2 visits from South End last week and 2 today from Town….

We have been employed making all sorts of shirts and chemises and planting our usual potatoes, and a good many sticks for future fruit. And now the eveng. shades prevent me so with love & kisses I must conclude ever your
aff^t. Mammy
I G C Thackeray[4]

Annie hints in a later letter that her mother was susceptible to depression and anxiety, which perhaps made it impossible for her to cope with living unassisted. 'I am so grieved you are saddened by the sad things & storms in the papers. You see they dont put the happy little things in, only the catastrophes! If they had described Billy waking up at 6 this morning & rushing to see what birthday presents were there I think it would have made you laugh.'[5]

In the summer of 1892, Isabella's increasing frailty caused Annie to visit her twice within a fortnight. On the first occasion, she found her mother 'very rational & sweet but I saw the D[r] who said she only just missed a stroke – However with care & quiet & calm so much can be done & M[rs] Thompson is about again & admirable – What a blessing those good people are.'[6] The costs of her care were met from Thackeray's estate by twice-yearly dividends derived from a lump sum invested on her behalf. In practice this may not have proved sufficient, for Annie and Richmond sought court approval to realise some of the capital to cover the excess. Their lawyers requested clarification about the arrangements for Isabella's upkeep.

> The Judge's chief clerk seems to be under the impression that the dividend on the Bank stock paid to you and M[rs] Ritchie half yearly ought to be amply sufficient for the maintenance and support of M[rs] Thackeray, and under these circumstances we shall be obliged to trouble you to make another affidavit. Will you be good enough to supply us with the following information to enable us to prepare the affidavit
>
> Where does M[rs] Thackeray live. In a private house or a private Lunatic asylum?
>
> The name of the Person at that House who is responsible for the custody & safety of M[rs] Thackeray.
>
> Amount paid for her maintenance during the last year, and whether such amount has increased or decreased during the time she has been at the house.
>
> Is M[rs] Thackeray entitled to any further money (the income of which is paid to you for her maintenance) besides the sum of £5565.13.5 India Stock paid into Court in the administration action on the death of M[r] Thackeray. The dividend on this sum is roughly speaking £108 odd a half year.[7]

During her 1892 visits, the Thompsons revealed to Annie that they had received an offer for their house, Eden Lodge (now demolished), as they were considering a move to a smaller, more manageable property. Annie was sure that the offer was lower than the market value, and urged them to hold out for more, but she also wondered whether it might not be sensible for Isabella herself to buy the house and its substantial plot of land so that the Thompsons could continue to look after her there. 'I told them [£1000] wasnt eno' & I said that they had better let Mama buy it than turn her out – I dont know if she could – but it w<sup>d</sup>. be a very nice thing to leave Billy.' Should the time come when Mrs Thompson had to stop caring for her mother, Annie and Richmond planned to pay her an annual pension of £12, just as they – and Thackeray before them – had provided for Isabella's former carer, Mrs Bakewell. 'You can get a lovely little old fashioned cottage at Leigh for £12 a year.'[8] In fact, when Isabella's estate was finally wound up, Julia Stephen stepped in to share the costs of the pension with Annie, presumably with Leslie's approval.

Visits to Leigh did not distress Annie, who drew comfort from her mother's gentle, guileless temperament. She was still able to draw upon the innate musicality which had so attracted Thackeray to the young Irish girl in Paris, and even after her stroke-like symptoms continued to play Gluck and Handel on the piano 'most beautifully – better than I have ever heard her'. Annie told her mother about a dinner with Millais, Leighton and Joachim, when the great violinist played Schumann (with Pinkie accompanying him at the piano), after which Annie had told him that 'I ought to love music for you were a real musician'.[9] During 1893, at the height of her concerns about Richmond's poor health and Billy's schooling, a visit to Leigh triggered a powerful emotional release as Annie experienced a rare role reversal, surrendering with an almost childlike dependence to the simple, trusting presence of the mother for whom she had been responsible for so many years. 'I was really floored one day with worry & nerves when I went to Mamas & lay on the sofa there while she played her sweet hymn tunes & I felt like a child again & all unlocked & cried & cried.'

After this lifetime of waiting, the end came quickly. Early in January 1894 a telegram summoned Annie, and by the time she arrived at midday Isabella was already unconscious and breathing heavily. She had suffered the threatened stroke. Annie took her mother's hand, and it 'felt like her & me together thro' it all'. Julia Stephen came for a while to be with Annie, who that night took turns with Mrs Thompson and the nurse to sit up. Writing to Margie in India later, Annie calmly records something of Isabella's last hours, privileged to have been with her at the end, something denied her when her father and Minny had died. This untroubled departure helped to make some sense of those earlier, frightful ones.

Pinkie will have told you that I was telegraphed for on
Wednesday & that when I got to Leigh my dear little mama
no longer knew me. She lay on her bed but she was not
conscious any more. She had been quite well & playing the
piano for some children to dance on Monday, & she was
sewing on Tuesday evening when M$^r$ Thompson came in
with that picture of Sedbergh w$^h$. she liked & w$^h$. he had
had framed and she looked at it & said 'very pretty' & then
suddenly she fainted. They carried her up to her room & sent
for help but tho' she rallied at first unconsciousness came
on. Thank God she was spared all suffering, for she might
have been paralysed had she lived. It was apoplexy of the
heart....

About 5 o'c in the morning I went for a rest for I did not
think her end so near. In about an hour I awoke & came back
& she lay quite still breathing heavily with Mary Anne the
lady help they have had of late attending to her & wiping
her face & putting hot bottles to her dear feet. About 8 in the
morning the doctor came by the train from Southend & we
pulled up the blinds. As he came into the room some change
seemed to come. Something so quiet & so mighty a light an
infinite revelation I thought the sunlight was dazzling my
eyes & I looked up at the window by her bed but there was
only dull dull grey & this glorious brightness & radiance in
her face.

Nothing has ever made me realise the hope of hopes &
the Kingdom beyond as that minute did & what my sweet
meek mother taught me, as if she had looked into the secrets
of God & lingered to tell them.

She looked very wise & stern in her coffin with a sort of
smile & a new face fine & different altogether. I should not
have known her but it seemed to me as if all a whole lifetime
of mind & power spoke though she was silent.[10]

Isabella, 'my kind, sweet, patient mother',[11] died on 11 January,
aged seventy-six. Before returning home, Annie agreed that the
funeral should proceed without delay, for 'the strain was great for the
poor kind Thompsons and I too longed that there should be no more
agitation'. Mr Thompson took charge of the burial arrangements
which would be at the Leigh cemetery, for Annie had decided against
returning her mother's body to join Thackeray at Kensal Green. It
was right to have decided in favour of Leigh, where her mother's last

contented years had been spent with her constant companions, and appropriate that Thackeray should rest undisturbed with his mother, whom Isabella had never really succeeded in replacing. Richmond met Annie at Fenchurch Street station, and on their way to Wimbledon they saw at Earl's Court the billboards already announcing the 'Death of Mrs Thackeray', surprising news to those unaware of her survival so many years after her husband's death. Most touching of all for Annie was the greeting from Hester and Billy. 'They really loved her & they cried & cried for two nights – Darling Hester reproaching herself & sweet little Bill breaking down utterly.'

In her several accounts of Isabella's last moments, Annie dwells on the wisdom which seemed to come at the end, a reward for a life lived so purely and so simply, the damaged mind made whole again. 'I saw her dear face so changed. <u>Stern</u> & tender & noble. I could hardly have known her. All her <u>sense</u> was there.' 'When my mother died I realised what she was and how little the shadow of her life had touched her dear radiant spirit. Her face was like the face of one who <u>knew</u> and was made great.' 'Her death was something far beyond peace. It seemed to me like a reality of Life and Knowledge, and her dear face looked translated, supreme. I have no words to tell you how great she seemed to me.'[12] They took the children to Leigh two days later for the funeral service at St Clement's church, and Julia Stephen and Margie's father, Edward Thackeray, also attended. 'As I went down in the train I found myself longing for Minnie & your mother & when y$^r$ Father came in it seemed like a dream & all so natural.'[13] Mrs Thompson, the companion of many years, was inconsolable, 'quite broken and overcome'.[14] Her husband played the organ, and the choir sang 'O rest in the Lord' from Mendelssohn's *Elijah*. A few months later, Annie arranged for an Irish cross to mark her mother's grave in the Leigh cemetery. With parents, grandparents and sister all dead, she was now the only survivor from her own childhood, yet as she tried to explain to Mrs Hart, her own children somehow carried that past forward within their lives. 'And my dear Mama's death seemed to make us realise only the more how the children have grown up to understand and share our lives, and even things which they could only guess at. Bill came with us to her dear funeral and Hester and somehow now I feel that the future inevitable partings won't be quite such partings for them.'

A few months later, after the brother of an old friend had died, Annie drew on the image of Isabella's face transfigured in death to give some meaning to the troubled years of her father's marriage. 'I felt that if my dearest Father could have seen her peaceful radiant look the bitter past w$^d$. have seemed less sad to him, & that one does not know – ever – ever what secret blessing & reassurance may be in store for the mourners or for those suffering under the dispensations of life.'[15] Only a few people fully understood the poignancy for her. Leslie reached out an affectionate hand. 'It seems very sad and strange.... It is a pang to see the old links snapping & feel that we are growing more solitary – let us keep the closer.'[16] For Henry James too, who had always admired Thackeray and by now was close to Annie, it was the link with her father's personal history which was here brought to mind. He read the announcement of Isabella's death. 'I can scarcely tell you in how friendly – in how affectionate a spirit, I enter into that sense, which I know must be strong in you today of the sadness of feeling that so long an interest has ended, so immemorial an element of your life.... All good lovers of your great father, too, must surely have been moved at thinking that something could still happen to-day to what was left of his so personal history. It makes us feel, that that history has lasted on – and that he himself might have remained.'[17]

During her mother's lifetime, Annie could never have written freely about her father's early life, and particularly of their marriage. As it was, she would only touch discreetly on Isabella's breakdown and removal from the family home, stressing instead the simple happiness of the early years of marriage, but it was at last something which could emerge, now that her mother's own story was complete. Yet the death knocked her back, and the good resolutions set out just days before Isabella's final illness – 'Determined to go on with the Edition sorting papers &ct' – were set aside. In any case, Richmond's abandoned Amherst book still needed some final work, after which her introductions to a clutch of Maria Edgeworth's novels preoccupied her. She would go with Hester to Ireland at the end of May, having contacted various Edgeworth relations. 'I thought I should <u>realise</u> it all so much better if I could see the places & spaces mentioned that I determined to take this little journey with my child.'[18] Twenty years later she was decidedly ambivalent about her own Irish inheritance, conscious of her father's difficulties with his mother-in-law during Isabella's decline into illness. 'I love Ireland & the Irish but I have absolutely no sympathy with my Irish half or their wild untidy cold blooded genius.'[19]

She had reached an agreement in 1893 with a dealer to sell the manuscript of Thackeray's *Philip* for £100 to a Mr Skeffington, part of the bargain being that for an additional £40 she would herself copy out those portions of the book which did not survive in her father's hand. She took the chore with them when she and Richmond visited Billy at Sedbergh late in February 1894. From there they travelled on to St

*Isabella Thackeray's grave at Leigh-on-Sea*

Andrews for the golf, Richmond having taken sick leave because of the depression brought on by constant bouts of nauseating giddiness, symptomatic of Ménière's disease. His doctor urged an extended period of specialist care in Switzerland as 'the nerves are concerned', which suggests that he was close to complete breakdown, but the golf at St Andrews certainly assisted him towards a short-term recovery. Annie sat up at night copying in hotel rooms – 'I am going on writing out Philip w[h] I like doing very much but it takes a most enormous long time'[20] – the £40 reward driving her to complete it on 15 March.

She rejoiced in Richmond's steady improvement at St Andrews, where a new friendship began in confused circumstances. He and Annie had yet to meet, but the admiration of the young Scottish writer J.M. Barrie for Thackeray had led her to invite him to Wimbledon. His reply, forwarded to St Andrews, warns of his likely shyness at their first meeting, reinforces his Thackerayan credentials, and concludes with the promise of a private entertainment for Billy.

> You had better be told in advance that for the first hour or so I shall present a semi-terrified appearance, as it will take me that time to get used to the great shade your name alone conjures up. That heading in Esmond 'I go to Cambridge & do but little good there' was the motto of my college days (with Edinburgh for Cambridge) except that I can add 'But read Thackeray about 16 times'. I used to wonder in the streets if people passing had read him, & cd scarcely resist raising my hat politely & saying 'Excuse me, sir or madam, but have you read 'The Newcomes'. But for all that it was for their own sake that I got to love your books. What an exquisite touch the eyeglass is to the picture of you & your boy … I am rather good at boys when I get them alone (mum before their parents as another boy wd be), & look forward to teaching this one certain Thrums revels that will give his mother fits, and probably spoil his father's hat.[21]

On the day that she received this, Annie was walking with Richmond around the old parts of St Andrews when they came upon Andrew Lang with a stranger, 'a short pale tiny silent little person & he mumbled something'. They all went on together, but it was some time before Richmond realised that this was Barrie himself. 'M[r] Barrie gave a faint cry of horror & said "I thought you were in Yorkshire – I thought you must be some other M[rs] Ritchie" – I like him very much but he is hardly bigger than a quill pen & most horribly pale with a little hair & two nice kind eyes.'[22] In this letter to Hester, who was staying with Leslie and Julia in her parents' absence, Annie adds a special message for the young Virginia Stephen, with whom she shared a taste for the absurd. 'Tell Ginia there are two epitaphs in the cathedral here so & so fell off the top mizzen into Jesu's arms, & then another. Here we lie horizontal like a ship in stays.'

During this same trip north Annie found herself dreaming frequently of her mother, 'always peaceful & tender. Oh my darling what a good invention daughters & mothers are'.[23] They read of FitzJames Stephen's death while they were away, which left Annie very sad, for Fitzy had been especially fond of both Thackeray sisters. She heard from Leslie two days later, a 'dear sad kind letter'.

> How good he always was – I remember how he tried to be kind in those dark days in 75 and how I always felt him to be a tower of strength to me.... The world is different for me henceforth. He has not really been here for a long time; but the final separation makes me feel the solitude. I have lost many of my best friends & but for the children it would be a desert I live in. That, however, is a large exception.
>
> Well, I hope that I love better all who are left. I think of you very often & I never think of you without a tenderness wh. I cannot always show.[24]

They returned to Sedbergh on their way south, in time for Billy's fourteenth birthday. As usual, they were financially stretched, the costs of the new house a particular drain this year. She would write to Billy in May about his hopes for a camera, regretting having to deny him anything. 'I always feel that to refuse you or Hester things is a real practise in self-education for Pop & me. We shall have to be very economical till we have paid for the move.'[25] But two years later, he received for his sixteenth birthday not just a microscope but his own bicycle, which Richmond and Hester took all the way to Sedbergh from where the three of them went on ambitious cycling expeditions.

Annie longed for building work on the End House to be completed, so that a new start might be made. 'I do feel we have gone on too long at the same groove, for our house is like a medical boarding house rather than a gentlemans suburban villa.'[26] The improvement in Richmond's health seen at St Andrews was only temporary, and his attacks began again after he returned to work and continued through the early summer. Just before they moved to the End House in June, Annie was called to the India Office to bring him home, although by August she struck an optimistic note. But she did not gloss over the reality of the debilitating symptoms of Ménière's disease, and was concerned to ease his comfort at work. 'I think if he gets a sofa there & can lie down flat the moment these giddinesses seize him he will be able to avoid better these horrid breakdowns which are such a handicap upon him & which certainly do spoil everything while they last.'[27]

There were other worries too. Laura's condition deteriorated, and Annie's visits to the Earlswood asylum troubled her. On 24 April she found 'my darling Laura very very ill. Home dreadfully

shaken & perturbed', and both in June and at the end of October
she returned 'very sad'. It really seemed that there was nothing to
be done, although a year later, when Annie took Stella Duckworth
with her, the sweet nature of Leslie's stepdaughter acted like a balm
on Laura. Annie recognised that if there was to be anything like a
hopeful future for Minny's daughter, it had to be as part of her new
family. After Stella's sudden death, she amended her account of the
visit, for even that possibility had now been lost. 'Went with Stella to
see Laureli at Earlswood. She was terribly excited at first, but when
her attaque de nerfs was over she began to listen to Stella looking at
her as if her little heart would break out of her body. It went to mine
– came home tired, jealous, thankful; Laura has so longed after them
all. Stella has all along been so wise & sweet about her, there seems
a hope of better things (It was but a flash. Laura has never come back
quite again).'[28]

Having despatched the last of the Maria Edgeworth introductions
to Macmillans and able to enjoy the prospect of 'going back to my
dear Papa today with a long breath of relief',[29] Annie was struck down
by flu in the autumn which left her exhausted for some weeks. Jane
Strachey helped out with the Edgeworth proof-reading. For a moment
Annie became convinced that the Edition would never be completed,
but at the end of the year, on another visit to the Bells at Redcar,
she was able to record that work on its first two volumes was at last
under way. 'Dec 7th. To Redcar viâ the George Smiths. Review of my
memoirs in P.M.G. Began Edition Vanity Fair … Began Pendennis.'
But still no publishing agreement had been reached with Smith, and
instead she was planning to write a series of prefaces to the novels
for America, where a lively interest in Thackeray had been sustained
ever since his two lecture tours in the 1850s. Lunch with the Harpers'
agent Richard Bowker in March 1895 led to a suggestion that she
should try to publish the prefaces simultaneously in America and the
Cornhill. This can only mean that Bowker envisaged that they might
be detached so as to appear in succeeding Cornhill numbers, and is
interesting only for indicating that whereas an American deal for the
Edition at this stage was Annie's principal target, nothing had yet been
agreed with Smith, Elder for the home market.

Word got around that Annie was contemplating a major new project. She heard from George Grove, the former editor of Macmillan's
Magazine, who offered to correct Thackeray's textual errors in any
new edition of his works, not realising that these kinds of details
were frankly of little concern to Annie. Strictly speaking, she was not
proposing to 'edit' the works at all. She must have blanched at his list

of amendments, it never having occurred to her that such pedestrian matters might be part of what editing could involve.

> I hear that you are going to do a new edition of your fathers immortal books. May I help you? – in a <u>very</u> small way – but I want – & have wanted for an immense time – to get the <u>text</u> correct; and if you would allow me should like to read it all right through again and show you what I think are the mistakes. There are a few that I have already noticed – but there must be more. To give you an instance in chap lxvii of Pendennis is the following sentence 'and he rather respected his adversary, and his courage in facing him, as of old days in the fencing-room; he would have admired the opponent who hit him'. This must be wrong. Of course the semi colon should come, not after 'fencing-room' but, after 'him' – There are worse errors in V. Fair – but for the sake of your father and of you I should be very much honoured if you wd. let me point them all out to you.[30]

On New Year's day 1895 Annie sat high up in a packed Albert Hall listening enraptured to Clara Butt in Handel's *Messiah*. Ten days later came the first anniversary of 'dear Mamas day', but it did not distress her, and she sat sleepily in the hall of the End House waiting for Hester and Billy to return from a dance, just as years before she had sat up half the night for Minny, leaning out of the window at Onslow Square to watch as the dawn crept in. In the evenings, Richmond read aloud Stevenson's last novel, *The Ebb-Tide*, and a couple of days later they maintained a seasonal ritual of all going to the pantomime, at the Lyceum Theatre. Then it was time for Billy to return to Sedbergh, a moment which Annie always dreaded, though this time he left in good spirits.

The calm start to the year seemed hopeful, but within a month or so there were money panics. She was still in bed when Richmond came to her room and they had an 'agitating talk', as he believed that they were not living within their income. It can have been neither a startling nor an unfamiliar conclusion. They made their usual promises to each other to keep regular household accounts, and as Annie wryly noted in her journal five years later, '1899 ditto'. More cryptically, she described a change in her behaviour towards their domestic staff in terms which suggest that she had been too informal with them hitherto. 'Determined to allow more company down stairs, to be more <u>mysterious</u> in my dealings with the Servants.'[31] She and Hester went to Sedbergh at the beginning of March where the snow-covered hills were dazzling, and seeing Billy again was like 'a delicious gulp of cold water'. She kept from her original diary the words she wrote whilst still in bed the next morning. 'How happy am I at this moment after my long bout of depression & discontent. Not yet up. Expecting Billy.'[32] It was touching to be told by one of his Sedbergh friends that 'I confide everything to Billy'. For the rest of her life her love for her son had a special intensity, so that being in his presence was always 'a blessing'. A few days after they had returned to Wimbledon she sent him a few lines copied from an early Thackeray letter, written before his marriage. 'He says to his Mother "When I marry I shall have more amusing things to tell you & all about Billy cutting his teeth & so forth". It looks quite natural tho' it was only a joke.'[33] It seemed like a magic connection across the generations.

Billy in turn adored her, something which his own children noticed in future years. His daughter recalls how 'he said she was so real. I think with others she laid on her Irish charm but with him she was entirely at her ease.'[34] As if to balance this, Hester drew unusually close to Richmond, offering him unquestioning devotion such that during one of his difficult periods of illness in 1894 Annie seriously contemplated removing Hester from school at Allenswood so that she might spend more time with her father. Marie Souvestre managed to dissuade her from doing this. This tendency for each child to side with one parent, perhaps prompted by Annie and Richmond themselves indicating an occasional partiality, led to tensions during Richmond's last years, causing Annie some unhappiness.

The death of Charles (Cheri) Carmichael in March resurrected memories of early days with Minny in Paris, for the birth of the Carmichael-Smyths' nephew in 1844 had been a moment of great excitement. Annie visited Cheri's widow a few weeks later and was immediately surrounded by ghosts. 'It was like a scene in Balzac all the old familiar faces on the walls.'[35] More shattering was the sudden death of Julia Stephen, news of which came by telegram on 5 May. Annie went to Hyde Park Gate two days later to lay her flowers on Julia's coffin, telling Billy of the prevailing sadness. 'Poor Thoby & Adrian are very brave & good & the little girls comfort their Father. I have lost the dearest friend that ever lived.'[36] As always, she gave herself up to the needs of others, looking after the younger children in the garden of the Hyde Park Gate house while Richmond and Hester attended the funeral, which Gussie wrote about later. 'It was all very simple & dignified with crowds of friends who cared. Henry James looked so kind so sad so understanding. I saw his face once & never liked him so much.'[37] Leslie was crushed by his loss and Annie did her best for him in the early days, knowing that he clung to her in his misery.

> It seems so sad now at H.P.G. that I hardly like to go, for I feel they are best alone tho' at first Leslie seemed to hanker after me a little – at least to ask for me. Stella is I fear quite overdone but the boys seem full of pluck & goodness indescribable. Trouble in the world seems to bring its own special goodness [and] unselfishness. Henry James wrote something Leslie liked. 'In this horrible world' he said 'the only happiness we really hold safe is that which is over.' But Leslie has those dear good children to see happy again, & started in life & then at least he will have fulfilled his mission.[38]

She was sensitive to the needs of the one person likely to be over-looked at such a time, but it was evident that Laura comprehended nothing of what had happened. 'On Wed^y. I went to see Laura who was much better & ran to meet me & threw her arms round my neck. But she cannot understand about dear Aunt Julia & I did not try to make her understand.'[39]

Through all of this she was determinedly putting together the early versions of the three first prefaces of the Biographical Edition, *Vanity Fair, Pendennis* and the *Yellowplush Papers*. A supreme irony underpins this vital shaping of the Thackeray legacy, undertaken over thirty years after his death and for which Annie's appropriateness was self-evident, it being work for which temperamentally and technically she could scarcely be less well equipped, requiring organizing skills which were almost beyond her. She seemed no more confident several years into the project than at its outset, and did not conceal her self-doubts, setting them out like a moment of confession by Mrs Hilbery in Virginia Woolf's *Night and Day*. 'I am not very good at facts & few people can feel more incapable than I do of following up a clear & sustained thread of history & dates combined.'[40] She lacked the eye for detail with which George Grove could triumphantly trap the errors in a text, and even the process of sorting her father's papers and assembling them into a coherent order threatened to defeat her. There are despairing notes in the journal, but fortunately Hester could be relied upon to sort things out.

> 18 [April] Writing h.ache & nervous. E.F.G. book. Hester helped me. I in a cobweb over it & rather despairing
>
> 19 Hopelessly confused. Got Hester to help. Cheered. She worked carefully sorted 1829. 30. 31. 32.

But she staged something of a coup when in sending off these first three drafts to Smith, Elder, she made it clear that it was her wish to publish the new edition in America whether or not it appeared at home. If they had been equivocal thus far about the enterprise, the firm now swiftly committed to her. In recent years, George Smith had handed over much daily business to his son-in-law, Reginald Smith, whose detailed reply to Annie tried to protect the firm's copyright interests whilst maintaining its customary generous dealings with her. The idea that the prefaces might be published as stand-alone essays 'in periodical and book form' is touched on – the point that Richard Bowker had put to Annie – but more important is the firm's implicit agreement to an entirely new Thackeray edition and an insistence that this should appear simultaneously with any American one. It signals Annie's most significant business triumph in stubbornly pursuing her 'little dream of an edition'. Reginald Smith thanked her for what he called the 'biographies', claiming to have read them with great interest.

> I found that nearly half of the MSS which you have sent consists of extracts from your Father's letters and diaries. These are clearly our copyright, as you will see from a quotation which I enclose from the deed of assignment executed in 1864. I think it is necessary to call your attention to this fact before you enter into any arrangement for the publication of your MSS.
>
> Our position is briefly as follows:– whatever may be our rights, we have no wish to interfere with the publication of your Father's letters and diaries in America so long as that publication does not interfere with our own copyright in this country. And in order that it may not do so, it will be necessary that publication should take place simultaneously in this country and in America.
>
> Nor have we any wish to assert our rights in respect of the publication of the extracts from letters and diaries in this country so long as our copyright is not impugned, – I mean that we could not consent to any publication as a part of your Father's works which would injure our existing editions.
>
> Having made this avowal, I wish to say that we are prepared to make such arrangements with you as we should make if we had no exceptional rights. We are ready either to pay you a sum for your entire rights in the series of papers, or else to publish them or arrange for their publication in

periodical and book form, and perhaps as a part of a new edition of your Father's works in which you might have an interest at all events covering the volume in which your introductory matter appears. I think I can see the way of dealing with the MSS which is most to your interest, and I should be glad if we could exchange our views upon the subject.

I may add that we were misled by the agent of an American firm when we told you that there was no room for a new Edition of your Father's works. We are now satisfied that there is room for a new Edition.[41]

And then there was the good news of a promotion for Richmond. With the collapse of Lord Rosebery's Liberal administration at the end of June and its replacement by the Conservatives under Lord Salisbury, Lord George Hamilton was appointed Secretary of State for India. As always with a change of administration there was an initial uncertainty about how jobs would be apportioned, but Sir Arthur Godley, the Permanent Under-Secretary, thought it likely that Richmond would be invited to be Private Secretary to the new Secretary of State. Annie had some doubts about this prospect, for Richmond had not entirely shaken off the bouts of depression. When the news of the appointment came she felt 'nervous excited glad anxious', having already confided in Billy that 'I dont know if I hope he will get it or not',[42] but as Richmond had pointed out, 'as likely as not the new Gov$^t$. will be in for 6 years, & £300 a year is a great difference'.[43] She took Hester and Billy with their cousins Arthur and Charles, sons of Willie and Magdalene Ritchie, to Brighton in August, planning to stay a fortnight but returning early because Richmond was 'profoundly depressed'. The Edition was now creating its own momentum, for although the interest of Smith, Elder had only lately been stirred, American prospects were altogether more encouraging. In mid-August the British agent for the Boston firm of Houghton, Mifflin wrote directly to ask 'what chance there is of their securing the introduction and notes by you for their edition'.[44]

This was not the only interest from across the Atlantic. She had already begun to explore with Macmillans the possibility of their American house taking on the Edition, for which they would offer an advance of £1,000 and royalties on sales. When visiting Europe with his wife, the writer and critic Charles Dudley Warner met Annie in September and recommended that she should consider Harpers as the best American publisher, undertaking to explore the possibilities on her behalf. After returning home he fleshed out their ideas into a very precise prospectus, upon which he urged her to stand firm.

> In pursuance of my promise in our conversations regarding a new Edition of Thackeray, I have had a long talk with Mr. J. Henry Harper, of Harper Brothers, who has just returned from England. I detailed to him my plan for you, as I opined it to you, and I may say, in a general way, that I found him heartily in favor of it, as a good move for you, for the sale of Thackeray's works, and for his firm. I found however that his firm had had some correspondence, or communication, with you on this subject through Osgood, McIlvain of London, and that Harper and Brothers have been ready and anxious to make an arrangement with you for whatever you may do.
>
> The plan, however, that I presented to you, in its fullness, had elements of newness, and it is this plan that I beg you now to understand, has the full approval of the Harpers. And I feel sure that they are ready to carry it out in a manner to be greatly to the benefit of you and your children. In speaking of this to you I think my communication should be regarded as confidential, and that you and Mr Ritchie should decide the matter for yourselves, and not complicate it with partial contracts, for single volumes, or with any reference to existing editions.
>
> Let me re-sketch the plan. A new and complete edition of Thackeray, containing everything that you would like to preserve of his for a final edition. To be illustrated fully and richly, not only with the old pictures, but with portraits and with views of houses and studio's [*sic*] connected with his work, and by a perfect reproduction of his drawings by a new process – a great improvement of them as at present engraved. (Take as an illustration the drawings in The Rose and the Ring. This, by the way, would make a splendid looking book, produced in <u>fac</u> <u>simile</u>, hand-writing and drawings. And this the Harpers would also undertake, I think).
>
> Each volume to have the sort of introduction you are now writing for special volumes, with notes by you, and as full details of his literary life as you can give. This would really be a sufficient biography of the <u>writer</u>, and such an account, incidentally, of the <u>man</u>, as would satisfy any legitimate public curiosity.

> This new material, so interspersed, would enable you to preserve on all the works a new and remunerative copyright. It would not forestall, of course, other editions, or single volumes, but it would in a manner protect itself, by being the most desirable and popular edition.

He urged her to act, believing that if she did not do so, someone else would, for enterprising publishers were on the lookout for reissues of classic authors.

> Suppose you, in a pure business way, state this plan for a new, complete, fully illustrated edition, to Smith, Elder & Co, as a plan you have fully determined on and will carry out. Give them the opportunity to take it up as the English publishers, to be executed, if they choose, in connection with Harper Brothers, upon terms as to expence that they can agree on. Do not be put off by tact, nor be pressured to drop the full new edition, and bring out from time to time detached volumes of the chief fiction. Do not throw away your splendid chance and materials in this dribbling way.
>
> If S. & E. decline, then drop the English market for the present altogether. Make a contract with Harpers for an American edition. You have full moral and legal rights to do that. And when the American edition is under way, you may be sure some English publisher will be glad to come into the arrangement. It is a very big market over here.[45]

It is to their September conversation and this subsequent proposal that the Biographical Edition owes much of its final format. Warner offered a belief in the worthwhileness of the project that had not initially been forthcoming from the Smith, Elder stable.

By the end of May 1895, Leslie had completed the first draft of what would become known as the Mausoleum Book, and during July continued to review his earlier life by going through old letters and papers. He reconsidered his role in the business of Annie's engagement, seeming to want reassurance that he had acted properly by her. '[O]n the whole, I was satisfied that I had substantially done my best to help you.... Naturally, at this time I feel as if I might die – though it is not a bit likely – and that suggests a desire that you should distinctly remember what we were to each other. I think these letters show it.' He also collected together for Annie a large group of Minny's letters to him, knowing just what they would mean to her – 'I am touched by their sweetness and by the affection for us'.[46]

In August he took the children to Freshwater, from where he wrote
again in a mood of deep despair, Annie having urged him to discover
something of Julia in the love of their children.

> I had a strangely vivid dream last night – strange for me
> who seldom dream. I met Julia & found that it had all been a
> mistake. She was going to explain to me how it had happened
> – the mistake, I mean – when I awoke to my misery. – That
> represents my waking state too.... I not only lose her but
> lose all that was most delightful in the rest of the world. I did
> not know before how much she made up my whole feelings,
> even when she was not directly concerned. I am getting
> stronger, though slowly, but even the strength makes me feel
> the blank.... Why should I tell you all this? Partly because I
> can tell it to no one else.... I feel, as you imply, the love of
> my children & a few more is the thing wh. may in time make
> the grief endurable; but at present it brings about as much
> pain as happiness.[47]

It was of course inevitable, but still painful for Annie to have to accept
that the times of Leslie's former happiness with Minny had been
erased from the record once he had become so intensely dependent
upon Julia, his rescuer from that earlier loss.

Richmond's acquisition of a bicycle at the end of the summer
became a new passion for him, to some extent even temporarily
pushing golf to one side. It was the ideal counterbalance to the long,
sedentary hours at the India Office, and he would go for long rides
from Wimbledon, often at night, refreshing himself after hours at his
desk. It lifted him and provided some respite from the episodes of
physical collapse and mental exhaustion. On one day at the end of
September, Annie made a particular note that 'R came home & cycled
by moonlight. It is delightful to see his enjoyment of his work.... Sat in
garden with R. Everything indescribably starry & beautiful.' But within
a fortnight, immediately before leaving for Holland and Germany with
Richmond and Hester, she complained of nervous exhaustion, what
she customarily described as being 'overdone'. A month abroad was
just what they needed. They spent their days in galleries and most
evenings at the opera, at Amsterdam (for the Rembrandts), then
Dresden (where during a performance of a long-forgotten opera, 'I was
thinking of everything else I had ever thought about Papa & Minny &
the old days'), and finally Berlin, where towards the end of their stay
they were invited by Joachim to attend his rehearsals with a student
orchestra. Richmond could not get too much music, sending Pinkie

detailed critiques of the Berlin performances of *Orfeo, Prometheus, Oberon* and *Die Zauberflöte*, for she was the one member of the family whose musical sensibility was equal to his. For Annie, it was the small details of their journeying which prompted a kind of childlike wonder, such as Richmond's command of the tram system in Amsterdam, or the way in which the streets of the Hague were crowded with 'soldiers children messengers carters', or simply when she got her first sight of the 'quaint flat fields, houses, cows in flannel jackets, quaint gables, distant spires'.

They arrived back in England in time for Annie and Hester to hurry to Sedbergh for Billy's confirmation in the school chapel, an occasion of spiritual significance despite doubts about its traditional sacramental meaning. 'He looked like Papa – He looked like Richmond at his age – Very dear pale shining eyed with high shoulders well set up. After tea we sat by the fire. I never can face great emotions but they are there & this was a great emotion – all the things it <u>wasnt</u> for me as well as all it really meant.'[48] A harder duty followed. On 28 November, the twentieth anniversary of Minny's death, she went to Hyde Park Gate to see Leslie 'in his den', and as she tried to lift him from his gloom her thoughts went back across the years which had done little to blunt the sharpness of the memories. And for Leslie too, freshly bruised by his second loss, there was added poignancy as he and Annie, the survivors and now sole witnesses of former happiness, sat together in his study 'remembering that awful day – now 20 years ago but present still minute by minute'.[49]

Seven

# THAT DIVIDED LIFE
## (1896-1899)

*There is only Denis Duval remaining to correct & then the work
will be done. How thankful I am & how I hope & trust my Father
wouldn't have thought I had been indiscreet. But even if he did I
could feel as sure of him as you could of y' Father & me.*

Annie to Billy<br>October 1898

Annie started writing her journal in 1898 or 1899, so we are already
moving within the years which were recent history when she was
putting it together. She added nothing to the journal after the year
1903, except to make occasional amendments to earlier entries,
although her original diary for 1907 survives, as do diaries for each of
the years from 1910 until 1918. The present state of the journal tells
its own story, some of the years from 1895 having been subjected to
later censorship. Individual pages have been removed, and judging by
the cleanness of the cut, a razor blade has been employed. Although
for 1895 this represents the loss of just one page, for 1896 five pages
have been excised (from different places), and a particularly brutal cut
has removed the entire section between June 1898 and mid-November
1899 (a sequence of eleven pages).

There can be no real doubt whose handiwork this represents. At
her death in February 1919, all of Annie's surviving papers passed
to her daughter, not just the archive of her own letters and journals
but also the precious mass of Thackeray letters and other manuscripts
which, in the right market, had significant commercial value. She saw
it as security for Hester, who after Richmond's death continued to live
with her mother during her last years. Billy married in 1906 and made
his career in the law, but Hester, unmarried, was entirely dependent
upon Annie's income. It was probably while working on her mother's

papers for her 1924 memoir that she excised some sensitive passages in the journal and destroyed particular letters. But despite all the care taken to cleanse the record, a few surviving clues throw light on the difficulties of the last years of the century.

One might assume that Hester simply wished to withhold the occasional unguarded journal remark from later eyes, and almost certainly the major deletion from mid-1898 included details of a medical nature, as a glandular condition led to surgery on Annie's neck and a period of convalescence. But this was not the principal cause of Hester's sensitivity. Her intervention was prompted instead by a desire to remove all hints of difficulties in her parents' relationship during these later years, especially as she must have found her own confused feelings and conflicting loyalties challenged when she read her mother's account of these events. It was not just a question of keeping private what should not be made public; a more multi-layered deception was being enacted.

By the start of 1896, events were already troubling Annie. Richmond's health continued to be a concern. She tried hard to shelter him from unnecessary stress, which included not having people to stay. Pinkie was an honourable exception to the rule, but as Annie explained 'except a stray <u>night</u> now & then & <u>you</u> – its quite clear I mustn't have anyone – it seems to make him so oddly nervous'.[1] Abroad, the news from South Africa was not good, with the foiled Jameson raid a crucial event in the approaching war with the Boers, while at home work on the Edition continued to be hard-going. It is remarkable that progress of any kind was made, so chaotic were her working-methods. 'Muddled over my papers & in many agonies finding & losing remembering & forgetting' (4 January). At the end of the year little seemed to have changed. 'Lost all my MSS – or confused it rather – so much for going away. Feel very frantic – H & I are going to sort everything over again' (21 November) – it was Mrs Hilbery and Katharine again. She at last came to a decision about an American publisher, although not without further confusion and the inevitable second thoughts, writing on 23 February to Smith, Elder to announce that she would put herself in Harpers' hands. Charles Dudley Warner's arguments appeared to have been persuasive, for he had written again to urge her 'not to lose sight of the big, <u>complete</u>, fully illustrated edition of Thackeray, for which you can arrange with Messrs Harper & Bros, in case the English publishers do not see their way to it. And do not, please, fritter away your material and your chance by publishing separate volumes.'[2] But she immediately began to doubt herself, a week later reversing her plans and asking Smith, Elder to consider overseeing the entire project, including the American negotiations with Harpers. 'Wrote to Reginald Smith retracting ab$^t$ America & telling him that if they <u>wished</u> it we were prepared to place ourselves in S & E's hands. Much relieved as I was dreading the business details.'[3]

Another crisis had occurred only the day before at the station, for realising that she had mislaid a packet of Minny's letters which Leslie had just given her, she jumped out of the train as it began to move, narrowly avoiding injury. Fortunately, the letters were retrieved a fortnight later – 'happy Saturday' – the day on which she also completed drafting her *Esmond* preface. During these same weeks of confusion and reversals, a time when she found herself short-tempered and generally out of sorts, she dreamt of being saved by Billy from falling – 'you & I were tumbling down a precipice last night & <u>you</u> pulled me up & neatly lugged up the side of a wall so I awoke & it was breakfast time'.[4] Her journal later recorded the 'odd chance' that on the same day that she wrote this to him, Billy had himself stumbled whilst walking up Winder Hill, near Sedbergh.

Meanwhile a new face had appeared to add a piquancy to their staid Wimbledon circle. On 15 February Charlotte Leigh Smith, 'lovely beyond words', came to dine, the rather discontented wife of the much older Benjamin Leigh Smith, an arctic explorer and brother of Barbara Bodichon. Charlotte Sellers was the younger sister of the academically gifted Eugénie Sellers, a former Girton graduate and friend of Barbara Bodichon, and it was through Eugénie and Barbara that Charlotte and Benjamin had met. He was forty years her senior, and the prospect of their marriage had caused predictable family disapproval. Another of Benjamin's sisters was blunt. 'I am sure it ought to be illegal for men to marry girls 40 years younger than themselves.… I feel that she must be doing it for the money.'[5] By the time the Ritchies came to know Charlotte, she was in her mid thirties and had been married for nearly ten years. They would see a lot of her over the ensuing months and years, the End House becoming something of a refuge during difficult patches in her marriage.

Annie's ready sympathy made her a convenient port in a storm, but there was a discomforting intensity about Charlotte's developing friendship with both Richmond and Hester. During the last weeks of Margaret Oliphant's life – she died during Queen Victoria's diamond Jubilee celebrations in June 1897 – Annie visited her old friend constantly, but she found her loyalty tested by the crisis of Charlotte's marriage and by the way in which Hester seemed to have succumbed to the surrounding hysteria. The episode survived Hester's purge of Annie's journal.

16 of June. Strange interview with Charlotte Leigh Smith who rushed in imploring me to speak to her husband who wished to divorce her – I went & found him very kind & quite ready to be kind. Came back & found her frantic against him & romantically excited about some M$^r$ W – strange creature – in the midst of all this scene M$^{rs}$ Carver met me saying M$^{rs}$ Oliphant was dying & Hester implored me not to abandon Charlotte & I went – gave up Cambridge (the Sidgwicks I think) my spirits quite done up & then I think I am dying....

22 Jubilee. Called them all at 5 – after they were gone early I went to dear M$^{rs}$ Oliphant held her hand & heard her talk cannot believe it is the end. 'If ever the sky looks brighter or a flower shines then think of me & of a sign from me she said – calm & almost gay – I could not have believed it was so easy to die' she said – Walked on the common at night with the vast bonfires burning to the sky.

Saturday 26 of June dear M$^{rs}$ Oliphant at rest for ever.

Charlotte's tendency to become 'romantically excited' is the key to the difficulties in the Ritchie household. There is no evidence, naturally, that she and Richmond had a sexual affair, but there were many occasions when he and Hester had dinner with Charlotte, or invited her to the End House when Annie was away recuperating in Brighton or elsewhere. This was a level of intimacy which seemed designed to exclude Annie. In 1899 she shared her distress with Billy in a letter from Brighton which showed that she was hurt not just by Richmond's casual thoughtlessness, but by Hester's willing complicity. 'I am rather miserable for I have written to implore Hester not to ask Charlotte to stay. I am so provoked with myself for being so jealous & yet I cant bear to think of having to be away & Charlotte there & it happens at least once a week.'[6]

It is evident that Charlotte's company intoxicated Richmond, while she felt flattered by the attentions of this intelligent and drily witty man. In 1897, Annie was sixty and Richmond forty-three, while Charlotte was younger still at thirty-five. Richmond was not resistant to being flirted with, and perhaps expected Annie to have seen it, rather like his bicycling and golfing, as nothing more than a distraction from the demands of the India Office and its many late nights. It seems that the intimacy of the earlier years of their marriage was now sufficiently rare for special moments to warrant recording. After working late one evening Richmond had come into her room where she was 'in bed very

bad ... I enjoyed seeing him look in', and the next night, having spent
the day on the sofa, she woke from a nightmare when 'R came in and
said "you are quite well aren't you tonight" & came back to his own
bed. Feeling him there I went off into peaceful slumbers.'[7] Recognising
her own jealousy, Annie was wise enough not to turn Charlotte into a
crisis. One Sunday in April, when Richmond and the children were all
out on their bicycles, she sat in the stillness listening to a thrush in the
garden, knowing that she had many reasons to feel contented. Though
nothing was permanent or assured, one had a duty to be optimistic.
'We cant <u>hold</u> anything but we can look up to the last.'[8]

She and Hester were invited by George and Mary Watts to stay
for a few days at Limnerslease, their house near Guildford, although
Annie found herself having to be uncharacteristically firm – 'a horrid
clap of thunder between Hester & me. She didn't want to come – but
at last I stuck to it for I would have to see them and she gave in.'
From Godalming station, the Watts took them to the new Charterhouse
school, which had left its former Smithfield location where Thackeray
had been a pupil, and where Annie had deposited the manuscript of *The
Newcomes*. Her visit to Limnerslease acted like a balm, and Watts's
description of its decorative paintings entranced her – 'everything
was fragrant, kind, suggestive; the ceiling meant one thing the walls
another. I listened & seemed to be refreshed & redipped in the waters
of life & hope.' They talked too about Frederic Leighton who had died
in January, 'one more old friend gone', and about a possible permanent
future for his house. She canvassed opinions when she returned to
Wimbledon, but was faced with the practical realities of costs. 'Sir T.
Martin to whom I went said he thought the idea excellent but that it
w[d]. take 20,000 or more, that people must be paid to live there & keep
it.... Leslie also took much the same view altogether the material facts
seems against the realisation but Signor has painted him & Swinburne
has sung him & his dear bright memory must live in his own works &
in the remembrance of what he <u>was</u> still more.'[9] A successful project
to preserve Leighton House had to wait a little longer.

The death of several old friends in 1896 – not just Leighton, but
Millais, Emily Tennyson and Jane Brookfield as well – made Annie
ever more conscious of her own infirmities. It was not a fear of dying,
but the incapacities of aging which she resented. 'Remember Huxleys
definition of Religion – accept the laws of life – think of Don Quixote,
of Col Newcome, of all that is noble & gentle & unselfseeking; accept
the laws, accept the laws.'[10] But she could not reconcile herself to
the death of the young. She was overwhelmed with grief when news
reached them that Theo, Gerald and Margie's daughter, had died from

peritonitis on the voyage from India, which was a cruel reminder –
not least for Gerald and Margie themselves – of the death of Lionel
Tennyson ten years before. Her body, like his, was committed to the
Red Sea. For days Annie felt detached from the life going on around
her, 'as if everything existed but without me any more. But thankful
that one has lived & Theo will be a light of God for ever. R & H
very dear & comforting & so is the thought of my Bill.'[11] In reading
through her father's letters for the Biographical Edition she found
herself being offered fleeting images of her own former life, viewed
as if through a prism. She was at last ready to let the past go, having
understood that its realities could not be recaptured, and she was
eager instead to grasp the vitality of the freshly-lived experience of
her own children. 'The best way is to put ones old self away with the
dusty packets & to live ones natural present self when one comes out
of the little writing room. It just occurs to me (for the 100th time) that
as so very much of oneself is dead & gone & yet so much still remains
that one need not ever fear the future – for nothing can be more past
than ones childhood for instance – & after all Hester's youth & the
dear young folks is more important to me now than my own a great
deal.'[12] So when Hester paid a short visit to Freshwater, Annie hoped
that her daughter might come to enjoy the landmarks once familiar
from her own past. In loosening her grip, Annie allows the possibility
of renewal and survival. 'I am imagining how everything seems to
you at FW. beloved spot. How often I have looked at those 2 rocks – I
dont know why but after my Papa died I used to feel as if they almost
talked about him when I looked at them f^m. M^rs. Camerons gate. Is the
sweet briar hedge still there.'[13]

And along with this new understanding of the limitations of memory,
she now began disposing of physical mementoes. Between April and
June, she sold various Thackeray manuscripts to the bookseller and
dealer John Pearson, despite feelings of disloyalty as she saw them
go, in the case of a group of 'dear drawings' experiencing something
like 'a torture'. Whilst she could release her father's drawings or
the occasional pages of manuscript, she refused to contemplate the
sale of any letters, for 'it goes against the grain'.[14] Pearson had first
approached her in 1891 for the original of *The Rose and the Ring*,
something which she regarded then as 'an heirloom & I wouldnt sell
it for £3000 – M^r Colvin always says we ought to give it to the British
Museum.' Things had changed five years later when she anticipated
the costs of seeing Billy through University, but she took many days
before deciding to sell. In March 1896 she still valued this particular
manuscript highly, perhaps too highly, and would not give way. 'I am

afraid I have nothing to sell at present. Someone asked me about the Rose & the Ring & I said 3300 for I am sure we get 100 a year pleasure out of it.' Two months later she was offering it for a much reduced price. 'Circumstances have arisen which may make it advisable for us to realise a large sum for my son, in the course of a year or two – This has determined me to make up my mind to part from my dear mss of the Rose & the Ring if a really good offer comes – by wh. I mean from £1800 to £2000.' Pearson offered £1500 which at Richmond's insistence she refused, only to write a few days later to accept. Even at this late stage she would not have been disappointed had Pearson chosen to withdraw. 'I feel if it is to be done I should like not to have it hanging over me, & tho' it seems a small difference your appreciation of my dear book does make it easier to part with it. But as I said before, if you have changed your views I shall not be sorry.'[15] It was difficult, but at least the cause was honourable. 'His grandfather shall pay for Billys College!'

As she recovered from the first sadness of Theo Ritchie's death, she felt able to work once more on the Edition. In June she planned *The Newcomes* volume, and also completed her article on the foundation of the *Cornhill*, drawing on correspondence to her father from some of its early contributors.[16] James Barrie congratulated her on the piece, finding himself caught up in her portrayal of times which were already passing into history. '[H]ow graciously they all move thro' your pages, what ladies & gentlemen they were in those days & (surely I may say it) how their courtly manner clings to you.' His admiration for Thackeray's writing is coupled with regret that he had not been a contemporary. 'Heighho! how I wish those had been my days, so that I might have followed a certain tall figure thro' the streets and touched him at the crossings.'[17]

There was reason for fresh anxiety after receipt of a letter which gave rise to serious concerns about Laura Stephen, for Dr Harold Corner, a medical officer on the Earlswood Asylum staff, feared for the future treatment of inmates following the appointment of a new director. Annie travelled to Earlswood where Dr Corner met her at the station. 'His plans seem hopeful. I sympathised with his indignation against the abuses there.' She wrote at once to Leslie. It is significant that ever since Minny's death Annie was the one who took a number of the initiatives about Laura's welfare and, as now, found herself having to prompt Leslie to act. Corner had told Annie of an intention to establish his own care home in north London – at Brook House, Southgate – to which Laura would indeed transfer early in 1897. Leslie's reply relieved her, although it is difficult to see why. 'Nice letter f^m. Leslie, who is not upset as I feared by the bad acc$^t$ D$^r$. C. gives of Earlswood.'[18] She set out with the children to Castle Malwood in the New Forest, Richmond following the next day in heavy rain. Perhaps her worries had made Annie unusually out of sorts, for she resolved 'to be gentle & loyal to my dear darlings', two days afterwards describing her mood as 'bitter. Say my prayers cultivate <u>stolidity</u>. 1 hour of work every day. Enter R well & jolly & quite unconscious of my vibrations. Seeing him all right I fought them & write this to remind myself another time.'

That Richmond could be so unaware of Annie's efforts to conceal her despair is curious. A couple of weeks in September at Littlehampton for the golf – 'there were nice moments but Littlehampton wasnt a success somehow' – were followed by Annie and Hester going to Cromer, while Richmond took his bicycle on the train to the Lake District and called on Billy at Sedbergh to discuss his university prospects. Oxford was the new goal. 'I went to see Fowler, Bung's master on Sunday who is a very sensible understanding man. He said he hadn't had enough time to form an opinion about Bill but that his position in the school was a good average, because although many older boys were below him they were stupid, but that boys really clever at their lessons would be higher. He said however that Bill would have no difficulty in matriculating at Balliol if we sent him there, but seemed to recommend Trinity.'[19]

Blanche Warre Cornish was also staying at Cromer, and Richmond was concerned that Hester would be exposed to his sister's occasionally overbearing manner. Her celebrated eccentricities and fascination with High Church ritual were endearing – the family looked on with weary tolerance when Blanche 'went over' to Rome – but there was a more worrying neurotic side which had resulted in breakdowns. By 1899 doctors feared that her mental health was permanently impaired. Richmond urged Annie to intervene should Blanche attempt to draw Hester into her customary soul-searching. 'Dont let Blanchie bother Hester if she goes on the rampage, but take Hesters side both with B & when alone with her. It does nothing but harm to young people to make them ask questions about themselves.' Charlotte Leigh Smith was also a Roman Catholic, and perhaps Richmond feared that Blanche's additional influence might draw Hester towards ideas of converting, which would certainly have been viewed as a step too far.

Annie saw a good deal of Jane Brookfield during 1896. In November she called and was struck by the way in which Jane fixed her with a long gaze and then said 'you have done me good dear'. The next day, feeling unusually light-hearted, Annie picked up a letter as she left the house and read on the train the news that 'JOB' had died two hours after she had left her. She and Hester had been going to the theatre, but Annie immediately made her way to Mrs Brookfield's, finding a strangely empty house, the room containing Jane's body locked and the nurse absent, with none of her immediate family there. One of the journal pages strategically removed by Hester covers this episode, almost certainly because it dwelt on the long years of Mrs Brookfield's friendship and what she had meant to Thackeray himself. Annie's reporting of the news to Billy in Sedbergh is expressed with an unusually detached restraint. 'Do you know that your dear Godmother M$^{rs}$ Brookfield is gone to her rest. I sat with her for an hour, & thought her so well & so bright – & she died quite gently & quickly after I had left her. M$^{rs}$ Page says Arthur [Ritchie] is very sad losing his dear Grandmama. I too shall miss her very much for I love her dearly.'[20]

It made sense for Richmond to decide to reduce his commuting time from Wimbledon to the India Office by remaining in town during the week, especially as he worked most evenings as well. From the start of 1897 various lodgings and flats were taken – in Suffolk Street, Queen Anne's Gate, Kensington Court Gardens and Queen Anne Mews. His letters during this time tend to be written either on India Office paper, or from the Garrick and the Athenaeum clubs, where he often took his breakfast and his evening meal. Weekends were spent at the End House, and during one of these Annie enlisted him 'to disentangle my Edition for me'.[21] The selection of what should be used from the wealth of available material and deciding exactly where to employ it caused constant interruptions and restarts. But the honed skills of this consummate civil servant, his clear thinking and ability to make sense of complex detail meant that Annie was able triumphantly to note within days of asking for his help that Richmond had 'finished the skeleton of [the] Edition', though she had decided on its basic thirteen-volume format at least a year before. When late in the year Pinkie also started helping at the proof-reading stage, including negotiating changes with Reginald Smith when Annie was ill or away from home, the Edition had become a real family industry.

The decision to move Laura from Earlswood and into the care of Dr Corner at Southgate was at last taken, and Annie felt much happier. 'Its very nice – nicer – much nicer & quieter than Earlswood & I felt I shouldnt mind going there myself – Earlswood I sh$^d$. have hated.'[22] Then, having despatched drafts of several of the prefaces to Reginald Smith, she set off with Hester for another of her extended visits to France and Italy, leaving Richmond established in lodgings at Queen Anne's Gate. She wrote to Pinkie from Paris, happy to be once more in the city where both women had spent significant portions of impressionable childhoods. '[W]e fly about & enjoy it all & I keep my own remembrance to myself for one does hanker after the past in an odd & yet delightful & most present way.'[23] At the great port of Marseilles she marvelled at the swarming masses and the ships bound for China and India, but was not well at Cannes where they rested for a few days – Richmond thought the town sounded 'as horrid as my firmest prejudices anticipated'.[24] In her absence Richmond was not feeling charitably disposed towards Reginald Smith who, not unreasonably, was asking questions about the material which Annie had sent him. 'I have answered that till you come back you had better not be bothered about business – <u>damn</u> Reginald.'[25] He did his best to stem some of the inevitable effusions which her encounter with Italy would bring forth – 'I will allow you to describe one sunset' – which Annie may have heard as an unconscious echo of a similar precaution sent to Venice by Minny twenty-five years earlier: 'dont describe the Tintorets nor the tints, for I know exactly what it is like & I like descriptions of people best'.[26]

At Bordighera they put up at a hotel near the house of Annie's old childhood friend Rosa Fanshawe, and she found herself regretting an earlier act of generosity. 'The bell w[h]. in a fit of enthusiasm years ago I presented to the Fanshawes for the chapel has driven me nearly mad with its Sunday clang. It w[d]. almost make a story – I begged Hester to shut the window & keep the horrid thing outside.'[27] They spent just one day at Genoa before reaching Florence, where they stayed in the Villa Guicciardini, the home of Sir John Edgar and his sisters who insisted on putting them up. The comforts of the villa and the kindness of the Edgars proved invaluable when Hester went down with influenza, which knocked her out for several days. It did not prevent Annie from revisiting sights last seen with Richmond in 1874. 'At the Uffizi I saw that wonderful Botticelli of Venus in a shell...& a splendid Albert Durer.'[28]

When Hester was well enough to travel again they began the long homeward journey, through Bologna and Milan, by lakes and mountains, territory familiar from past travels with Minny and Leslie, '& I thought of the old days when we walked & drove alternately'.[29] As they approached Zürich through the St Gotthard pass, the remarkable scenery left her breathless, and she made no attempt to curb her enthusiasm in describing it to Richmond. 'You simply must, must, must, see it. I seemed to have forgotten what beauty was. Codge never said a word but her cheeks got pink again & her eyes danced.'[30] She wanted to stop off at Zürich to see whether it would do as a place to send Billy to learn German once he had left school. It was rich in memories, 'the beautiful hotel I remembered with Papa and Minnie & <u>Leslie</u> in the garden looking without speaking'. But she was thinking ahead too, and whilst in Zürich it occurred to her that Billy might train to be 'a scientific barrister – If he has a speciality he w$^d$ be much more likely to get on & his bent is a little that way'. The plan was that Billy should leave Sedbergh at the end of the summer term and prepare for entry to Oxford, but other plans were also under consideration. Richmond passed on an idea of Jane Strachey's, who, recognising that Lytton was still young for Oxford planned to send him to St Andrews – 'not to the University but to live with a Professor'[31] – and thought that this might also suit Billy. In the event, he stayed an extra term at Sedbergh, not leaving until Christmas, and Lytton went to Liverpool University College for two years. Billy matriculated for Trinity College, Oxford, in the following April.

After leaving Zürich on the last loop back to Paris, Annie and Hester paused in Basel long enough to note the announcement of Brahms's death. They were home in time for Stella Duckworth's marriage to Jack Hills, the prospect of which Leslie hated for he had rather assumed that Stella would continue as his housekeeper, her role since Julia's death. The day before the wedding Annie went to see Stella and felt miserable, 'for she looked so ill & so pale & wan'. It was not a good omen. For Annie, all too conscious of Julia's absence and Leslie's misery, the wedding day was 'very sad', though Stella's beauty gave a brilliance to the occasion that was almost worthy of her mother. A few short months later she was dead, and Annie had one of her vivid dreams in which she relived the wedding day which turned without warning into a funeral.

Having returned to a London which was excitedly anticipating the Queen's diamond jubilee celebrations in June, Annie's labours to find a good viewing point for Sir John Edgar's sisters had a triumphant outcome. 'It was simply impossible at the I.O. but to my joy I heard of a very tidy spot in the W$^r$. Bridge Road where the Oliphants are going..... If the dear beloved women get better ones I shall be possessed of 3 excellent & cheap points de vue from a nicely tiled butchers shop. The meat is to be cleared away for the occasion – or eaten perhaps by the loyal crowds, anyhow I have obeyed the weird enchantment by w$^h$. Sir John makes everyone do that he chooses.'[32] The weeks on the continent and now this resumption of 'the usual va et vient' all served as distractions, perhaps welcome ones, from the Edition. There is almost a cry of despair recorded in the journal, two days after Stella's wedding – 'When am I going to begin my work?' The question is rhetorical and familiar, but is worth a moment's consideration, for though there was still much to do, this surely meant the reworking and amplification of draft prefaces rather than a beginning. After all, versions had already gone to Reginald Smith, and by September proofs for the first volumes were arriving. What it may instead reveal is her lack of confidence that she would adequately acquit herself in this self-imposed task. Having expended so much energy on resisting the intrusions of others into her father's history, her own desire judiciously to circumvent his objections now needed to be carried out with the right mix of openness and discretion. It was this responsibility which troubled her, and her confidence was not increased when in mid-June Richmond managed to be 'most discouraging about my work'.

Even when the job was over, she remained unconvinced that she had done it justice. This is revealed by a note added to the journal after the Edition had been published; when deciding a possible sequence for the volumes back in 1896, she added 'all this was eventually done, but the Edition itself was never thoroly done. Is it too late? 1899.' In one sense, it was not too late, for the later Centenary Edition, in twenty-six volumes rather than thirteen, allowed for revisions and further material to be added, but this was not quite what she meant. Perhaps she began at last to appreciate the implication of George Grove's insistence that a 'thoroly done' edition ought to depend as much upon the integrity of Thackeray's texts as upon the introductory material. But if so, she still shied away from this specialised task, for the texts for the later Centenary Edition remained largely untouched, and old errors were preserved. Perhaps at one stage she did consider making textual corrections, and her American publishers certainly seemed to have expected it. It was a matter which Harpers raised with Smith, Elder in September 1897, when they were arranging for simultaneous publication in the United States. The understanding was that copyright royalties attached to the new material in Annie's prefaces – in other words both to her own writing as well as to the substantial extracts from her father's previously unpublished papers. But there was also the matter of Thackeray's original texts. 'We have been informed that throughout the volumes there are more or less of corrections made by Mrs. Ritchie. If our information is correct, those matters might supply a fair basis for a copyright in this country on the edition as a whole.'[33] If Harpers' understanding had ever been accurate, it no longer was, for far from making 'more or less of corrections' Annie made none. Issues of editorial principle are never mentioned in her prefaces, because they never entered her thinking.

At the end of May a lightning storm caused the collapse of the church tower of St Clement's, Leigh-on-Sea, and Annie's thoughts at once went to her mother. 'I have written to the Thompsons who will

I fear be dreadfully shaken for they lived next door almost. I thought first "O Mama will have been frightened" & then I remembered she w^d. never be afraid again.'[34] There was also an incident this year concerning her father's final resting place, for it had troubled her to read of a man complaining that Thackeray's Kensal Green grave looked neglected. 'I had had some ivy planted which grew over the stone. I wrote for it to be clipped and we went yesterday to see that it had been properly done. The busy body had <u>again</u> written to the papers to say that he was pleased to see that "in consequence of his recommendation" the ivy had been seen to. He also put a horrid little scrubby geranium in a flower pot upon the stone – I said to Hester I cant think what my Papa would have advised me to do. Hester said "I think he would have laughed Mom." I felt inclined to laugh and cry too & I still do when I think of it all.'[35] It was thoughtful of Leslie to have written when Annie was abroad to say that he had attended to other restorations at Kensal Green. 'The gravestones are put straight & a railing set up round him & some things planted, wh. will, I hope, grow. It does not look so deserted & abandoned as it did & I hope that it will be kept in order.'[36]

After all her uncertainties about the Edition, Annie was elated when Smith, Elder finally made their contractual proposal, after years of doubt as to whether they would publish it. She had made her first approach to George Smith as long ago as 1892, when the firm had seemed unconvinced that another Thackeray edition was justified. But once they had committed themselves to her, the offer which followed was exceptional. It reflected George Smith's personal intervention and his always generous treatment of Thackeray's daughter, despite her nearly having left his firm for Harpers. Just days after Stella's funeral came 'Mr Smiths splendid offer for the Edition' of £4,000, a remarkable sum for the time. Reporting the good news to Billy, she had doubted this happy ending until the last moment. 'Did Hester tell you of my <u>splendid</u> offer f^m. M^r Smith. I am so pleased & so pleased <u>he</u> has done it for I was afraid he wasnt going to publish the notes – But this makes everything easy & delightful if only I can get it all finished.... If all goes well I hope this next year will see me through & you all will benefit by y^r mama & still more by your dearest grandpapa.'[37]

Personal triumph was then set aside, for she was doing her best to comfort Leslie and the mourning family. Nor did she forget Laura, to whom of all the young people at Hyde Park Gate Stella had been the kindest. 'Went to see Laura then I went to Leslies & the dear little girls ran into my arms.'[38] The matter of who would oversee Laura's care in future years now began to concern Annie, while Leslie seemed only

too happy to let her decide things as she saw fit, a further shuffling
off of responsibility for his unfortunate daughter. 'I take it for granted
that you will settle about Laura's guardianship as you think right.'[39]
It would be a considerable relief to Annie when Jack Hills assumed
this role, though Leslie's niece, Kate Stephen, was also considered.
Leslie was on securer ground when advising about the Edition, both
as to its name and its appearance. His own Thackeray article from the
*Dictionary of National Biography* was to be republished in the final
volume.

> I would not think of 'Jubilee': the word has been hopelessly
> spoilt; and does not convey the real point of the undertaking.
> I should say that his daughter's edition is not only the most
> taking but the simplest & most straightforward way of
> putting it.
>      All that I will add at present is that I hope that you will
> impress upon GS the desirability of having a really nice
> form – I dont think that the firm is strong upon that matter....
> I should like to see something wh. would be attractive in
> appearance; handy to read, with a good clear type &c & yet
> not aesthetically pretentious. – I am sure that that would go
> for a good deal; and I am also of opinion that you should not
> trust to GS's unmediated taste.

But Annie's rather weary lament to Gussie Freshfield suggests that, far
from being indifferent to matters of presentation, George Smith was
to her mind rather too preoccupied with how the volumes would look.
'GS. is all that is splendid about the money but oh! dear he is adamant
about print, shape, order of printing.'[40] She worried over a title for the
Edition until almost the last moment, ideas being proposed, rejected
and then reconsidered, whereas in his correspondence with her Smith
was principally concerned with getting the sequence of publication for
the volumes right. 'I have been considering the question of adopting
a chronological order for the "Daughter's Edition" (the title which
grows on me) of your Father's works. There is much to be said in
favour of it, but I am still afraid that it will not suit the public.'[41] His
publisher's instincts appear to have won the day, in that *Vanity Fair*
and *Pendennis* would be the first volumes to appear, with Thackeray's
earlier writings coming after. Nevertheless, the major novels were
published in the correct chronological sequence, interspersed amongst
other volumes.

      This was the summer in which Charlotte, having become 'ro-
mantically excited about some M^r W', asked Annie to intervene in

her threatened divorce. It blew over, and just a month later Annie
and Richmond borrowed the Leigh Smith's handsome Sussex country house for their holiday in late August and September. Scalands
Gate near Robertsbridge, 'a lovely house among woods & fields',
had been built by Barbara Bodichon and bequeathed to her brother,
Benjamin Leigh Smith, whose offer to the Ritchies was perhaps a way
of thanking them – and perhaps especially Annie – for calming his
young wife, whose role in the arrangements Annie remembered with
a waspish humour. 'Charlotte exclaimed it was what I longed to do.
She would not say so to me now!'[42] Their stay at Scalands Gate was
a mixed success, 'a happy time & yet it <u>wasnt</u> happy. R[d]. was out of
spirits & not like himself. I was easily upset & un-nerved, everything
was beautiful autumnal homelike but confusing.' The recent deaths
of Stella Duckworth and Margaret Oliphant left Annie saddened, and
the thought of the approaching return of Gerald and Margie to India
distracted her. And there were deadlines to meet. Proofs of her *Vanity
Fair* and *Pendennis* introductions were checked at Scalands Gate,
and manuscripts for the next two volumes despatched. Friends came
to stay, as well as various Ritchie nephews and nieces. But the house
held some fascinating distractions, 'books & people & interesting
things', including letters to Barbara Bodichon from George Eliot
about her marriage. Richmond played golf, and admitted to enjoying
the 'agreeable female sympathy'.[43] This coded remark by Annie to
Billy may be unpicked a little by her ambiguous journal comment
about Charlotte, who 'received us & went away & then came back'.
Annie had probably not foreseen that Charlotte would be part of the
arrangements at Scalands, and it became apparent that the difficult
relationship between the Leigh Smiths was far from being repaired.
At some stage Richmond seems to have insisted that Charlotte should
be made welcome at The End House, if there were occasions when
she needed a refuge. 'I dont think we need be afraid that Charlotte
will take our invitation too literally: & it is more gracious in the circs
to ask her to come when it suits her.'[44] Billy, now in his final term
at Sedbergh, was kept abreast of some of the fluctuating fortunes of
this tempestuous marriage. 'Charlotte Leigh Smith came to <u>lunch</u>
looking very well & handsome & I think things are going rather well
for her for she & Ben are giving dinner-parties, only Ben doesn't
behave nicely to his sister-in-law she says.'[45]

As Annie struggled through the final stages of her work, a compa-
rably long period of dutiful devotion ended when Hallam Tennyson
published the *Memoir* of his father in October. Their projects could
scarcely be less alike, his the standard late-Victorian life and letters,

monumental and imposing, hers a series of sketches characterised by their informality and lightness of touch. Annie's copy of the *Memoir* arrived as Gerald and Margie started on their return voyage to India, and she lay in bed 'aching and confused' as a friend read it to her, but she told Billy the next day not only that she thought it 'good decidedly' but that she had checked the final proof of *Vanity Fair* – 'It looked nice I thought'.[46] It was a happy decision to involve Pinkie in these final stages of checking and proof-reading, as her careful attention to detail – a Ritchie rather than a Thackeray trait – proved essential in the months to come. At Redcar, shaking herself free from headaches in the bracing sea air, and having taken Henry James's memorial essay on George du Maurier to read on the train – 'as I had 5 uninterrupted hours to understand his language I was able to make it out & I like it <u>very much indeed</u>'[47] – she was thankful for Pinkie's encouragement. 'She says they get better as they go on, & that the article on Punch is the best of all.'[48] Annie was painfully aware of her own technical inadequacies, and did not hide them from Billy. 'I make the most extraordinary slips & omissions & if ever you do you may thank y$^r$ mama for it. But one is all right if one has the time to go over. It is not carelessness so much as gabbling I mean trying to get on too quick.'[49] Two months later, Pinkie's real value had emerged, as Annie still worried over the Edition's name. 'It is really wonderful how Pinkie has gripped it all. We are steadily getting on – she is working at the Newcomes now – then comes Rome & the Christmas books then Virginians & the 2$^d$. journey to America.... Instead of the Roundabout Ed. w$^h$. S & E don't like I wrote about <u>the Gold Pen</u> Edition which is a pretty name I think & w$^h$. S & E incline to. Pinkie & R$^d$ want "The Memoirs' Edition" w$^h$. isnt nearly such a good name, but more descriptive certainly.'[50]

She saw the ludicrousness of all of this 'fumbling' indecision, just a week later telling Margie that 'it will end by being The Rumpelstiltskin Edition – I still want Gold Pen Edition[51] – Pinkie & R dont like it – I shall suggest the Ritchie Edition w$^h$. isnt very pretty but distinctive. There was Colliers Shakespear & Chapmans Homer.' For her, there was quite a lot in a name, and in the end it was called the Biographical Edition, described on each title page as 'The Works of William Makepeace Thackeray with Biographical Introductions by his Daughter, Anne Ritchie.' It is a declaration of independence, a clear assertion of the biographical intent of her contribution, and even while she claimed her rights as 'daughter', she omitted her maiden name, satisfied with her married status as Anne Ritchie. There is thus something a little disingenuous about the prefatory note to the first volume, dated 28 November 1897, written whilst this fussing over a name was still at its height. Her claim that her work is not primarily biographical is unconvincing.

> My Father never wished for any Biography of himself to be written, and for this reason I have never attempted to write one. It is only after a quarter of a century that I have determined to publish memories which chiefly concern his books. Certain selections from his letters are also included, which tell of the places where his work was done, and of the times when he wrote. So much has been forgotten, so much that is ephemeral has been recorded, that it is my desire to mark down some of the truer chords to which his life was habitually set. For this reason I have included one letter to my Mother among the rest: it will show that he knew how to value the priceless gifts of home and of happiness while they lasted, as well as to bear trouble and loneliness when they fell upon him.

Of all her writing, this was unquestionably the project that she most needed to get right, and she continued to doubt that she had succeeded. It represented a complex personal investment, and she could only hope that her father would have understood. She worked on through the proofs and final drafts, weary but deeply moved, declaring to Billy that 'I cant tell you how I do feel more & more as I go on what a courageous & tender hearted Papa I had & how proud I am of him'.[52] The first volume was published on 15 April 1898, others appearing regularly until March 1899, and after each one she received from Smith, Elder a cheque for a little over £300. The timing of the American publication was put at risk by the Spanish-American war of 1898, and though she turned it into a joke she feared for the royalties if the edition did not get a good start. 'Alas for the war. I sympathise but I long for it to be peace. It will seize our poor ships I fear the Vanity Fair the Pendennis all prevented from sailing peacefully or should I write it sale-ing into their American docks.'[53]

Each of the red covers bears the distinctive WMT monogram, placed centrally, and tucked below, to the right, are her own initials AIR in matching gold, the hand familiar from her correspondence. She wrote to Gussie Freshfield with all the pride of a new parent – 'I cant help wanting to tell you how the Edition is <u>born</u>'[54] – but here the stale cliché of artistic production has real meaning. The daughter had given new life to all of the father's works, a last triumphant act for the 'Miss Williamson' persona which she had sometimes chosen

*Portion of illustrated letter from Thackeray to Edward FitzGerald, 1831*

for herself in her earlier fiction. The launch had its public dimension through reviews and announcements in the daily papers, but it was the family meaning which Annie dwelt on. '[I]t is nice to realise that Thackeray is a name to conjure with – I find myself longing for Minnie to tell her about it – My sweet Codge is no less sympathetic than if she had known & lived with her, & our Father.'

As her task reached its conclusion, she could allow herself this moment of triumph. On a personal level, it had redefined her understanding of what her duty to her father might be. Having for years been unable to contemplate being his chronicler, since the early 1890s it became an ambition to which Annie became increasingly committed, needing only to decide how it might be done. In her short 1891 piece for *The Illustrated London News*, 'Thackeray and His Biographers', she argued that writing the biography of a great man was more about timing than taste, in that something attempted too soon fails through being too much in awe of its subject or is constrained by the sensitivities of those still living.

> Memoirs and biographies are, as it has been said, like wine, and improve by keeping. But they are apt to come out too crudely, far too soon, as a rule, after the man or woman has passed away whom they are intended to honour. Very often the good taste and good feeling with which they are edited destroy the likeness, and prune and restrain all spontaneous grace of truth and simplicity.
>
> There are people to be considered, natural feelings to be allowed for; there is not enough space left between us and the picture to put things in their proper proportions. Or,

again (and this happens not infrequently), other people's
feelings are *not* considered, passing chance irritations and
foibles are photographed; moods are pointed out, dilated on,
and lectured about.

But she is quick to concede that each of the existing studies of her father
had their value, and that 'there are few … which do not convey something
of him reflected from each different mind'. Surprising nonetheless is
her description of Mrs Brookfield's book, which had initially provoked
such anxiety, as 'the nearest approach to an autobiography', her point
being that here her father could be encountered directly, through his
own words. As she was quick to emphasise, understanding the life
was more than a matter of sorting out the facts and drawing upon the
memories of acquaintances – 'all these are but memoranda'.

> And yet in some inexplicable way – as often as not without
> the help of printer's ink – how surely the real essence of a
> real existence reaches us at last! In the case of any good man
> (and I am not speaking only of my father), the date of his
> birth means so much good service come into the world, so
> much goodwill to others, and constancy in toil and adversity,
> experience accepted with courage, disillusion realised with
> charity. These are the facts of his life, and its details sink
> into insignificance beside them. The date of any such man's
> death marks the hour when we lose him and the joy of his
> presence; but it does not mean that his work is dead, or that
> it is not here still among us.

With her manifesto laid down, exactly a year later she had suggested
to George Smith her embryonic idea for a 'final' Thackeray edition
drawing on his letters, 'with notes biographical or otherwise by me', an
outline that did not change in any significant way from what eventually
she supplied. Her personal authority is stamped very markedly upon the
result. Each introduction is written in the first person, with Annie the
intimate narrator of her father's story. Of course, for the later writings
she is an indispensable and, one must presume, a reliable witness, but
even for the years before she was born, she constantly validates her
presence with reminiscences of what her father told her. The tendency
to situate these conversations within an on-going present, with her
father at her shoulder to lend authenticity, is a technique which helped
reassure her of their currency. 'My father has sometimes told me that
he lost his heart to my mother when he heard her sing; she had a very
sweet voice and an exquisite method.'[55] But elsewhere her writing is

coloured by ambiguity and allusiveness, as if to acknowledge that the past – her own, as well as her father's – throws up survivals in the form of artefacts, but that its true meaning is preserved only in the partial and passing memories of the individuals affected, and that facts and details cannot contain 'the real essence of a real existence'.

> Turning over the pages of *Punch*, and looking at the familiar titles and histories and pictures, the circumstances under which all these were devised come vaguely back to my mind again. Suns long set begin to shine once more through the old Kensington study windows. My father's silvery-grey head is bending over his drawing-board as he sits at his work, serious, preoccupied, with the water-colour box open on the table beside him, and the tray full of well-remembered implements. To the writer her own childhood comes back and fills her world.... The cane-bottom chair, 'that bandy-legged, high-shouldered, worm-eaten seat,' is gone, though one of its contemporaries still survives in our home; and as I look at the pictures of that time, and recognise one and another of the objects depicted there, I am always carried away from now to then. Why, the very coal-skuttle which Becky brought in with her own two hands still serves to warm the hearth where my family is assembled.[56]

Edith Sichel's long appreciation in *The Quarterly Review* understood well the collective value of the introductions. 'They are not a biography – in the circumstances they could not be one – but they are a Life.... [W]e get something better than chronology – a breathing picture.'[57]

A month after the volumes of the Edition began to appear, Richmond was appointed a Companion of the Order of the Bath, a significant acknowledgment of his years of service. The Secretary of State, Lord George Hamilton swept Annie up into his congratulations, pointing out that it was a rare honour for India Office civil servants. 'He has been my right hand ever since I have been here, & I could not have got through the troubles of the past if I had not been able throughout to rely upon his exceptional powers of work & observation, & the invariable high quality of the work he does.'[58] Annie was proud of this reward for dedication and integrity, and that Hamilton was delighted to have secured something 'for someone who has never once asked for it'.[59] It was some compensation for the heavy labour which continued to affect Richmond's health. The death of Gladstone did not spoil their happiness, though Annie noted the formalities of the funeral, Hester and Billy having gone up early to Westminster Abbey to try to view the procession. '[T]hey seem to have seen the great sea of life flow in & carry away the solemn ship of death.'[60]

Unsettled by an 'odd swelling of throat', she consulted doctors who ordered a three-week cure at Ramsgate, but her neck glands continued to cause her much pain. Dr Jeafferson did not detect any malignancy, diagnosing 'a wholesome abscess not a bad sort', but surgery was necessary. She relayed the details to Billy.

> Chloroform is certainly a most astounding invention. For an hour I was <u>nowhere</u> nothing. I didnt like the morning at all but it was done early & I had hardly any time to wait – D[r]. Jeafferson appeared & offered me his arm & when I came in I felt exactly like Mary Queen of Scots.... Then the nurse invited me to mount the scaffold (a little high wooden sofa). Then they popped softly on a pointed felt cap over my nose & I thought of you, Codge & Wizz & my prayers somehow – & then I couldnt quite think what I was thinking only something I cared about – & then <u>nothing</u>. At the end of an hour or more I awoke cold far far way like a dream – tucked up in bed neatly mended – absolutely unconscious of everything that had been happening – The nurse told me the chloroform Doctor & D[r]. Jeafferson had carried me into bed.[61]

She stayed on for several days in the nursing home in Upper Wimpole Street where the surgeon had operated, and then went to Harrogate to recuperate.

This entire episode coincides with Hester's major deletion to the record, but the period covered by the destroyed pages extends well beyond this time, the journal not resuming until the very end of 1899. It is legitimate to suppose that Charlotte's impact upon the Ritchie household necessitated the censor's knife. Annie was learning to cope with the disruptive impact of this undeniably attractive if unpredictable personality, and there was an occasion early in 1898 upon which she remarked cryptically. 'Thursday 6 [January]. With Billy to Village Fancy ball. Preparations. Stillmans insisted on coming to help – also Charlotte Leigh Smith came. battle royal between them all.' She fought to suppress her own jealousy. In the weeks before her surgery, Richmond went with Charlotte and the children to the Lyceum to see the French actor Coquelin perform, famous for his creation of Rostand's role, Cyrano de Bergerac, and all but Lisa Stillman (whose own innocent attachment to Richmond had been supplanted by Charlotte's more ominous intrusion) were charmed by their companion. 'Charlottes visit is being a great success. She is really <u>very</u> nice & can't help being so lovely – They all went to Cyrano last night & enjoyed it enormously – They supped jovially on their return – She is just like somebody out of the play itself & certainly her audience is most enthusiastic. Lisa still refuses to speak to her.'[62] In August Hester went to join Charlotte across the Channel in Ouistreham, a visit meant to last a few days but which extended into something closer to a fortnight, Annie rather bitterly remarking that 'as she is with Charlotte she is bewitched'.[63]

A bigger test followed, for as Annie recuperated in Harrogate, Richmond also took a holiday in France, meeting Billy who was there learning the language, and for at least some of the time Charlotte and her son, Philip Leigh Smith, were of the party. It seems that Annie, an invalid and now in her sixty-second year, was meant to be reassured when her husband wrote from Normandy to say of Charlotte that 'nothing could be nicer or cleverer than the way she manages us & the meals & comforts she provides are simply astonishing. My inside is blossoming like the rose under the succulence & plenty of the food.'[64] Whilst Annie could sometimes find Charlotte's company as refreshing as everyone else appeared to, there were moments when things grated, such as on the occasion when she had to make another recuperating visit to the seaside. 'Charlotte came yesterday – we were both on our very best behaviour. She said I hope you will enjoy yourself a great deal while you are away. I very cross – enjoy myself! I shall bear being away with what patience I can muster.'[65]

It was an unfamiliar luxury for Annie to feel wealthy, and it was good whilst it lasted. Her intention had always been that the Edition should help provide some financial stability, but she had not imagined that it would pay so handsomely. It offered an opportunity to honour old debts, and she wrote at once to repay Leslie the money advanced in 1877 for the Young Street house. He had given her £500 then, and she was insistent that she should now pay him £800, a figure which he was unwilling to accept. 'But as you are so anxious to give me something, I will take <u>half</u>. I will write to S & Elder to that effect. – I am not at all sure that I ought to do this; but I yield to your pressure. If the other half were paid to me, I should send it in your name to the Salvation Army or whatever more loathsome I could think of.'[66] During the months of Annie's illness and convalescence, Leslie was aware that she was trying to complete the Edition's later introductions whilst at the same time having to check proofs for the earlier volumes. He helped her with proof-reading, at the end of July in looking over *The Newcomes* and *Christmas Books*, and also offered to assist with the final introductions. It was perhaps his way of acknowledging a

lifetime of support, particularly evident since the deaths of Julia and
Stella. 'How are you situated in regard to the later prefaces? Are they
all finished? If not, could I help you in any way?' But he was cautious
about interfering with her style. 'A patch of my flat prose would jar
with your poetical inflexions.... However, I will do what a creature
can do whose mind is chiefly occupied just now with an imposition
of Mill's Political Economy.'[67] His judgments were invariably good,
derived from years of editorial work on the *Dictionary of National
Biography*, and he advised against publishing Thackeray's notebooks
as a separate volume. She also sought advice from others whose
opinion she respected. Henry James came to dinner and was 'not only
ornamental but useful & really truly kind & gave some hints'.[68]

But her most loyal helper continued to be Pinkie. As astute as
she was diplomatic, she could make her points forcibly and Annie
was usually persuaded. When they looked through the first proofs
for *The Virginians*, Pinkie had very clear ideas about what should be
included, perceiving that a skewed view emerged from Thackeray's
constant dwelling on the money that he hoped to make from his
second American tour. She also knew how to put her doubts forward
with subtlety. 'In reading the delightful American letters over in
print, it has struck me that there are rather too many mentions of the
dollars & of the weariness & I have just marked them with a query.
There are so many letters that one or two paragraphs the less won't
matter.'[69] Annie called Pinkie a 'born Editor'. The same instinctive
skills came to the fore in the later production of a memorial volume
of Edith Sichel's writings, and then again when she oversaw the
publication of Annie's own posthumous collection of essays, *From
Friend to Friend*.

During this summer of anxiety and discomfort, George Curzon,
the newly-appointed viceroy, invited Richmond to accompany him to
India. Richmond showed no obvious desire to return to the country of
his birth, and despite spending all of his career in senior roles at the
India Office, he never would go back. But for a time there seemed a
real possibility that he might be persuaded, and Annie was torn in her
feelings, for she would of course have accompanied him. She gave
Billy the news. 'M$^r$ Curzon – of course – wants him to go to India –
But happily y$^r$ Father has not got the slightest intention of going. It is
certainly very nice to have Gov-Generals & Secretaries of State all
trying to keep him with them.'[70] In her more considered reflection to
Pinkie, Annie was generous enough to want Richmond to set aside
family considerations and seek the rewards of personal ambition.
She (and he) may also have reflected that absence from England was

also time away from Charlotte. 'My impression is that he <u>has</u> made up his mind to refuse – He doesn't like talking of it. He is evidently immensely pleased. If I wish anything it is for him to take it – for life doesnt hold so many things & this seems so full of meaning & interest. But you know that in big things he is absolutely unselfish & I am sure he is chiefly thinking of his family's sake. He came in last night & lay on the sofa so tired out that I didnt say a word.'[71] Leslie told Annie that Richmond was right to have refused. He feared for her health, and for Richmond's too perhaps, had they gone. 'It seemed to me all along that it would be the height of rashness for you. Of course it is a pity that Richmond should not take anything he could get, but he has, at least, had a very high compliment &, I hope, though I know nothing about such things, that he may get a lift in some other way.'[72] Leslie was dead before Richmond rose to become head of the India Office, the ultimate affirmation of his intervention in 1877 when he had steered Annie's young fiancé towards a public office.

Once the first few volumes of the Edition had appeared Pinkie observed that the story of Thackeray's life, like his novels, was emerging as if in a serial. 'People cannot I think fully realize the delightfulness of it all till they have read the next three or four numbers as they always say it is so tantalizingly short and they don't get the continuous strain.'[73] The real pleasure for Annie came from people's renewed or restated admiration for her father's writings. Richmond passed on Lord George Hamilton's praise for the early volumes. 'He said Dizzy told him years ago that he cdn't understand Dickens but that your father's style was so magnificent that he would never cease to be read and admired.'[74] The widowed Sir Theodore Martin believed that Annie's choice of Thackeray's letters revealed the essence of the man, and he was touched by her comments on his wife in the final volume – 'Her gracious gift of genius belonged to the world, the charm of her goodness was for her home and for those who loved her' – subsequently using this text on her monumental slab.[75] Leslie, too, was surprised 'by the beauty of your father's letters. M[rs] B[rookfield]'s correspondence did not do him justice, somehow: & I read it with jaundiced eyes. Anyhow he is a continual proof that the art was not forgotten in his days, as idiots repeat.'[76] In words which placed them both in the company of an earlier generation, she would thank Swinburne, her 'dear old friend', for praising the Biographical Edition in the *Quarterly Review* in 1902. 'As Tennyson once said to my Father "it is because you are the old friend that you are & also because you are the great man that you are that I feel all the fullness of your praise". These were not quite the words but it was the sense & I who am I am grateful to think the friend

& the daughter of great men send you my love & my thanks for this bit of new life, & pride & happiness, for mine & me & I am yours – <u>decorated by you</u>.'[77]

Although Annie eventually made a full recovery from the glandular surgery, she experienced some further discomfort during the early months of 1899, warranting extended stays in Brighton and Tunbridge Wells. The incisions in her neck did not heal easily, continuing to reopen. But as work on the Edition began to decrease, she was at last able to get the rest that she needed. There is something decidedly poignant about Annie's life during these years, quite apart from the state of her health. Her children had grown up. Billy was no longer a schoolboy but an Oxford undergraduate in whom she took great pride. On a visit to Trinity College she watched him in the chapel and had one of those revelatory experiences which came to her at moments of heightened emotion. It was an occasion of almost mystical significance, and one which she could not easily explain. 'I went to Chapel on Sunday & saw my dear boys happy face & stately figure in the opposite stalls. He really looks stately among the rest. I did feel so thankful & I feel as if all the rest of my life will be different for having had this happy realisation.'[78] Hester meanwhile grew ever closer to her father, often accompanying him when Annie was away from town. It was perhaps not unlike the role which Annie herself had acted out for her own father towards the end of his life, although the circumstances were very different. Not to be outdone by Billy, Hester pointedly embraced Richmond's interests and pursuits. She enjoyed bicycling and golf, and like her brother took up fishing, these activities representing, for Annie, an unfamiliar and resolutely non-intellectual world, as mysterious to her as the rules of the sports which Billy had played at Sedbergh, and in which she rejoiced when he did well.

Meanwhile, a more subtle shuffling of the cards was occurring. During 1898 Richmond was still addressing Annie as 'sweetheart' in his letters, but during the course of 1899 this became less frequent, and by 1900 his letters, though not noticeably less affectionate, carried no salutation at all. Towards the end of 1902 he was addressing her as 'Dear Momm', just as Hester and Billy had always done, and he kept to that until his death. Perhaps Annie performed a role for Richmond which was as much that of mother as wife, offering unconditional love to the sometimes wayward child. She never wavered in calling him 'my heart'. They now rarely took holidays together. The demands on Richmond's time at the India Office were such that his periods of leave were few, and could not always be planned well in advance. In his last decade he tended to go to France in the late summer for a few weeks, alone or with Hester; there would also be two extended trips in order to take the waters at Carlsbad. Perhaps it was inevitable that things should have developed along these lines, and that as Annie moved into old age the great affection which they still felt for each other lacked that mix of intellectual energy and passion which had sparked the tenderness of the early years of marriage. It is in this context that the Charlotte Leigh Smith problem should be understood. It pleased him to be seen in the company of this good-looking, energetic, younger woman, and although he was unreasonable in expecting Annie not to demur, it cannot be assumed that anything more than friendship was involved.

It seems unlikely that she would have confided in Billy – which she was doing from March 1899 – had Annie really feared for her marriage. Part of her distress was that Hester had been drawn in, and that sides appeared to be being taken. There is something pathetic about her blaming herself for her jealousy and subsequent gratitude for Richmond's attempt to put her mind at rest. Writing from Tunbridge Wells, she told Billy that 'I am not quite in such a fluster as usual, tho' they <u>are</u> both going to stay with Charlotte, for Wizz told me so charmingly & kindly that I said I w$^d$ try not to feel so fussy as usual, & meanwhile I did so enjoy a pipe or two with him last night by the fire'.[79] It was unavoidable that she should spend time away from home to recuperate, but both Annie and Richmond knew that it was not good to be apart for such extended periods. 'As he says that divided life is unwholesome for us all.'[80] The other part of this equation was Richmond's being based in town during the week and returning to Wimbledon only for the weekend, an arrangement which had made good sense initially but which became increasingly unsatisfactory. By 1899 it was evident that this enforced separation could only be resolved by a move into town, so after much searching they let the End House and took a house in Grosvenor Road, Westminster, transferring a year later to Embankment Gardens in Chelsea.

Not until the autumn of 1901 would they make their final move to a large house in St George's Square just off the Embankment, a short walk from the Tate Gallery. It had been pleasant to live in Wimbledon's village community, but London's social attractions would be more accessible. It took them a full two years to decide to leave the End House, which had been as close as they would get to having their own country idyll. In June 1900, Richmond expressed dissatisfaction with their uncertain status, committed neither to staying or moving. For Annie's part, 'I said very positively I hoped

we <u>should</u> stay, every summer & make this <u>home</u> & go to London
for the winter & to this he agreed.... It certainly is the nicest prettiest
sweetest little garden that ever was. The stag beetles are beginning
to buzz about & Ben selects her favourite plants to sleep upon.'
But just a month later this unrealistic compromise was abandoned,
again largely because of Richmond's insistence that the End House
was beginning to seem more like a rented property than their home.
'Wizz inclines more & more to London, & our last arrival was so
revolting with all the mess that I feel as if it w$^d$. be a mercy to have
no more lettings & to settle down in S$^t$. Georges Sq$^r$. or somewhere
handy.'[81] When they finally did move, financial motives helped in
sealing the deal, for the End House earned more in rent than they
would themselves have to pay for St George's Square. But as she told
Billy, the move was a wrench.

> The more the days go by & the more Wizz doesnt eat his
> dinner the more I feel we are right to go. I think S$^t$ G's Square
> will really suit us very well – You will have a room & a good
> bed-room & so shall I, and so will Codgie & Wizz & its only
> £130 w$^h$. we are going to keep to ourselves & if we can get
> £210 for this or £220 – it really would be very economical
> indeed..... Of course the garden is heart rending! The fig
> tree is all over figs the apple tree of apples the peach tree of
> peaches and a lot of lovely new roses have come out but man
> cannot live by gardens alone.[82]

It was during the months when she was not really strong enough for
much else that Annie started compiling her journal. Through summary,
omission and occasional amplification, a narrative of her past was
constructed. She was engaged in destroying some of the original
diaries when the news of the death of her old friend Mary Cunliffe
was received. 'I had been thinking of Mary all day for as I burnt these
old diaries I had read of her constant kindness & help & coming & I
thought I must write & tell her <u>what</u> a help & friend she was to me for
years.'[83] A process of summing up was under way, with Annie sensing
that in having acquitted herself of a duty to her father's memory the
best was now behind her. As the old century died, ending a 'troubled
year with happy interludes', Hester and Billy were with their parents
to hear the bells at midnight, New Year's day bringing a welcome thaw
in the icy weather. The progress of the South African war preoccupied
London, with troops constantly passing through the capital, and Annie
recorded each setback including the bad news from Ladysmith. Fifteen
years later she would make a rare late amendment to these journal

entries, as the news of fresh horrors of cataclysmic war seized the country. 'What was that to now & the terrible anxiety (1915 May).' The insertion has a wider resonance which puts personal difficulties into perspective. Annie would survive into a world immeasurably changed from the confident certainties of her childhood, but though she thought of the past with fondness she did not fear the present. Her optimism and desire to see the goodness in people carried her through, and experience had taught her that love was indeed the greatest of the human virtues. It can be left to Leslie to suggest just how effective was her ability to transform the lives of others. 'It is often strange to me to think of our past history. I have not always been all that I ought to have been to you: but I know at least now all that you have been to me & these last years will be cheered & soothed by your wonderful goodness to me.'[84] The edges of even his tough agnosticism were softened as death drew closer and he prepared to leave the stage.

# Eight

# THE CONTINUANCE OF LOVE
## (1900-1909)

*I didn't know it again when I saw it! – but it enchanted me even more than it did 25 years ago – only I had remembered it smaller & a different colour; how odd it is the way things slip into a difference.*

Annie to Billy on a picture at the Pitti Palace
14 March 1900

The century turned. A lifetime of visiting France and Italy had not lost its magic, and even the prospect of leaving behind an over-worked husband in poor health did not make Annie postpone her plans. In February 1900 she prepared to travel with Hester to 'the land of Parasols & I'm sure it will do us both good – but I do hate leaving Whizz & being so far away from my Bill. O why are we not American millionaires travelling about all comfortably together!'[1] Italy made her think 'of earth air & water & ancient stones & ancient wares & ancient painted virgins & marble & the old Gods coming to life once more';[2] she temporarily left behind England's preoccupations with the South African war, news of which they followed carefully when they were abroad. It was a revisiting of old territory – Avignon, Marseilles, Cannes (where at the Chateau Thorenc she was allocated Gladstone's former room, slept in his bed and 'quite melted to him'), Genoa, Pisa and finally Florence, staying once again with Sir John Edgar and his sisters. Their arrival in Florence coincided with the sudden death of the Marquese Simone Peruzzi de' Medici, husband of the former Edith Story, and Hester witnessed the impressive funeral procession of 'hundreds & hundreds of Florentines with torches & the priests & a mass of carnations, winding across the bridge & the piazza'.[3] Annie made a point of spending time with Edith, 'who is absolutely pathetic & simple'.[4]

Annie's birthday was celebrated that year with a party and concert, and games in the Wimbledon garden after the music. For someone who always took an interest in the lives and welfare of her servants, who would give a present to a maid when she married and a gift when she left, her journal record of that day is oddly jarring. 'Our poor cooks young man had died suddenly & not one of the tradesmen told her till after for fear of spoiling my birthday party.' It is a reminder of the real separation in the lives of servants and masters in late Victorian England, not least when they lived under the same roof. Annie's extensive charitable work for hospital welfare and for schools – she served on the management committee of the Horseferry Road schools for many years and took the work very seriously – was not in itself sufficient to allow her to understand the circumstances of the lives of those beyond her social circle.

She felt unable to object to Richmond and Hester going to Ouistreham in Normandy where Charlotte was spending the summer, but it was hard to stay positive. 'However I console myself by thinking how bored he is at seaside places here, & what an excellent change it is & how comfortable Charlotte makes him.'[5] Annie reserved for the privacy of her journal her painful jealousy when Richmond made a second visit to Charlotte, this time with Billy – 'R & B to Ouistreham alas' – but some weeks later queried a proposed third trip. 'I told R how much I minded his wanting to go again. I think he understood & I have felt much happier.'[6] She took another holiday herself during August, rather unusually joining a small party on a private yacht for a fortnight's voyage around the coast from Southampton in the south to St Helens in the north-west. Pinkie wrote to tell her that Edith Sichel had also been invited by Charlotte to Ouistreham, adding with gentle but nonetheless well-aimed sarcasm that 'strange to say she is not accepting'.[7] Pinkie remained loyal to Annie, even when it involved implicit criticism of her brother. Annie's continuing relationship with Charlotte is hard to fathom, for she seems to have gone out of her way to be friendly, whilst the rare mentions of Benjamin Leigh Smith have a kind of knowing significance. 'All these days I have had a most curious run of Charlotte. First I called, then she came to lunch, we had Ella Merivale M$^{rs}$ Reeve Char & Molly to meet her. It did very well indeed ... then tomorrow <u>Ben</u>! is coming.' She was fond of Charlotte's two boys, but in the end confided to Billy to being perplexed about her feelings, whereas Hester and Richmond were simply bewitched.

> Phil, Val & Charlotte came to tea & fortunately M$^{r}$. Sydney Colvin also arrived: it made it like an afternoon party. Its so pretty to see Phils adoration for Val. Charlotte is a most extraordinary mixture – sometimes I love her sometimes she

puts every one of my nerves on edge, if only Hester wasnt
so absorbed I shouldnt mind her & if Wizz took her more
lightly I sh$^d$. be almost thankful that there was anybody who
distracted & amused him as she does – Anyhow it must be
far better that she should come here sometimes & yesterday
went off very well on the whole.[8]

Even Leslie Stephen seemed to notice something a little curious going
on, calling on Annie at Cambridge where she was staying with his
sister, Caroline Stephen, and finding her 'in a characteristic state:
wildly looking for a cheque-book & vague about things in general.
Richmond with Hester had gone off to stay with their particular friend,
Mrs Leigh Smith.'[9]

With the new century came thoughts for a new project, a return
to the mix of personal recollections and memoirs about individuals
which Annie had made her own. Early in January she began to plan
the series of occasional *Cornhill* essays which appeared over the next
seven years and then in book form as the *Blackstick Papers* (1908),
the name taken from the Fairy Blackstick character in *The Rose and
the Ring*, a strange instance of Annie inhabiting the persona of one of
her father's imaginative creations. The pieces are slight, sufficient to
charm her old readers but unlikely to win new ones; the formula was a
little too comfortable and provided no fresh challenges for her. But nor
was she seeking them. Rather more energy was invested in her long-
standing irritation about her father's memorial bust in Westminster
Abbey, culminating in the ritual trimming of its extraneous whiskers.
She eventually won the agreement of the Dean, George Bradley, for
alterations to the piece by Carlo Marochetti to be done, under her
supervision, on a day in July. As a surviving witness to the modest
dimensions of her father's facial hair, she hoped that George Smith
might join her in the Abbey, and also took Molly Warre Cornish with
her to steel her resolve. 'If you had time & could meet me at the <u>clerk
of the works</u> office <u>at 11 in the cloisters</u> for 5 minutes how grateful I
should be. Of course my Father had whiskers but nothing prominent &
sitting <u>under</u> the bust they seem the most prominent thing. You are one
of the people who would know.'[10] She later wrote in triumph to Hester
that the mason had chipped away skilfully and 'removed for ever the
horrible weepers – I felt more happy than I can tell you'.

Smith's customary New Year present for 1901 would be his
last. 'They are like jewels & fairy food combined & you are a dear
enchanter to send us such a festival of bonbons & to make me young
again.'[11] His health was failing, and by March she told Billy that 'dear

George Smith is passing quietly away'. This most loyal friend of the
Thackerays survived the Victorian age by just a few weeks, the queen
dying on 21 January and he early in April. Born in the year the queen
came to the throne, Annie was in the fullest sense a Victorian, but
there is no expression of personal loss in her account of the solemn
events of the royal succession and funeral. If anything, there is a sense
of expectation as she bore witness to the potency of change, joining
the crowds to watch the new king pass by. 'Saw history in the streets
crowds in black waiting for the K. blinds down everywhere. Cabmen
with bits of crepe.' And she felt a certain distinction that the Ritchie
household was variously represented on the day of the funeral. She was
at Westminster Abbey for a service timed to coincide with the funeral
at Windsor, Richmond having earlier been at Buckingham Palace in
his uniform as a Companion of the Bath attending the new king, whilst
Billy, now a lance-corporal in the Oxford University Volunteer Corps,
was at Windsor Castle with his platoon close to St George's Chapel.
The coffin had been brought back from Osborne House, crossing the
Solent from Cowes to Portsmouth, and early on the day of the funeral
had travelled by train to Victoria where it was transferred to a gun-
carriage and drawn ceremonially through the streets to Paddington for
its final rail journey to Windsor. 'All the maids went – Hilda saw 15
ladies fainting & Mary saw the crown on the coffin: I went to the
Abbey w$^h$. was really extremely fine & impressive.... Sir Theodore
[Martin] said to me "who preached" & I said Handel preached &
Beethoven preached.'[12]

Amidst these grand solemnities, the prosaic challenges of living
within their means again preoccupied the Ritchies. There is a beguiling
innocence about Annie's confusion as to why they were so short of
funds. We are entitled to be puzzled too, for within two years the
Biographical Edition money of £4,000 seems all to have gone. In
October 1900, having just seen their balance at the bank, she had written
to Billy to postpone a visit to Oxford – 'only about £150 left lots to pay
so we must all be economical & wait for larks till Wizz's salary & the
divs are paid in'. It was rather a hand to mouth existence, for she was
already counting on the payments for her new *Cornhill* essays, and in
February was pleased to receive 'a small but very welcome remittance
f$^m$. America'. In consultation with his Oxford tutors it was decided
that Billy should leave in the summer of 1901 and become articled
to their friend Charles Plumptre Johnson, the solicitor and Thackeray
bibliophile. 'We are being agonizingly economical as we have hardly
any balance till Wizz's next salary & it is rather a good thing for us that
you wont have another year.'[13] No unrealistic pressures had been put

on him, Richmond having long stopped hoping for academic brilliance from his son, though he acknowledged that Billy had worked hard. 'I find I shdnt be surprised if he got a Second but I dont suppose he will.'[14]

When Gussie Freshfield had the first of the operations for the cancer which ten years later would kill her, Annie recommended the surgeon who had treated her own glandular condition, and shared her hopes with Pinkie at a time of great anxiety. 'O what a comfort it will be if she is as fortunate as I was & comes out of this pass.'[15] May was spent in Paris with Hester, whilst Billy took his last Oxford exams and faced the viva voce. They now made final preparations for leaving Wimbledon, completing the long-contemplated move to St George's Square in September. Annie left the logistics to Hester and Richmond and retreated to Brighton. There she took inspiration from the resilience of an old Thackeray friend, Eliza (Tisey) Smith, who was enthusiastic about the prospect of her ninetieth birthday in November. 'The Fifth Act my dear she says but not the last scene O no.'[16] Richmond went his own way, to Brussels and Paris, spending his days in galleries and evenings at the theatre and opera. Hester remained alone to get the house in order. Annie increasingly relied on Hester now, involving her in decisions about the future of the Thackeray materials, for the time was drawing nearer when the legacy would pass into the care of others. Annie had been approached about selling more manuscripts. 'I dont quite know what to advise. Denis [Duval] & D[r]. Birch are for Billy & there are 2 notebooks for each – & the Scrap books & there is the book of the Virginian drawings – on the whole I feel inclined to keep it & even if the fashion for mss goes off the mss itself will be just the same as it is now.'[17]

The onset of Leslie's final illness began in 1902. 'How nobly he bore it! With what courage.' He told Annie of his condition in the spring, resigned to the likely outcome even before hearing the specialist's prognosis. As he suspected, the growth was cancerous. 'My case is serious & I could not help wishing for your sympathy. The doctor at Hindhead discovered that I had an obstruction in the bowel which will probably require an operation – He said that time was important & I am to see a specialist tomorrow morning at 11.15. I shall then know what are my prospects.'[18] Annie's devotion to his welfare over the next two years was exemplary, the more so as she had worries enough at home. Although there are fewer references to Richmond's attacks from Ménière's disease, his general digestion became a new concern, and especially the condition of his liver. If the symptoms were less dramatic, they were still sufficiently serious for his doctor to insist on his spending three weeks in the Austrian spa town of Carlsbad in order to take the waters, a regime that was repeated the following year. The source of the problem was overwork, and the medical opinion was that 'he must spare himself in every way & take any amusement he can'.[19]

As he prepared himself for Carlsbad, Richmond was reassured by his doctor's prognosis. 'He said with Carlsbad & a good rest I ought to be all right next winter – that I had a bad but not a very bad liver & that the really disagreeable symptoms were due to the effect in the line of nervous exhaustion which was due to overwork – & that after Karlsbad the virginity of the stomach should tell for my good when I got back to work.'[20] He was under additional pressure now because of his involvement in preparations for the king's summer coronation, for he was responsible for the visiting Indian delegates. Annie and Hester were on the continent when he wrote to tell them of the drain on his time, of 'frivolous Coronation problems with the Chiefs arriving'. Despite the impressive rituals of the occasion, Richmond was diverted during the service by the presence of Sarah Bernhardt, 'got up as for her First Communion, & as full of fervent emotion'.[21] It rather thrilled Annie to glimpse the masculine world of politics through Richmond's work, so removed from her natural habitat. She stood with Billy in July to watch Lord Kitchener pass by, returning in triumph from South Africa following the surrender of the Boers, and then Richmond provided a balancing human glimpse of the war leader. 'R says a tall pasty strange looking man marched into his room unannounced today in a shabby white waistcoat. He said Im Lord Kitchener & I want to know what the exact date of my return to India will be – Perhaps you will kindly telegraph at once to Lord Curzon about it…. He says L$^d$. K has an odd schoolboy manner. I thought he was a demi-god on Satdy when he went by.'[22]

The original plan for Carlsbad was that Richmond would join Annie and Hester on the continent and continue south with them, but that he should then be left to 'start his cure alone'. In fact it would be Annie who, leaving Richmond and Hester in Switzerland to undertake the final leg without her, returned slowly through Germany and France, having watched their departure by train and imagining herself in a scene from *Vanity Fair*. 'I saw y$^r$ handkerchiefs waving & waving & then when I had got into bed again I felt exactly like Becky after the troops went to Waterloo & I began to think what a delightful trip it ought to be & then I blew my nose & had a nap.' She wrote daily, sending off a letter from each town she reached, anxious for details of the benefits of the curative springs. She was back in London by

6 September, and the next day Richmond sent off a detailed account
of the Carlsbad water regime which involved regular imbibing and
occasional baths. It certainly was no holiday.

> The waters make me feel so wretchedly ill, always headache
> or backache & the same sort of feeling as after influenza
> …The doctor whom I went to see this morning … told me
> when I first went that there was a decided though very slight
> enlargement of the liver & that I had a good deal of uric acid
> in me (due no doubt to the wine drunk in Switzerland) so
> that there is something definite for the waters to do. He is
> giving me what he says is the mildest course & that I want
> no reducing & I only lost 5 oz in weight in 3 days which is
> nothing – but Im thankful Im not being treated drastically – &
> I am thankful poor Hester wasn't embarked on it. The baths
> are so delicious (they cost 5 francs each) that I treated her to
> one yesterday with the result that she absolutely collapsed
> for the rest of the day – though enraptured with the sensation
> at the time – with very much my symptoms, but today she
> is all right, vowing however that nothing will induce her to
> take another.[23]

Once the Carlsbad treatment was over, he and Hester would take
a few more weeks holidaying in Italy before returning to London,
and he made tentative plans that Charlotte might join them for part
of that time. When he wrote on 16 September, this was Annie's first
inkling of what he had in mind, and he knew that it would hurt her.
It remains the only piece of evidence to show that, however innocent
his intentions, he was conscious that this friendship was open to more
salacious interpretations. The awkwardness of the letter is indicative
of the wider gulf that remained largely unspoken.

> I now want to tell you about our plans. Charlotte is coming
> to Italy when her boys holidays are over, & we propose to
> meet: to which I hope you will agree. I know that it will give
> you pain that I say this: but without telling you beforehand,
> I should not feel justified in carrying out the plan. I know it
> gives you pain, but nevertheless I say I hope you will agree
> – You know me well enough to know I would not say this if
> there was any real reason why you should object –
>     You may be reassured that we shall do nothing to provoke
> criticism – not stop at the same hotels etc – nor shall we be
> together all the time as Charlotte has to go to Miss Lowndes

at Florence. Hester too as you know is looking forward to Charlotte's coming: & is really glad to have her as a third.

Dont think me unfeeling because I have written in this matter of fact way – It is the only way now in which I can express myself – & if you think, you know what I feel & that there is nothing that in my own way I dont say – but the consciousness that my silence & matter of factness is sometimes misunderstood, only makes it more difficult for me to say things – But that is my nature which cant be changed I fear even by waters more drastic than those of the wells here.

His search for approval was disingenuous, for on what grounds could Annie have withheld it? It was unavoidable that she should feel some sexual jealousy, but more hurtful was her exclusion from this special friendship in which Hester had also become implicated. It had showed no signs of diminishing as the years went by, during which she felt herself growing older. The reply which she sent by return does not survive, but Richmond's response to it does, and there is no doubt who emerges with the greater dignity. He had confidently appealed to her best nature. 'I am most grateful for your letter which however is what I expected from you. You will understand what I mean by this & by being grateful. Nor need you be under apprehensions. I will behave with perfect prudence, & from this point of view the fact that you trust me is what makes the difference. I had thought it all over and come to the determination that if you did not agree I would return from Munich alone at once, leaving Hester to make a tour with Charlotte.'[24] What Annie found distasteful was being drawn into the arrangements and having publicly to make light of the supposedly chance Italian encounter. To one of her nieces who had learnt of the likelihood of the meeting, Annie simply maintained a discreet silence, but to Hester she could not resist a dig at having to field the family queries. 'I consider I have been as wise as a serpent & as harmless as a dove tell Wizz.'[25] Writing from Fasano on 7 October he addressed Annie as 'My heart' rather than 'Momm', a once familiar endearment which now reads as an awkward acknowledgement of what he owed her. She crossed back to France at the end of the month to meet them on the return lap, and they spent a last few days in Paris. Richmond had noticeably benefited from Carlsburg, though Hester seemed rather wan. As Annie told Pinkie, one topic was best avoided. 'Charlotte I dont talk about – She is gone back to England all those friends & visits having melted into thin air.'[26]

On his return to the India Office, Richmond was given the important position as Secretary of the Political and Secret Department by Lord George Hamilton, whose own resignation as Secretary of State less than a year later caused considerable consternation. Change at the top always made the positions of others uncertain, and despite his many years of service it was inevitable that Richmond should be wary of the ambitions of younger, fitter men. He knew that he owed a lot to Hamilton, who had valued his judgment and support, for 'it is real good fortune (apart from the merits) to be one of the chosen'.[27] In fact, it is unlikely that someone of Richmond's experience and ability would have been overlooked, and he continued to be valued by succeeding Secretaries of State, especially John Morley.

Annie and Richmond threw a party on New Year's day 1903 to celebrate twenty-five years of marriage (they were already well into their twenty-sixth), surrounded by 'kind guests, flowers, crowds, friendship'. William Ritchie died quietly in his sleep later that night, news which, though not unexpected, was saddening. He was the oldest of the four Ritchie brothers, the one whom Annie and Minny had got to know more then forty years before, when as a boy he stayed in Onslow Square during holidays from his preparatory school. It was another link broken. Willie's illness had become apparent at about the same time as Leslie's, so that his death made Annie even more alert to her brother-in-law's slow decline. During Leslie's last months she went to him almost daily, visits which he valued more than those of any other person – to Charles Eliot Norton he called her 'my beloved Anny Ritchie' – for her love was not spoiled by sentiment. Knowing that his time was limited made it easier for them to communicate without awkwardness. As Leslie wryly put it, their letters were like an exchange between a dove and a gorilla, but the fact that they were unalike in so many ways was no hindrance. With Annie, he could share intimacies that he probably held back from other friends and family. 'He is gentle & cheerful – & his eyes look so young. The dear children flit round & are so good. It is such a strange repetition of dear Willys illness last year. Leslie said It is nice to think of the new young life following us.'[28] After one visit in October she set down their exchange in her journal. 'I said I dont think the world will be nearly so nice without us. Leslie said It will go on. You have others. Life will go on. I said Dear Leslie I love you I dont know what else to say. He said I know it dear Annie. They say it cannot last beyond Christmas.'

In fact it lasted a little longer than that, until the end of February 1904, but Annie was not distressed by the vigil, for only with him could she revisit the now largely unspoken memories of their shared life with Minny. She tried also to ease things for Vanessa and Virginia – 'the nurse made a sort of appeal to me to try to get the girls away. She says they are always waiting shyly on the stairs.'[29] She arranged for Billy to take them to a play at Drury Lane, and found other temporary distractions from the oppressive gloom of Hyde Park Gate. Pinkie saw the value of what Annie was trying to do. 'How good for Virginia to be taken by you to see things.'[30] In her devotion to Leslie's comfort she put aside other engagements to spend time with him. 'I go every day to Leslie & that is as much as I can do almost – I shall not have him very long to go to.'[31] When the end came, a gentle note from Vanessa was enough. 'Father did not rally or become conscious again & died very peacefully & quietly at 7 this morning. Nothing could have been more absolutely peaceful.'[32] Virginia expressed something of their lasting debt after Annie's own death. 'I feel as if we owed more than we can ever say to Aunt Anny for what she was to mother & father as well as for what she was to us. I think they loved her better than anyone.' Although Virginia doubted 'the sincerity of my own emotions', she had no need to.[33]

Several letters of sympathy came from those who understood something of what Leslie's death meant to her, including Gussie, who knew that Annie would inevitably be reliving the time after Minny's death. 'I am thinking very very sadly of you tonight for I know what this passing away of dear Leslie means to you! How the years roll away & one feels back at Southwell G[dens] with him & you left desolate!' Touched, Annie replied at once. 'It is so strange about feeling. I begin to think of everything else of Minnie most of all. Has he not been magnanimous & outcoming to the last & what a sense of the continuance of love it gives one as note after note is struck.'[34] As she had done when Minny died, she retreated to Brighton for a while.

In the months leading up to Leslie's death, Annie had managed to get some time away. Late in May 1903, Pinkie and Edith Sichel lent her their house near Godalming, and in August she went with Billy and a couple of her Ritchie nieces for a few weeks to Sedbergh, their first visit back since he had left school. Billy fished and walked and entertained his Oxford friend, the young pianist and composer Donald Tovey, and she worked on two of her 'Blackstick' essays. Hester came briefly before returning to London to accompany Richmond on his second Carlsberg visit. A suggestion that Richmond might first visit them in the north seems not to have gone down well. 'I said why not come to us at Sedbergh – but that was rash of me!'[35] There is no mention of meeting Charlotte abroad this year, although in June Annie cryptically noted 'C.L.S. too interfering'. But Charlotte could be thoughtful too, and she was among those who wrote sympathetically after Leslie died.

The Stephen children experienced real trauma. His stepsons were old enough to cope with the loss, but his daughters by Julia were another matter – particularly the fragile and susceptible twenty-one year old Virginia. Annie would seek out and pass on any reassuring news concerning Virginia during her periods of nervous collapse, such as in October 1904 when, with their move from 22 Hyde Park Gate to Gordon Square not completed, the Stephen sisters first took up the offer of the loan of Charles and Mary Booth's London house – 'Virginia is there quietly reviving'[36] – and again when Caroline Stephen threw open her Cambridge home to her. As one of the first visitors to Gordon Square, Annie's interest in the welfare of the Stephen children went so far as trying to fix them up with servants. 'Did I tell you how perfectly charming I thought their house with a bright open back & pretty french windows. Ginia got wrong in London & is rapidly reviving at Carolines. I want her to have Leahs sister – a perfect <u>darling</u> woman merry handsome & gentle 37 a dressmaker who has had to give up for the long hours.'[37]

She encouraged Sidney Lee, Leslie's successor as editor of the *Dictionary of National Biography*, to arrange for an engraving of the Watts portrait of Leslie to be made, so that a copy might be given to the London Library, where it is still displayed on the stairwell. 'It will be nice to send it to Trinity & to America.'[38] The legal historian, Frederic Maitland, got in touch seeking letters for the 'short memoir' which Leslie had hoped that he might one day undertake, Maitland and Leslie having been related by marriage. His request for materials is a model of modesty and caution, for he was of course aware of Annie's closeness during Leslie's last months, as well as her likely sensitivity about things relating to the first marriage and its sad conclusion. '[I]t seems to me possible that you have some letters which do not fall within the sacred class and which might help me in my difficult endeavour.' Later he thanked her for letting him have sight of Leslie and Minny's 1868 American trip correspondence, which made clear the bond with Annie left at home – 'you have enabled me to make some outsider's guess of the weight of sorrow that fell on you and Leslie many years ago'.[39] His fear of saying anything at all which might open old wounds led him to ask Leslie's sister to decide how the first marriage might be handled, and Caroline Stephen wrote a few lines which were then passed to Annie for approval. 'What I care for is chiefly that M<sup>rs</sup>. Ritchie should be satisfied or not dissatisfied.'[40]

Although Leslie's was the death which touched her most closely, there were other departures during 1904. Watts died in July, and

Mary wrote to Annie, 'his dearest of friends', pleased that there were permanent mementos in the form of the portraits which Watts had done of her and of Minny. 'I am so glad you have those two pictures, the second made precious three times over to you! Your beautiful flowers were near him – he was surrounded by love & honour!'[41] In the same month Sir John Simon died, his pioneering improvements in public health having won him a national acclaim which never got in the way of his affectionate interest in Billy, his godson. Annie was less close to the painter Val Prinsep, but she had followed his career since the early Freshwater days. He died on 11 November whilst undergoing a prostate operation, and Annie heard that Mary Watts, who went to the funeral, was 'half rent by it'.[42] But once again there were troubles closer to home, this time with Hester, who seems to have suffered some kind of breakdown. Annie packed her off to Berlin during the autumn to learn German, uncertain that she was doing the right thing. 'I think Im glad & thankful on the whole & that it will be a new start for my darling Hester.'[43] The possibilities of inherited illness must have been a concern, with the histories of her own mother and Laura ever present. Two years later, Richmond took Hester to convalesce in Hyères, and sent encouraging reports. 'Hester gets visibly stronger every day and takes an interest, and there is no doubt that in a comparatively short time, nature will complete the cure.'[44] On the other hand, these collapses – for there would be others – perhaps struck Annie as no more serious than her own tendency towards a sort of hysteric reaction at moments of intense crisis, from which she always seemed to recover with rest and a change of scene.

She longed for her family to be free from their current worries. Billy was preparing for his Inns of Court examinations, but escaped when he could to the country – 'tomorrow thank goodness he will have his free day with the Beagles…. It will be splendid when you too have passed in German & when I have finished my novel! … & when this wretched Tibet no longer worries Wizz.'[45] She does seem to have worked on a piece of fiction to which she turned periodically during her last years, but would never complete. In 1906 she told the American publisher George Putnam that there might be a book on the way, and he expressed a decided interest in 'the romance that you have in preparation which is to be published under some such title as "The Wishing Well"'.[46] But that is about all we ever learn about it. Reginald Smith had told her that there were not yet sufficient 'Blackstick' essays to warrant republishing as a book, recalling Frederick Macmillan's similar comment from ten years earlier concerning her *Chapters from Some Memoirs*. In both instances, she had to write additional

material to make up a viable volume. As the years had gone by and
the energy which she could devote to writing had receded, she had
begun to depend upon this recycling of her essays into collections.
She hoped to persuade Smith, Elder to bring out all of her old fiction
in a new collected format, even if she knew that sales were likely
to depend as much upon the illustrations as on the pull of her own
name. 'Wizz & I settled last night that I should apply to R. to bring
out a pretty Edition of my stories with the <u>Walker pictures</u>. They are
all the fashion & I might just as well get the fun of it as wait till I
die.'[47] Smith must have found a way to steer her away from this idea,
not convinced by its commercial viability. Yet he does seem to have
promoted the plans for a revised version of the Biographical Edition,
and Annie devoted much energy during 1905-6 to reworking some of
the Introductions, incorporating additional materials from her father's
letters and drawings. It would eventually be born as the twenty-six-
volume edition published to coincide with Thackeray's centenary in
1911, having been temporarily aborted in 1907 with the withdrawal
of Harpers from the contract.[48]

Knowing that the productive years were behind her, and with the
loss of old friends a constant reminder of her age – sixty-eight in 1905
– her former capacity to retreat into the past was easily triggered. Her
correspondence touches on times when things were more certain, and
perhaps happier. When Lucy Baxter made a return visit from America,
'so taking & gracious still', Annie organised a tea party to welcome
her, as her father's representative. 'I know he w$^d$ have wished it.' She
felt a little shy of inviting Joseph Joachim to attend, as she would
have liked. '<u>He</u> remembers those days & spoke to me so charmingly
of my dear Father the other night that I admired him more than ever.
Dear light in the fogs of life as he ever has been.'[49] It was important
for her to keep up with those who, however transiently, had featured
in her past. She contacted Ellen Terry through a mutual friend. She
had seen the actress on stage in recent years, but it was to earlier times
that she now went back. 'I have such old links with her & her early
girlhood belongs to my youth & I have always <u>ached</u> for her poor soul
but I do hope she has some sunshine in her life as well as cares.'[50]
From Freshwater, the elderly Mary Brotherton sent Annie a portrait
of Mrs Carmichael-Smyth which as a child she had copied from a
picture, together with a little anecdote about the legendary good looks
of Thackeray's mother. 'How beautiful she was. When we were in
Rome, and your father came to see us, and I asked after her, he said
"Oh she's quite well" – adding, "She's still the <u>second</u> most beautiful
woman in the world".' Mary Brotherton also had a good story about

the positivist philosopher Frederic Harrison and Mrs Cameron. She had once come across the two of them in earnest conversation at the gate of Dimbola Lodge. 'When she saw me she said, "O do come and talk to M<sup>r</sup>. Harrison. I <u>must</u> go for half an hour" – & whispered as she kissed me, "Do, <u>do</u>, persuade him of the divinity of Christ – I know you can if you try – Goodbye, I shall be back in half an hour" – & she was off.'[51]

And when herself at Freshwater, Annie was struck by the way in which the patterns of history formed and reformed, for on seeing Hallam Tennyson with his own young child she was swept back decades to a time when not just the poet was alive, but when Lionel and Minny and that lost generation were still young and hopeful. 'Hallam has been so kind that it quite affects me. He looks like his Father & there is the little boy & the tutor & it might be all thirty years ago for any great change of aspect in the dear old place.'[52] With someone like Kate Perugini, Dickens's daughter, she had much in common despite the very different lives they had led. Kate was no less shielding of her father's reputation than was Annie of hers, robustly expressing her view of those who offended. Occasionally Kate felt even more protectively towards Thackeray than did Annie herself, such as when the novelist Mrs Eliza Linton was injudicious enough to publish some memories. 'How did she know who were our father's loves? Of this I am certain; that neither of them ever loved <u>her</u>, and what she says of <u>my</u> father seemed to imply that he did! But I am always angry with M<sup>rs</sup>. L.L. since reading what she had to say about George Eliot to whom she ought to have been on her knees!'[53]

With both of Laura Stephen's parents dead, future arrangements for the funding of her care came under fresh scrutiny. Two documents survive drawn up by Hills & Halsey, Jack Hills' own legal firm, he being Stella Duckworth's widower and principal trustee of the Trust fund established under Leslie and Minny's marriage settlement drawn up in 1873. Investments generating an annual income of nearly £470 were available to cover Laura's care costs, which in 1905 at £221 had left a surplus of about £240. The first of the documents, dated 1 March 1906, set out to establish whether Laura was likely ever to be in a position to make decisions for herself, of the kind involved in drawing up a will, and to determine who was her legal next of kin. Medical advice was taken from Dr Corner, into whose direct care Laura had passed in 1897, and he reported on 11 February 1906 that 'Miss Laura Stephen is quite unable to make a will or transact business of any description and there is not the slightest chance of her ever being able to do anything of the kind'. An expert ruling was sought from Counsel, which was that, in the event of Laura dying intestate, her property would become divisible between her next of kin, identified as the children of Leslie's second marriage.[54] A meeting quickly followed, on 19 March, involving Adrian, Thoby, Vanessa and Virginia Stephen, Gerald Duckworth and Jack Hills (the trustees), Billy (representing Annie)[55] and Katherine and Herbert Stephen, Leslie's niece and nephew. It was agreed that costs of up to £300 for Laura's care must continue to be covered 'and it was decided that Mrs. Richmond Ritchie and Miss Katharine Stephen should each year determine the actual amount'. There remained some unspent monies, and 'it was unanimously agreed that the surplus annual income should be accumulated by advancing it at 4 per cent interest to Miss L. M. Stephen's half brothers and sisters, secured upon a Mortgage of their freehold house, 22 Hyde Park Gate'.[56]

Fortunately, Annie was not a witness to this division of the spoils, for she would surely have found it intensely distasteful to see the future of Minny's vulnerable daughter become entangled with the financial self-interest of her half-siblings in this somewhat mean-spirited picking over of the bones. The condition of Laura herself was remarkably changeable, and her behaviour unpredictable. Sometimes things seemed quite hopeful, such as when she 'looked radiant to see me: & so well & even tried to talk a little', but just a few months later, when Annie took her to stay with her for a short holiday in Hampstead, the situation seemed much bleaker. 'I am thankful to have had my Laura but O much less well she is. Just a flash of herself – at one moment I could see Minnie in her merry peeping face & then this cruel nightmare again.'[57]

One event in 1906 brought unqualified happiness. In May Billy became engaged to Margaret (Meg) Booth, who had already turned down proposals from two of the Llewelyn Davies brothers. Meg was the daughter of Charles and Mary Booth, whose marriage had united new money with a distinguished intellectual pedigree. Charles Booth was the wealthy founder of a Liverpool shipping line, but is now better known for devoting much of his later life to philanthropic work and as the author of the immense *Life and Labour of the People in London*, a work which helped shape the direction of the British welfare state. Mary Booth was a daughter of the Macaulay who in 1860 had been touched by the *Cornhill* obituary for his better-known brother, a tribute which he described as 'the outpouring of a tender, generous, noble nature', unaware that Thackeray was its author. 'I should much like Thackeray to know that the last book my Brother read was the 1st. number of the Cornhill Magazine. It was open, at Thackeray's story, on the table by the side of the chair in which he died.'[58] This was the kind of detail which would not have passed by Annie unnoticed, now that Thomas Macaulay's great-niece was to marry her son.

The only concern which Annie and Richmond had about Billy's engagement related to his prospects, for he had still to achieve a secure position within the law. Hard experience had taught his parents that their ability to provide him with a financial cushion was decidedly limited, but the Booths' characteristic generosity – one which they could readily afford, admittedly – ensured that this would be no hindrance. The Ritchies undertook to provide Billy with £200 a year, and Charles Booth matched this sum, adding it to the £400 annually which he already allowed to Meg. Booth was taken by Billy, acknowledging that his daughter 'has won the heart of a good & true gentleman'.[59] Annie wrote with a full heart to Mary Booth.

> Billy came home last night after seeing M^r Booth & told us how kind how <u>very</u> extraordinarily kind he had been – We at home know what Billy is but of course we know that he is not at all a good match as far as material things go – he has but a very small portion, – he has only made the first step in his profession and unless you or M^r Booth make it possible, no marriage could be thought of for years, & this of course w^d. be hard on him tho' he w^d have no real reason to complain.
>
> Dear M^rs Booth when I think what it w^d be to realise the thought of so dear a love for my dearest boy my heart feels full of thankfulness & how shall I say it I feel that those who belong to him (& he is not universal in his affections) have a true gentleman & friend in him and this comes of his beloved self & is his Fathers inheritance also.[60]

The wedding followed in early August at Gracedieu, the Booths country house at Whitwick in Leicestershire. But before that, there was the usual hasty round of visits to enable friends and family to meet the intended bride or bridegroom. Annie took Meg to see Howard Sturgis at his house near Windsor. 'He says if we dont mind one very small room he can gladly take us in & that he is particularly glad to make your acquaintance & that he has asked "dear Henry James" to meet us.'[61] It made Annie very happy to contemplate the good fortune of her beloved son, even if she had to surrender him to the care of another woman. 'I have just ordered Billys & my wedding dress! Smoke gauze over silk to match. I <u>cant</u> get used to it! Billy a married man! its just impossible.'[62] As the families gathered

*Wedding of Billy and Meg Booth at Gracedieu, Leicestershire, August 1906.*
*Meg sits between her mother Mary Booth, and Annie; behind her stands Billy,*
*and behind him, on either side, stand Charles Booth and Richmond.*

at Gracedieu for the marriage we glimpse an image of Edwardian
leisure and privilege, so soon to be swept away. Writing to Pinkie,
Annie was even persuaded that Hester was stronger again.

> It is all so kind so <u>really</u> kind. The family comes & goes & the
> motors, & the boys play cricket (including the bridegroom)
> & the girls look so charming in their muslin dresses &
> Richmond sits under the trees discoursing & Hester is her
> old self again. I feel very very thankful.
>
> It is like a Swiss table d'hote with all the immense family
> down either side Macnaghtens & Ritchies & George now
> expected with his bride. Adeline looks well & very pretty.
> M^{rs} Booth says she gets better looking every day. Hester is
> my old Hester.[63]

Billy and Meg began their honeymoon in Sedbergh, hill-walking
and revisiting his schoolboy haunts – in a letter to her mother Meg
described it as 'a sort of home to Billy'[64] – while Richmond and Hester
went to France and Annie made her own summer plans. Immediately
after the wedding came news that Billy had been appointed by the
Lord Chancellor to a legal position in the Chancery Registrar's Office.
The duties were relatively light, and the prospects good, as Richmond
pointed out. '£250 a year, rising £25 annually – never kept at work
later than 4 – holidays, the long Vacation plus pickings at Xmas &
Easter – Was there ever such luck?'[65]

At the end of the summer Gussie Freshfield faced further surgery for the recurrence of her cancer. She bore the years of her illness with dignity and resignation, and urged Annie not to be anxious. 'Life cannot be all beer & skittles. And I constantly feel I have had more than my share of sheer enjoyment.... Darling come & see me very soon. I do implore you not to be unhappy.'[66] But then came Thoby Stephen's death on 20 November from peritonitis, news which Annie relayed to George Meredith whose reply spoke of the great hopes that many had placed on Leslie's eldest son. 'All who loved the family must feel that this death of their bright boy has thwarted the hope of father & mother. They might be alive, so conscious am I of them in our day of mourning. The children will have inherited fortitude. But Vanessa must still be weak, & anxiety continues .... When I read of peritonitis the shadow came over me. – Thoby's article on Compulsory Chapel promised much of his father. I have been used to see lights extinguished. This one is the saddest to survivors. Always the question comes to me – Why not I? for I am useless, & ready.'[67]

Annie was there, as always, to support Leslie and Julia's surviving children. She visited them at Gordon Square, finding Virginia and Adrian in the garden. 'I was quite overcome yesterday by their gentle, noble courage & tenderness it was so simple and so <u>wise</u> somehow.'[68] It was an affection returned in kind. Virginia in particular seems to have been alert to the small gestures which would please her father's ageing sister-in-law, giving her 'the dear old Punch spoon' which had once been Thackeray's, and had come to Leslie through Minny.[69] It was a scene which surely contributed to Virginia's later characterisation of Mrs Hilbery. 'I found Nessa & Ginia dividing the silver & like angels they asked me if I sh$^d$. like any & I said yes the old spoon in the Roundabout Papers & they have given it me. I <u>am</u> so pleased to have it again. I had often wished for it. It was most sweet of them & Ive brought it home.'[70] Annie's own sureness of touch ensured that Caroline Stephen's shyness about meeting Clive Bell for the first time was smoothed over. Vanessa took Clive with her to visit her aunt in Cambridge, and Caroline was grateful to Annie for preparing the way. 'It does make me a little nervous, but y$^r$. dear words help me – Vanessa is always sweet & perfect to me – but Clive is unknown ground, & I am so thankful for what you say of him.'[71] It was what Annie was good at – seeing the best in people and enabling others to do the same. If there was a downside it was her tendency to be blind to their weaknesses. But her intuitive understanding about how people's actions impinge upon the lives of others cannot be faulted, for the day following Vanessa and Clive's wedding she and Hester called on

Virginia, perhaps remembering her own confused feelings in the first days after Minny had married Virginia's father.

Richmond's experience and exactness was not lost on his political masters. Early in 1907 he turned down the chance of promotion which would probably have taken him to the Foreign Office. John Morley, by then Secretary of State for India, came to Richmond's room to make the offer, 'at the same time saying what a boon it w$^d$ be to him & to the I.O. if R <u>didnt</u> take it!'[72] His loyalty had its reward, for at the end of June his name was put forward for a knighthood, the KCB. On their way to a party at Windsor Castle he showed his 'secret letter' to Annie and Hester in the train. Their shared joy at his pleasure went a long way to heal the hurt that Annie continued to feel at her tendency to be kept at arm's length. Only in March her diary had recorded him setting out once again to France without her to meet up with Charlotte and her sons. 'R goes off alone with Hester always & I feel so far off – cant be cured. Must be endured.' But at the end of June, as she and Hester embarked for Christiansund in Norway to stay with the naturalist, Edith Cole, they were excited at the prospect of the news that would become public in their absence. Annie took a childlike delight at the trappings which went with the honour, replying to two ladies on board ship who asked whether she was Miss Thackeray 'no I was M$^{rs}$ Ritchie & then as the ship had started I told them I believed I sh$^d$. be Lady Ritchie tomorrow morning', later signing 'Lady R' for her soda water at dinner and playfully closing her letter to Richmond as 'Her Ladyship'. She described Bergen as 'the birthplace of Ibsen & of <u>Lady Ritchie</u>', and Richmond had to rein in her excitement a little, pointing out that protocol would not permit her to be known as Lady Richmond Ritchie – 'I am afraid it won't do' – plain Lady Ritchie would have to suffice. Mary Brotherton understood Annie's simple pleasure in the reflected glory of the title. 'I am sure you <u>enjoy</u> it, and don't pretend you don't, – like affected common people.'[73] Richmond himself was perhaps a little hurt at the jealousies of some of his relatives – 'the family has on the whole been very grumpy' – but he was in no danger of taking himself too seriously. One of the housemaids at St George's Square, rather overwhelmed by his title and uncertain how to address him, started by calling him 'Miss'.[74]

Annie was a seasoned European traveller, but she had never experienced anything quite like the stark beauties of Norway and 'this noble new world ... like Switzerland but softer & bigger & not overrun'. Her visit coincided with a period of considerable political change, for just a few months earlier the union between Sweden and Norway had been dissolved, and Norway became the first European nation to embrace women's suffrage. But it was the mystery and magic of the landscape which struck her, as well as its primal power. One night at Christiansund Hester stayed out fishing alone until late, and at about midnight Annie decided to go out to look for her, rather losing her way. 'Everything was O so still & beautiful & luminous. I dont think I was ever more frightened – for the river rushed below & I couldnt find the wooden bridge – Then I called & again & then I thought I heard her answer & lo there she was close to the bridge. It was not a tree as I feared but Hester very calm & warm & having caught nothing & not at all ready to come back. It was about <u>one</u> when we got back meeting Miss Cole halfway & I tried to pretend it was all in the days work.' As they left Christiansund behind and travelled to Bergen, she and Hester went on deck to witness the spectacle of the phenomenon of the midnight sun. It was hard to find words to describe it to Richmond. 'It was dim luminous twilight the great rocks with pointed spires rose sheer up on either side the end of the pass opened into floating opal Monte Rosas, & suddenly at a break in the great wall a round red moon hung over a gigantic pass.... We <u>longed</u> for you to see it, & wondered whether to rush in to the saloon & call all the people out from their Bridge, but while we were hesitating the supreme moment was passed.'[75]

Towards the end of their trip they received the appalling news of Reginald Balfour's suicide, husband of Charlotte Warre Cornish. It made Annie anxious to return without delay, yet she feared that at seventy her capacity for doing good was limited. 'I am too old to do anything for anyone except love you all, only I long to be back.' She was determined to assign noble motives to Balfour, who had suffered from depression, and recalled her last time with him. 'Reggie drove back to town with us perfectly gay & charming but deadly pale. I can imagine his wanting to spare them all.' She embraced Huxley's maxim, 'that it is so great a thing to have <u>lived</u> at all that even such premature death does not un-make the boon of living'.[76] To Edith Peruzzi, whose eldest son had taken his own life in February following a rumoured homosexual scandal, she showed once again how even such a low moment as this could offer a degree of comfort. 'Now that I am an old woman I feel more & more that we are meant to take any happiness that comes along with these terrible griefs & anguishes – and how one <u>loves</u> those who die young & how their memory lives year after year.'[77] She and Hester were back in London in time to dine with Billy and Meg on their first wedding anniversary, but Joseph Joachim's death was another sadness. Knowing its poignancy for Pinkie, Annie found the right words to comfort and encourage his close friend and frequent accompanist. 'You have been one of the people to give him most happiness in his interpretation & you have to go on making people love great & beautiful music.'[78]

When the first of Annie's grandchildren was born, it was like the page turning on a fresh but final chapter in her life. James Makepeace Thackeray Ritchie, a 'placid beautiful boy', arrived at about teatime on 5 November. He was christened at Westminster Abbey a month later, surrounded by his Ritchie great-aunts and great-uncles. Annie was struck by Meg's likeness to the statue of her Macaulay great-uncle in the Abbey – 'the same round outlooking face' – but it was Meta Gaskell who deftly touched on the new baby's mixed Thackeray/Macaulay pedigree. 'If the Darwinian theory has a grain of truth in it, it ought to be a paragon – considering its forbears.'[79] As the year drew to its close, Annie and Richmond seemed as busy as ever, much to Meg's amusement. She told Mary Booth that her parents-in-law 'drive out and give dinners perpetually. The KCB pretends to hate it; he says when it comes to going my wife is as bored as I, but on the arrival of the invitation a madness seizes her! She however says he loves it.'[80] Richmond's knighthood and her new status as a grandmother does seem to have given Annie renewed optimism. On New Year's eve she quietly recorded her thoughts in her diary. 'Thank God for the blessings of this old year. The end of my life is happier than I ever dared to hope.'

The last of her 'Blackstick Papers' appeared in the *Cornhill* in June 1907, and in 1908 Smith, Elder issued the short anecdotal memoirs as a collection. It had taken seven years to produce sufficient material for a book, her first since *Chapters From Some Memoirs* in 1894. Writing tired her now, certainly, but one cannot escape the crueller reality that she had run out of ideas. Every now and then a glimmer of something might come, but it was rarely developed. During a short stay in Newhaven in September 1907 she had the idea for a story about 'little girls in Paris', all too familiar territory perhaps – '[I] realise that writing is like gambling for me & carries me off my legs – write very little'.[81] There were fewer loyal readers, and even they must have missed the spark of the successes of earlier days. By the end of 1908, just over eleven hundred copies had been sold, earning her royalties of £66. Graceful praise from a reader such as George Meredith was received gratefully, but his admiration of Annie's familiar virtues merely underline the comfortable nostalgia from which she seemed unable to escape. 'In reading the discoveries of the Fairy Blackstick one has the pleasure of seeing the features & hearing the voice of the most benevolent of Fairies as well as the lovable subjects she brings before us. I had a liking for all of them. She has brought them more tenderly home to me.... These things are <u>felt</u> as the doings of the gracious Fairy, to whom is given full homage, with the knowledge that she would not be her father's daughter if she could not at a touch exhibit pretenders in their colours only she prefers to step in sunny fields.'[82]

The birth in December 1908 of Billy and Meg's second child, Belinda, saw Annie and Richmond fully entering into their roles as doting grandparents. Their own uncomplicated enjoyment of Billy and Hester's childhood was replicated now in the lives of this happy young family growing around them. Catherine would be born in March 1911, and Mary a few months after Richmond died, in June 1913. During 1908 Billy and Meg took on a cottage in the grounds of Gracedieu, the Booth's estate in Leicestershire; their London base was in Durham Place where Annie and Richmond were constant visitors, together and separately, checking on James and sending reports back and forth. 'He is a darling little toad so merry & well'; 'Gussie said there are two sorts of babies the grave ones & the laughing ones & the laughing ones were perfectly irresistible w[h]. is quite true of James.' The first sighting of Belinda prompted a letter to Mary Booth in which Annie reflected on genealogy. 'I have seen <u>our granddaughter.</u> – Just as James is a Booth or a <u>you</u> rather so Belinda (is she Belinda) is a Ritchie. She was stretching & yawning comfortably with her dear little mouth. I have not looked long enough to realise more than that the dearest little being gave her beloved mother as little trouble as possible & eased all our hearts by coming so quickly.'[83]

As Annie's family continued to grow, daughter-in law followed by a succession of grandchilden, another player moved aside. We hear no more of Charlotte Leigh Smith, not even passing mentions in correspondence or diaries, other than Annie and Hester's one chance encounter some years after Richmond's death. At some point after Billy's marriage, probably during 1908 or 1909, Charlotte and Richmond's friendship came to an end, and probably at his instigation. It may be that an increased Roman Catholic commitment, eventually leading to Charlotte joining the English community in Rome, was not unconnected with the cooling of the relationship, particularly if it was felt that Hester might be susceptible to influence. Whereas Blanche Warre Cornish's conversion was regarded as a characteristic eccentricity, neither Richmond nor Annie would have been sanguine about such a move in their own daughter, whose emotional fragility during these years made her vulnerable. Later in her life Hester continued to be susceptible to religious enthusiasms, after her mother's death embracing a form of American Unitarianism with a branch in London.[84] Memories of the upset caused by Charlotte's appearance in the Ritchies' lives survived long after the protagonists' death, for Annie's eldest granddaughter remembered her father's story of how, one Christmas Day, Richmond and Hester decided to take their lunch with Charlotte, leaving Billy and Annie to eat theirs alone. This is likely to have been the same year in which Billy hurled his Christmas gift from Charlotte into the pond at Wimbledon Common, where presumably it still lies.[85] A further reason for Richmond's closing of the friendship may have been his fresh commitment to Billy's family, for the delight he took in his small grandchildren and his affection for his daughter-in-law was very strong. Annie recognised the special bond with his grandson, such as when Billy and Meg returned from a trip away to collect James and Belinda. 'Wizz rather wistfully handed Jimps over to Billy & then came home with me – Jimps looking wistfully after his G: Papa – such are life's happiest moments.'[86]

It is not unlikely that Hester's breakdown during the latter part of 1908 related in some way to Charlotte's withdrawal, and she stayed for a while at Dr Harley's nursing home to benefit from massage therapy. But nor can one dismiss the possibility of a failed love affair, particularly in the light of a casual comment by one well-wisher – 'I trust the rest cure will quite set her up – but I am sure the heart will need prolonged care now.'[87] Significantly, none of Annie's letters to Hester between 1905 and 1908 have been preserved, for they would certainly have revealed something of her troubles.

Hester responded well to treatment, and when Annie and Richmond were not able to visit they were sent daily bulletins.

> I saw her masseuse, & Hester says she is an artist – very gentle but very efficacious & that the after effects are most soothing & she goes to sleep. By good luck R[d] went at 7.30 after the Office & paid her a visit for they say for a time now she must see no one. I had one blissful happy hour & she told me all about it & all the histories each nurse in turn seems to confide in her. She has a clock & her eiderdown & her little sketch of Titmarsh & various familiar odds & ends. I didnt say goodbye I was so afraid of crying for she was on the point of it but as the masseuse came in I left the room – One goes all ones life giving out & being tugged in.[88]

After all these years, Annie remained as sensitive as ever to people wanting to publish her father's letters. When in 1909 her sister-in-law Blanche started putting together the materials which two years later appeared as *Some Family Letters of William Makepeace Thackeray*, it prompted the familiar doubts. It seems that after Annie's intervention

Blanche destroyed her first draft, but not without some resistance. 'Dear poor Blanche. I <u>am</u> so grieved she minded & so grateful to her for burning what made us very unhappy. It was absurd but I seemed to live it all over again when I saw it <u>typed</u> for all the children.'[89]

In October 1909 Richmond finally scaled the heights of the India Office, when on the retirement of Sir Arthur Godley he succeeded him as Permanent Under-Secretary. He had worked there since 1877, the year in which he had given up Cambridge to marry Annie, and nobody could have been better prepared for the post. On 6 October he saw the Secretary of State, Lord Morley, and later that day told Meg and Billy the news. The promotion brought an additional £800 a year, but ruling the administrative machine of the largest and historically most emblematic part of the British Empire carried enormous responsibilities. Richmond was gratified when Morley told him that he had consulted the great and the good – Asquith, Balfour, Grey, Lansdowne and Curzon, as well as the heads of the Treasury and the Colonial Office – and that their opinion had been unanimous: 'they all without exception said that there was no question of going outside, while I was available. Very agreeable, let the Lord have mercy on me! I am more afraid than elated.'[90] Annie was moved by his success, and could only hope that his health would bear it. The knighthood had been fun and a worthy honour, a tangible reward for loyalty, but this responsibility was daunting. A couple of days after his appointment had been made public she wrote to Meg, having left Richmond still working at papers after midnight – 'when I looked in & saw R sitting writing & writing I felt that Promotion is all very well but one has to pay for it'.[91]

Proudest of all was Hester, whom Annie described without exaggeration as having been made '<u>ill</u> with happiness'. Richmond's was an entirely self-made success, and owed nothing to his being the husband of Thackeray's daughter, a late reminder, if one were needed, that this rather unconventional marriage was a union of equals who in their pursuit of independent careers had survived intact to the end. That was something which Annie might not have predicted all those years ago. As she confided to Pinkie, 'I do feel thankful that it has come in my time'.[2]

# Nine

# SUCH A LITTLE TIME FOR ME
# (1910-1914)

*The fresh time of all their lives is springing again & you would not wish it otherwise, but yet I know how the effort to take part in all with them must react when you withdraw into yourself; & the curtain is so thick & drawn so close. Sometimes, it seems to part for an instant, but before one has time to taste the comfort, it is drawn again.*

Mary Booth to Annie
8 January 1913

In the last decade of her life, Annie rediscovered Freshwater. A frequent visitor in the first years after her father's death, since her marriage she had only been back two or three times. When she learnt from Hallam Tennyson that the same cottage rented from Julia Margaret Cameron nearly forty years before was available again, she decided to take it, and The Porch became the haven of her last years. It was not just Annie who sought its refreshing consolations. Before his death in October 1912 Richmond went more than once to rest, and Hester too would slip away there to be alone when her frail nerves demanded change. Freshwater became the ideal holiday retreat for Billy's young family, and Annie counted amongst the keenest pleasures of her last years the times spent with them all during summer months, she and Hester perhaps joining the extended family at nearby lodgings when there were too many to fit in The Porch. She came to love the Island all over again, and the cottage became the 'dear little home' which she became increasingly reluctant to leave, and where she would die.

Early in 1910 they prepared The Porch for occupancy. Hester went on a few days ahead, and when Annie arrived on 13 January was there to greet her in the doorway. 'I found my room prepared, flowers, comforts, a fire, Hester beaming welcome.' New linen came with them, bought in Sloane Street, as well as Margie Ritchie's gift of a dinner service. They celebrated by buying new fireguards, an extra chair and a clock, and within days Annie was sufficiently established to be able to report to Pinkie that a ritual sorting of old family letters was under way. 'Of a morning we go on reading & tearing & tying. What a flood of loving-kindness it has been for years & years from you all. Hester said "I never should have known what Aunt Blanche really was, if I had not read these old letters".' Amongst them was one in which Pinkie had scolded Annie for placing too much significance upon words and looks, and Annie destroyed it rather than leaving it for the grandchildren to read later. 'I rather like <u>my moods</u> to die with me.'[1] She was invited with Hester to Farringford by Hallam and Audrey Tennyson, and visited other old Freshwater friends, including the housebound Mary Brotherton. But a telegram from Richmond took them back to London where they found him depressed and listless.

By the time Annie returned to Freshwater late in March, it was her turn to feel 'used up'. She wanted Richmond to join her for Easter, but he had other ideas, preferring the comforts of Gracedieu and the company of his grandchildren to the more Spartan pleasures of The Porch. He was not beyond seeking his daughter-in-law's complicity, if it meant he could get his own way. 'My coast will not be clear at the Office till Thursday – when I think I shall come to Gracedieu, shedding the Island ruthlessly. But this will require some more courage & I should be obliged of your moral support.'[2] This stubbornness, harmless enough in this instance perhaps, hints at something dysfunctional in Richmond's behaviour towards his wife in these years. There is a telling recollection in Leonard Woolf's autobiography, the description of a dinner party at the Ritchies' a month before he married Virginia in August 1912. It was the first time that he had seen Annie and Richmond together in their own home, and there is something disconcerting about his account. He came to regard Annie as the most interesting of Virginia's 'relatives', 'a rare instance of the child of a man of genius inheriting some of that genius ... [which] like most things about her and in her, was a shade out of control'. And it was that erratic quality, on display that night as Leonard sat 'slightly oppressed and depressed by the solid Victorian gloom of their dining-room', which triggered in Richmond a reaction discomforting to witness.

> He was an extremely able, formidable man and, sitting at the head of his table, he seemed to me to be rather saturnine.... That evening in 1912 she sat at one end of the dining table ... looking very frail, living not entirely in the same

world as we were living in, and suddenly from time to time saying one of those things which no human being could possibly mean, but which she meant. From time to time too Richmond from the opposite end of the table heard one of these strange pronouncements which obviously irritated him like a little thorn which had been for so many years domestically and matrimonially embedded in his mind, and he put her somewhat sharply in her place. The curious thing was that when I thought about what she had in fact said, the absurdity remained, but through the absurdity I seemed to see something imaginative, something which only Aunt Anny had seen and which we could not quite get at, and Richmond's irritation irritated me.[3]

It is only a snapshot, though a compelling one. Perhaps this was un-characteristic behaviour – Richmond may have been unwell, and his brother was dying – but Annie also notes in her diary a couple of weeks earlier an occasion when 'R & I sparred. But something made rough places smoother thanks be to God.' That Richmond could be difficult is undeniable. He was compelled to suffer fools at the India Office, but was less willing to tolerate foolishness at home. Gertrude Bell's half-sister, Ella, also remembered him as 'a curious, saturnine creature, and although delightfully humorous and at bottom very kind-hearted, was not always easy to get on with'.[4] We know the date of the Leonard Woolf dinner at St George's Square, for Annie records having 'Virginia & her nice young Jew to dinner' on 5 July, an occasion which Annie probably enjoyed rather more than did either Leonard or Richmond, telling Pinkie that 'last night came Virginia & Daniel Deronda both quite charming'.

If over the years Richmond had found it harder to conceal his impatience with Annie's flights of fancy and impracticalities – the very qualities of her character which endeared her to those who did not have to live with her – her own affection was undimmed. His failing health distressed her and she worried for the future, for she never doubted that he would outlive her. Neither of them was particularly well during the early part of 1910, and at the start of May he suffered a severe gastric attack which kept him in bed for some days, Annie bringing the news of the death of Edward VII upstairs to him. The doctor advised another foreign rest cure, something which his office duties made impossible. Annie urged him instead to get away to Freshwater to join Hester, and was triumphant when at last he agreed to go. He departed for the Island while she settled things at St George's Square, including that

well-rehearsed ritual of the Victorian middle classes, the depositing
of the silverware at the bank. Billy and Meg had already taken the
children to Freshwater, so there was a happy reunion when Annie saw
them all coming up the road to meet her. Richmond was content, 'like
a fly in amber', and her plans for The Porch seemed to be working out.
'It is very sweet & calm & more successful than I dared to hope!'[5]
Richmond had to return temporarily for the king's funeral at Windsor,
and Annie went to a special Freshwater memorial service with the
rest of her family, joining 'all the country people coming along the
flowering lanes'.[6]

The formal ceremonies for the king were moving, but another death
in the late summer touched Annie more pointedly. Sylvia Llewelyn
Davies, daughter of the late George du Maurier and the widow of Arthur
Llewelyn Davies, died from cancer on 27 August aged just forty-four,
prompting from Annie words which might have been written by her
father. 'Death is not all terrible when it comes as a peace & a rest
after living but these dear young people – so full of life & loving &
eagerness, that joint life just starting – Where has it gone to – How
everyone will have to love the boys.' The news made her want to write
to Henry James, for she knew that he would have been saddened. 'How
fond he was of the Du Mauriers.'[7] Her customary sensitivity to the
fragility of human happiness had not diminished over the years. There
were moments when she was stopped short by the almost unbearably
poignant contrast between her own long life drawing towards its close,
for which she was perfectly prepared, and the trusting optimism of her
grandchildren whose own share of hopes and suffering all lay ahead.
She observed in Belinda 'that eager wistful look w[h]. almost frightens
me for her, dear little girl'.

And there was still Laura to fear for. Hers was a different kind
of innocence, one which had not been touched by the years: in 1910
she became forty. As she did each summer, Annie took Laura away
for a few days, this year staying near Dorking where they could take
walks together. Richmond could only admire Annie's selfless patience
in surrendering herself to this duty. 'I am afraid it is very trying – &
it must be depressing. However the change must be good in a way for
Laura, even though she only perceives it vaguely. The only way to
regard it is as a sort of failure to get beyond the very earliest stages of
childhood.'[8] Things took a turn for the worse in 1911. Early in June,
Annie was told that Laura might need to face an operation for some
unspecified condition, and a month later she underwent surgery. She
appeared to recover well enough to be able to go to Annie, but it soon
became evident that her behaviour was more erratic than normal, her

distress spilling over into bouts of uncontrollable shouting. Things came to a head on a day when growing political unrest contributed to Annie's own anxieties, and longing for Freshwater's refreshing calm she abandoned Laura and her nurse in Surrey. The guilt she felt at leaving them cannot hide her relief in finding the normalities waiting for her. '11 August. Alarming papers full of strikes & Lords abolished by Commons. Neighbours came in to complain of poor Lauras cries. Sorry I lost my temper – moved Laura into back room – Suddenly came off to FW – a long journey 6 hours. Meg met me. Dined out of doors, children delicious in their nurseries.' When she returned to the Haslemere cottage three days later, things were stable again. But this brief crisis had been a stark reminder of the hopeless nature of Laura's case. Annie had been unsparing in her care over the years, giving up afternoons to drive with Laura in Richmond Park or through the lanes of Roehampton. It was all too evident just how colourless Laura's life would be once Annie was not there to brighten it.

Thackeray's approaching centenary – he had been born in July 1811 – brought a fresh commitment from Smith, Elder and Harpers to issue a revised version of the 1898-9 Biographical Edition, reassigning the content of the originally thirteen volumes to occupy the twenty-six of the Centenary Biographical Edition. During the summer and autumn of 1910, Annie returned to revising her previous introductions, the task aborted in 1907 after much work had been completed. Additional Thackeray letters and drawings were incorporated, and account taken of relevant critical material published since the earlier edition. Relatively little new writing was required from Annie, other than adjustments necessary to fit the different sequence in which the works would now appear. She worked closely with W. J. Williams at the Smith, Elder offices, Reginald Smith being consulted only about major matters of principle, and she relied closely upon Hester for advice and proof-checking. This had benefits for them both, for when the project was all but done she made a diary note about Hester that 'work is what she needs to keep well'.[9]

The first volumes were planned to appear in November 1910, the sequence spreading over nearly a year so as to end a couple of months after the centenary itself. She stood firm about the use of previously unpublished Thackeray material, for she was reluctant to release too much without securing a good price for it. She told Pinkie about a poem which had not been reprinted since an American appearance in 1853. 'I spent £4 trying to make sure the poem had not been published here by some one else.... I have been reading all this admirable unpublished mss. of w$^h$. this may well spoil the market; but it shall be kept back for

James & Belinda if we cant get fair terms for it now.'[10] Her instinct for
protecting her father's interests or those of her own descendants never
weakened.

Annie again showed no editorial interest in Thackeray's texts, all
of her many communications with Williams at Smith, Elder being
concerned with her own prefaces. Most are trivial if business-like;
several are charming, such as one concerning the *Yellowplush Papers*.
She provided a photograph for the volume, taken to show the table
and chair at which her father had written *Vanity Fair* and *Pendennis*.
Beneath the chair is the Ritchies' tabby cat, comfortably curled up
on an elaborately patterned carpet. At the last moment Annie doubted
her selection. 'On second & third thoughts we sh$^d$ like to omit this
picture I enclose w$^h$. is rather <u>theatrical</u> & brings in too much of our
drawingroom chintz cat & carpet!' But the photograph had been sent
to Harpers, and Reginald Smith had to intervene. 'Only let me plead,
if I may, for the historic chair and table. The photograph has already
gone to New York: and all eyes I am sure will be fixed on the chair
and the table – which are so very interesting – while the chintz and
the cat will escape notice. <u>Please</u>, may the picture stay in!' It did.[11]
It is not difficult to see how Virginia Woolf's witnessing of this mix
of earnest reverence and endearing chaos inspired her portrait of Mrs
Hilbery in *Night and Day*, published in the year of Annie's death. The
early volumes met with Annie's approval, prompting a formal note of
thanks to Smith, Elder – 'we have appreciated the care & delightful
form, which we owe to your interest & effort to make the Centenary
Edition worthy of my Father's name. I am writing for myself & also
for my daughter who has helped me so much.'[12] With the appearance
of this revised edition, the family duty to Thackeray's reputation had
been paid in full.

The Thackeray centenary prompted other commemorative gestures.
Early in 1911, Annie paid several visits to the Chelsea studio of the
sculptor Leonard Jennings who was preparing a new bust for the
cathedral in Calcutta, Thackeray's birthplace. Jennings worked from
photographs provided by Annie, who urged friends like Kate Perugini
to view the likeness before it was shipped out to India. Hallam Tennyson
and Montague Butler, the Master of Trinity College, Cambridge, were
persuaded to come up with an appropriate inscription for the Calcutta
pedestal. A fortnight-long Thackeray exhibition, opened by the former
Prime Minister, Lord Rosebery on 30 June, was organised by the
Titmarsh Club at the old Charterhouse, which, the *Times* observed,
'must have changed little, if at all, since the great writer was a boy
at the "Greyfriars".'[13] Rosebery's speech was carried in full by the

Times, prompting a leading article a couple of days later. A reception jointly hosted by Annie and Smith, Elder was held in the garden of the Middle Temple on 18 July, when the Temple choir sang some of Thackeray's ballads in settings by Walford Davies. Kate Perugini had enjoyed spotting the family likenesses during the opening ceremonies of the Charterhouse. 'There is just a look in your boy of your father, and yet not of yourself, through we all agreed there is much in the bust that reminds us of you.' Just a few days later she was congratulating Annie on being sounded out as a possible President of the English Association, unable to hide her enjoyment at Mrs Humphry Ward being eclipsed for once. 'We dont know what it is called but we do know you are the only woman who has ever received it – as you should be of course – and that Mrs. H– W– is left out in the cold – as she should be of course. Hurrah!'[14]

The protracted mood of celebration, aided no doubt by the birth of Billy and Meg's third child in March 1911, was checked by Gussie Freshfield's death in May, her several operations for cancer having only delayed the progress of the disease. Her courageous resignation was exhausting for all those who went through the last months with her. Gussie valued Richmond's quiet, watchful support, but she discouraged Annie from visiting. 'I do not ask you to come just now because I am very suffering – the exhausting breathlessness (but it is better than the horrible pain). I know it would make you sad to see me – but go on writing.'[15] When the end was near, Richmond wrote to Freshwater to tell Annie.

> I saw her yesterday afternoon and again today – perfectly serene, & not then in a state of suffering, & in perfect possession of her faculties – talking & listening with pleasure. One could not have guessed, if one had not known. She said very little about the impending stroke of fate, & that quite cheerfully, with no repining & no wish for a prolongation of life. They say it cant be more than a week or two now, and may come suddenly at any time.... This is a disturbing letter to write, but it is much better to face the facts without circumlocutions, as both she & Douglas & Eleanor do.[16]

Annie wrote to Gussie of the golden times at Freshwater when they had all been young, but she did not pretend that the situation was other than it was.

> 'I think of you so that writing seems but a little bit of what is in my heart & in all our hearts – That Richmond was able

to come in and see you seems better than any letter from me.
I think he told us all…. The little Porch seems so silent &
far away but everything speaks to us of you in one way, &
the birds & the waves & all the familiar things…. Last night
after the rain everything flashed with beautiful illuminating
rays.'[17]

Gussie asked for Annie in her last few days, and they had a final time
together. Annie stood for a last moment at the door as she left, and
from her bed Gussie kissed her hand to her. 'How heartfelt it was. How
tender & beautiful in every word & thought. Home at night with stars
shining.'[18] The end came on 26 May, and Annie's thoughts were for
Gussie's children and for others in the family. She went with Richmond
and Hester to the funeral, the 'lovely sad meeting', and tried to find
words to strengthen Pinkie for the years ahead. 'Last night I looked for
help & what <u>was</u> comfort were Minnies type written letters & when
you are in sorrow the thought of Gussie & of all who belong so nearly
to you will be your comfort, you dear comforter.'[19]

When early in 1912 Annie looked back over the previous twelve
months, there seemed to be little to regret, for coming to terms with
one's losses was part of the price exacted by life. 'This has been a
wonderful year full of sadness & loss and also with so much blessing
& interest & the delicious spontaneous tribute to my dearest Father.'
But she was weary and finding it harder to adjust to change. 'I get
older & more slow, & it seems to me the world gets younger & more
quick, & rushing.'[20]

Elderly though Annie may have felt, the indignities of age en-
croached with far greater rigour upon Richmond, despite his being
seventeen years her junior. Probably a mixture of malice and fantasy
played a part in Virginia's letter to Clive Bell, written late in 1911. 'I
have just come back from having tea with Richmond Ritchie, who has
lumbago. He became so lecherous that I had to leave. When old men
are very lecherous, their beards and jowls are so unpleasant.'[21] During
the first months of the new year his health appears if anything to
have been stronger, and his decline in the late summer at first seemed
nothing more than one of his usual bad spells. Certainly there was
nothing to prevent Annie and Hester from arranging a trip to Venice
in early March to take up a long-standing offer to stay at the Palazzo
Barbaro with Ariana Curtis, Browning's old friend. It had been thirty-
five years since Annie had visited Venice, when she and Minny were
hurried through by Leslie who was anxious for the Alps – 'he seemed
on fever and as if some supernatural power was driving him into the

mountains'.[22] As they now set out for Paris, she and Hester left behind an England simmering with industrial unrest, including a miners' strike, and Richmond told them to linger abroad until the situation was clearer. Together with many in official positions, he thought violent disorder to be almost inevitable. '[It] is not safe to count on being back by the end of the month. Because if the strike isn't over by then, the serious business will only then be really beginning & it will not only be very disagreeable but also perhaps dangerous.'[23] In Venice, Annie enjoyed reacquainting herself with pictures last seen in 1874, when she had been scolded by Charlotte Ritchie for monopolising the attentions of the schoolboy Richmond. She sought out Giorgione, Carpaccio and Bellini and visited the Accademia, and there was one memorable evening at the opera when, after hearing Rossini's *Barbiere*, they returned 'in a starry gondola'. The Rudyard Kiplings were also in Venice and Mrs Curtis's gondola took Hester to their hotel to bring them to tea, 'but the ladies were laid up with cold.... [Kipling] says the end of this coal strike will be that people will only burn oil & he made her smell the smell of the East coming f$^n$ Constantinople – she said she could quite well define it when he made her notice it.'[24]

Annie fought the cold which troubled her for most of their stay, which perhaps prompted Hester to take a grim interest in celebrated Venetian misadventures, of 'Alfred de Musset & Johnnie Cross jumping into the Grande Canal &ct &ct but my chill has subsided without any sensational events'. A collection of Edith Wharton's stories, *The Hermit and the Wild Woman*, proved diverting, though one of them had offended the Curtis family. 'The Verdict is the story of M$^{rs}$ Curtis's eldest son she told me. His wife was so angry she made M$^r$ Ralph Curtis write & remonstrate & there was a crisis.'[25]

Once the British government had introduced emergency legislation to force the strikers into arbitration, Richmond could advise returning home as things were calmer. He had maintained an active social life in their absence, dining out most evenings, and paying a memorable call on Rhoda Broughton. 'Rhoda also told me (but under promises of more than complete secrecy) how poor Henry James is in a terrific quandary, because it appears that when Robert Elsmere came out he though loathing the book, wrote as an author of European fame 2 letters full of humbugging praises to the aspirant, with no hope of success as she then was: and now, oh horror, M$^{rs}$. Ward is bringing out her works with prefaces & has printed the two damning documents.'[26] These letters from Richmond, noticeably affectionate and rather longer than normal, are amongst his last surviving ones to Annie. The moments of irritability which Leonard Woolf witnessed a few months later at St George's Square need to be balanced against such solid evidence of an enduring sympathy which sustained this unusual marriage.

The Italian trip was shadowed by sadness, for the unassuming Edward Ritchie was dying from cancer. The least ambitious of the Ritchie brothers, a successful medical practice had won him considerable local respect. Annie and Hester were on their way home, taking in Geneva and then Paris, when Richmond described a visit to his brother. It was all so reminiscent of Gussie's last days just a year earlier. 'He was a little stronger yesterday & the end may not be for some days but it has really come & there will be no more suffering.'[27] In fact, Edward survived until early July.

One of the pleasures of Venice had been the opportunity to share memories of Browning, including listening to Ariana Curtis reading out some of the notes which her husband had kept of the poet's talk. In May, Annie was amongst those who attended the Browning centenary celebrations organised by the Royal Society of Literature at Caxton Hall, and knowing that the occasion would interest Mrs Curtis she sent details to Venice. The highlight had been the address by Henry James. 'He made a most beautiful sympathetic & original speech as full of reality & generous appreciation – as one knew it would be .... "Shelley was a light" Henry said "Swinburne a sound Browning was an Atmosphere". Pen must have loved all this & it <u>must</u> I think have done him real good. And also those delightful messages from the Venice City to the City of London.'[28] As she and Henry James grew older, they also grew closer. She saw him the month after the Browning commemoration, when time seemed to be taking its toll. 'Met H James who said How does old age stretch you. It is not that I dont take interest in things & people – but I no longer take interest in the interest I take.'[29]

Towards the end of July Richmond was ill once again, and it was serious enough for Annie to have to represent him at a dinner with the king and queen. A diary note that he was in bed on 23 July led her subsequently to wonder – 'was this the influenza which brought on his great illness'. She was at Freshwater during August so missed Virginia's wedding, but provided flowers and instructed Budd, her carriage driver, 'to fetch M$^r$ & M$^{rs}$ Wolf [sic] after the ceremony to Victoria'.[30] Richmond was well enough to attend the civil ceremony at St Pancras Town Hall on 10 August. At the end of the month he snatched a break from the India Office to come to Freshwater, but after only a couple of days the symptoms of his final illness had begun, and on 1 September he was 'quite floored after luncheon'.

They were back in London within days, and after this briefest of interruptions Richmond resumed work, though clearly he was not at all strong. A veneer of normality was preserved until he became ill again at night. For the next few days Annie 'pottered out' with him to the India Office, happy to think that he and Hester would soon be able to get away to the continent, but he began to experience considerable pain, and during the night of 15 September he was in 'cruel torture'. In the early hours Annie sent for the doctor, and his niece Adeline Ritchie, who had previously acted as his housekeeper when both Annie and Hester were away, prepared poultices. She and Annie took turns to sit with him, whilst Hester hurriedly returned from a holiday in the Lake District. Billy came back on 18 September from a fishing trip to Norway, by which time his father was very weak though not in pain. Another day passed without improvement, and it became evident that professional nursing and proper medical supervision was required, so Richmond was conveyed by private ambulance to Dr Vaughan Harley's nursing home in Harley Street. For a few days his condition stabilised under the new regime, and Annie would sometimes return from Harley Street quite encouraged by his appearance. The debilitating weakness continued, however, and on 1 October Dr Harley issued a certificate requesting his release from work for six months. His continued absence from the India Office justified mention in the *Times* of 3 October, where the Court Circular announcements reported that he was suffering from overwork, and 'taking a rest cure' in a London nursing home.

Annie actually managed to do some writing during this protracted period of worry. She got books from the London Library and planned her Presidential address to the English Association, 'A Discourse on Modern Sibyls', fitting in a visit to the Post-Impressionist Exhibition on 3 October. But Richmond was deteriorating, and on 6 October she watched as he groaned in his sleep, his nurses 'very grave'. On the following day Vaughan Harley admitted for the first time to being very anxious. Annie went to Fortnum and Mason to buy champagne for Richmond, for she placed great faith in its restorative properties, reminded, perhaps, of the occasion in 1841 when her father took a bottle of 'chimpong' to cheer Isabella at a clinic in Ivry. She put off a visit from Clive and Vanessa Bell, but did her best to be positive. 'The news is good on the whole – but it is so depressing to think of him ill & we shall please God be much happier when the pain is better.'[31] But by this time Richmond's breathing and pulse were 'so faint and difficult', and on 10 October he was given oxygen. Then came another respite. Meg took James to see his grandfather, and as Annie arrived 'Jamie came running out a little pink flash'.

Things really seemed more encouraging, and Harley told her that Richmond's pulse had strengthened. It proved to be a cruel hope, and when Annie woke anxiously and very early in the morning of 12 October she at once wrote down words from the funeral sentences – 'O Lord in the last hour let us not fall from thee for any fear of death. Hester came in after I had written this & told me.'

Richmond had slipped into unconsciousness through the night, and his body had given up the fight. Death was caused by heart failure resulting from toxaemia and septic pneumonia. Annie at once returned with Hester to the nursing home where she experienced a profound peace. 'He lay there himself O more himself than ever ever in this life – Strong tenderly wise gentle with a look of such great sympathy & knowledge of love that it cannot be put into words. He did not seem in another world but in this world & with us and at rest here & holding us in his great gentle might & Heart. Once I saw the snow mountains through breaking clouds just for a few instants at Lucerne, & so it was then & while I live to remember. Holy, Divinely Him. 8$^{br}$ 12 1912 about nine o'c in the m$^g$.'[32]

The rituals of death took their course. Annie communicated with Lord Morley at the India Office about the *Times* obituary notice. The next day was Sunday, and she went with Hester and Billy to Hampstead parish church, where they had secured a plot in the 'kind and peaceful graveyard', and that night Annie returned to view Richmond's body for the last time in Harley Street. 'It was like meeting not parting. So himself fatherly great noble. After that he was carried to the chapel at night.' Early on Tuesday the body was removed from the Baker Street undertakers, and taken first to Golders Green crematorium. Annie was a supporter of cremation, having said some years before that 'if it wouldnt give too much trouble that is what I should like myself'.[33] She and Meg went straight to the Hampstead church whilst Hester and Billy attended the cremation, which they told their mother was 'nobly magnificent – not terrible'. The ashes were transferred later on Tuesday morning to Hampstead for the committal at midday. 'My Richmond was brought to rest in the church yard for ever and ever.'

Hester collapsed under the weight of her grief, for in recent years she had been her father's unswervingly devoted companion. On Wednesday, Annie took her to see Harley, who advised rest, and then she went on alone to Hampstead to the fresh grave, 'all beautiful still'. It was comforting to see the grandchildren on the following day, and James saying to his mother 'let us pretend Grandpapa is at S$^t$ Georges Square. I walked round but he was not there'. Hester's nervous condition had worsened by Friday, and Harley insisted that she should go to her cousin Eleanor Clough in the New Forest for a fortnight. It allowed Annie to start the business of house-hunting without delay, for St George's Square was too large now for her likely income. Richmond's pension rights had died with him.

She received many letters of sympathy, one of the most thoughtfully reassuring coming from Dr Harley, who had known the Ritchies long enough to mourn the loss of a friend. 'One comfort is you can know he had actually no suffering in the end. During the night he was quite unconscious & his heart simply found the power not sufficient so stopped. There was none of the air hunger which is so distressing to the poor patient – Up to the end it seemed he even then might pull through.'[34] Of the family letters, that from Richmond's youngest sister, Elinor Paul, seemed to speak for them all.

> There seem to be no words only aching silence – and yet in all the overwhelming sorrow there is thankfulness – He had all that life could give – he was spared what you and Hester & Billy & Meg have to bear & he died at his work as every man would wish to die in the fullness of his powers and honour. Except for his health, & over that he was so nobly victorious, he had all that every mother would wish for her son, every wife for her husband, the fullness of love of friendship of success, of achievement – and all the sweet young joys of life in his children & Billys children.... I hope Pinkie will be with you once you have this – She has lived through so much with you & her love will enfold you.[35]

In fact Pinkie was away when Richmond died, making it the more painful for her, and in a second letter Elinor commented on how broken her sister was. 'She has lost more than any of us outside his home & life will never be what it was to her again.'[36] But Elinor was right in supposing that it would be to Pinkie that Annie turned most for quiet understanding. 'Bless you my darling Pinkie & dont ever think of being different from yourself, and your dear loving heart – and let things be in peace & thank God for Richmond & for you & all those living & dead who are such a heritage.'[37]

A simple note came from Virginia Woolf, who had always loved Annie. Whatever private comments she had previously made about Richmond, she knew the right thing to say now. 'It was only the other day that Uncle Richmond wrote to me. He has always been extraordinarily kind to us, & I cant believe that he is dead. Leonard wants me to send his love. I am so glad that we both saw him, & darling Aunt Anny we both send our love to you & would do anything for you we could.'[38]

Vanessa wrote in similar vein, but also thought back over the years to the support Annie had given Leslie in his last illness – 'you have always been one of the people who could help most'. She reflected on how her mother would have been able to provide some comfort at a time like this, 'such as I know you gave to her'.[39]

The high regard in which Richmond had been held in the India Office was best expressed by one of the juniors in the department, who told Hester that 'I cannot see the future at all clearly now that his never failing help and encouragement is to be withdrawn'.[40] There were many tributes from more senior figures and other friends, and a telling one from Baron von Hügel, whose Hampstead home the Ritchies had often used in earlier years. He cannot have been the only witness of how the passing years had taken their toll. 'There was only one thing about him that truly pained me. I felt that, somehow, this my junior by two years was considerably my senior physically; that, tho' really only in later middle life, there was a bodily condition there which made him, in these respects, my senior by, say ten years or so.'[41]

Set apart from these personal messages and more public statements is Henry James's private observation, shared with his friend Margaret Prothero, which, much as Leonard Woolf had done, hints that Annie had deserved something fuller from her marriage, and that Richmond had somehow failed her. 'One thinks ever so tenderly of poor dear Anne R. – little as one had ever felt (or at least I had) that her marriage had brought her the full measure of intimate consideration that her exquisite nature seemed to ask for. However, Richmond was a great public servant – and she sits there in abundant honour.'[42] His reservations in 1878 about Annie's 'boy-husband' had never wholly retreated.

Annie directed much of her grief into a concern for Hester, drawing on her own experience of suffering after the deaths of her father and Minny. This time she was better able to cope, for as she confided to her diary on the last day of the year, it was not as if she had so very much time left. 'Life is over for me. I can just love them on a little longer. Amen.' She was more explicit to Violet Hammersley. 'It is such a little time for me it really doesnt matter. It is Hester I ache over. Fogs come, wars come, nonsense is talked in the House about the dear & noble India Office & now I think he is not troubled by it all any more. But when the children are merry & sweet it seems to be a chord between us.'[43] Billy and Meg sat with her in the evenings, and he would read *Vanity Fair* aloud. It was Billy too who found a Chelsea house for Annie and Hester in St Leonard's Terrace, costing £1,000 and very near his own in Durham Place. They spent some time getting it ready before eventually moving there in May 1913. A fear that she lacked capital led Annie just ten days after Richmond's death to send various Thackeray manuscripts to America for £720. She went on worrying for some weeks about what might be sold now and what should be kept as an inheritance – on 6 December she and Hester were 'choosing & indexing my Fathers picture books to sell'.

On 26 October she wrote separately to Billy and to Hester, explaining her intentions for the large collection of remaining Thackeray letters, manuscripts and drawings. Hester had lived with her parents all of her life and had no independent income. Unless she were to marry this was unlikely to change, so it was essential that her future should be secured. Annie had already given Billy the manuscript of *Denis Duval*, from the sale of which he purchased a farm – 'It makes him happy & so I'm glad tho I <u>hated</u> selling it'[44] – his school and university education also having been funded through previous disposals, including the manuscript of *The Rose and the Ring*.

> I have been writing to Billy to tell him that I am settling my affairs & that I now give him the Fitzgerald book which – with the Denis Duval MSS that I gave him last May – will be I think a fair share of his grandfathers things.
>
> I now give <u>you</u> all the rest – as your share. I hope you will think this a fair division of all the delightful fun and genius. You have earned the correspondence by the work you did with me for the Edition.[45]

She asked her maid to witness this letter to Hester, but in any case a few days later she arranged to see her solicitor and finalised her will. The End House in Wimbledon would be left to Billy, though at his own insistence he assigned to Annie for her lifetime the income from his share of his father's estate.

Rhoda Broughton had been a good friend to Richmond, and when she heard that Hester was convalescing she wrote to her. 'I know & always knew what he was to you & you to him; & can in some degree estimate your measureless loss. Need I say how I shall welcome you when you come to see me on your return? My dear love to your mother. Thank you <u>so</u> much for putting my flowers near his grave.'[46] Annie called on Rhoda early in December, and came away with fresh confirmation of what she already knew to have been Richmond's undemonstrative character. 'She said Wizz said if people understand one another even a minute a day was eno.'

That first Christmas they all decided to return to a scene associated with happier times. Together with Billy, Meg and the children, Annie

*Annie with James, Belinda and Catherine, her three eldest grandchildren,
taken especially for* The Bookman, *April 1912.*

and Hester hired lodgings in Littlehampton for a fortnight, where
Richmond had enjoyed his golf so much. Hester and Billy golfed in
the stormy weather, and Annie took solitary walks. The children made
it a surprisingly contented if subdued Christmas, James dressing up
as Father Christmas in his red dressing gown, so that Annie was
reflective but not miserable. '[I]ndeed I feel as if Wizz <u>had</u> been here
this Christmas. He will always seem there when the children are round
about.'[47] On the last day of the old year she felt as if 'Richmond's
blessing was there in Jamie's room'. Hester clung to her nephew, who
was a reminder of all that was most affectionate in Richmond. 'Hester
adores that little comforting boy. Richmond did so love him – so
happily, so tenderly.'[48] Earlier in December, Herbert Stephen, son of
FitzJames and Mary, had written about the burial of his mother in the
Stephen family plot in Kensal Green. 'That little company of graves
in the corner hurriedly chosen in 1859 after Sir James's death is now
closed.... There are nine persons altogether in the old place, & how
little to regret in the lives of any of them, except that some of them
ended so early.'[49] He was thinking in part of Minny, of course, whose
grave lies to the left of the main family group.

Annie did not feel up to attending the English Association on 10 January, so she asked that her address be read out for her by Ernest von Glehn. The subsequent appearance of 'A Discourse on Modern Sibyls' in the *Cornhill* in March brought a graceful tribute from Edmund Gosse. 'You are yourself the one authentic Sibyl left, with your delicate wavering style that is like shot silk. Is it not so? I have only just thought of it, but I am sure that is right. George Eliot is satin, M^{rs}. Gaskell is velvet, but you are chatoyant – you are the dove's neck.'[50] By the early spring ordinary life of a kind had been resumed, although Hester was far from recovered. Clearly she was enduring the effects of some kind of nervous breakdown and was sleeping badly, and there continued to be difficult times in the months to come. In early March, she declared that she needed time alone at The Porch, and as Billy thought that this was sensible Annie let her go. She certainly seemed improved a month later, overseeing the alterations for the new house. 'It is the best <u>rest cure</u> she c^d. have – Yesterday she was collapsed & today she is alive once more'.[51] Henry James was consistently sympathetic, perhaps even discussing Hester with Annie when she called on 27 March and she received 'kindness and advice'. Whilst she remained focussed on practical concerns, the ghosts slipped through occasionally. During the Palm Sunday service at Westminster Abbey she caught sight of 'a distant figure like R^d.' Easter Sunday night was clear and starlit, the kind of sky which in their early courtship days she and Richmond would have written to each other about. The beauty had not retreated, but 'how it aches'.

She joined the grandchildren at The Porch for the first week of April, picking primroses with them just as she had done with Minny fifty years before, and as Richmond had done as a boy. She raised with Billy the idea of giving some Thackeray materials to the British Museum, amongst them the notes to the *Four Georges* lectures which subsequently were sold at Sotheby's the following year.

> A letter from Pinkie came with yours with a bit about long long ago when he had been as a boy to that very wood where we went yesterday to gather the Primroses – It seemed so extraordinarily beautiful & the childrens figures passing between the slender trees & the golden shining flowers quite reckless with light & profusion.
>
> All your letter was so very interesting. I have been thinking whether it might not be well to send the enclosed to the British Museum about the Book of notes for the lectures. It might be patriotic to give them the chance for

they have nothing much of your Grandfathers – Shall we <u>give</u> it altogether if they wont buy – I do like the idea of the museum at Harvard so much and those kind Americans helping and taking an interest.[52]

The smaller St Leonard's Terrace house was not able to accommodate all of their furniture from St George's Square, but disposing of anything with associations with Thackeray or with Richmond proved difficult. Distributing things within the wider family circle was a happy solution, and it was with a sense of relief that she sent chairs off to Pinkie and to Elinor Paul. 'I like to think of you each owning a little scrap of this dear home which loves you as it says goodbye & God bless you.'[53] In a similar vein she sent to George Smith's daughter the silver teapot which Thackeray had given to her. 'I know no one to whom it should so naturally belong. Was not Ethel Newcome your Godmother (will you ask your dear Mother for me) and have you not always been a niece to me in kindness & response.'[54] When she closed the doors on St George's Square for the last time, it was with a 'sad wrench … thankful for all mercy there'. It ended all that her life with Richmond had represented, the house having originally been taken in order that his work at the India Office might allow the possibility of a home life of sorts. From here Billy had left to start his own married life, and it was where his children had each in turn become regular visitors. Annie's own last chapter had begun.

Billy and Meg's fourth and final child, Mary, was born at the end of June, and a month later Annie took Richmond's KCB star to the christening and laid it on the baby during the ceremony, a touchingly emblematic gesture. During the summer months she revised some of her previous essays for republication in what, with the exception of the posthumous collection *From Friend to Friend,* would be her final book. *From The Porch* indicates by its title where her heart and sentiments now lay. She was at Freshwater for August, but saw rather less of Hallam and Audrey Tennyson than usual, their encounters limited to acknowledging each other as they passed. The problem was again Hester, who was content to have Billy's children around her, but could not cope with more demanding society – 'as we came back rather late we met a drag, Hallam on the box, waving figures inside. It is so complicated that we chiefly wave & dont meet much at all. Hester shrinks from visits & with the children in & out there is little room to ask anyone <u>here</u>.'[55] It was therefore encouraging that Hester felt up to accompanying her mother to Normandy early in September, although within days she had returned to Freshwater leaving Annie in Trouville. Perhaps it had always been the plan that Hester should only ensure her mother's safe crossing. Certainly Annie enjoyed her three weeks away, receiving a 'delightful letter' from Hester on 8 September, who had gone to stay with the Birrells. Eleanor's health was declining, and Hester became her most intimate friend in the last months of her life. Annie returned home on 23 September, having taken the overnight sailing, and spent that first evening with Pinkie and Hester who was 'at her best'.

As the anniversary of Richmond's death approached, Hester seemed stronger, and they were able to welcome a fresh face at St Leonard's Terrace. Richard (Dick) Norton's name appears in Annie's diary for the first time on 25 September 1913, although just two days later comes the cryptic entry – 'M$^r$ Norton to tea sad sad talk in evening suddenly realised it all.' Assuming her discussion in the evening was with Hester, did it touch on Norton? He was the son of Charles Eliot Norton, who next to James Lowell had been Leslie Stephen's closest American friend. What Annie may have found disturbing was not that Hester was attracted to him, but that he was divorced. Annie herself certainly became fond of Norton, who was intelligent and personable, an archaeologist by training and director of the American School of Classical Studies in Rome, but there was a decided ambivalence in her affection. She may have feared not unreasonably that Hester would wilt under the scrutiny which a growing intimacy with a divorced man would bring. So whereas Dick Norton called frequently during the remainder of 1913 – Annie was decidedly grateful for his presence as 'an invaluable guest' at her Boxing Day lunch party[56] – at one point during the following year she confided to Meg that she doubted the wisdom of encouraging him. 'O dear me. Hester says it will be interesting to ask Dick Norton to come & see us here, & tell us what he has seen. I shant prevent her but I wont unless she urges it.'[57] But nor can one entirely dismiss the possibility that Annie's fears for Hester had more selfish motives, for in losing her to marriage she would be left alone. It may never have previously occurred to her that Hester might find someone of her own. But her principal concern was surely for Hester's health. Even as things seemed to be so much more positive there was a new scare in December when Miss Bennett, who seems to have been a health consultant, told Annie that Hester was ill again. After a day's reflection Annie felt that Miss Bennett was being over-cautious, 'perhaps too professional in detail, but right in the main', and told Billy that 'Hester says she is <u>quite well</u> this morning & that she is going for a drive with E Birrell so I do hope Miss B took too melancholy a view yesterday but it is well to be warned'.[58]

1914 began quietly enough, but it was not the best of omens when at the end of January Annie slipped and fell in the Hampstead graveyard. From Edmund Gosse she received a 'bewildering letter', which seems to have hinted that she was about to be recommended by Asquith for a civil pension. She was in two minds about whether such an offer would be appropriate, and wrote to Gosse 'almost refusing the grant'. But it came to nothing in any case, and on 21 February she simply recorded that it was 'all nonsense about Prime Ministers pension'. Old wounds were opened with news of the New York sale of a major collection of Thackeray manuscripts owned by Major William Lambert, scheduled for 25-27 February. They included the manuscript of *The Rose and the Ring*, which Annie had originally sold in 1896 for £1,500 – it now fetched $23,000 (£4,600), claimed by the *Times* to be 'the highest price ever realized in an American market for a modern manuscript'. But it was the inclusion in the auction of a large group of Thackeray's letters to Jane Brookfield, and the public interest which they excited, which disturbed Annie, although the wording of the subsequent 'soothing article' in the *Times* of 25 February reassured her. 'No doubt these unpublished letters will create some stir, and apart from their inevitable attraction for the vulgarly curious, they undeniably possess a legitimate interest. There is not one of them moreover that does not redound entirely to the honour and credit of the parties involved.'[59]

Annie was not precious about selling heirlooms at auction, for she herself sent a number of items to Sotheby's for sale on 9 April, the four lots realising £1,520. These included the quarto volume of drawings and letters given her by Edward FitzGerald after Thackeray's death, and which she had given to Billy. It went for £730 to the dealer Sabine, Annie only regretting that she hadn't agreed a private deal with him the year before as this would have saved the auction commission. It seems that she also put some books up for auction, but a number were returned unsold. But once the prices realised for the manuscripts were known she remained optimistic, for it suggested that the market for Thackeray was reasonably buoyant, auguring well for their future value. 'Years hence you will find the remaining MSS. go up again. There ought to be still a drawing book or two w$^h$. we will lock up altogether for the present. We certainly owe a candle to dear old E.F.G.'[60] Her concern over money meant that she encouraged Billy to make a private arrangement with Reginald Smith to sell him some Thackeray drawings and books, and hoped to raise upwards of £600. As rumours of war grew louder, the negotiations continued into the summer. Billy acted as the go-between, for she retained a coy reluctance to become involved directly in money discussions. When Smith made an offer, she urged Billy to accept. 'M$^r$

Williams said M$^r$ Smith had ceased to buy but he wished to go on with me – the last of the purchases & he said without the war he thought 400 guineas was as much as he c$^d$. give.'[61]

This year Billy moved his family to the country, giving up their London house in Durham Place on the recommendations of their doctor. Probably this was to minimise the children's exposure to diseases such as whooping cough and scarlet fever, but Billy's own health was not robust, and during the Great War much to his distress a heart weakness prevented his being passed fit for the front. They chose Hertfordshire, taking the Old Vicarage in Ware, and in the first year or two Annie and Hester helped out financially by renting out their own Chelsea house for extended periods and dividing their time between London, Ware and Freshwater. Even before Billy and his family had given up Durham Place, the five-year-old Belinda extolled the benefits of country life during one of her Freshwater visits. 'I like being here. I dont like London people are always ill & they die. Here we play & go to the sea.'[62] For two days in July, Annie sat to John Singer Sargent for her portrait, a group of 115 friends having subscribed to 'my beautiful picture'. He completed the charcoal drawing on 8 July, and in her excitement Annie went straight off to see Henry James, whose own portrait by Sargent, a 'noble picture', she had admired just the year before. She sent a printed letter to the subscribers, thanking them for their gift. 'It has come bringing gracious sympathy and comfort and kindness – May others find the same help in their lives as that which has been given me and mine!' For much of the summer Hester was at Walton in Surrey, where Eleanor Birrell had been moved to a nursing home for the final months of her illness. Hester lodged nearby and visited daily, sending regular reports to Augustine Birrell whose government responsibilities kept him in London. Annie paid Hester and Eleanor visits, anxious for the health of them both. 'Hester certainly better – only better not well. Eleanor less well again after three good days.'[63]

The prevailing mood of the papers was not good and by late July, with troops mustering across Europe, war seemed inevitable. Having tried to maintain an optimistic outlook in his letters to Hester, even Birrell became gloomy. 'It is too terrible to believe – that at any moment Germany, France, Russia & Austria may be at a bloody issue.'[64] During the weekend of 1-2 August the cabinet met to review the threat to the territorial integrity of Belgium, underwritten by Britain, France and Russia, and put at risk by Germany's intention to cross its borders to gain a corridor to French territory. Annie's diary for that final weekend of peace, when she was a guest of the Booths at Gracedieu, gives a

snapshot of England on the eve of war, of an old order about to pass for
ever, and we glimpse a family routine threatened by events unfolding
with their own terrible momentum. By 4 August Belgium had been
invaded, and England was at war with Germany.

> *1. August.* happy day war notwithstanding. children, deli-
> cious Gracedieu – cricket dinner all nice – only this grim
> suspense beyond. M$^{rs}$ Booth says their great business ab-
> solutely <u>stopped</u> & their fleet idle.
> *2. August.* pouring rain. Wrote letters, finished Rhodas
> story 'the vow' in nursery. Tea at Gracedieu. Lawn-tennis,
> childrens games. M$^{rs}$ Booth better – all charming but very
> anxious. About 7.0 Meg came back with the terrible news
> that the Germans had invaded France. Dreary evening but
> together all by the fire. Alas Billy must join the Reserves.

Edith Sichel died in mid-August. She had been Pinkie's companion
for many years, and the end was mercifully quick. They had been
staying in Cumberland with the music critic John Fuller Maitland and
his wife, when Edith was suddenly taken ill. Already in the final stages
of cancer, only then did she become incapacitated, and she died within
hours of Pinkie writing to tell Annie that the end was close. 'Yesterday
I was dreadfully distressed to receive the saddest tidings from Pinkie
of Edith's illness dear dear Edith is passing away in sleep & without
pain.'[65] It was Annie's turn to support Pinkie, who returned to London
after the funeral at Carnforth. Amidst this deep sadness Annie scanned
the papers for details of the bigger conflict – 'news of the beginning of
the awful battle at the frontier f$^{m}$. Holland to Switzerland' (12 August);
'fighting everywhere' (14 August); 'Read the papers & the terrible
news in the peaceful garden. Namur taken. Retiring movements of the
allies' (25 August); 'ominous news. The French & English opposed
by the hordes of Prussians' (1 September). The memories were still
fresh when Pinkie returned in the following July to revisit the Fuller
Maitlands and the scene of Edith's last days. 'We were here together
before when she was well and I don't dwell on the day when she ceased
to know me and fell into that long drowsiness when already Divine
Mystery seemed to enfold her.'[66]

One of Annie's strangest letters dates from this time. She had never
demonstrated any great sentimental attachment to her earlier writings,
and rarely referred to them or attempted to explain her writing processes.
Indeed, most of her fiction had been completed upwards of fifty years
before, when Minny was still alive and before she herself married,
belonging to that earlier life which more recent events had made

unimaginably remote. The letter which she now wrote to Constance Smith about the composition of *Miss Angel* (1875) is therefore a rarity. It is unusually detailed, but more remarkable are the oddities it outlines, not just regarding the coincidences which she claims took her to residences associated with Angelica Kauffman, but also in suggesting that the book grew as if from some kind of unconscious knowledge of the painter's life. Nowhere else in her correspondence or journals does she even hint at such irrational possibilities, but it helps lend credence to the claim that Annie 'had the power of clairvoyance, which bothered her and which she heartily mistrusted', and that in the 1850s she had been inducted by Mrs Browning into the practice of automatic writing, proving herself to be a potent medium.[67]

> It is a long time since I wrote the story of Miss Angel – I was dining with Constance Leslie in Stratford Place, & after dinner Sir John said Do you know that Angelica Kauffman painted these ceilings – we were sitting in the great drawing room. I said I dont know anything about Angelica. He answered, there was a romantic story about her – you ought to write it down. She was a very charming woman & she was secretly married. The paintings I saw over-head & what Sir John told me of the painter interested me – & I bought a little book from a catalogue; it was by a man called Rossi in Italian and it interested me still more. I had just come back from Venice & I was able to make the Italian out. I had to send a story to the Cornhill <u>at once</u> or wait for two years, & I thought I w$^d$ send it in at once & risk being able to learn more about Angelica as I went on. And this is the curious part of the story. I wrote a-head – it was very wrong – but some unknown luck was with me. Whatever I wrote was true as I afterwards found. I had written notes of what I had seen in Italy – of Venice especially & as I had little time to spare I used them up for copy. I thought she must have been in Italy. To my great relief I found when I bought Rossi's pamphlet that Angelica & her Father <u>had</u> stayed in Italy & then in Venice & that she had studied in the gallery there – then I had to bring her back to England & I invented a grand English lady who brought her in her train – I called her 'Lady G.' then I remembered there was a Lady G in Sir Charles Grandison so I changed the G to W. Then I found that it was actually Lady Wentworth the ambassadors wife who brought Angelica home. Then I thought she <u>must</u> have known Sir Joshua and I read about 'Miss Angel flowers' in his diary. I knew I had

a far away aunt Kitty Thackeray who died young of love &
one of my cousins said casually she cared for a painter called
Zucchi who cared for someone else. This bygone great aunt
was the daughter of an Eton dignitary – I think he was Vice
Provost. The only house I knew at Eton in those days was one
where my cousin S$^t$ John Thackeray was living & when I read
that it was in Windsor Castle itself that Angelica discovered
that she was not really married as she thought, to de Horn
but to his secretary I brought her to Eton to the only house I
knew. My cousins wife (who had never heard of Kitty) said
to me the front room has been whitewashed lately there used
to be frescos in it once, but they were all faded & discoloured
– They say they were painted by an Italian drawing master
– you know D$^r$. Thackeray & all his daughters lived in this
house a hundred years ago. I <u>didnt</u> know it – but as I wrote on
& on that winter I seemed possessed & and as if all the fancies
were alive. My Father when we first came over to England
to pay him a visit took a lodging in Golden Square for us & I
was again assured that Angelica had lived there, when I went
to find out <u>where</u> she lived I recognized our lodging.

So many moving things have happened lately that I
can hardly remember all the curious coincidences as they
occurred one by one over the little story of so long ago....

I have always thought that my relationship to Kitty had
something to do with my seeming to <u>remember</u> all that had
occurred to Angelica, rather than collecting the facts out of
books & hearsay.[68]

By September of this first year of war, the streets and parks of
London offered evidence of mobilisation, of 'long processions of men
drilling in the open spaces', who though not yet in uniform, marched
by in ranks whilst passers-by raised their hats to them. 'I c$^d$. only cry.'[69]
A further link with the past was dissolved with Lizzie Smith's death,
widow of George Smith, and it was very touching to learn a few weeks
later of her £500 bequest. News of the bombardment of Rheims with
its significant destruction of the cathedral fabric brought a new kind of
horror for Annie, so many of whose formative years had been spent in
France. She was not unaware of the realities of conflict, having visited
Paris during the hostilities of the Franco-Prussian war more than forty
years before, but this new threat was of a different order, overturning
the shared values of European civilization that she had been handed
from her father's and grandmother's generations. It appeared that such

continuity could no longer be taken for granted, and Annie felt unable to sit by as a helpless spectator. Much as her grandmother had done during the Crimean War sixty years before, she now threw herself into war-work, firstly by helping to organise relief for the Belgian refugees who began to arrive in London from early October, Brussels itself having been occupied on 20 August. She was seeing the young men of her acquaintance leaving for the front. Arthur Ritchie, the son of William and Magdalene Ritchie, had gone on 25 September as a reservist with the British Expeditionary Force, a captain with the Cameronians. On that day too, Dick Norton came raising money for an ambulance, a week later setting out for France in the company of Desmond MacCarthy, son-in-law of Blanche Warre Cornish, who would serve with the Red Cross. Like a number of young educated New Englanders in London and Paris during the years when America was still unaligned, Norton felt a strong loyalty to the British and French cause. He would oversee one of the several American motorised ambulance corps which provided vital support behind the lines throughout the war years, and of which Henry James was a prominent supporter.

Billy was a reservist officer with the North Midland Mounted Brigade of the Leicestershire Yeomanry, and in the early months of the war was based at Diss for training. He was depressed that successive medical boards would not pass him fit for active service, but Annie found it hard to conceal her relief. Her niece, Eleanor Clough, had gone to France by the beginning of November to start a field hospital; Eleanor's sister Katia Freshfield would also nurse near the front for much of the war and in June 1918 would be badly injured when a bomb fell on her hospital in Etaples. The speed with which the lives of ordinary people had been transformed was remarkable, and the appalling costs were felt almost at once. Within two months of his departure for the front, Arthur Ritchie was dead, wounded near Ypres and dying in the military hospital at Boulogne. There was a memorial service for him on 30 November, but Annie was too ill and upset to attend. 'Hester went – I read the litany & the beautiful chapter at home.' Arthur had left a war diary which was recovered after his death, and sent back to England. When it was shown to Annie she was 'deeply moved by it', touched by the casual bravery and decency of Billy's favourite cousin whom she had known and loved since he was a baby. She scarcely needed this reason to understand the personal horrors of the European tragedy. She wrote to Marie Belloc Lowndes early in December, with Arthur's diary before her. 'I am shaking today with the letters & journals of my nephew w[h]. I have just seen.... What heroes they all are – what gentlemen.... In all my long life it seems to me there never was war till now.'[70]

# Ten

# THE END OF A LONG DAY'S WORK (1915-1919)

*It is all the same a comforting sight to see now and then a complete picture, as it were, spread out before our eyes; to listen to the end of the story. It would seem somehow as if this were the case when we hear of a life, which can be best counted by long years of usefulness and conscientious labour; of kindness, simplicity, contentment; of early endeavours and aspirations, matured and executed in later days; of success well and hardly earned, and interest enduring to the last.*

> Annie's tribute to Nassau Senior
> 'The End of a Long Day's Work'
> 1864

In *Mr Britling Sees it Through*, H.G. Wells conveys with an uncomfortable honesty what living during the uncertainties of wartime was like. After serialisation in the Nation, the book appeared in September 1916 and went through thirteen impressions by the end of the year. It gripped its first readers, who within the conventions and artifices of fiction encountered a contemporary reality in which they too were participants. The opening chapters sketch out the last weeks of peace, leading to that fateful weekend at the beginning of August 1914 when hope finally died, but the novel deals essentially with events whose outcomes were still unresolved. Wells's willingness to confront political complacencies and to highlight Britain's military unpreparedness resonated with his liberal readership, even if they doubted his new world order based on reason and internationalism. In the war journal which she kept from September 1916, Hester Ritchie mentioned the book and admired its author's 'tremendous denunciation of the Government & what incompetent idiots they have been. His descriptions are all written in flaming passion of those first days of war – he puts down just what we all felt, it will tell everything to future generations if they ever want to know the psychology of the English at that time.'[1] In 1920, in words close to Hester's, Thomas Hardy would promote Mr Britling as 'the best war book we have had. It gives just what we thought and felt at the time.'[2]

It had soon become clear there would be no sudden end to conflict, the Western Front establishing instead that directionless stalemate, unprecedented at the time, which has come to be characteristic of trench warfare. Although conscription would not arrive until 1916, enormous numbers volunteered in the first flush of an excited patriotism, but the heavy attrition rate kept the demand for fresh troops high. Billy was involved in training the Leicestershire Yeomanry in musketry, many of whom were killed during the first year. '[H]e has lost friend after friend', Annie told Alan Cole.[3] The weakness in his heart which kept him from the front was a bitter disappointment, but at the end of July 1915 his hopes were raised when he was at last assessed as fit. 'We have had a <u>choke</u> for the medical board has now passed Billy who is not really one bit for the front tho' he can <u>do</u> anything quietly & instruct & drill & all that sort of work.'[4] Within days a relieved Annie recorded in her diary that the 'authorities object to Billy going & it may be avoided after all'. Towards the end of 1916 he would be appointed to the Quartermaster General's staff, responsible for preventing waste and the recycling of materials for the war effort or, as Hester put it, 'turning dripping into explosives'.[5] Annie was sensitive to other sons departing for France and elsewhere. All three of Hallam Tennyson's boys had gone, and she confided to Pinkie how Richmond's absence made things harder to bear. 'The Darwins & the Ll. Davies haunt me. Poor M[rs] Booth sent off 2 sons in one week.'[6]

Annie was at Ware when news of the 'haunting nightmare of the Lusitania' came in May 1915. The nation was horrified by the liner's sinking off the coast of Ireland, hit by a U-boat on its voyage from America. Twelve hundred passengers died, about a tenth of them Americans. Some returning Thackeray manuscripts were lost, which Annie had probably sent with a view to their possible sale in New York, or perhaps for inclusion in an exhibition. It was painful to accept, but she kept things in proportion when she wrote of it to Billy. 'I am so glad [Charles] Lauriat escaped, but the poor beloved drawing books A & B went down in the Lusitania – I wonder if he insured them? If he didnt shall we give him all or half the Cornhill to Cairo books w[h]. he still has in N York – There is no hurry, but what do you think?'[7] She decided to write a brief memoir of Richmond for his grandson, and once again read through old diaries and letters with 'a grateful heart'. She told Pinkie that she was 'doing a little chewing of the cud <u>boiling</u> down old diaries',[8] which probably required some further adjustments to her journal, originally compiled in the late 1890s. Certainly, it was only in January 1915 that she 'finished diary and burnt [18]63', and as late as August she called another diary 'wonderfully interesting all the past <u>present</u>'. But now it was almost as if she was reading someone else's words, the story of a life in which Pinkie featured prominently. 'I am so touched to realise how you have ever ever come in my moments of stress & anxiety & ever brought music & hope & faith & charity & O what a piled up happy if anxious life it has been what dear & blessed things.'

The first months of 1915 were gloomy ones as Hester witnessed Eleanor Birrell's decline. During the evening of 10 March, Alfred Tennyson phoned with the news that his mother had died peacefully. 'H. very sad and pale.'[9] In the years since Richmond's death, the former Eleanor Tennyson had been close to Hester, which just occasionally pained Annie. It was almost as if Hester needed to be associated with whatever had once been important for her father, and although the problem of his own former intimacy with Eleanor had been over even before her remarriage, twenty-five years previously, in a curious way Hester managed to resurrect it. A week after the funeral at Golders Green, attended by Annie, Augustine Birrell sent Hester his wife's bracelet. 'I hardly ever saw her without it. Please wear it for her sake.'[10]

A happier kind of future for Hester seemed possible, the friendship with Dick Norton having continued during his absence in France with the American Ambulance corps. It was a relationship sustained by correspondence, although no letters have survived. If Annie remains silent on the subject of marriage, Kate Perugini is more forthcoming, regarding herself as Dick's honorary aunt, and in more than one letter to Hester she linked them closely. Hester probably confided things to Dickens's daughter that she felt unable to raise with her own mother.

> I think it is so very sweet and touching of you to treat me with such entire trust and affection, as if I were indeed a much loved Aunt Kitty and not only one of your mother's oldest and most intimate friends – but it strikes me Hester, that if I am Dick's aunt I must be your aunt too, for you and he are now inseparable in my mind and it is a very pleasant thought that I have lately gained a dear new niece as well as a nephew!... Your mother has several times said that

she thought we were rather alike, you and I, in our way of thinking and in a way we have of coming to quick decisions, and though it may not flatter you to hear it – I think she is right. And we were certainly never meant for door mats! Any way all these things, led by Fate, have thrown us into each others' arms as it were, and it makes me very happy that you speak to me as a daughter of my own might have spoken. Bless you and thank you for it.

I hope to see you soon and I hope also that the day is not very far distant when you and Dick will both dine with us. He must bring that cross to show us, tell him, or I shall not believe he's really got it.[11]

Yet if the possibility of marriage was in Hester's mind, it is unlikely that she expected anything to become clear before the war ended. Meanwhile, the ongoing bouts of nervous anxiety continued for months, sometimes spilling over into criticism of her mother. 'Hester bilious & bothered & cross. Alas what can I do. I only jar upon her in these moods of irritation.'[12]

For the first six months of 1915 Annie lent The Porch to the writer and critic Desmond MacCarthy, now married to Molly Warre Cornish, allowing him (according to Virginia Woolf) to 'live cheaply & write a novel'.[13] It meant that Annie and Hester were at Freshwater only once this year, during September and October. The tranquillity of life there was still magical, but even Freshwater could not ignore the war's realities. One day Annie watched a destroyer searching for mines out in the channel, and then returned to The Porch to help prepare bandages for the local hospital. Eleanor Clough, Gussie's daughter, came to visit for a few days, and they climbed up High Down together to admire the view which fifty years earlier Annie had enjoyed with Minny. 'Lovely & holy gleam over the sea – Very thankful to find myself there once more.'[14] She and Hester followed the war news keenly, poring over the daily papers and pouncing on anecdotes. London's Zeppelin raids had begun, and Annie recounted to Rhoda a story that they had picked up about Lady Buckmaster's gardener. 'He got in to the train [from Hertford] in the dark & as they went along they heard a Zeppelin over head, on & on following them to London. The red smoke f$^m$. the funnel was guiding it. The clever engine driver stopped short outside London in a suburb, all the passengers alighted & presently down came the bombs comparatively harmless. Yesterday at Farringford we heard of a general from Gallipoli – most hopeful & saying we are sure to get thro' before October. This general takes Vanity Fair to read in the trenches.'

Virginia's first novel, *The Voyage Out*, had appeared in March. Annie's early interest in Leslie's imaginative child was bearing fruit, even if her diary comment about the book is non-committal – 'Read Virginias novel good quite'. She was herself still picking over the bones of a story from which she hoped that a novel might yet emerge, but it was destined never to work out quite satisfactorily. Virginia was a witness to this ambition, after Annie's death remembering an episode from about 1916 when she and Leonard called at St Leonard's Terrace.

> [U]nlike most old Aunts she had the wits to feel how sharply we differed on current questions; & this, perhaps, gave her a sense, hardly existing with her usual circle, of age, obsoleteness, extinction. For myself, though, she need have had no anxieties on this head, since I admired her sincerely; but still the generations certainly look very different ways. Two or perhaps three years ago L. & I went to see her; found her much diminished in size, wearing a feather boa round her neck, and seated alone in a drawing room almost the copy, on a smaller scale, of the old drawing room; the same subdued pleasant air of the 18th Century & old portraits & old china. She had our tea waiting for us. Her manner was a little distant, and more than a little melancholy. I asked her about father, & she said how those young men laughed in a 'loud melancholy way' & how their generation was a very happy one, but selfish; & how ours seemed to her fine but very terrible; but we hadn't any writers such as they had ... She put her hand down I remember, into a bag or box standing beside the fire, & said she had a novel, three-quarters written – but couldn't finish it – nor do I suppose it ever was finished.[15]

The quick, sympathetic intelligence remained on both sides, though it is scarcely surprising that Virginia and Annie were far apart on 'current questions' concerning the war. A matching recollection of perhaps a year or two earlier comes from Annie's granddaughter, who would often visit St Leonard's Terrace with her brother. 'Upstairs in the double-drawing room we always found Grandmama sitting by the fire in long black silk skirts and a lace cap. There was a round red-japanned box at her feet known as the great Panjandrum, in which her novel, our toys, her French newspaper, which came daily, and some pages of manuscript were all jumbled together.'[16]

Annie and Hester decided to transfer to The Porch for much of 1916, returning in September to spend the winter months in London.

But Annie was still at Littlehampton when the 'cruel news' reached her on 1 February of Harold Tennyson's death, his ship having been struck by a mine a few miles off the coast of Boulogne.[17] Harold was the youngest of Hallam and Audrey Tennyson's sons, 'the most charming devoted boy gallant & tender'.[18] She felt keenly for Pinkie, for Harold had been a talented amateur violinist, and she had played the piano for him. His parents were grief-stricken, and Hallam replied to her note of sympathy. 'How he prized your 'Esmond' which you gave him and how proud he was of winning the prize for it. Audrey is bearing up bravely. She keeps saying, "My darling, my darling – oh the pity of it"'.[19] Once Annie and Hester were installed at Freshwater again, the romance of the place worked its magic. One day they both stood and watched a scene of ploughing, and for a moment the horrors of the fields of Flanders could not break into this ancient English idyll, the image offering an innocence which might yet survive untouched. As she told Billy, it had brought her young grandson to mind.

> I wish I could pack up all the breath off the downs & all the light off the sea & O the beautiful sight H fetched me to see this morning, six pairs of carthorses dragging ploughs along the great field leading down to the bay & all the old men driving them & a little bit of a boy with fair hair turning one of them. I said to Hester 'well done James'. She laughed. The little boy turned sharp round & stared. His name must have been really James.[20]

Another friend was bowing out. Henry James had suffered a stroke on 2 December 1915, and another two days later. Just a few months before, on 28 July, James had taken the Oath of Allegiance and became a naturalised British subject. 'The post brought me the most touching charming letter from Henry James who says the <u>relief</u> of what he has done is so great to him that he realises more & more how glad he is he did it.'[21] A week after his second stroke Annie paid what she thought might be her last visit. '12 December. To say goodbye to dear Henry James.' In fact, she managed to see him again on 12 January, but news of his death now reached her in Freshwater. She wrote at once to Billy about 'dear dear Henry James's death. Is it good news? – To live on at half power is only wretched – I go on thinking my stock phrase to myself. Life is worth dying for – For <u>us</u> his death is all loss. He sent us a message not long ago "– My love – always, always" – he said – so his niece told me.'[22] It was a thoughtful gesture to invite James's secretary, Theodora Bosanquet, to stay with them at The Porch for a fortnight, ostensibly to undertake some copying work. 'If you could bring a type writer I should be glad but otherwise I w$^d$. dictate & you should write say f.$^m$ 11 to 1.'[23] The duties were light indeed, and it became a chance for Annie to share memories of her old friend. 'Miss Bosanquet talks to us most interestingly of dear H.J. She is very nice indeed – an <u>on-looker,</u> like one of his characters quite a lady.'[24] Theodora was amused by the regime, but it took a day or two for her to fathom Hester, whom she found 'distinctly "intense"', dressing 'in the roughest country clothes and [who] bolts down chunks of food in an appropriate manner'.[25]

In these last years Annie's sight was not good, and to read a book she had to hold the page up close to her face. A visit to an oculist in early August reassured her that there was no sign of cataracts, although later in the year her doctor thought he detected the start of one, only for the eye specialist to confirm the original diagnosis. Her gratitude to Hester, 'my dear help thro it', is touching.[26] Despite her poor sight, there were occasional striking experiences, including one which brought Richmond before her again. '23 September. I saw Rs picture shining <u>coloured</u> – blue sky for a few minutes as I lay in bed vividly bright. Then it faded.' It was the same night as a Zeppelin raid on London, when Hester watched excitedly from her bedroom window as one airship was brought down by tracer fire, 'a great burning red mass like a comet'.

During a brief visit to Eton with Margie Ritchie in May, Annie saw where a memorial brass to Richmond would be erected a week later in the chapel. It was probably the last time that she saw Frank Warre Cornish, who died on 29 August. Writing to Pinkie on the day of Frank's funeral she wished 'good speed on the great journey – to the dear friend & <u>host</u> for so many of us in life'.[27] Gerald Warre Cornish was serving at the front when he heard of his father's death, unable to return for the funeral. Of all the letters which Blanche received, 'nothing more beautiful has come than Captain Gerald's letter from a lonely evening in a French village his regiment resting after its great battles, – he says amongst other things full of upliftedness "There is a peace which the world cannot give or take away before which all these European troubles sink away, and to that peace belongs the inexpressible beauty of Father's life; … his last words to me when we parted last were: <u>We shall meet again</u>".'[28] So it was especially poignant when, within the month, Gerald was reported missing. He had been wounded on 16 September, 'had his wounds bandaged & then ran back into the battle, & he has never been heard of since'.[29] Hester accompanied her aunt Blanche to the Wounded and Missing Enquiry Department of the Red Cross, but the news was not hopeful, for they were told that 'prisoners are only taken when the

Germans advance over our ground'. With notable resilience, Blanche accepted the grim probabilities. 'It is so like Gerald to have vanished in the curtain of fire that it is vain to search for him now among the wounded living. Your letter of last Monday has the word – the word Gerald leaves us – <u>Peace</u>. Keep it dearest in your heart for it is <u>with us</u>.'[30] There had been times when some in the wider Ritchie family had been irritated by Blanche's Romanist proselytising. Now the comforts of her simple faith were inspiring. She stayed at St Leonard's Terrace with Annie and Hester for a few weeks and 'melted our hearts'. It was her own decision to leave Eton and take a flat in Kensington, and Annie was profoundly moved by her stoicism. 'Husband – Son – home – all are swept out of her busy moving life.... She is nobly courageous & dignified in her sorrow. She has many to love & to turn to – but this seems like the heart of her life <u>not</u> destroyed but pierced thro' & thro.'[31] They reminisced about the first days of the war, Blanche recalling the large crowds of returning French nationals at Charing Cross. Amongst them was 'a jolly Breton, who said to the crowd "<u>moi</u>, je suis marchand d'onions [*sic*] et je repars pour la France." Aunt Blanche said "I could not help saying to him Vive la France at which to took my hand in his, & said Merci Madame & I then added Vivent les onions" & he beamed.'[32]

Listening to eye-witness accounts of the wounded was sobering. A fellow officer of Gerald's told them that after relentless artillery fire and the ferocity of the German advance 'there is absolutely nothing left of anybody or anything'. They heard of Harold Macmillan, wounded and in hospital – 'he spent from 8 a.m until dark in a shell crater, then he managed to crawl out & get back to our lines. He said he passed the time watching the battle & reading Aescalus [*sic*].'[33] At the end of October Hester went once more with Blanche to the Wounded and Missing office, hoping that Gerald's identity disk might have been returned, but there was nothing. 'They say so many of the lost are never found again. Sometimes a shell comes & blows away those who are burying the dead.' A year later the extended Ritchie family would face another loss when the 'heartbreaking cruel news' reached them of the death of Algy Villiers, husband of Annie's niece Beatrix Paul, killed leading his machine-gun section into action at Bourlon Wood.

The war work went on. Annie involved herself in fund-raising to support a group of nuns at Rheims, who despite the destruction of their convent were caring for injured soldiers sheltering in the ruins of the cathedral. She wrote seeking money from American supporters of the allied cause. 'I would gratefully forward it to Rheims for darning &

*Annie in later life*

renovating & reclothings cost money & the sisters live from hand to mouth.'[34] And in August she would appeal in the pages of the *Spectator* for subscriptions to support the Surgical Requisites Association, a group of mainly female volunteers in Chelsea making artificial limbs and surgical devices. To assist the efforts of the Belgravia War rooms in Grosvenor Crescent, Kate Perugini joined Annie in running a bookstall at Hyde Park House on 22 November, selling items from their own collections as well as contributions from literary friends. She asked Thomas Hardy for autographs to paste into copies of his books, gently reminding him of one 'who knew you years ago with Leslie Stephen, & George Smith & in old days'. Hardy sent the autographs, and reminisced with her. She was grateful for his recollections, and even more for his ready support. 'I can vaguely remember the junketting of my youth thank you for remembering. A bookseller told my daughter that yours was one of the only autographs that had any value. I shall hope for 4 Bank notes.'[35]

In sorting through some of her father's manuscripts for the sale, she came across 'a stray most characteristic page of Vanity Fair' which a dealer valued at £40, but then began to doubt whether it was hers to sell. Having seen Virginia recently she started a letter, seeking the acquiescence of Leslie's children. 'Suddenly <u>seeing</u> you it occurred to me that the page was either all of yours I mean you three, – y$^r$ father having chosen V.F. for his share or Laura's – <u>not</u> mine to dispose of. Laura's I sh$^d$. think on the whole – If it is <u>hers</u> I think it might possibly be contributed <u>for</u> her for the fund – But it is beyond my powers to decide.' She then converted the letter into one to Jack Hills, who could provide the proper legal advice. 'I suddenly feared to disturb that dear calmly restored Virginia & I thought I would ask you instead to help me.'[36] At one stage, it seems that the bookstall risked an effeteness not quite appropriate for the occasion. 'Dearest Kate Perugini wanted to have a picture of her Father with a wreath of laurels – I said of course if she liked it but I couldnt possibly do anything of the sort & to my great relief she has given it up.'[37] The day's schedule is suggested well by Louisa Lee Schuyler, who was not even there. She wrote with characteristic enthusiasm from the Hudson Valley, north of New York city, recreating the scene from Annie's itinerary.

> [T]his is the day of the 'Sale and Concert' at Hyde Park House – when the daughters of Thackeray & Dickens open their book stall and sell their precious heirlooms, for the wounded heroes of the hour.
>
> George & I have been counting the hours (in accordance with your inventory) – Now the Princess Christian opens the sale; now Queen Alexandra appears at the Concert; now Lady Ritchie and Mrs Perugini – the attractions at the bookstore, receive their many friends and the jumble; and now the Canadian Military Choir is singing.[38]

The bookstall was the success which Louisa imagined for it, attracting many buyers, including the queen herself, as well as dealers bidding for the rarer items.

A political crisis at the end of the year saw Lloyd George resigning from Asquith's coalition administration, quickly followed by his elevation to the premiership in a coup as skilful as it was ruthless. A surge of short-term confidence in Lloyd George won him broad popular support, Hester's trenchant criticism of Asquith being the view shared by their set.

> Dec 5th. No one talking of anything but new War Council. Thunderbolt evening papers announce Lloyd George's resignation as M[r] Asquith will not accept his Council scheme.... The most cheering sign that the German newspapers already angry at this change in our politics. Mama & I discuss & discuss, we feel all is up for England if Asquith carries the day. Miserable to bed with the uncertainty only longing the night to be over quick....

> December 6<u>th</u> Wednesday All is well. Asquith has res-
> igned. The King sends for Bonar Law to form a new
> ministry.
>     <u>Dec 7 Thursday</u> Lloyd George sent for by the King to
> form a ministry, universal joy & hope.

But all was not quite well with Hester. The nature of her feelings for Dick Norton, probably kept from her mother, the loss of the father whom she still mourned, and with victory still very far from certain, all this weighed heavily on her. A week after the new ministry was established, Billy and his cousin Humphrey Paul dined at St Leonard's Terrace. Hester kept to her room, so Annie discussed 'plans' with Billy, including finding a companion for Hester. The idea was not pursued, but Annie clearly feared that she was unable to provide her daughter with sufficient distraction. It must have been a hard realisation. In leaving the bulk of the Thackeray materials to Hester, she had made whatever financial provision she could, but what would the future hold? A later diary entry suggests a more resigned outlook. '16 July 1917. Thinking of Hester when I died. She will make her own place in life, bless her – low all the same.'

It was not exactly a cheerful time for anyone. As Christmas approached, the darkened streets and empty shop windows seemed to mock the plenty which had been taken for granted before the war. Once again, it was Hester who remarked this. 'Sunday 24th Xmas Eve & anything less like it cannot be imagined. No light in the streets & the shops even if they had any lights they have no goods nothing to put in the windows. Everything is coming to an end at the A & N Stores; they told me in a month there will be nothing more to be had. How could we all take the plenty & profusion of pre war days with such indifference!'

In 1917 Annie reached the age of eighty. Having believed five years before that there remained 'such a little time for me', to be a witness now to the loss of a generation of young men was a cruel irony. Nor could she ever have imagined that she would live for so many more years than her father – aged only fifty-two at his death – outlive her sister by more than forty years, or that her husband, seventeen years her junior, would go before her. The past, which once had seemed like an almost tangible reality, had finally retreated from her, leaving her stranded. There were still moments which would take her back to earlier memories, but they seemed almost impossibly remote now. She came across a lock of Minny's hair cut when she was a child, put away and forgotten for decades, yet which '<u>shone</u> in sun after

70 years – as nothing'.[39] Another such occasion was the arrival of a uniformly-bound set of Annie's books, a gift from Charles Johnson to Belinda, his goddaughter. Annie charmingly describes the scene when the volumes were unpacked and the pages turned, but they seemed like artefacts from a past now lost to her and unimaginably distant for her grandchildren.

> It was very cold and quite dark when Billy arrived & after he had had his tea, & settled down by the fire he said 'now children' & they rushed away & came back bringing in the hamper, & opened the lid & lo! there were the beautifully bound books! Did any authoress in her old age ever see such a droll touching sight as her beloved grandchildren – & Linny in particular – eagerly turning over the leaves of all her past days, exclaiming at the pictures, & obediently putting the books down when their Father cried 'beware of fingers'. What a kind old friendly god paternal thought, what an apotheosis for my life long chatter to find itself so kindly honoured & decorated. I hardly knew which were the grandchildren & which were my stories so much of the past was written in each one of them. And Walkers lovely drawings & George Leslies & M^rs Allingham's all seemed alive too & thankyou & thankyou again dear M^r Johnson.[40]

She was happy to live in whatever present was left to her, if frustrated by her frailties. 'I wish how I wish I could be cut into four active young women of twenty to come & go. I should like wings to fly with and intelligence to know what might be of some use.'[41] She was at Ware for 9 June, a happy birthday which began when James pushed a wheelbarrow filled with roses and presents into her bedroom, steered by Hester, and after she had come downstairs the grandchildren, dressed as pirates, carried still more armfuls of flowers to her. It was the kind of homemade pleasure that she had always loved, the sort of inexpensive treat that she and Minny had shared with their father, and which Hester and Billy had been shown in turn by their parents. At the end of her life, her father's enduring gift was as valuable as when she had herself been a child, a straightforward, uncomplicated love, costly only in time and generosity of imagination. Florence Bell, helping out with hospital work at Northallerton, nicely caught what Annie really does seem to have represented for those who knew her well:

> is it conceivable that you have reached 8 on that dial? – but you're a very long way behind on the dial that marks the age

of one's heart and sympathies and all the things that really matter. You are of those whom the Gods love and who die young – to the end. Dear, you won't mind my saying this – & telling you what an inestimable thing you are doing for the world in showing it the sweetness and wisdom that come with the years – or that <u>may</u> come, at any rate, to the privileged.[42]

In these last years, Annie was still visiting Laura, and taking her out when she could. This was less often now, but only because she was away at Freshwater for weeks at a time. Laura seems at last to have achieved some kind of stability in her life, and Annie was more resigned about the future. They probably saw each other for the last time on 25 September 1918, and it was a good meeting. 'With P[inkie] to Laura a lovely day lovely drive in Richmond Park.'

America had finally entered the war at the beginning of April 1917, the first troops stepping on French soil in June. Annie and Hester were at The Porch, having let St Leonard's Terrace for five guineas a week to Major Bowes-Lyon, and Hester struggled through heavy snow to buy newspapers. They had travelled by train from Waterloo to Southampton before crossing by boat, and the stations had been full of soldiers, including a large group of German prisoners being transferred under escort to Dorchester. Hester did not conceal her contempt. 'A revulsion of hate went up against them & a man called out "Lynch them". But they were such wretched underdeveloped men with such evil faces one felt only dislike & a longing for them to be marched off to their carriages. One wondered what they felt, Waterloo Station swarming with magnificently built Canadians and Australians in the prime of manhood. Such splendid men, with warm cheerful kind ways & manners.'[43] Hester's reaction was probably widely-shared, but Annie was conscious of the prisoners' hopelessness, victims as much as aggressors.

For those Americans who had long supported the Allied efforts, President Woodrow Wilson's commitment to the war was a milestone. A cable came immediately from Louisa Lee Schuyler in New York, asking Annie to 'congratulate us that at last we are allowed to fight side by side with the Allies'.[44] But at Farringford the mood was subdued, for at the end of the previous year Audrey Tennyson had died after a short illness, and Hallam now cut a lonely figure. He would send his motorcar to The Porch to fetch Annie and Hester, one day relating how from the downs he had seen a plume of white smoke rising in the Solent, later discovering that a hospital ship had been torpedoed by a U-boat as it entered Southampton Water. A naval officer who was spending some of his leave at Farringford told them that a defensive boom had been laid in an attempt to keep out the U-boats, but that they slipped through by following the liners coming into Southampton. The losses of merchant shipping to German patrols had declined somewhat by this time, and although there were significant shortages in some foodstuffs, such as sugar, potatoes and bread flour, the country was not going to starve. But people disliked changes to their eating habits, as Hester's journal suggests. 'Lord Devenport urges us to give up afternoon tea. I am having oat cake for breakfast to save bread. It is absurd to find oneself missing bread for b.fast though before rations one had never imagined one did care for it. With so many things one finds this. Potatoes rare as peaches. But when tea comes to an end that really will be a blow. Parsnip & swedes which we've been having instead of potatoes have come now to an end. We are having barley & rice instead' (2 April 1918).

Pinkie joined them for a couple of weeks in July. Her presence rekindled some of Annie's hopes from forty years earlier, when she had thought that Pinkie and Hallam might have made a go of things. He came to The Porch to invite Pinkie to dinner, and she also called at Farringford the day before she crossed back to Southampton. But Hallam sought consolation for his loneliness elsewhere, a year later marrying rather suddenly an old Freshwater friend, May Hichens, daughter of Sara Prinsep (Julia Margaret Cameron's sister) and widow of Andrew Hichens. Hallam gave his news to Pinkie before anyone else, which was special consideration of a kind. 'We are all getting quite used to the new Lady of Farringford. Hallam wrote to Pinkie ten days ago. I'm glad he did: & I think she was touched by his confidence in her first of all.'[45] It pleased Hallam's friends that he could find some happiness again, particularly after the death of his second son, Aubrey, who was killed just months before. 'Lord Tennysons marriage makes everything much less sad somehow for all of us who care for him & one can speak out loud at Farringford again. All last year this Lady Tennyson who loved Audrey Tennyson had been running the hospital & then to everyones relief L^d Tennyson & she eloped.'[46] Nonetheless, the news provoked some less charitable comments, including a predictably acid one from Rhoda Broughton. 'Have the Triumphal Arches yet been erected for the homecoming of the Bride & Bridegroom? Someone wrote me that a convenient letter from the late Lady T. begging him to marry again, was found after her death! I dont much believe in these Post Mortem requests to be replaced. But I suppose it made everything pleasanter for both parties.'[47]

Ever since their initial deployment, Zeppelins had rarely caused more than a few casualties in their bombing raids on London and other English towns. The main excitement for those on the ground was the occasional sighting of an airship being brought down. Mary Cholmondeley witnessed one destroyed above her Suffolk cottage. 'We heard the enemy pass over us twice amid a deafening cannonade, and at last when the dawn came we saw him hanging tilted and wounded above the Ufford chimneys. He struggled a few miles, and then fell slowly in flames.'[48] Germany now began to send aeroplanes more frequently on bombing missions. Margie Ritchie wrote of a major raid over London in which perhaps twenty planes had been deployed, although little damage was done. Incidents like this helped persuade civilians that they too had been drawn into the conflict. Nor did the fighting across the channel seem that far away. There were times when Billy and Meg, as far inland as Hertfordshire, could hear the firing of the larger artillery guns in Flanders.

After pondering the risks, Annie and Hester returned to St Leonard's Terrace late in the summer, only to face more raids. On 24 September Hester listened to what the newspapers reported as the 'worst air raid yet', though the damage was relatively minor – a crater in Green Park and smashed windows at the Ritz. The sporadic attacks continued for some weeks, and during the night of 1 October bombs dropped on Eaton Terrace with a gas main hit near Grosvenor railway bridge, the explosion knocking them off their feet in their Chelsea house. Hester walked out the following morning to see the damage. 'Incredible desolation of the bombed places – they look as if it was a hundred years ago that they had been destroyed, not 12 hours ago. You can't quite believe its true, & yet one knows it is – Crisp beautiful autumn morning with brilliant sunshine.'

In late October, Annie was distressed to hear of the retreat of the Italian army and Venice threatened by the German and Austrian advance. She thought at once of Ariana Curtis, with whom she and Hester had stayed at the Palazzo Barabaro in the spring of 1912. As recently as July they had exchanged letters, recalling those happier pre-war times. '[I]t brings back all your kindness to us, & all the wonderful charm of every thing when we lived, in those delightful places & times when war was not with us, & did not keep us awake at night and bring sorrow & anxiety to friend after friend.' Now she worried for Ariana's safety, and for the city which in 1874 had seen the first stirrings of her romance with Richmond. 'My dear kind beloved friend how often we think of you & of all you have had to go through & to witness. I read the papers, I seem to live it all as I read.... Venice seems like a mirage when I look back at our blessed stay with you. Will it ever be the same again! How glorious the stand has been.'[49]

And yet, the banalities of ordinary life continued. Blanche Warre

Cornish held an 'at home' to which Annie and Hester went, only to encounter Charlotte Leigh Smith for the first time in ten years. Blanche and Charlotte had little in common beyond their religion, so it was a surprise to see her there with her son. It had unfortunate if predictable consequences. 'Enter Phil & Charlotte. H turned pale & left so did I first shaking hands & glad to greet Phil.' Blanche expressed her disapproval through Pinkie, who told Annie that she had been 'vexed at our flight'. If she had known of Richmond's former friendship, she can have had no conception of what it represented.

War work kept Hester busy. At Freshwater she was involved in an organisation encouraging local women to take on farm work, and in Chelsea she helped to set up a communal kitchen, one of many established in London and other urban centres. Bulk purchasing and centralised cooking contained

*Hester in later life, about 1955*

food costs for hard-pressed families, who would buy precooked meals and take them home to eat. Although they were targeted at the poor, these wartime takeaways were sought out by others too.

> Hesters present interest is a communal Kitchen for Chelsea which she & a friend are trying to start. They save food firing expence & the fatigue for poor women of catering & going from shop to shop in search of food. Hester heard a lady imploring a pound of dripping – I am Viscountess so & so, she said & carried it off in her basket, or as much as she could get.[50]

More than once Annie was a customer herself, such as when Billy called for lunch one day. 'We <u>bought</u> it at the Communal Kitchen today, & kind Miss Hayes brought it home in a basket.' It had all the fun of a treat. After Annie's death, Mary Cholmondeley's sister recalled the pleasures of visiting St Leonard's Terrace. 'I often think of that very happy evening I spent there – & you had such a clever meal obtained from the communal kitchen … & your Mothers joyousness & lightness of heart over it all. She made all simple things seem delightful & radiant.'[51] Hester's voluntary work took on a more sombre tone in the last two months of the war. On 11 September she began to work for the Red Cross, trying to establish details of the war missing by interviewing wounded soldiers in hospital, who might have seen their comrades fall. The difficulties in establishing what had happened to Gerald Warre Cornish had introduced her to this harrowing but necessary work.

In early 1918, Annie and Hester themselves became victims on the home front when a single bomb from a stray German plane fell close to St Leonard's Terrace, at about 10 pm on the night of 16 February. Collateral damage was caused from a direct hit on a house in the grounds of the Royal Hospital at Chelsea, killing the occupants. Hester furnished Marie Belloc Lowndes with details.

> We are all safe and unhurt, though the explosion broke every window in the house, and also blew in the framework of the drawing-room windows. Two men were blown into the area from the road by the force of the explosion, but this was rather a comfort from our point of view, as we had to look for them, and this distracted us from what was going on outside. There were terrible fumes, and the children's governess, by way of cheering us up, suggested they must be poison gas! The house rocked backwards and forwards, and upwards, and down, and from all sides came sounds of falling masonry, crashing glass, and the shooting down of tiles.[52]

Annie faced the trauma with remarkable composure, receiving her granddaughter on the morning after the bomb fell. 'Broken glass cracked underfoot and the curtains flapped continually. Grandmama lay on a sofa in the dark looking tired and bored. Lots of people came in with flowers and condolences. She answered their queries in a distrait manner.'[53] The house was put into the hands of builders for repairs, and having transferred to Billy and Meg in Hertfordshire, Annie wrote to Rhoda. 'This is a real Bombers letter. Crash went all the windows, and all the room was full of smoke and fury on my part. I rushed up to Hester and met her flying downstairs, she had heard the bomb coming – it was that one Bomb which killed a poor family, Major Ludlow, his wife, and two children in the pretty old

house Fanny d'Arblay used to go and write letters from.'[54] She tried
to dismiss the incident later, but there was no mistaking its impact.
'I forget … if I told you how we had been bombed ourselves before
we came away. It doesn't improve one's nerves. Hester suffered far
more than I did, and I was glad to take a poor offer for the house and
to come off, first to Billy's home and now to the faithful little Porch.'
From the island, Annie watched a cargo ship burning for days off
the Needles, until eventually it struck rocks and the spilt cargo came
drifting towards the shore. The slow death of the stricken vessel held
her, an emblem of war's impact on ordinary lives.

> There was a fleet of ships, and in the confusion as they tried to
> escape the coming attack two of them collided, of which this
> was one. There was a sunset. It was church-time, and the people
> going to the little chapel here turned towards the beach.… The
> crew had been taken off – the ship burnt and burnt. Then came
> a glorious night, and the great flames leaping and reflected in
> the water. About one o'clock I was told the great ship, as if
> manned by a phantom crew, stood off and made the circuit of
> the bay, and them came back as if steered towards the rocks,
> blazing all the time under the stars.
>
> Then after two days the fire went out in smoke, and then
> on the waves came sacks and sacks of fine white flour, boxes
> of lard and pork, and horrible streams of petroleum from some
> other ship. Today the sea has been tossing up barrels of oil.[55]

The last year of the conflict saw a series of major setbacks, such
that few could have predicted quite how quickly the end would come.
Pinkie was depressed at what seemed to be the ineffectuality of the
English military command in the face of enemy successes. '[O]ur hope
must rest on Foch's tactics for we cannot count on any inspiration
in our own Headquarters though Haig's proclamation today is fine
enough. We must keep courageous hearts and not yet think of Defeat
whatever the terrible cost.'[56] But the real possibilities of defeat could
not be dismissed, certainly during April and May, and Hester was in
low spirits. 'April 13th. 1918 Blackest days ever known in English
history. Germans winning everywhere. Battle of Armentieres at its
height.' She conveys the widely felt despair at the extent of the losses
and the apparent hopelessness of the task. '[Aubrey Tennyson] was
seen commanding his platoon with greatest coolness & brilliancy until
he fell. The Germans were only 250 yards off. He was hit by machine
gun fire & from the way he fell they knew he was mortally wounded.
They could not stop for him. Noble noble Aubrey.… Appalling our

lists of killed, and appalling our lists of missing.'[57] At the beginning of June there was a service at the parish church to honour the 'dear dead boys & men of Freshwater', and the Bishop of Southampton dedicated a memorial in the churchyard. The names of the local fallen were read out, and everyone present was overcome.

Amidst the terrible losses, a new menace, invisible and undiscriminating, spread across many parts of the world, including Europe, India, South Africa and America. A virulent strain of influenza took hold in 1918, which for no convincing reason came to be called the Spanish flu, or in moments of black humour, the plague of the Spanish lady. The pandemic would kill many millions over the next two or three years. During peak weeks, hundreds would die in each of the major British conurbations, so that on 18 December the medical correspondent of the *Times* estimated the death toll to have been five times more costly than the war. 'Never since the Black Death has such a plague swept over the face of the world; never, perhaps, has a plague been more stoically accepted.' With so many medical staff away serving with the army, nursing facilities at home were woefully inadequate. In Freshwater, the hospital was overflowing with victims, and special influenza camps were established. Although the epidemic seemed to be receding late in 1918, there would be another serious outbreak in February 1919.

Annie could still savour the small comic moments in what now passed for ordinary life. 'Hallam starts tomorrow with his butler his gardener his cowman both called up. The immaculate butler goes on opening the drawing room doors & announcing Lady & Miss Ritchie just as if his wife wasnt packing for him.'[58] Just before *Eminent Victorians* appeared, with its deliberate debunking of reputations, Lytton Strachey had told Ottoline Morrell that he wanted it to 'burst upon an astonished world'. Perhaps Annie was astonished, but this particular Victorian was not shocked by mere naughtiness. 'I am amazed by Lytton Strachey's book. Diable à quatreically clever & amusing.'[59] It is a generous appreciation, not what one might have predicted from one whose discretion and circumspection was so very different from Strachey's approach to biographical writing.

There was considerable popular resentment at the royal family's Germanic genealogy, and private criticism could be virulent. Rhoda Broughton relished being able to pass on to Hester a story about Queen Alexandra enquiring of a wounded soldier whether he would like to return to the Front. '"Well Mum, I should like to 'ave another 'it at them Bloody 'Uns!"... The poor Tommy, seeing that he had made a blunder corrected it thus. "Beg pardon, Mum! I forgot as you was 'alf a 'Un yourself!'"[60] The prejudice existed even in those close to government. Augustine Birrell was at the St Paul's service to celebrate the royal silver wedding, and told Hester of the 'fearful German guttural grunts & noises [which] came down from the Royal pews when our 40 royal Huns sat in a bunch. It was apropos of the wild cry everywhere that every German is to be interned & to be forced by law to go back to their German names … It is rather absurd with the German Jews having taken the most blue blooded names of England, Cholmondeley, Greville, etc etc.'[61]

During the late summer, Hester registered her relief as the war news at last began to improve, but about the death of Dick Norton she remained eloquently silent. When America entered the war, he left the ambulance corps which he had led with such distinction. In the spring of 1917 he had been awarded the Cross of the Legion of Honour, the highest French decoration available to a foreigner. He was not killed in the hostilities, but succumbed suddenly to meningitis and died in Paris. The news must have devastated Hester, and Annie finally understood something of what it meant for her. '6 August. Poor Hester came in crying. Dear Dick Norton is dead a sad day.' In writing to Ariana Curtis, Annie's affection for Dick becomes clear, but there is no allusion to Hester's closer bond. It is of course possible that that fuller friendship had faded before he died. 'I cannot tell you how kind he was when my husband died & he has written to us & kept up with us ever since.'[62] Kate Perugini and Annie arranged for a memorial tribute to be sent to Norton's American relatives, a framed inscription carefully written out by Hester and signed by his English friends. Kate engaged a London frame-maker to do the work, and then sent it on to Freshwater. '[The] frame will not be very ornate, but extremely simple which was what Dick liked – and it will not be expensive. We will share all expenses, you and I dear, as we arranged and I will let you know when everything is sent off.'[63]

The Porch now felt more like home than did anywhere else, and during her final trip to the mainland in September Annie saw Laura and a number of old friends, as well as visiting Richmond's grave in Hampstead, returning to the island with a sense that she was leaving things in good order – 'thankful for month in London & for having seen everyone there for getting to Ware Hampstead Charterhouse for seeing Bells Annie everyone. I grow too fussy, need [to] <u>dip</u> into friendship every now & then.' It was enough to have lived to see the longed-for peace approaching, for by the beginning of November it was clear that hostilities would end within days. She was not at all well during this time, affected by neuralgia and digestive problems.

Her back gave her pain and she slept badly, 'but nothing matters if Peace is come'. She was also troubled by the old problem in her neck, visiting a local surgeon for advice. Though she would live for a few more months, the final decline had begun. '[My gland] doesn't hurt & is only uncomfortable and rather weakening. But O what a good thing is the preparation of Peace to cure everyone of everything.'[64]

On 10 November the Freshwater vicar declared that news of the armistice would be signalled by the pealing of the church bells, the call for an immediate service of thanksgiving. Hester recorded the events of the next momentous day.

> Monday Nov: 11th Suddenly at 9.45 the church bells suddenly ring. No words can ever say what one's feelings were – I rushed to Mama, who was still not yet up – she hurried into her dressing gown, I ran for my boots and started pell mell for Church Mama following. Everyone streaming in, from the Beach, the village the farms, officers off duty from the submarine listening House. There was no joy, everyone crying, & very grateful for long pauses in which to say our own prayers. First God save the King, then the cxxiv Psalm, the Doxology, then the Lord's Prayer, & prayer for the liberated people....
>
> Free tea & concert for the soldiers in the Tin House. Awful rumour in the afternoon that the news is not true, for the newspapers have not got it in today's issue, only description of the ex-Kaiser's flight to Holland – but later on a telegram from Billy who says the news is true, & that he went to Buckingham Palace to celebrate it.

For his mother and sister at Freshwater, Billy captured something of the excitement of the huge London crowds who gathered to see the king and queen.

> Queen Victoria's monument was black with enthusiasts, one youth sat upon her knees in the most friendly manner. After a bit the Guards band came through the crowd & then the King & Queen stepped out onto their balcony. The band played Rule Britannia & then Home Sweet Home. The crowd cheered & sang & wept & the King waved his hat & Queen Mary ever incongruous waved a little flag. It was really a most splendid ovation.... By the Law Courts the King & Queen caught us up in their carriage. It was pouring by then but noone seemed to mind. There were about 2 mounted

policemen in front of the carriage & the rest of the escort
was composed of loyal subjects hanging on to the back.
Mary had exchanged her flag for an umbrella, but the King
was just the same & beaming. He must enjoy having downed
William as much as any of us.[65]

The long agony was over, and there was nothing left to hold on for. In
one last attempt at industry, and just a week after the armistice, Annie
began to pull together the essays that would form her final book, *From
Friend to Friend*, which appeared posthumously and which Pinkie
would steer through the press. On 14 December she accompanied
Hester to the polling station and voted for Lloyd George's candidate
in the general election which saw Asquith and his supporters lose their
seats. Annie had lived to see the 1918 Representation of the People
Act extend the franchise for the first time to women. It is difficult
to determine her views on the struggle for female suffrage. In earlier
years, it would seem that she had actively endorsed the cause, in 1889
subscribing to the Manchester National Society for Women's Suffrage,
but her commitment to democratic change was perhaps fragile.
Leonard Woolf tells of how he invited her to support the Adult Suffrage
movement in 1916, and of receiving a reply that was charmingly in
character. 'O my dear Leonard What will you think of me. It seems
to me ten thousand pities to give equal votes to unequal men. I should
like to give 100 to one man and ¼ of a vote to another. I would give a
great many to you and to Virginia too and my love to her.'[66]

During her final weeks, Annie became weaker and more frail,
increasingly reliant upon Hester who in the end had found a role for
herself as her mother's carer. In earlier years, Hester's outward affections
had been directed elsewhere – towards Richmond principally, but also
to Charlotte Leigh Smith, and, more recently, to Eleanor Birrell during
her final illness. Now that her own mother needed her, her love was
unstinting. Pinkie was astute enough to perceive the importance of
these last weeks for Hester's peace of mind, and after Annie's death
wrote admiringly. 'To have been all you have been to her through these
months of her entire dependence on you is happiness beyond words for
you I know and you will go on living for her.'[67]

Annie wrote her final diary entry on the last day of this momentous
year, when Billy and his family, recuperating from influenza, had
come over to Freshwater. It was their last time together. 'Happy
happy thanks to God for the happiness of seeing them all here &
recovered.' On New Year's Day she wrote to Virginia, delighted at
the news of the birth of Vanessa's daughter, Angelica, 'the beautiful

little baby with grey eyes', and past and present somehow seemed to jumble up happily.

> I remember Richmond saying when Nessa was a little girl what lovely grey eyes she had. It makes me happy to see Hesters eyes shine up, with all the joy of having [the] dear 4 here & Billy who is looking better & Meg too after their ordeal of Flu upon Flu.
>
> Accept this Nickleby letter, – I cant be consecutive in my words but I <u>am</u> in my heart when I think of the past which has been so good to me & is so dear past & present in one.

In a further letter to Virginia a week later, she calmly considered whether any semblance of consciousness would survive in whatever lay ahead. 'You dear creatures how you all come & go in ones thoughts how I wonder if I shall carry them on with me.'[68] With Annie already in a weakened state during the autumn, there had been some risk to her own health in Billy's family coming to Freshwater over the New Year. She would have been susceptible to any new flu infection, and although her death certificate records 'mitral incompetence [for] 5 years' as the cause, during February a new wave of the previous deadly strain took hold again across Britain. In the week before she died, the *Times* reported that 'the influenza position is again very bad.... From all parts of the country comes news of the disease – and of the deadly pneumonia which follows it.' And yet there was no sudden crisis or collapse, but rather a gradual decline and a resigned acceptance that at last her time was near. She would not have fought it. We do not know when she took to her bed, but she was already very weak when she wrote what was probably her last message. On 24 February she sent a picture postcard of Alum Bay and the Needles to her granddaughter, a brief note of thanks for an embroidered dressing gown. Characteristically, the note of optimism was for the recipient's benefit – 'I think the <u>embroidery</u> will cure me' – for Annie herself was patiently waiting.[69]

She died two days later, in Hester's arms. Hester sent telegrams to the family, and Billy and Meg made arrangements to join her at Freshwater. She wrote at length to Margie Ritchie and to Pinkie, wanting to assign an almost visionary intensity to Annie's final moments.

> The last thing she ever did was to send you those flowers – & she pulled the violets herself out of the vase.
>
> She is looking so wonderfully happy & radiant, that when I feel I cant bear not having her, I go and give her a kiss and feel quite comforted.

<u>Your</u> flowers came by the second post & I unpacked them
for her, and we were quite peaceful together when at ¼ to 4 in
the afternoon, the change came, and she said to me with the
sweetest smile 'How dark it is getting', then I supported her
in my arms, she was quite conscious, and I said my darling
my darling & she smiled & looked at me so tenderly – One
felt God was calling her to come to him very quick, she kept
looking upwards, or else at me, & though she couldn't speak,
I spoke and told her how I was so thankful she had been my
mama, and how blessed that she & I were with each other at
that moment. How we all loved her.

I did not know when she actually passed, it was so gentle
& beautiful and now she is looking radiant & Billy & I think
she must have looked like that when she used to take you all
for outings. Bless her, & she said to me 'You don't know how
one doesn't mind going when the moment comes' 'Before it
comes one can't imagine what it is like.'

And she said 'Remember I can't explain it, everything is
God, even this horrible mucous, from the bronchitis.'

She loved your letter telling her what George Booth said
about Billy. One can only say God bless her & everything
she has given to us all. Billy has settled it, she said how she
wanted to be buried with Papa, & to be cremated just like
him, & all this Billy will have done. And her funeral will be
just like Papa's. Billy will let you know the day. He & Meg
came by the 5 a.m. train this morning. I think of you darling
so much, & as you aren't here, say things to her from you &
your flowers are by her side.[70]

None felt the loss more than Pinkie, who had taken on something
of Minny's sisterly role and been told things that Annie would have
spoken of to nobody else. Through Richmond's favourite sister, and
the love of music which they had shared, Annie had continued to feel
close to him. Profoundly grieved, Pinkie now wrote words of courage
for Hester, deeply thankful for her account of Annie's departure.

I have no words to say what your letter is to me.

I can only bless & bless you for writing it and giving me
this most wonderfully beautiful vision of what surely is a
sunrise for her – She has been the sunshine of all our lives
and this radiance is like her whole life and can reach us all
through you. It was just right you and she should have been
like that absolutely together at the end.

And now dear Bill can feel through you as if he had been there to have the blessing she was giving him all his life. This is what she wrote to me after Gussie died 'Let us realize our own pang of mortality and realize the Blessing of God beyond.' No-one had more lovely apprehensions and revelations of it all at times and at the end she left this divine message of what she had found.

I write this with the violets she touched keeping still the sweetest freshness before me and what touches one infinitely is that you thought of me and how I should have given much to be with her at this last – you comfort me entirely as it could not be. I am glad that her wish can be arranged for by dear Bill about Hampstead. She constantly spoke about that to me as an easing thought. Hallam has sent me a few lines with the true words 'Her wonderful life of triumphant loving kindness'.[71]

Annie lay for a few days longer in the quiet Freshwater cottage. She had died on the Wednesday, and on Sunday evening there was a simple ceremony as finally she was taken from the much-loved Porch. A group of Freshwater men proudly transferred her coffin to the parish church of St Agnes where it would rest overnight. It was a clear night, and the stars shone brilliantly.

I have never seen them more beautiful than that last Sunday, Jupiter, Orion, the Plieades [sic], & all the others, & as Mama says to you 'the sky all dizzy with stars & unimaginable distance' & the men carried her dear coffin, (the men asked to be allowed to carry her) & we followed & there was nothing but the stars & the darkness & the deep silence of night, and the tramp tramp tramp of the men. The Dimbola Ilex seemed to sweep down a benediction upon us as we passed. At the little church all the people were drawn up & saluted her, & inside her favourite little church, it was all so sweet & loving.

Hallam Tennyson, in recent months a constant visitor during Annie's illness, grieved for the mercurial personality who had been a presence from his earliest childhood, and whom his father had loved. He asked that on her coffin should be placed Tennyson's own cream-coloured funeral pall, 'emblazoned with roses, a rose for each year of his life, & his initials A.T. & it was dear to think they were mama's too',[72] signalling not just his respect but his father's also. Pinkie told Hester how Hallam 'was happy to have been able to show his life-long love and honouring and also his great father's love for her. "Annie Thackeray can command the world" I remember hearing him say in the early days.'[73] It would be Hallam, too, who devised the memorial tablet in the Freshwater church where Annie had been a regular worshipper, its wording combining affection with a more formal admiration.

> Her writing reveals the inheritance of Genius,
> Her life the inspiration of loving kindness.

After resting overnight in the dark silence of the church, surrounded by family flowers, on Monday morning Annie crossed the Solent one last time. There had been so many crossings in the years since that sad occasion when she and Minny had taken refuge with Mrs Cameron after Thackeray's death, Tennyson coming down from Farringford to comfort them. It was a journey crowded with memories. Hallam's discreet thoughtfulness ensured that her return was unfussy and dignified, and Hester was alert to the kindness which made 'what might have been so dreary & terrible, so bright & beautiful'. He supplied the same horse-drawn wagon that had pulled his father's coffin from Aldworth, so that Annie's body might be taken to the Yarmouth boat. Finding the flags at half-mast, Hester at first assumed that Hallam had arranged even this, but he assured her that it was Yarmouth's own doing, a response to the news of the departure of this much-loved Freshwater resident who had always had a word for everyone. The ship's flag, too, was lowered, and once it had arrived in Lymington the coffin was transferred to the London train, in a compartment set out like a chapel. Hester placed a few last tokens from Freshwater with her mother's body, fresh snowdrops from Farringford and the laurel wreath given by Lionel Tennyson's son and his wife, Alfred and Cisley. Where Hester might have been exhausted and overwrought, this inspiring, almost triumphant last journey buoyed her. Her Thackeray inheritance had taught her that the passing of one who had lived well and honestly was not something to be mourned. 'And there was only beauty & sweetness all the way', she wrote to Pinkie, describing the simple ceremonies of that final return, but the words capture the whole of Annie's life journey.

The next day, 4 March, Annie was cremated at Golders Green and her ashes interred at Hampstead, alongside Richmond's. It was raining as family and friends stood together in the churchyard, led by Billy, Hester and Meg. Margie noted that 'it was all beautiful & like her – & what she would have liked – The rain did not matter in the least if only you all kept well. Your mother's dying has seemed throughout just like her living. She was able to pour out happiness & love up to the last moment – & yesterday we were all borne along on the great stream of her overpowering love & goodness.'[74] The elderly Mary Booth also ignored the rain. 'It was sad that the day was so gloomy, unlike her sweet, happy spirit, and yet I felt it mattered little. The love felt for her was shining in so many faces. There was no one who did not care; & that is as she would have had it.'[75]

Hester kept many of the letters of condolence, and two themes dominate. Old friends, as well as those who had come to know her only more recently, dwelt on an exceptional capacity for love, bestowed generously and freely. And there was frequent mention of her age, or rather how her outlook and spirit had remained youthful to the last. Lady Constance Battersea, a Rothschild by birth, declared that 'She was so young in her affections, so brilliant in mind that years did not seem to count with her. I never thought of her age, but only of her loving warm nature, her beautiful imagination, her wonderfully kind heart. And now she is gone! but we are the poorer.'[76]

All had felt the special grace of her friendship. Many had valued her sustained support at times of bereavement or illness, and a proliferation of nephews and nieces and their own children had all enjoyed her active interest in both the trivial and the serious issues of their lives. In the midst of her own busy life, the concerns of others had come first. She was one of those rare people who had the capacity to make someone feel more alive in her presence, so that, as Gerald Ritchie observed, 'everything seemed better, purer, holier'.[77] Leslie Stephen had understood this, having described Annie as 'the most sympathetic person I ever knew … Everybody who knew her loved her. Her extreme openness, her quick sympathies and her bright perceptions made her one of the most delightful of persons in all social intercourse.'[78] It was a theme now picked up by Leslie's friend, James Bryce, who had met Annie in the early days of Leslie's marriage to Minny. 'Never have I known any one with quite the same charm, inexhaustible kindliness and sympathy with a freshness and genuineness which made everybody feel wiser & better than themselves when they were in her company.'[79] And Herbert Paul remarked on this same generosity of spirit. 'The brilliance of her wonderful talk was always so fresh, and wise, and spontaneous, that one felt as if it were meant especially for oneself.'[80]

Adeline Thackeray perceived that something irreplaceable had been taken from them.

> She sometimes spoke to me of the great company in heaven,
> & all our large family & some of them in Heaven & some on

earth, & one always felt she brought something from Heaven
& belonged to it.... You both know how I loved her, no one
in the world has ever been the same as she has been to me,
no one can ever fill up the blank for me.[81]

But few knew better the character of the woman than Margie Ritchie,
who with her sister had been brought up by Annie and Minny when
their mother Amy had died in India, and in more recent years had lived
nearby in Chelsea.

> I find that all the <u>happy</u> things come back to one – all the
> countless countless delightful doings she has poured into
> one's life – all the delicious things she always said and wrote
> – Whoever had the smallest letter or meeting without her
> saying or writing something that no one else in all the world
> could have done. How intensely happy it has been for me to
> have been permitted this long spell of living constantly near
> her since we left India – I like to think that I did know how
> wonderful it was.
>
> Gerald has been remembering the first time he saw her.
> I daresay you have often heard of it. The three boys arrived
> from Paris to stay at Palace Green, & Aunt Annie always
> described how she went in & found Willy brushing Gerald
> & Richmond's hair.
>
> One of the things she said when I was at Freshwater was
> 'I am not going to let myself be unhappy when I think of my
> Hester after I have gone. I feel so sure it will all be right for
> her.' She knew well how you could carry her love with you
> wherever you go – just as she lived always with her Father
> and Minny even through so many years – so she will live
> with you always.[82]

Margie realised that Annie had been tranquil, even content, in the
prospect of her own death. 'That is just what one knows – She is so
happy. She who gave & gave of happiness and love all her long life – I
think of those marvellous days of hers when she used to go about from
one house to another taking always help & love. Or when she sat at
her writing table & the pile of letters meant this one and that cared for
and difficulties smoothed out or blessings sent. Has one ever imagined
genius turned into love as she contrived it.'[83] Eleanor Clough, Gussie's
daughter, was recovering from bronchitis and unable to attend the
funeral, but in recalling many past incidents was especially grateful
for Annie's support during her mother's last illness. 'I remember too

Mamma saying to me at the time that Aunt Anny was the only person now who could remember her as a little child. I remember also her saying one day "Anny is so wonderful. It is so wonderful the way she carries her Dead about with her, <u>alive</u>, in her life".'[84]

Louisa Lee Schuyler read the news in the New York papers, words which 'sent a cold chill to my heart.... I look upon my friendship with your mother as one of the great blessings in my life.... On the 9th of last June she was 81; and I on the 26th of last October. We used to pretend that from June to October she was one year older; from October to June we were "twins".'[85] And from Washington, a long letter arrived from Emerson's daughter, Edith Emerson Forbes, an occasional correspondent since first meeting Annie in 1888 and who over the years had tried, in vain, to get her to visit America. Annie's most recent letter to Edith had been written after Christmas. 'She ended her dear letter with these words "I am doing a delightful warm rest-cure in bed during the cold weather! I hope to appear with Spring." It sounded so comfortable and hopeful – and just a week ago I read that it was over.' After praising the early novels and the interest they provoked in America, she finds a way of offering comfort to Hester in the knowledge that Annie was reconciled to death.

> I have gone on writing these pages about my love for and interest in your Mother because I feel every word about her and the love her lovers have for her must interest her daughter, but I hardly dare to draw nearer, and offer my sympathy to you and your brother, whose loss is so tender and so great. You two were the light of her eyes and heart. She has shown it in every letter and every talk we have had. In this last letter she says 'At 81 one takes short views and my dear Hester looks anxious if she sees me fail. I have to accept my destiny & feel that for her too will come help and the friendship of the past.'[86]

Virginia Woolf offered a measured assessment of Annie's public career in her *Times Literary Supplement* obituary notice. It appeared anonymously, and Blanche Warre Cornish found much to admire in it. 'A young forcible writer, I guess, the writer to be, and all whom I have seen who had read it find truth in every line.'[87] Without over-praising her writing, Virginia admired Annie's 'highly cultivated instinct', so that although none of the novels ranks as a masterpiece, 'each one is indisputably the work of a writer of genius'. The originality of the writing is its allusiveness, its tendency towards atmosphere and suggestion, of delicate brushstrokes and of 'opal tinted lights', whilst underneath lay a sharpness and humour which stopped any drift into mere whimsy and sentimentality. It was the same quality which *The Graphic* had isolated half a century before, admiring for example the 'picturesqueness' of *Old Kensington*, where 'atmosphere, flowers, and sunlight are with her integral parts of her pictures, and are brought into some strange, subtle harmony with the emotion that is being expressed'.[88] Virginia avoided obvious comparisons between father and daughter, knowing that Annie would not have wanted it, being content, as she always was, to sit in his shadow. But in turning from the fiction to the biographical work, she assigned to her 'aunt' a status which still has resonance.

> She will be the un-acknowledged source of much that remains in men's minds about the Victorian age. She will be the transparent medium through which we behold the dead. We shall see them lit up by her tender and radiant glow. Above all and for ever she will be the companion and interpreter of her father, whose spirit she has made to walk among us not only because she wrote of him but because even more wonderfully she lived in him.

The years pass, and those who understood Annie's sense of family and duty, and how it framed her life, disappear from view. As one of the last to perceive it, it is entirely appropriate that Virginia should have been the author of such an astutely balanced judgment. The daughter of a literary man, and linked to Thackeray through her father's first marriage, she too would spend a crowded life-time working through the responsibilities of inheritance and memory.

# NOTES

## Prelude and Acknowledgements

1. VW to Vanessa Bell (6-1921) and to C.P Sanger (2-12-1919). Nigel Nicolson, ed, *The Letters of Virginia Woolf*, II.

## Chapter One:
## THIS SOMETHING COME INTO MY LIFE (1875-1877)

1. AI to ET, early 12-1875, *TRC.*
2. LS to CN, 8-8-1876, *HL (bMS Am 1088[6909]).*
3. AI to CR, before 13-12-1875, *E.*
4. AI to Mrs Baxter, ?12-1875, *Shankman.*
5. AI to RR, ?1-2-1876, *E.*
6. AI to JS, ?2/3-1876, *Y.*
7. *J.*
8. AI to RR, 4-1876, *E.*
9. AI to RR, summer 1876, *E.*
10. *Mausoleum*, 24-5.
11. *J*
12. AI to Mrs Field, 7-4-1886, *P.*
13. AI to RR, 14-2-1875, *E.*
14. Obituary notice, *Eton College Chronicle*, 17-10-1912.
15. *Cornhill*, November 1919.
16. Howard Sturgis to RR, 20-10-1909, *E.*
17. Howard Sturgis to HR, 14-7-1919, *E.*
18. AI to RR, 1876, *E.*
19. MO to Frank Wilson, 5-5-1876, *Autobiography.*
20. AI to RR, ?April-1876, *E.*
21. RR to AI, 5-1876, *E.*
22. AI to ER, 23-5-1876, *E.*
23. AI to MO, 29-5-1876, *E.* There is no reason to suppose that Mrs Oliphant was drawing on recent experiences. In *Carita*, James Beresford's wife takes her own life to avoid a protracted illness, leaving a daughter; his subsequent innocent friendship with his neighbour causes gossip. Annie's intimacy with Richmond, and its perception by friend and family, may be what was in her mind, as well as the widowed Leslie left with Laura.

24.  AI to RR, 4-6-1876, *E.*
25.  RR to AI, ?summer 1876, *E.*
26.  AI to GS, 7-1876, *JMA.*
27.  AI to RR, 7-1876, *E.*
28.  AI to BC, 7-1876, *E.*
29.  *J,* 28-7-1876.
30.  *J.* 1-1-1877.
31.  LS to AI, 29-1-1877, *E.*
32.  Leslie's recollections of the engagement from *Mausoleum,* 45-6.
33.  *J,* 3-2-1877.
34.  AI to MO, 9-4-1877, *E.*
35.  AI to RR, 3-1877, *E.*
36.  AI to ER, late 3-1877, *E.*
37.  AI to RR, ?18-4-1877, *E.*
38.  LS to JJ, 5-4-1877, *Mausoleum,* xxv.
39.  AI to RR, 1-5-1877, *E.*
40.  LS to AI, 5-5-1877, *Bicknell.*
41.  LS to AI, 9-5-1877, *E.*
42.  AI to RR, 10-5-1877, *E.*
43.  LS to AI, 11-5-1877, *E.*
44.  *J,* 11-5-1877.
45.  Mrs Ritchie to A, 12-5-1877, *E.*
46.  LS to CN, 20-5-1877, *HL (bMS Am1088[6915]).*
47.  AI to ER, 5-1877, *E.*
48.  AI to Nina Lehmann, 3-6-1877, *P.*
49.  AI to Joseph Milsand, 17-5-1877, *BU.* Transcription kindly supplied by Michael Meredith.
50.  *Trewman's Exeter Flying Post or Plymouth and Cornish Advertiser,* 30-5-1877.
51.  AI to CR, 5-1877, *E.*
52.  RR to CR, 18-5-1877, *E.*
53.  RR to AI, ?May-June 1877, *E.*
54.  MG to AI, 25-5-1877, *E.*
55.  AI to W.W.F. Synge, 5-1877, *Shankman.*
56.  FS to AI, 16-5-1877, *E.*
57.  AI to MO, 21-5-1877, *E.*
58.  AI to BC, 7-1877, *E.*
59.  AI to RR, 15-4-1877, *E.*
60.  LS to CN, 20-5-1877, *HL (bMS Am1088[6915]).*
61.  CN to AI, 20-7-1877, *E.*
62.  LS to AI, 25-7-1877, *E.*
63.  *J.*
64.  Henry Bradshaw to GS, 11-8-1877 (copy by GS), *E.*
65.  ER to ET, 8-1877, *Daughter,* 151-2.
66.  AI to IT, 28/9-8-1877; *E.*
67.  George Eliot to AI, 19-8-1877, *Daughter,* 153.
68.  AI to AF, about 21-8-1877, *E.*

## Chapter Two:

## SHADOWS OF THE PAST (1877-1881)

1.  *J*, 2-10-1877.
2.  LS to AI, 29-10-1877, *E*.
3.  AI to MO, about 10-12-1877, *E*.
4.  RR to AI, 23-1-1878, *E*.
5.  AI to ER, 1-1878, *E*.
6.  AI to ER, ?30-1-1878, *E*.
7.  ER to AI, ?3-1-1878, *E*.
8.  AI to HT, 27-3-1878, *E*.
9.  AI to Lord Houghton, 4-4-1878, *TCC*.
10. AI to MO, 16-4-1878, *E*.
11. Confusion has arisen concerning *From an Island*. Gérin, Shankman and Garnett all regard the piece as one written during Annie's engagement, but it dates from nine years earlier, and was first published in the *Cornhill*.
12. *J*.
13. KD to AI, 5-6-1878, *E*.
14. ER to AI, about 10-6-1878, *E*.
15. George Crowe to AI, 14-7-1878, *E*.
16. *J*.
17. JC to AI, 6-1878, in Victoria Olsen, *Julia Margaret Cameron and Victorian Photography*, London: Aurum Press, 2003, 258.
18. AI to ER, late summer 1878, *E*.
19. *J*, 1-1879.
20. Matthew Arnold to AI, 26-3-1879, *E*. His *Mixed Essays*, London: Smith, Elder, 1879, included his 1877 essay 'On Memories of Nohant and George Sand's Qualities as a Writer'.
21. *J*, 4-1-1879.
22. HJ to Grace Norton, 4-1-1879, in Leon Edel (ed), *Henry James Letters, vol 2. 1875-83*, London: Macmillan, 1975.
23. HJ to Alice James, 17-3-1878, Edel, II, 157.
24. HJ to his father, 25-3-1878, Edel, II, 160.
25. HJ to Howard Sturgis, 27-6-1906, *HL (bMS Am1094[1243])*.
26. AI to ER, ?spring 1879, *E*.
27. AI to LS, 5-1875, *E*.
28. LS to AI, 16-1-1878, *Bicknell*.
29. 'Madame de Sévigné', *Encylopædia Britannica*, University of Chicago, 1947 edition.
30. *J*, 29-5-1879.
31. *J*, 11-7-1879.
32. AI to RR, 14-7-1879, *E*. She means 'The Lifted Veil', 1859. 'Brother Jacob' was written in 1860.
33. AI to MO, 30-7-1879, *E*. Frederick Greenwood edited *Pall Mall Gazette*, for which Richmond undertook some reviewing.
34. AI to FK, 10-8-1879, *E*.
35. FK to AI, 15-8-1879, *E*.

36. AI to HJ, ?12-8-1879, *Shankman*.
37. Victoria Glendinning, *Trollope*, London: Pimlico, 1993, 471-4.
38. Glendinning, 472.
39. *Pall Mall Gazette* review, 18-8-1879, cited in John Hall (ed.) *The Letters of Anthony Trollope*, Stanford: Stanford University Press, 1983, II, 855.
40. Glendinning, 473.
41. *J*, 11-2-1882. Hall is incorrect. Annie did date this note in her journal.
42. AI to JF, 5-1871, *HU (FI 4287)*.
43. EF to Frederick Pollock, about 1-3-1882, Alfred McKinley Terhune and Annabelle Burdick Terhune, *The Letters of Edward FitzGerald*, Princeton University Press, 1980, IV, 491. 'I think her Irish blood comes out in her – may it not prove too much of the Mother's.' 16-3-1879.
44. AI to HR, 27-11-1879, *E*.
45. MO to AI, 12-2-1880, *NLS*.
46. *J*, 13-14-3-1880.
47. RR to BC, 18-3-1880, *E*. *J* (written much later) records the time as 2 a.m. Richmond's time is presumably accurate.
48. AI to MO, 10-4-1880, *E*.
49. AI to RR, 30-5-1882, *E*.
50. AI to ER, 5-1880, *E*.
51. AI to ET, 6-6-1880, *E*.
52. *J*.
53. AI to AT, 27-11-1880, *E*. The collection was *Ballads and Other Poems*.
54. RR to AI, 5-1880; *E*.
55. *J*.
56. John Ruskin to AI, 24-7-1880, *E*.
57. RR to AI, 31-7-1880, *E*.
58. ER to A, 2-4-1881, *E*.
59. *J*, 18-1-1883.
60. AI to RR, 19-1-1883, *E*.
61. AI to ER, 28-10-1880, *E*.
62. AI to John Cross, late 12-1880, *Y*.
63. AI to ER, 1-1881, *E*.
64. AI to FK, ?7-1886, *E*.
65. AI to ER, 2-1881, *E*.
66. AI to ER, 8-3-1881; ER to AI, 2-4-1881, *E*.
67. *Mausoleum*, 44.
68. *J*, 23-7-1881.
69. AI to RR, 5-1882, *E*.
70. *J*, 25-12-1882.
71. AI to Mrs Field, 5-3-1887, *P*.
72. ER to AI, 14-4-1881, *E*.
73. AI to ER, ?early 1881, *E*.
74. MO to William Blackwood, 1-3-1881, *Autobiography*.
75. *Times*, 9-6-1881.
76. AI to ER, ?5-81, *E*. After the initial print run – probably of about a thousand in March 1881 – *Miss Williamson's Divagations* was not reprinted until December 1882.

77. AI to RR, 30-5-1882, *E. The Spectator* reviewer had been enthusiastic, believing that the subject was one for which Annie was 'eminently fitted, not only by genius, knowledge, and taste, but by that swift, penetrative sympathy which was, above all things, needful for such a task' (10-9-1881).
78. ER to HT, 19-12-1881, *TRC.*
79. AI to AF, 12-1881, *E.*

## Chapter Three:
# AFTER ALL A LIFETIME (1882-1885)

1. AI to Lady Houghton, 6-9-1865, *TCC.*
2. Edmund Gosse, *The Life of Algernon Charles Swinburne*, London: Macmillan, 1917, 95-6.
3. AI to JF, 16-7-1885, *E.*
4. AI to AF, 1905, *E.*
5. AI to BC, ?1-1882, *E.*
6. AI to AS, 19-3-1891, *B.*
7. *J*, 18-7-1885.
8. Clara Watts-Dunton, *The Home Life of Swinburne*, London: A.M. Philpot, 1922, 266.
9. AI to Mrs Lucy Robinson, 12-1-1882, *E.*
10. *J*, 18-1-1882.
11. AI to HT, 14-3-1882, *TRC.*
12. HT to AI, 30-10-1892, *E.*
13. AI to Henrietta Litchfield and Elizabeth Darwin, 24-4-1882, copy, *BNB.*
14. WMT to Magdalene Brookfield, 26-2-1850, *Ray.*
15. *J*, 26-6-1883.
16. AI to AW, 22-7-1883, *TCC.*
17. AI to GS, 29-6-1883, *JMA.*
18. AI to AW, 4-12-1883, *TCC.*
19. AI to AW, 6-12-1883, *TCC.*
20. William Aldis Wright, *Letters and Literary Remains of Edward FitzGerald*, London: Macmillan, 1889, I, xii.
21. HR's note on a transcription of a letter by FK, *BNB.*
22. AI to GS, 2-9-1883, *JMA.*
23. *J.* He died on 11 December.
24. AI to JF, 1-1-1884, *P.*
25. AI to HT, ?late 11-1883, *E.*
26. The six volumes include Annie's annotation: 'Anne Ritchie bought at the sale of M^r Fitzgeralds books. The pencil markings are all his & the notes'. *JM.*
27. This copy with EF's annotations survives. *JM.*
28. *J*, 8-8-1883.
29. From *Tiresias.*
30. George du Maurier to AI, 6-5-1884, *E.*
31. *Punch*, 24-5-1884.
32. Note of December 1846 in presentation copy of *Trilby, JM.*
33. *J*, 12-1881.

34.   Gertrude Bell would later achieve fame in several fields, as writer, foreign
      political diplomat and archaeologist. A daughter of the Ritchies' friend, the
      industrialist Hugh Bell, she was unrelated to Clive Bell, later husband of
      Leslie and Julia's elder daughter, Vanessa.
35.   GB to FB, 20-10-1884, in Elsa Richmond, *The Earlier Letters of Gertrude
      Bell*, London: Ernest Benn Ltd, 1937, 27.
36.   AI to FK, c.11-5-1885, *E.*
37.   AI to JO, 15-7-1885, *E.*
38.   *J*, 1-1-1885.
39.   AI to RR, 1-1885, *E.*
40.   LS to AI, ?1-1885, *E.*
41.   LS to AI, 29-5-1885, *Bicknell.*
42.   AI to SA, 13-9-1885, *Shankman.*
43.   SA to AI, 19-9-1885, *E.*
44    SA to AI, 29-11-1885, *E.*
45    LS to AI, 29-7-1885, *E. Bicknell* has significant omissions.
46    AI to RR, 9-1885, *E.*
47    *J.*

# Chapter Four:
## THE LIGHTS OF THE HILLS (1886-1889)

1.    GS to AI, 17-3-1864, *JM.*
2.    AI to Mrs Baxter, 24-10-1864, *Ray.*
3.    AI to CJ, 13-7-1885, *E.* Lucy Baxter (ed), *Thackeray's Letters to an American
      Family*, New York: Centaury Co., 1904.
4.    LS to GS, 2-9-1886, *Bicknell.*
5.    RR to AI, 25-9-1885, *E.*
6.    AI to CJ, 10-11-1885, *E.*
7.    AI to CJ, ?summer 1887, *E.*
8.    AI to FK, 9-1887, *E.*
9.    Emma Taylor Lamborn to AI, 2-4-1887, *E.*
10.   *Pall Mall Gazette*, 20-9-1887.
11.   AB to AI, 1887, *E.*
12.   Lytton Strachey to Dora Carrington, 28-5-1917. Paul Levy (ed), *The Letters
      of Lytton Strachey*, London: Viking, 2005, 354.
13.   AI to Savile Clarke, 1-10-1890, *Shankman.*
14.   AI to FK, 6-1886, *E.*
15.   RR to AI, 5-1882, *E.*
16.   *J*, 28-12-1882.
17.   AI to JO, 1-1-1884, *P.*
18.   Ann Thwaite, *Emily Tennyson: The Poet's Wife*, London: Faber & Faber,
      1996, 556.
19.   ER to HT, 25-2-1886, *E.*
20.   Thwaite, 564.
21.   MT to ER, 15-4-1886, transcription by ER within her letter to HT, 20-5-1886,
      *TRC.*

22.  ER to HT, 26-4-1886, *TRC, 4187.*
23.  AI to Mrs Field, 7-4-1886, *P.*
24.  AI to the Fields, 12-7-1886, *P.*
25.  AI to RR, 23-10-1890, *E.*
26.  RR to AI, ?about 8-1895, *E.*
27.  AI to MC, ?1883, *E.*
28.  AI to FK, 6-1886, *E.*
29.  RR to AI, 6-1886, *E.*
30.  RR to AI, 22-6-1886, *E.*
31.  AI to ER, ?7-1886, *E.*
32.  RR to AI, 7-1886, *E.*
33.  Annie knew Marie Souvestre through Jane Strachey, who was intimate with this 'brilliant and irreligious woman', as Michael Holroyd describes her. Both of the younger Strachey daughters attended Allenswood, as would the young Eleanor Roosevelt. Holroyd, *Lytton Strachey. A Biography*, London: Penguin: 1979, 57.
34.  Jane Simon to RR, 24-8-1886, *E.*
35.  RR to AI, 25-8-1886, *E.*
36.  RR to AI, 7-1886, *E.*
37.  Peter Gunn, *Vernon Lee*, London: OUP, 1964, 85.
38.  ER to AI, ?10-1903, *E.*
39.  AI to HR, 27-8-1886, *E.*
40.  AI to RR, 3-9-1886, *E.*
41.  AI to RR, 9-1886, *E.*
42.  RR to AI, 15-9-1886, *E.*
43.  Winifred Gérin, *Anne Thackeray Ritchie*, Oxford: OUP, 1981, 214-15.
44.  RR to AI, ?late 1886, *E.*
45..  RR to AF, 5-1891, *E.*
46.  ER to AI, 4-1889, *E.*
47.  AI to GW, 8-11-1886, *NPG.*
48.  GW to AI, 10-11-1886, *E.*
49.  AI to RR, 12-11-1886, *E.*
50.  AI to AT, 15-12-1886, *TRC*
51.  Joan Severn to AI, ?1887 or 1888, *E.*
52.  AI to Octavia Hill, ?early 1887, *P.*
53.  MW to AI, ?1887, *E.*
54.  AI to FK, 3-1887, *E.*
55.  AI to ?, 10-1-?1887, *E.*
56.  AI to MC, 30-5-1887, *E.*
57.  *J*, 11-12-1887.
58.  AI to FK, 9-1887, *E.*
59.  AI to ER, ?10-1887, *E.*
60.  AI to AW, 16-12-1887, *TCC.*
61.  AI to RR, 3-1888, *E.*
62.  *J*, 9-6-1888.
63.  AI to ER, 5-1888, *E.*
64.  *J*, 1886.
65.  AI to ER, 13-11-1888, *E.*

66. AI to ER, 11-1888, *E.*
67. AI to MO, 28-11-1888, *E.*
68. *J*, 14-1-1889.
69. AI to FK, 4-1889, *E.*
70. AI to AW, 21-4-1889, *TCC.*
71. AI to FK, 23/24-6-1889, *E.*
72. AI to ER, 6-1889, *E.*
73. AI to AW, 4-7-1889, *TCC.*
74. AI to ER, 7-1889, *E.*
75. Annie Kerrich to AI, 7-1889, *E.*
76. SA to AI, 20-7-1889, *E.* For more on this episode, see Stefan Hawlin and Michael Meredith (eds) *The Poetical Works of Robert Browning*, vol 15, 'Parleyings and Asolando', Oxford: Clarendon Press, 2009, 506-9.
77. AI to ER, 30-5-1891, *E.*
78. SA to AI, 26-8-1891, *E.* When Annie's own essay on the Brownings was published, her niggling concern was reserved to a footnote. 'An ambiguous extract in Mrs. Orr's *Life of Browning* has only recalled my own most vivid impression of the happy relations between my father and Mrs. Browning'.
79. AI to ER, 9-1889, *E.*
80. RR to HR and WR, 18-9-1889, *E.*
81. AI to HR and WR, 25-9-1889, *E.* The allusion is to Trollope's novel, *The Struggles of Brown, Jones and Robinson.*
82. AI to RR, 5-11-1889, *E.*
83. AI to ER, ?21-5-1888, *E.*
84. *J*, 2-12-1889.
85. 'The Boyhood of Thackeray', *St Nicholas*, 17, December 1889.
86. ET to AI, 14-12-1889, *E.*
87. MA to AI, 18-12-1889, *E.*
88. AI to SA, 16-12-1889, *E.*
89. SA to AI, 15-1-1890, *E.*
90. AI to SA, 16-1-1890, *E.*
91. AI to FK, 14-12-1889, *E.*

# Chapter Five:
## MY LITTLE DREAM OF AN EDITION (1890-1893)

1. AI to ET, 3-3-1890, *E.*
2. GW to AI, 1-3-1890, *E.*
3. AI to ER, 17-11-1881, *E.*
4. ER to AI, 2-4-1881, *E.*
5. AI to JO, 15-7-1885, *E.*
6. *J*, 4-1890.
7. AI to RR, 4-1890, *E.*
8. AI to GS, about 19-6-1890, *JMA.*
9. AI to IT, 6-1890, *E.*
10. Frederick Locker-Lampson to AI, 2-7-1890, *E.*
11. AB to AI, 25-7-1890, *E.*

12. AI to GS, 8-1890, *JMA.*
13. AI to ER, 9-1890, *E.*
14. AI to AF, 28-11-1890, *E.*
15. AI to GS, 4-12-1890, *JMA.*
16. AI to ER, 12-1890, *E.*
17. *J*, 26-12-1890.
18. CS to AI, 6-2-1892, *E.*
19. AI to RR, ?3-1891, *E.*
20. AI to CJ, 25-2-1891, *E.*
21. Herman Merivale and Frank T. Marzials, *Life of W.M. Thackeray*, London: Walter Scott, 1891.
22. AI to RR, 2-3-1891, *E.*
23. 'Thackeray and His Biographers', *The Illustrated London News*, 20 June 1891.
24. RR to AI, 1-3-1891, *E.*
25. AI to ER, ?4-1891, *E.*
26. AI to Jane Freshfield, 5-1891, *E.*
27. AI to AF, 5-1891, *E.*
28. AI to ER, 3-4-1891, *E.*
29. AI to SA, 18-8-1891, *E.*
30. MG to AI, 2-7-1891, *E.* The drawings were by Hugh Thomson, one of Macmillan's regular illustrators. Ironically, his style is not unlike Thackeray's own.
31. AI to IT, 8-11-1891, *E.*
32. *J.*
33. AI to RR, 6-9-1891, *E.*
34. RR to AI, 1891, *E.* Rhoda's novel, *Nancy*, was published in 1891. Mrs Ward's *David Grieve* had been in progress since 1889, and rumours of the sexual frankness of its French episodes had spread.
35. AI to HT, 25-3-1892, *E.*
36. William H. Forbes to AI, 17-9-1891, *E.*
37. Frederick Macmillan to AI, 2-8-1893, *E.*
38. AI to ER, 14-4-1892, *E.*
39. AI to AF, 18-4-1892, *E.*
40. AI to ER, 5-1892, *E.*
41. AI to AT, 6-8-1892, *TRC.*
42. KD to AI, about 25-6-1892, *E.*
43. AI to RR, 5-6-1892, *E.*
44. AI to AT, 6-8-1892, *TRC.*
45. AI to Eleanor Birrell, ?17-7-1892, *LP.*
46. 'Thackeray and His Biographers'.
47. Andrew Lang, 'Thackeray and His Biographers', *Longman's Magazine*, April 1891, 673.
48. Review of *Thackerayana. Notes and Anecdotes*, in *The Nation*, 9 December 1875.
49. AI to GS, 17-7-1892, *JMA.*
50. RR to AI, 12-7-1892, *E.*
51. AI to AF, 19-7-1892, *E.*
52. *J*, 7-1892.

53. AI to RR, 3-8-1892, *E.*
54. AI to GS, 8-1892, *JMA.*
55. AI to RR, 8-1892, *E.*
56. RR to AI, 8-1892, *E.*
57. AI to RR, about 7-10-1892, *E.*
58. HT to AI, 30-10-1892, *E.*
59. AI to HT, 1-11-1892, *TRC.*
60. AI to ET, 26-11-1892, *TRC.*
61. AI to MW and GW, 25-12-1892, *NPG.*
62. GW to AI, 28-12-1892, *E.*
63. H.G. Woods to A, 15-2-1893, *E.*
64. AI to RR, ?2-1893, *E.*
65. Mowbray Morris to AI, 10-11-1892, *E.*
66. AI to ET, 17-1-1893, *TRC.*
67. Itemised account from the architect, J Ransome, 7-1894, *JM.*
68. A to RR, late 1892 or early 1893, *E.*
69. William Hunter to RR, 23-3-1893, *E.*
70. William Hunter to RR, 18-7-1893, *E.*
71. AI to GS, 11-1893, *JMA.*
72. AI to ER, ?4-1893, *E.* James's piece on Fanny Kemble, who had died on 15 January, appeared in *Temple Bar.*
73. Mowbray Morris to AI, 31-5-1893, *E.*
74. *Lord Tennyson and His Friends: A Collection of Photographs*, London: T. Fisher Unwin, 1893.
75. AI to RR, 3-9-1893, *E.*
76. AI to RR, 4-9-1893, *E.*

# Chapter Six:
# THAT HISTORY HAS LASTED ON (1894-1895)

1. AI to IT, 7-10-1892, *E.*
2. Related to me in October 2007 by Belinda Norman-Butler, to whom HR had recounted it.
3. IT to AI, 21-12-1887, *E.*
4. IT to AI, 20-3-1889, *E.*
5. AI to IT, 18-3-1891, *BNB.*
6. AI to RR, 12-7-1892, *E.*
7. Fladgates to RR, 16-6-1892, *JM.*
8. AI to RR, 26-7-1892, *E.*
9. AI to IT, 18-3-1891, *BNB.*
10. AI to MT, 19-1-1894, *E.*
11. AI to BC, 1-1894, *Letters.*
12. *J*; AI to Mrs Hart, 23-1-1894, typed transcription, *BNB*; to BC, 1-1894, *Letters.*
13. AI to MT, 19-1-1894, *E.*
14. AI to FB, 20-1-1894, *Letters.*
15. AI to Susan Scott, 11-4-1894, *E.*
16. LS to AI, 11-1-1894, *E.*

17. HJ to AI, 12-1-1894, *E.*
18. AI to unidentified Edgeworth relation, 14-5-1894, *E.*
19. AI to ER, 7-7-1914, *E.*
20. AI to WR, 2-3-1894, *E.*
21. J. M. Barrie to AI, 25-2-1894, *E.*
22. AI to HR, 28-2-1894, *E.*
23. AI to HR, 24-2-1894, *E.*
24. LS to AI, 13-3-1894, *E.*
25. AI to WR, 14-5-1894, *E.*
26. AI to MT, 22-2-1894, *E.*
27. AI to JST, 20-8-1894, *E.*
28. *J*, 11-1895.
29. AI to ER, 10-10-1894, *E.*
30. George Grove to AI, 19-12-1894, *E.*
31. *J*, 26-2-1895.
32. *J*, 2-3-1895.
33. AI to WR, 9-3-1895, *E*, quoting WMT to AC, 10-1833, *Ray.*
34. Unpublished recollections of Belinda Norman-Butler.
35. *J*, 2-4-1895.
36. AI to WR, 7-5-1895, *E.*
37. AF to AI, 9-5-1895, *E.*
38. AI to Douglas Freshfield, 11-5-1895, *E.* 'There is no happiness in this horrible world but the happiness we have <u>had</u> – the very present is ever in the jaws of fate.' HJ to LS, 6-5-1895, Edel, *Letters*, IV, 13.
39. AI to WR, 18-5-1895, *E.*
40. AI to ?, 13-4-1897, *P.*
41. Reginald Smith to AI, 7-6-1895, *E.*
42. AI to WR, 29-6-1895, *E.*
43. RR to AI, 24-6-1895, *E.*
44. Alexander Watt to AI, 15-8-1895, *E.*
45. CW to AI, 5-12-1895, *E.*
46. LS to AI, 28-7-1895, *E.*
47. LS to AI, 20-8-1895, *E.*
48. *J*, 18-11-1895.
49. *J*, 28-11-1895.

## Chapter Seven:
## THAT DIVIDED LIFE (1896-1899)

1. AI to ER, 4-1-1896, *E.*
2. CW to AI, 4-1-1896, *E.*
3. *J*, 29-2-1896.
4. AI to WR, 29-2-1896, *E.*
5. Anne Leigh Smith in 1887, quoted in Pam Hirsch, *Barbara Leigh Smith Bodichon*, London: Chatto & Windus, 1998, 316.
6. AI to WR, 2-1899, *E.*
7. *J*, 13-3-1896.

8.   *J*, 26-4-1896.
9.   AI to MW, 23-3-1896, *NPG*.
10.  *J*, 25-4-1896.
11.  *J*, 10-5-1896.
12.  AI to ER, ?1896, *E*.
13.  AI to HR, 22-5-1896, *E*.
14.  AI to John Pearson, 2-3-1896, *M*.
15.  AI to John Pearson or to his business partner C.E. Shepheard, 27-10-1891, 2-3-1896, about 17-5-1896, 30-5-1896 and 4-6-1896, *M*.
16.  'The First Number of the "The Cornhill"' appeared in the July *Cornhill*.
17.  Barrie to AI, 28-6-1896, *E*.
18.  *J*, 17/20-8-1896.
19.  RR to AI, 5-10-1896, *E*.
20.  AI to WR, 11-1896, *E*.
21.  AI to WR, 7-2-1897, *E*.
22.  Ibid.
23.  AI to ER, 24-2-1897, *E*.
24.  RR to AI, 6-3-1897, *E*.
25.  RR to AI, 1-3-1897, *E*.
26.  HM to AI, 9-1874, *E*.
27.  AI to RR, 14-3-1897, *E*.
28.  *AI to RR, 3-1897, E.*
29.  *J*, 1-4-1897.
30.  AI to RR, 2-4-1897, *E*.
31.  RR to AI, 2-3-1897, *E*.
32.  AI to ER, 8-6-1897, *E*.
33.  Harper Brothers to Smith, Elder, 2-9-1897, *JMA*.
34.  AI to WR, 26-5-1897, *E*.
35.  AI to WR, ?11-1897, *E*.
36.  LS to AI, 15-3-1897, *E*.
37.  AI to WR, 23-7-1897, *E*.
38.  *J*.
39.  LS to AI, 6-8-1897, *E*.
40.  A to AF, 8-1897, *E*.
41.  GS to AI, 12-8-1897, *E*.
42.  *J*, 14-7-1897.
43.  AI to WR, 9-1897, *E*.
44.  RR to AI, 1897, *E*.
45.  AI to WR, 3-12-1897, *E*.
46.  AI to WR, 7-10-1897, *E*.
47.  AI to HR, 13-10-1897, *E*.
48.  AI to WR, 16-10-1897, *E*.
49..  AI to WR, ?10-1897, *E*.
50.  AI to MT, 3-12-1897, *E*.
51.  See *Biographical*, IX, xlvii. 'I have called this chapter of Christmas Books the Gold Pen Chapter, because so much of the work was done by one favourite pen. It lasted for some six years, and produced besides the "thousands of funny women and droll men," most of the drawings for the later Christmas books.'

52. AI to WR, 3-12-1897, *E.*
53. AI to Annie Fields, ?4-1898, *HU.*
54. AI to AF, ?15-4-1898, *E.*
55. *Biographical*, III, xxxvi.
56. *Biographical*, VI, xxv-xxvi.
57. 'The Sentiment of Thackeray', *The Quarterly Review*, January 1900, 143.
58. Lord George Hamilton to AI, 19-5-1898, *E.*
59. AI to ER, 21-5-1898, *E.*
60. AI to ER, 29-5-1898, *E.*
61. AI to WR, 8-1898, *E.*
62. AI to ER, ?10-7-1898, *E.*
63. AI to WR, ?1-9-1898, *E.*
64. RR to AI, 10-1898, *E.*
65. AI to WR, 1898, *E.*
66. AI to LS, 10-6-1898, *E.*
67. LS to AI, 28-7-1898,, 27-9-1898 and 2-11-1898, *E.*
68. AI to RR, ?1898, *E.*
69. ER to AI, 10-1898, *E.*
70. AI to WR, 13-8-1898, *E.*
71. AI to ER, 8-1898, *E.*
72. LS to AI, 30-10-1898, *E.*
73. ER to AI, 2-6-1898, *E.*
74. RR to AI, 1898, *E.*
75. Theodore Martin to AI, 19-11-1898 and 30-4-1899, *E.* Annie's comment on Helena comes in *Biographical*, XIII, xx-xxi.
76. LS to AI, 8-1-1899, *E.*
77. AI to AS, 22-7-1902, *B.*
78. AI to ER, ?1899; *E.*
79. AI to WR, 3-1899, *E.*
80. AI to ER, ?4-1899, *E.*
81. AI to WR, 6-1900 and 7-1900, *E.*
82. AI to WR, 9-1901, *E.*
83. AI to ER, 9-1899, *E.*
84. LS to AI, 1-5-1899, *E.*

## Chapter 8:

## THE CONTINUANCE OF LOVE (1900-1909)

1. AI to WR, 9-2-1900, *E.*
2. AI to BC, 14-2-1900, *E.*
3. AI to WR, 23-2-1900 and 14-3-1900, *E.*
4. AI to ER, 17-3-1900, *E.*
5. AI to WR, 20-5-1900, *E.*
6. *J*, ?19-10-1900.
7. ER to AI, 8-1900, *E.*
8. AI to WR, 2/3-1901, *E.*
9. LS to Mary Fisher, 30-3-1902, *E.*

10.  AI to GS, 16-7-1900, *JMA.*
11.  AI to GS, 3-1-1901, *JMA.*
12.  AI to WR, 3-2-1901, *E.*
13.  AI to WR, 3/4-1901, *E.*
14.  RR to AI, 6-6-1901, *E.*
15.  AI to ER, 4-1901, *E.*
16.  AI to ER, 9/10-1901, *E.* Annie's memories of Tisey featured in her November 1903 *Cornhill* paper, 'Links with the Past'.
17.  AI to HR, 11-1901, *E.*
18.  LS to AI, 13-4-1902, *E.*
19.  AI to HR, ?7-1902, *E.*
20.  RR to AI, 6-8-1902, *E.*
21.  RR to AI, 30-7-1902 and 10-8-1902, *E.*
22.  AI to ER, 15-7-1902, *E*
23.  RR to AI, 7-9-1902, *E.*
24.  RR to AI, 16-9-1902 and 20-9-1902, *E.*
25.  AI to HR, 8-10-1902, *E.* The allusion is to Matthew, X, 16: 'Behold, I send you forth as sheep in the midst of wolves: be ye therefore wise as serpents, and harmless as doves'.
26.  AI to ER, ?31-10-1902, *E.*
27.  RR to AI, 27-9-1903, *E.*
28.  AI to ER, 10-1903, *E.*
29.  AI to HR, 22-9-1903, *E.*
30.  ER to AI, autumn 1903, *E.*
31.  AI to Walter Senior, 5-11-1903, *Y.*
32.  Vanessa Stephen to AI, 22-2-1904, *E.*
33.  VW to HR, 4-3-1919, *E.* See also Anne Olivier Bell (ed), *The Diary of Virginia Woolf*, London: The Hogarth Press, Vol 1, 1977, 5-3-1919, 247-8.
34.  22-2-1904 and 23-2-1904, *E.*
35.  AI to ER, 8-1903, *E.*
36.  AI to H, 13-10-1904, *E.*
37.  AI to ER, 30-10-1904, *E.*
38.  AI to ER, 18-4-1904, *E.*
39.  F.W. Maitland to AI, 9-8-1904 and 16-11-1904, *E.*
40.  Maitland to CS, 25-3-1905, *E.*
41.  MW to AI, 16-7-1904, *E.*
42.  AI to HR, 11-1904, *E.*
43.  AI to ER, ?29-9-1904, *E.*
44.  RR to AI, 4-4-1906, *E.*
45.  AI to HR, 21-10-1904, *E.*
46.  George Putnam to AI, 25-5-1906, *E.*
47.  AI to HR, 11-1904, *E.*
48.  Gérin (263-4) refers to legal correspondence I have not been able to locate.
49.  AI to JST, 24-5-1905, *E.*
50.  AI to Elizabeth, Lady Lewis, 19-10-1905, *BD.*
51.  MB to AI, 13-3-1906 and 4-4-1906, *E.*
52.  AI to ER, 15-2-1906, *E.*
53.  KD to AI, 13-2-1905, *E.*

54. Typed statement 1-3-1906, *JM.*

55. Hilary Newman supposes that the William Ritchie at the meeting was Richmond's elder brother, but he had died in January 1903. *Laura Stephen: A Memoir*, London: Cecil Woolf, 2006, 40.

56. Typed account of meeting 19-3-1906, *E.*

57. AI to ER, 3-6-1906 and late summer 1906, *E.*

58. Charles Macaulay to Thomas Taylor, 1-2-1860, *JM.*

59. Charles Booth to RR, 4-5-1906, *JM.*

60. AI to Mary Booth, 5-1906, *E.*

61. AI to MR, 6-1906, *E.*

62. AI to ER, 5-6-1906, *E.*

63. AI to ER, 7-8-1906, *E.*

64. MR to Mary Booth, 2-9-1906, *E.*

65. RR to AF, 9-8-1906, *JM.*

66. AF to AI, 30-9-1906, *E.*

67. George Meredith to AI, 23-11-1906, *E.*

68. AI to AF, 29-11-1906, *E.*

69. *DI*, 16-1-1907.

70. AI to WR, 1904, *E.* This ornamental spoon, now owned by *JM*, served to inspire Thackeray's initial letter illustration for 'On a Joke I Once Heard from the Late Thomas Hood'.

71. CS to AI, 18-1-1907, *E.*

72. *DI*, 24-1-1907.

73. MB to AI, 8-8-1907, *E.*

74. Correspondence between AI and RR, 27-6-1907, 28-6-1907, 3-7-1907, 6-7-1907 and 15-7-1907, *E.*

75. AI to RR, 10-7-1907 and 21-7-1907, *E.*

76. AI to ER and RR, 27-7-1907, *E.*

77. AI to Edith Peruzzi, 30-7-1907, *HRC.*

78. AI to ER, 11-8-1907, *E.*

79. MG to AI, 8-11-1907, *E.*

80. MR to Mary Booth, ?12-1907, *E.*

81. *DI*, 22-9-1907.

82. George Meredith to AI, 2-3-1909, *E.*

83. AI to RR, A to B, 1/3-1908 and AI to Mary Booth, 12-1908, *E.*

84. Information about her great-aunt supplied by Juliet Murray.

85. These family memories were recalled for me by Belinda Norman-Butler.

86. AI to HR, ?8-1909, *E.*

87. Julia Sterling to AI, 3-1-1909, *E.*

88. AI to ER, 12-1908, *E.*

89. AI to ER, ?6-1909, *E.*

90. RR to MR and WR, 6-10-1909, *BNB.*

91. AI to MR, ?8-10-1909, *E.*

92. AI to ER, 6-10-1909, *E.*

## Chapter Nine:
## SUCH A LITTLE TIME FOR ME (1910-1914)

1. AI to ER, 14-1-1910 and 20-1-1910, *E.*
2. RR to MR, 22-3-1910, *BNB.*
3. Leonard Woolf, *Beginning Again. An Autobiography of the Years 1911-1918*, London: Hogarth Press, 1964, 70-73.
4. Elsa Richmond, *The Earlier Letters of Gertrude Bell*, 28-9.
5. AI to ER, 15-5-1910, *E.*
6. *DI*, 20-5-1910.
7. AI to ER, 31-8-1910, *E.*
8. RR to AI, 7-1910, *E.*
9. *DI*, 29-7-1911.
10. AI to ER, 10-9-1910, *E.*
11. A to W. J. Williams, 14-11-1910, *P*, and RS to AI, 15-11-1910, *E.* For the photograph, see *Centenary*, V, facing p. xxiii.
12. AI to Smith, Elder, 13-11-1910, *JMA.*
13. *Times*, 1-7-1911.
14. KD to AI, 1-7-1911 and 4-7-1911, *E.*
15. AF to AI, 25-4-1911, *E.*
16. RR to AI, 30-4-1911, *E.*
17. AI to AF, 3-5-1911, *E.*
18. *DI*, 24-5-1911.
19. AI to ER, 27-5-1911, *E.*
20. AI to Annie Fields, 29-1-1912, *HU (FI 3749).*
21. Nigel Nicolson, ed, *The Letters of Virginia Woolf*, London: Hogarth Press, I, 1975, 487.
22. AI to CU, 2-3-1912, *DNH.*
23. RR to AI, ?5-3-1912, *E.*
24. AI to ER, 19-3-1912, *E.*
25. AI to MR, 21-3-1912, *E.*
26. RR to AI, 24-3-1912, *E.*
27. RR to AI, 5-4-1912, *E.*
28. AI to CU, 8-5-1912, *DNH.* James's Browning address is 'The Novel in *The Ring and the Book*', *Henry James, Literary Criticism*, New York and Cambridge: Library of America, 1984.
29. *DI*, 21-6-1912.
30. AI to RR, 10-8-1912, *E.*
31. AI to Clive Bell, 9-10-1912, *KCC.*
32. 'Notes of Happy Things', manuscript notebook, *BNB.*
33. AI to HR, 6/7-1901, *E.*
34. Vaughan Harley to AI, 12-10-1912, *E.*
35. EP to AI, about 12-10-1912, *JM.*
36. EP to AI, ?13-10-1912, *E.*
37. AI to ER, 10-1912, *E.*
38. VW to AI, 12-10-1912, *E.*
39. Vanessa Bell to AI, 15-10-1912, *JM.*

40. Frank Lucas to HR, 12-10-1912, *E.*
41. Baron von Hügel to AI, 15-10-1912, copy, *BNB.*
42. HJ to Margaret Prothero, 13-10-1912, in Susan E. Gunter (ed), *Dear Munificent Friends. Henry James's Letters to Four Women*, Ann Arbor: University of Michigan Press, 1999.
43. AI to Violet Hammersley, 5-11-1912, *E.*
44. AI to ER, 12-9-1912, *E.*
45. AI to HR, 26-10-1912, *E.*
46. RB to HR, 20-10-1912, *E.*
47. AI to ER, 26-12-1912, *E.*
48. AI to Walter Senior, 23-1-1913, *Y.*
49. Herbert Stephen to AI, 8-12-1912, *JM.*
50. Edmund Gosse to AI, 3-3-1913, *E.*
51. AI to ER, 4-1913, *E.*
52. AI to WR, 3-4-1913, *E.*
53. AI to ER, 17-4-1913, *E.*
54. AI to Ethel Murray Smith, 27-12-1913, *JM.*
55. AI to ER, 20-8-1913, *E.*
56. AI to ER, 26-12-1913, *E.*
57. AI to MR, 1914, *E.*
58. AI to WR, 10-12-1913, *E.*
59. *Times*, 25-2-1914.
60. AI to WR, 10-4-1914, *E.*
61. AI to WR, 7-8-1914, *E.*
62. *DI*, 9-6-1914.
63. *DI*, 23-7-1914.
64. AB to HR, 29-7-1914, *JM.*
65. AI to MR, 14-8-1914, *E.*
66. ER to AI, 3-7-1915, *E.*
67. See *The Inheritance of Genius*, ch 4, pp. 109-10.
68. AI to Constance Smith, 1-9-1914, *E.*
69. *DI*, 5-9-1914.
70. AI to ML, 4-12-1914, *HRC.*

Chapter Ten:

# THE END OF A LONG DAY'S WORK (1915-1919)

1. *HRWJ*, 14-11-1916.
2. Samuel Hynes, *A War Imagined. The First World War and English Culture*, London: The Bodley Head, 1990, 133.
3. AI to Alan Cole, 8-6-1915, *E.*
4. AI to HT, 31-7-1915, *E.*
5. *HRWJ*, 2-10-1916.
6. AI to ER, 5-5-1915, *E.*
7. AI to WR, ?25-5-1915, *E.*
8. AI to ER, ?5-1915, *E.*
9. *DI.*

10.  AB to HR, 22-3-1915, *JM.*
11.  KD to HR, ?summer 1915, *E.*
12.  *DI*, 3-2-1916.
13.  24-1-1915. Anne Olivier Bell, *The Diary of Virginia Woolf*, I.
14.  *DI*, 10-10-1915.
15.  5-3-1919. *The Diary of Virginia Woolf*, I.
16.  Unpublished recollections, *BNB.*
17.  AI to WR, 6-2-1916, *E.*
18.  AI to Robert Underwood Johnson, 13-3-1916, *HRC.*
19.  HT to AI, 4-2-1916, *E.*
20.  AI to WR, ?3-1916, *E.*
21.  AI to JST, 13-8-1915, *E.*
22.  AI to WR, 29-2-1916, *E.*
23.  AI to Theodora Bosanquet, 9-3-1916, *HL (bMS Eng1213.3 174).*
24.  AI to WR, 17/18-3-1916, *E.*
25.  Theodore Bosanquet's journal, 15-3-1916, *HL (bMS Eng1213.2).*
26.  *DI*, 8-11-1916.
27.  AI to ER, 1-9-1916, *E.*
28.  ER to AI, 9-1916, *E.*
29.  *HRWJ.*
30.  BC to AI, 2-10-1916, *E.*
31.  AI to ML, ?9-10-1916, *HRC.*
32.  *HRWJ.*
33.  *HRWJ*, 3-10-1916.
34.  AI to Robert Underwood Johnson, 27-1-1916, *HRC.*
35.  AI to Thomas Hardy, 3-11-1916 and 9-11-1916, *DCM.*
36.  AI to Jack Hills, 16-11-1916, *KCC.*
37.  AI to RB, 5-11-1916, *E.*
38.  LL to AI, 22-11-1916, *E.*
39.  *DI*, 30-10-1917.
40.  AI to CJ, 22-1-?1917, *MM.*
41.  AI to AD, 6/7-1917, *E.*
42.  FB to AI, 22-6-1917, *E.*
43.  *HRWJ*, 20-3-1917.
44.  *HRWJ*, 4-4-1917.
45.  AI to WR, 30-7-1918, *E.*
46.  AI to Elizabeth Robins, 7-8-1918, *Shankman.*
47.  RB to AI, 9-8-1918, *E.*
48.  MC to AI, 16-7-1917, *E.*
49.  AI to CU, 13/14-7-1917 and 15-1-1918, *DNH.*
50.  AI to CU, 15-1-1918, *DNH.*
51.  Victoria Cholmondeley to HR, 22-3-1919, *E.*
52.  Marie Belloc Lowndes, *A Passing World*, London: Macmillan & Co, 1948, 204.
53.  Unpublished recollections, *BNB.*
54.  AI to RB,19-2-1918, copy, *E.*
55.  AI to LL, 1-4-1918, copy, *BNB.*
56.  ER to AI, 13-4-1918, *E.*
57.  *HRWJ*, 13-4-1918.

58.   AI to MR, 25-7-1918, *E.*
59.   A to ER, 14-6-1918, *E.* Strachey's letter to Morrell (3-3-1918) in Paul Levy (ed), *The Letters of Lytton Strachey.*
60.   RB to HR, 27-5-1918, *E.*
61.   *HRWJ*, 9-7-1918.
62.   AI to CU, 8-8-1918, *DNH.*
63.   KD to AI, 10-1918, *E.*
64.   AI to WR, 9-11-1918, *E.*
65    WR to AI, 14-11-1918, transcription in *HRWJ.*
66.   Leonard Woolf, *Beginning Again. An Autobiography of the Years 1911-1918,* 72. This letter probably dates from about October 1916.
67.   ER to HR, 1-3-1919, *E.*
68.   AI to VW, 1-1-1919 and 8-1-1919, *KCC.*
69.   AI to Belinda Ritchie, 24-2-1919, *E.*
70.   HR to MT, 27-2-1919, *E.*
71.   ER to HR, 28-2-1919, *E.*
72.   HR to ER, 7-3-1919, *E.*
73.   ER to HR, 2-3-1919, *E.*
74.   MT to HR, 5-3-1919, *E.*
75.   Mary Booth to HR, 5-3-1919, *E.*
76.   Lady Constance Battersea to HR, 28-2-1919, *E.*
77.   Gerald Ritchie to HR, 28-2-1919, *E.*
78.   *Mausoleum,* 12 and 14.
79.   Lord Bryce to HR, 1-3-1919, *E.*
80.   Herbert Paul to HR, 8-3-1919, *E.*
81.   AD to HR, 28-2-1919, *E.*
82.   MT to HR, 3-1919, *E.*
83.   MT to HR, 1-3-1919, *E.*
84.   Eleanor Clough to HR, 4-3-1919, *E.*
85.   LL to HR, 2-3-1919, *E.*
86.   Edith Emerson Forbes to HR, 6-3-1919, *E.*
87.   BC to HR, 14-3-1919, *E.*
88.   *The Graphic,* 21-6-1873.

# THACKERAY AND RITCHIE FAMILY TREE

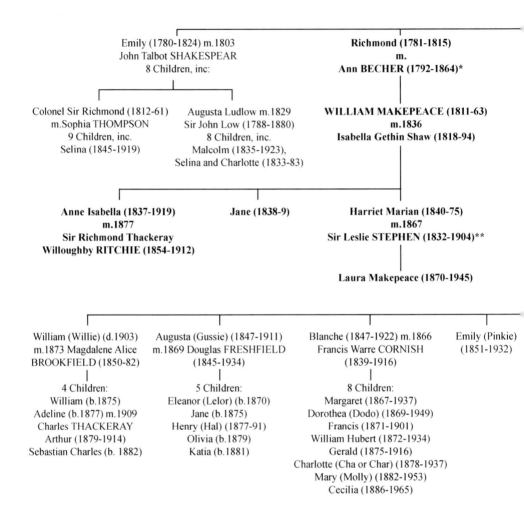

Emily (1780-1824) m.1803
John Talbot SHAKESPEAR
8 Children, inc:

**Richmond (1781-1815)**
**m.**
**Ann BECHER (1792-1864)\***

Colonel Sir Richmond (1812-61)
m.Sophia THOMPSON
9 Children, inc.
Selina (1845-1919)

Augusta Ludlow m.1829
Sir John Low (1788-1880)
8 Children, inc.
Malcolm (1835-1923),
Selina and Charlotte (1833-83)

**WILLIAM MAKEPEACE (1811-63)**
**m.1836**
**Isabella Gethin Shaw (1818-94)**

**Anne Isabella (1837-1919)**
**m.1877**
**Sir Richmond Thackeray**
**Willoughby RITCHIE (1854-1912)**

**Jane (1838-9)**

**Harriet Marian (1840-75)**
**m.1867**
**Sir Leslie STEPHEN (1832-1904)\*\***

**Laura Makepeace (1870-1945)**

William (Willie) (d.1903)
m.1873 Magdalene Alice
BROOKFIELD (1850-82)

Augusta (Gussie) (1847-1911)
m.1869 Douglas FRESHFIELD
(1845-1934)

Blanche (1847-1922) m.1866
Francis Warre CORNISH
(1839-1916)

Emily (Pinkie)
(1851-1932)

4 Children:
William (b.1875)
Adeline (b.1877) m.1909
Charles THACKERAY
Arthur (1879-1914)
Sebastian Charles (b. 1882)

5 Children:
Eleanor (Lelor) (b.1870)
Jane (b.1875)
Henry (Hal) (1877-91)
Olivia (b.1879)
Katia (b.1881)

8 Children:
Margaret (1867-1937)
Dorothea (Dodo) (1869-1949)
Francis (1871-1901)
William Hubert (1872-1934)
Gerald (1875-1916)
Charlotte (Cha or Char) (1878-1937)
Mary (Molly) (1882-1953)
Cecilia (1886-1965)

\*    *In 1817, Anne Becher Thackeray remarried, Henry CARMICHAEL-SMYTH (1780-1861), stepfather to WMT*

\*\*    *In 1878, Leslie Stephen remarried, Julia Jackson DUCKWORTH,*
       *becoming stepfather to the children of her first marriage:*
       *George, Stella and Gerald de L'Etang. The children of this marriage were*
       *Vanessa (1879-1961), m. Clive BELL*
       *Thoby (1880-1906)*
       *Virginia (1882-1941) m. Leonard WOOLF*
       *Adrian (1883-1948) m. Karin COSTELLOE*

\*\*\*    *Edward Talbot Thackeray remarried, Elizabeth PLEYDELL*
        *Four children, inc. Charles THACKERAY, m. Adeline RITCHIE*

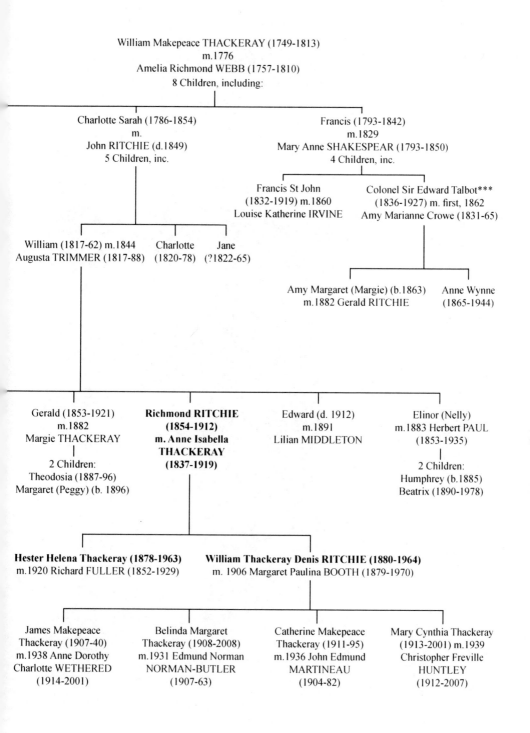

William Makepeace THACKERAY (1749-1813)
m.1776
Amelia Richmond WEBB (1757-1810)
8 Children, including:

Charlotte Sarah (1786-1854)
m.
John RITCHIE (d.1849)
5 Children, inc.

Francis (1793-1842)
m.1829
Mary Anne SHAKESPEAR (1793-1850)
4 Children, inc.

Francis St John
(1832-1919) m.1860
Louise Katherine IRVINE

Colonel Sir Edward Talbot***
(1836-1927) m. first, 1862
Amy Marianne Crowe (1831-65)

William (1817-62) m.1844
Augusta TRIMMER (1817-88)

Charlotte
(1820-78)

Jane
(?1822-65)

Amy Margaret (Margie) (b.1863)
m.1882 Gerald RITCHIE

Anne Wynne
(1865-1944)

Gerald (1853-1921)
m.1882
Margie THACKERAY
|
2 Children:
Theodosia (1887-96)
Margaret (Peggy) (b. 1896)

**Richmond RITCHIE**
**(1854-1912)**
**m. Anne Isabella**
**THACKERAY**
**(1837-1919)**

Edward (d. 1912)
m.1891
Lilian MIDDLETON

Elinor (Nelly)
m.1883 Herbert PAUL
(1853-1935)
|
2 Children:
Humphrey (b.1885)
Beatrix (1890-1978)

**Hester Helena Thackeray (1878-1963)**
m.1920 Richard FULLER (1852-1929)

**William Thackeray Denis RITCHIE (1880-1964)**
m. 1906 Margaret Paulina BOOTH (1879-1970)

James Makepeace
Thackeray (1907-40)
m.1938 Anne Dorothy
Charlotte WETHERED
(1914-2001)

Belinda Margaret
Thackeray (1908-2008)
m.1931 Edmund Norman
NORMAN-BUTLER
(1907-63)

Catherine Makepeace
Thackeray (1911-95)
m.1936 John Edmund
MARTINEAU
(1904-82)

Mary Cynthia Thackeray
(1913-2001) m.1939
Christopher Freville
HUNTLEY
(1912-2007)

*A family group, about 1883, labelled by Billy*

*Francis:* Francis Cornish *B.C.:* Blanche Cornish *Lelor:* Eleanor Cornish *D.F:* Douglas Freshfield *Mama:* Annie *Papa:* Richmond *Uncle Gerald:* Gerald Ritchie *William:* William Ritchie *Aunt Margy:* Margie Ritchie *Annie:* Anny Thackeray *Mag:* Margaret Cornish *Uncle Frank:* Frank Warre Cornish *G. Cornish:* Gerald Cornish *H. Cornish:* Hubert Cornish *Janie:* Jane Freshfield *Grannie:* Mrs Augusta Ritchie *Hal:* Henry Freshfield *A.C.R:* Arthur Ritchie *W.T.D.R:* Billy *H.M.R:* Hester *Aunt Pinkie:* Emily (Pinkie) Ritchie *Char:* Charlotte Cornish *O.F:* Olivia Freshfield

# ABBREVIATIONS AND SOURCES

## 1. Names of Correspondents

| | |
|---|---|
| AI | Anne Isabella Thackeray (Annie), Anne Thackeray Ritchie after her marriage in 1877 (elder daughter of WMT) |
| AB | Augustine Birrell |
| AC | Anne Carmichael-Smyth (mother of WMT) |
| AD | Adeline Ritchie (Adeline Thackeray after her marriage) |
| AF | Augusta (Gussie) Ritchie (Gussie Freshfield after her marriage) |
| AP | Anne Procter |
| AS | Algernon Swinburne |
| AT | Alfred Tennyson |
| AW | Aldis Wright |
| BC | Blanche Ritchie (Blanche Warre Cornish after her marriage) |
| CJ | Charles Johnson |
| CN | Charles Eliot Norton |
| CR | Charlotte Ritchie (cousin of WMT) |
| CS | Caroline Stephen |
| CU | Ariana Curtis |
| CW | Charles Dudley Warner |
| EF | Edward FitzGerald |
| EL | Eliza Field |
| EP | Elinor (Nelly) Ritchie (Elinor Paul after her marriage) |
| ER | Emily (Pinkie) Ritchie |
| ET | Emily Tennyson |
| FB | Florence Bell |
| FK | Fanny Kemble |
| FS | James FitzJames Stephen |
| GB | Gertrude Bell |
| GW | George Frederic Watts |
| GS | George Smith |
| HJ | Henry James |

| HM | Harriet Marian Thackeray (Minny), Harriet Marian Stephen after her marriage in 1867 (younger daughter of WMT) |
| HR | Hester Ritchie |
| HT | Hallam Tennyson |
| IT | Isabella Shawe, Isabella Thackeray after her marriage in 1836 (wife of WMT) |
| JB | John Brown |
| JC | Julia Margaret Cameron |
| JF | James Fields |
| JJ | Julia Jackson (then Julia Duckworth and finally Julia Stephen) |
| JO | John Field |
| JOB | Jane Octavia Brookfield |
| JS | Jeanie Nassau Senior |
| JST | Jane Strachey |
| KD | Kate Dickens (then Kate Collins and finally Kate Perugini) |
| LL | Louisa Lee Schuyler |
| LS | Leslie Stephen |
| MB | Mary Brotherton |
| MC | Mary Cholmondeley |
| MG | Meta Gaskell |
| ML | Marie Belloc Lowndes |
| MO | Margaret Oliphant |
| MR | Margaret Meg Booth (Margaret Ritchie after her marriage) |
| MS | Mary Stephen |
| MT | Margie Thackeray (Margie Ritchie after her marriage) |
| MW | Mary Watts |
| OH | Oliver Wendell Holmes (Jr., unless noted) |
| RB | Rhoda Broughton |
| RR | Richmond Ritchie |
| SA | Sarianna Browning |
| VW | Virginia Stephen (Virginia Woolf after her marriage) |
| WMT | William Makepeace Thackeray |
| WR | William Ritchie (Billy) |

## 2. Sources and Locations

### *PUBLISHED*

| *Adversity* | Gordon N. Ray, *The Uses of Adversity 1811-1846*, London: OUP, 1955 |
| Autobiography | Mrs Harry Coghill (ed), *The Autobiography and Letters of Mrs M.O.W. Oliphant*, Edinburgh and London: W. Blackwood & Sons, 1899 |
| *Bicknell* | John Bicknell (ed), *Selected Letters of Leslie Stephen*, 2 vols., Columbus: Ohio State University Press, 1996 |

| | |
|---|---|
| *Biographical* | Anne Isabella Ritchie, *The Biographical Edition of the Works of William Makepeace Thackeray, with Biographical Introductions by his Daughter, Anne Ritchie,* 13 vols., London: Smith, Elder, 1898-99 |
| *Chapters* | Anne Isabella Ritchie, *Chapters from Some Memoirs,* London: Macmillan, 1894 |
| *Centenary* | Anne Isabella Ritchie, *Centenary Biographical Edition of the Works of William Makepeace Thackeray, with Biographical Introductions by his Daughter, Lady Ritchie,* 26 vols., London: Smith, Elder, 1910-11 |
| *Daughter* | Hester Fuller and Violet Hammersley, *Thackeray's Daughter,* Dublin: Euphorion Books, 1951 |
| *Harden* | Edgar Harden, *The Letters and Private Papers of William Makepeace Thackeray* (supplement to *Ray*) 2 vols, New York and London: Garland Press, 1994 |
| *Letters* | Hester Ritchie, *Letters of Anne Thackeray Ritchie,* London: John Murray, 1924 |
| *Mausoleum* | Alan Bell (ed), *Sir Leslie Stephen's Mausoleum Book,* Oxford: Clarendon Press, 1977 |
| *Ray* | Gordon N. Ray, *The Letters and Private Papers of William Makepeace Thackeray,* 4 vols, Cambridge, Mass.: Harvard University Press, 1946 |
| *Records* | Anne Isabella Ritchie, *Records of Tennyson, Ruskin, Browning,* London: Macmillan, 1892 |
| *Shankman* | Lilian Shankman, *Anne Thackeray Ritchie Journals and Letters,* Columbus: Ohio State University Press, 1994 |
| *Wisdom* | Gordon N. Ray, *The Age of Wisdom 1847-1863,* London: OUP, 1958 |

## *MANUSCRIPT*

| | |
|---|---|
| *B* | Brotherton Library, University of Leeds |
| *BD* | Bodleian Library, University of Oxford |
| *BNB* | Estate of Belinda Norman-Butler (private collection deposited at *E*) |
| *BU* | Joseph Milsand Archive, Armstrong Browning Library, Baylor University, Waco, Texas |
| *CUL* | Cambridge University Library |
| *D* | Duke University |
| *DCM* | Thomas Hardy Memorial Collection, Dorset County Museum, Dorchester |
| *DI* | Annie's year diaries (*BNB*) |
| *DNH* | Dartmouth College, New Haven |
| *E* | Eton College Library |
| *HL* | Houghton Library, Harvard University |
| *HRC* | Harry Ransom Center, University of Texas at Austin |
| *HRWJ* | Hester Ritchie's War Journal (*JM*) |
| *HU* | Huntington Library, San Marino, California |

| | |
|---|---|
| *J* | Annie's Journal (*BNB*) |
| *JM* | Juliet Murray (private collection) |
| *JMA* | John Murray Archive, National Library of Scotland |
| *KCC* | Charleston Papers, Kings College Cambridge |
| *LP* | University of Liverpool |
| *M* | Pierpont Morgan Library, New Yor |
| *MM* | Michael Millgate (private collection) |
| *NLS* | National Library of Scotland |
| *NPG* | National Portrait Gallery, London |
| *P* | Princeton University Library |
| *TCC* | Trinity College Cambridge |
| *TRC* | Tennyson Research Centre, Lincolnshire County Council |
| *Y* | Beinecke Library, Yale University |

# SELECT BIBLIOGRAPHY

*Items described in the list of principal sources do not appear here.*

Aplin, John, *'A True Affection': Anne Thackeray Ritchie and the Tennysons*, Lincoln: The Tennyson Society, 2006

Aplin, John, *The Correspondence and Journals of the Thackeray Family*, 5 vols, London: Pickering & Chatto, 2011

Baxter, Lucy (editor), *Thackeray's Letters to an American Family*, New York: Centuary Co., 1904

Bell, Anne Olivier (editor), *The Diary of Virginia Woolf*, London: The Hogarth Press, Vol 1, 1977

Benson, A.C., *Memories and Friends*, London: John Murray, 1924

Cornish, Blanche Warre, *Some Family Letters of W. M. Thackeray together with Recollections by his Kinswoman*, London: Smith, Elder, 1911

Dakers, Caroline, *The Holland Park Circle. Artists and Victorian Society*, London: Yale University Press, 1999

Edel, Leon (editor), *Henry James Letters*, 4 vols, London: Macmillan, 1974-84

Fenwick, Gillian, *Leslie Stephen's Life in Letters. A Bibliographical Study*, Aldershot: Scolar Press, 1993

Fisher, Hervey, *From a Tramp's Wallet. A Life of Douglas William Freshfield*, Banham: The Erskine Press, 2001

Garnett, Henrietta, *Anny. A Life of Anne Isabella Thackeray Ritchie*, London: Chatto & Windus, 2004

Gérin, Winifred, *Anne Thackeray Ritchie*, Oxford: OUP, 1981

Glendinning, Victoria, *Trollope*, London: Pimlico, 1993

Glyn, Jenifer, *Prince of Publishers. A Biography of George Smith*, London: Allison & Brisby, 1986

Gosse, Edmund, *The Life of Algernon Charles Swinburne*, London: Macmillan, 1917

Gunn, Peter, *Vernon Lee*, London: OUP, 1964

Hawksley, Lucinda, *Katie*, London: Doubleday, 2006

Hirsch, Pam, *Barbara Leigh Smith Bodichon*, London: Chatto & Windus, 1998

Holroyd, Michael, *Lytton Strachey. A Biography*, London: Penguin: 1979

Howe, M.A. Dewolfe (editor), *The Harvard Volunteers in Europe. Personal Records of Experience in Military, Ambulance, and Hospital Service,* Cambridge MA: Harvard University Press, 1916

Hynes, Samuel, *A War Imagined. The First World War and English Culture,* London: The Bodley Head, 1990

James, Henry, *Literary Criticism,* New York and Cambridge: Library of America, 1984

James, Henry, *William Wetmore Story and his Friends,* 2 vols, Edinburgh and London: Blackwood, 1903

Lang, Andrew, 'Thackeray and His Biographers', *Longman's Magazine,* April 1891

Leigh Smith, Philip, *Record of an Ascent. A Memoir of Sir Richmond Ritchie,* London: Dillon's University Bookshop Ltd, 1961

Leslie, Shane, *Long Shadows,* London: John Murray, 1966

Levy, Paul (editor), *The Letters of Lytton Strachey,* London: Viking, 2005

Lowndes, Marie Belloc, *A Passing World,* London: Macmillan & Co, 1948

Mackay, Carol Hanbery, *Creative Negativity. Four Victorian Exemplars of the Female Quest,* California: Stanford University Press, 2001

Martin, Robert, *With Friends Possessed. A Life of Edward FitzGerald,* London: Faber and Faber, 1985

Merivale, Herman and Frank T. Marzials, *Life of W. M. Thackeray,* London: Walter Scott, 1891

Newman, Hilary, *Laura Stephen: A Memoir,* London: Cecil Woolf, 2006

Nicolson, Nigel (editor), *The Letters of Virginia Woolf,* London: Hogarth Press, I, 1975

Olsen, Victoria, *Julia Margaret Cameron and Victorian Photography,* London: Aurum Press, 2003

Pope-Hennessy, James, *Monckton Milnes, The Flight of Youth 1851-1885,* London: Constable, 1951

Richmond, Elsa, *The Earlier Letters of Gertrude Bell,* London: Ernest Benn Ltd, 1937

Ritchie, Gerald, *The Ritchies in India,* London: John Murray, 1920

Rose, Phyllis, *Parallel Lives. Five Victorian Marriages,* London: The Hogarth Press, 1984

Sichel, Edith, 'The Sentiment of Thackeray', *The Quarterly Review,* January 1900

Sturgis, Howard, 'Anne Isabella Thackeray', *Cornhill,* November 1919

Terhune, Alfred McKinley and Annabelle Burdick Terhune, *The Letters of Edward FitzGerald* vol 4, Princeton University Press, 1980

Thwaite, Ann, *Emily Tennyson: The Poet's Wife,* London: Faber & Faber, 1996

Turner, James, *The Liberal Education of Charles Eliot Norton,* Baltimore: Johns Hopkins University Press, 1999

Watts-Dunton, Clara, *The Home Life of Swinburne,* London: A.M. Philpot, 1922

Wood, Marilyn, *Rhoda Broughton. Profile of a Novelist,* Stamford: Paul Watkins, 1993

Woolf, Leonard, *Beginning Again. An Autobiography of the Years 1911-1918,* London: Hogarth Press, 1964

Wright, William Aldis, *Letters and Literary Remains of Edward FitzGerald,* London: Macmillan, 1889

Zuckerman, Joanne, 'Anne Thackeray Ritchie as the model for Mrs Hilbery', *Virginia Woolf Quarterly,* I, part 3, 1973

# INDEX

Lightning Source UK Ltd.
Milton Keynes UK
17 January 2011

165844UK00001B/9/P